THE MICROECONOMICS OF INCOME DISTRIBUTION DYNAMICS IN EAST ASIA AND LATIN AMERICA

THE MICROECONOMICS OF INCOME DISTRIBUTION DYNAMICS IN EAST ASIA AND LATIN AMERICA

François Bourguignon

Francisco H. G. Ferreira

Nora Lustig

Editors

A copublication of the World Bank and Oxford University Press

1818 H Street, NW
Washington, DC 20433
Telephone: 202-473-1000
Internet: www.worldbank.org
E-mail: feedback@worldbank.org

A copublication of the World Bank and Oxford University Press.
Oxford University Press
198 Madison Avenue
New York, NY 10016

ISBN 0-8213-5861-8

Cataloging-in-Publication Data has been applied for.

Contents

Figures

Tables

Preface

The process of economic development is inherently about change. Change in where people live, in what they produce and in how they produce it, in how much education they get, in how long and in how well they live, in how many children they have, and so on. So much change, and the fact that at times it takes place at such surprising speed, must affect the way incomes and wealth are distributed, as well as the overall size of the pie. While considerable efforts have been devoted to the understanding of economic growth, the economic analysis of the mechanisms through which growth and development affect the distribution of welfare has been rudimentary by comparison. Yet understanding development and the process of poverty reduction requires understanding not only how total income grows within a country but also how its distribution behaves over time.

Our knowledge of the dynamics of income distribution is presently limited, in part because of the informational inefficiency of the scalar inequality measures generally used to summarize distributions. Single numbers can often hide as much as they show. But recent improvements in the availability of household survey data for developing countries, and in the capacity of computers to process them, mean that we should be able to do a better job comprehending the nature of changes in the income distribution that accompany the process of economic development. We hope that this book is a step in that direction.

By looking at the evolution of the entire distribution of income over reasonably long periods—10 to 20 years—and across a diverse set of societies—four in Latin America and three in East Asia—we have learned a great deal about a variety of development experiences, and how similar building blocks can combine in unique ways, to shape each specific historical case. But we have also learned about the similarities in some of those building blocks: the complex effect of educational expansion on income inequality, the remarkable role of increases in women's participation in the labor force, and the importance of reductions in family size, to name a few.

We have learned that the complexity of the interactions between these forces is so great that aggregate approaches to the relationship between growth and distribution are unlikely to be of much use for any particular country. We have also learned that some common patterns can be discerned and, with appropriate care and humility, understanding them might be helpful to policymakers seeking to enhance the power of development to reduce poverty and inequity. We hope that readers might share some of the joy we found in uncovering the stories behind the distributional changes in each of the countries studied in this book.

François Bourguignon
Francisco H. G. Ferreira
Nora Lustig

Acknowledgments

This book started as a joint research project organized by the Inter-American Development Bank (IDB) and the World Bank, and we are grateful to the many people in both institutions who supported it throughout its five-year lifespan. We would like to thank particularly Michael Walton, who supported the birth of the project when he directed the Poverty Reduction Unit at the World Bank, as well as Carlos Jarque and Carlos Eduardo Vélez of the IDB, who supported the project's completion.

We are also very grateful to Martin Ravallion, who commented on various versions of the work, from research proposal to finished papers; to James Heckman, who acted as a discussant for three chapters at a session in the 2000 Meetings of the American Economic Association; to Ravi Kanbur, who provided very useful suggestions at an early stage of the research process; and to Tony Shorrocks, who gave us many insights into the nature of the decompositions we undertook. We are similarly indebted to a number of participants in seminars and workshops that took place at various meetings of the Econometric Society (in particular in Latin America and the Far East); of the European Economic Association (in Venice); of the Network on Inequality and Poverty of the IDB, World Bank, and LACEA (Latin American and Caribbean Economic Association); and at the Universities of Brasília, Maryland, and Michigan, The Catholic University of Rio de Janeiro, the European University Institute in Florence, and DELTA (Département et Laboratoire d'Economie Théorique et Appliquée) in Paris.

Our greatest debt, of course, is to the authors of the seven case studies, who really wrote the book. Their names and affiliations are listed separately in the coming pages, and we thank them profoundly for their commitment and endurance during the long process of producing this volume. Finally, the book would not have been possible without the dedication, professionalism, and attention to detail of Janet Sasser and her team at the World Bank's Office of the Publisher.

Contributors

Vivi Alatas   Economist in the East Asia and Pacific Region at the World Bank, Jakarta, Indonesia

César Bouillón   Economist in the Poverty and Inequality Unit of the Inter-American Development Bank, Washington, D.C.

François Bourguignon   Senior vice president and chief economist of the World Bank, Washington, D.C.

Walter Sosa Escudero   Professor of econometrics at the Universidad de los Andes, Buenos Aires, Argentina, and at the Universidad Nacional de La Plata, Argentina; researcher at Centro de Estudios Distributivos, Laborales y Sociales (CEDLAS) at the Universidad Nacional de La Plata

Francisco H. G. Ferreira   Senior economist in the Development Research Group at the World Bank, Washington, D.C.

Gary S. Fields   Professor of labor economics at Cornell University, Ithaca, New York

Martin Fournier   Researcher at the Centre d'Etudes Français sur la Chine Contemporaine (CEFC), Hong Kong, China, and associate professor at the Université d'Auvergne, Clermont-Ferrand, France

Leonardo Gasparini   Director of CEDLAS, as well as professor of economics of income distribution and professor of labor economics at the Universidad Nacional de La Plata, Argentina

Marc Gurgand	Researcher at the Département et Laboratoire d'Economie Théorique et Appliquée (DELTA) at the Centre National de la Recherche Scientifique (CNRS), Paris, France
Adriana Kugler	Associate professor of economics at the Universitat Pompeu Fabra, Barcelona, Spain, and assistant professor of economics at the University of Houston, Texas
Arianna Legovini	Senior monitoring and evaluation specialist in the Africa Region at the World Bank, Washington, D.C.
José Leibovich	Assistant director of the Departamento Nacional de Planeación (Department of National Planning), Bogotá, Colombia
Nora Lustig	President of the Universidad de Las Americas, Puebla, Mexico
Mariana Marchionni	Professor of econometrics at the Universidad Nacional de La Plata, Argentina, and researcher at CEDLAS
Jairo Núñez	Researcher at the Universidad de los Andes, Bogotá, Colombia
Ricardo Paes de Barros	Researcher at the Instituto de Pesquisa Econômica Aplicada (IPEA), Rio de Janeiro, Brazil
Sergei Soares	Senior education economist in the Latin America and Caribbean Region at the World Bank, Washington, D.C., and researcher at IPEA, Rio de Janeiro, Brazil
Carlos Eduardo Vélez	Chief of the Poverty and Inequality Unit at the Inter-American Development Bank, Washington, D.C.

Abbreviations and Acronyms

CPI	Consumer price index
DANE	Departamento Nacional de Estadística (National Department of Statistics, Colombia)
DGBAS	Directorate-General of Budget, Accounting, and Statistics (Taiwan, China)
EH	Encuesta de Hogares (Household Survey, Colombia)
EHIP	Equivalized household income per capita
ENIGH	Encuesta Nacional de Ingresos y Gastos de los Hogares (Household Income and Expenditure Surveys, Mexico)
EPH	Encuesta Permanente de Hogares (Permanent Household Survey, Argentina)
GDP	Gross domestic product
IBGE	Instituto Brasileiro de Geografia e Estatística (Brazilian Geographical and Statistical Institute)
ICV-DIEESE	Índice do Custo de Vida–Departamento Intersindical de Estatística e Estudos Sócio-Econômeios (Cost of Living Index–Inter Trade Union Department of Statistics and Socioeconomic Studies, Brazil)
IGP-DI	Índice Geral de Preços–Disponibilidade Interna (General Price Index, Brazil)
INEGI	Instituto Nacional de Estadística, Geografía y Informática (National Institute of Statistics, Geography, and Informatics, Mexico)
INPC-R	Índice Nacional de Preços ao Consumidor–Real (National Consumer Price Index, Brazil)
MIDD	Microeconomics of Income Distribution Dynamics

OLS	Ordinary least squares
PNAD	Pesquisa Nacional por Amostra de Domicílios (National Household Survey, Brazil)
Progresa	Programa de Educación, Salud y Alimentación (Program for Education, Heath, and Nutrition, Mexico)

1

Introduction

François Bourguignon,
Francisco H. G. Ferreira, and Nora Lustig

This book is about how the distribution of income changes during the process of economic development. By its very nature, the process of development is replete with structural change. The composition of economic activity changes over time, generally away from agriculture and toward industry and services. Relative prices of goods and factors of production change too, and their dynamics involve both long-term trends and short-term shocks and fluctuations. The sociodemographic characteristics of the population evolve, as average age rises and average family size falls. Patterns of economic behavior are not constant either: female labor-force participation rates increase, as do the ages at which children leave school and enter employment. Generations save, invest, and bequeath, and so holdings of both physical and human capital change. But although change is everywhere and although some patterns can be discerned across many societies, no single country ever follows exactly the same development path. The combination, sequence, and timing of changes that are actually observed in any given country, at any given period, are always unique, always unprecedented.

Each one of these processes of structural change is likely to have powerful effects on the distribution of income. Social scientists in general—and economists in particular—have long been searching for some general rule about how development and income distribution dynamics are related. Karl Marx (1887) concluded that, under the inherent logic of capital accumulation by a few and relentless competition in labor supply by many, social cleavages would grow increasingly deeper, until revolution changed things forever. Simon Kuznets (1955)—drawing on W. Arthur Lewis (1954)—believed that the migration of labor and capital from traditional, less productive sectors of the economy toward more modern and productive ones would result first in rising inequality, followed eventually by declining inequality. Jan Tinbergen (1975) argued that the crucial struggle in modern economies was that between the rival forces of (a) technological progress—ever raising the demand for (and the pay of) more educated workers—and (b) educational expansion—ever raising the supply of such workers. More recently, economists have developed models with multiple equilibria, each characterized by its own income distribution, with its own mean and its own level of inequality.[1] These models show that different combinations of initial conditions—and of the historical processes that might follow them—could lead to diverse outcomes.

In this book, we do not suggest yet another grand theory of the dynamics of income distribution during the process of development. Instead, we propose and apply a methodology to decompose distributional change into its various driving forces, with the aim of enhancing our ability to understand the nature of income distribution dynamics.[2] In fact, rather than searching for a unifying explanation, we explore the incredible diversity in the distributional experiences and outcomes across economies. Why do changes in inequality differ so markedly across economies that have similar rates of growth in gross domestic product (GDP) per capita, such as Colombia and Malaysia (see table 1.1)? Why do we observe rising inequality both in growing economies (Mexico) and in contracting ones (Argentina)? Why do educational expansions sometimes lead to greater equality (as in Brazil and Taiwan, China) and sometimes to greater inequality (as in Indonesia and Mexico)?

The microeconomic empirics reported in this volume suggest that this diversity in outcomes results from the various possibilities that arise from the interaction of a number of powerful underlying social and economic phenomena. We group these phenomena into three fundamental forces: (a) changes in the underlying distribution of assets and personal characteristics in the population (which includes its ethnic, racial, gender, and educational makeup); (b) changes in the returns to those assets and characteristics; and (c) changes in how people use those assets and characteristics, principally in the labor market.

At a general level, our approach to addressing these themes consists of simulating counterfactual distributions by changing how markets and households behave, one aspect at a time, and by observing the effect of each change on the distribution, while holding all

Table 1.1 Selected Indicators of Long-Run Structural Evolution

Indicator	Argentina[a]	Brazil	Colombia	Indonesia	Malaysia	Mexico	Taiwan, China
Period analyzed	1986–98	1976–96	1978–95	1980–96	1984–97	1984–94	1979–94
GDP per capita in 1980 (purchasing power parity in US$)	6,506	4,499	2,520	1,430	5,548	5,758	3,786
Annual growth rate of GDP per capita (1980–96, percent)	0.0	1.0	3.7	5.7	4.0	2.4	6.0
Growth rate of mean household per capita income[b] (percent)	−1.0	0.2	3.8	5.1	5.2	1.1	5.7
Average years of schooling							
Initial year	8.7[c]	3.2	4.6	3.8	7.9[c]	5.6	6.0
Terminal year	9.8[c]	5.3	6.9	6	8.3[c]	6.9	9.5
Urbanization rate (percent)							
Initial year	86	68	57	23	42	63	70
Terminal year	88	77	61	35	55	58	84
Participation of women in the labor force (percent)							
Initial year	45	28	27	32	60	33	46
Terminal year	56	42	41	48	58	41	50
Family size							
Initial year	4.4	4.6	5.4	5.0	4.9	5.3	4.9
Terminal year	4.4	3.6	4.3	4.4	4.4	4.9	4.2
Gini coefficient (household income per capita, size-weighted households)							
Initial year	0.417	0.595[d]	0.502[d]	0.384	0.486	0.491	0.271
Terminal year	0.501	0.591[d]	0.544[d]	0.402	0.499	0.549	0.290

a. Apart from the GDP and urbanization data, all Argentine data refer to Greater Buenos Aires only.   b. As given by household surveys in initial and terminal years.   c. For population age 14 and over.   d. Urban sector only.

other aspects constant. We construct a simple income generation model at the household level, which allows us to separate the observed changes in the distribution of income into the three key forces just described. The first force comprises the changes in the sociodemographic structure of the population, as characterized by area of residence, age, education, ownership of physical and financial assets, and household composition (collectively referred to as *endowment effects*, or *population effects*). The second force comes from changes in the returns to factors of production, including the various components of human capital, such as education and experience (*price effects*). The third force has to do with changes in the occupational structure of the population, in terms of wage work, self-employment, unemployment, and inactivity (*occupational effects*).

Of course, those causes of changes in the distribution of income are not independent of one another. For instance, a change in the sociodemographic structure of the population—such as higher education levels in some segments of the population—will probably generate a change in the structure of prices, wages, and self-employment incomes, which may in turn modify the way people choose among alternative occupations. Conversely, exogenous changes in returns to education (say, from skill-biased technological change) are likely to induce some response from households in terms of the desired level of education for their children. Like all of its relatives in the Oaxaca-Blinder class of decompositions, the technique discussed in this volume is not designed to model those general equilibrium effects. It simply separates out how much of a given change would not have been observed under a well-defined statistical counterfactual (for example, if returns to education had not changed), without making any statement about the economic foundations of that counterfactual (for example, the conditions under which no change in the returns to education would be consistent with the other observed changes, in an economic sense). Nevertheless, as we hope the case studies in chapters 3 through 9 will show, the insights gained from the statistical decomposition and some basic microeconomic intuition allow analysts to improve their understanding of the nature of changes in income distribution in a particular economy.

The microeconometric approach applied in this volume should be seen as complementary to the more prevalent macroeconometric (cross-country) studies of the relationship between growth and inequality (or the reverse). (See, for instance, Alesina and Rodrik 1994; Dollar and Kraay 2002; Forbes 2000.) Cross-country regressions can, if well specified and run on comparable data, tell us much about average relationships between measures of income dispersion and other indicators of economic performance (such as economic growth). However, for two reasons they should be complemented by more detailed country studies of the sort included in this volume.

First, one can argue that endogeneity and omitted variable biases inevitably plague most macroeconometric cross-country studies. Suppose, for instance, that inequality is on the left-hand side of a regression, and growth is treated as an explanatory variable.[3] Various case studies in this volume suggest that changes in the distribution of years of schooling affect income inequality. Standard growth and wealth dynamics theory suggests that such changes would also affect the rate of economic growth. Those changes cannot be adequately captured by the mean years of schooling alone. If they are not somehow included as explanatory variables (which they usually are not), then their correlation with growth would bias the estimated coefficient of mean schooling. Even if the changes were not correlated with growth (which is unlikely), their omission would increase the variance of the residuals, inflate standard errors, and compromise hypothesis testing.

Second, even if the average relationships identified by the cross-country studies were true, they might not be particularly relevant to individual countries whose specific circumstances (some of which may not be observed at the macro level) place them at some point other than that average. Although useful lessons can be learned from the average relationships estimated macroeconometrically, specific country analysis and policy recommendations should also be informed by more in-depth country studies.

The method proposed is applied to seven economies in this volume: three in East Asia and four in Latin America.[4] The East Asian economies are Indonesia, Malaysia, and Taiwan (China). The Latin American ones are Argentina (Greater Buenos Aires), Brazil (urban), Colombia, and Mexico.[5] Latin America and East Asia have had rather different experiences with trends in the distribution of income and with the pace of economic development (see table 1.1). For example, during 1980–2000, growth in GDP per capita was considerably higher in East Asia than in Latin America. Also, Latin America showed higher initial levels of income inequality and (with the exception of Brazil) sharper upward trends as well. In most economies, however, the average years of schooling, the share of urban population, and the participation of women in the labor force rose, while the average size of households fell. Given the similar demographic and educational trends in practically all the economies, what explains the differences in the evolution of inequality? We hope that learning about the forces at work in the Asian and Latin American contexts will provide new insights for development analysts and policymakers.

The volume is organized as follows. In this introductory chapter, we first review the broad changes in structure observed in the economies under study. We then present a nonmathematical description of the methodology, placing it within the context of the literature. The formal presentation of the method is found in chapter 2. Chapters 3 to 9 contain the analyses for each of the seven economies. Chapter 10 presents a synthesis of the results and some concluding remarks.

Indicators of Structural Change in Seven Selected Economies

The magnitude of the structural changes that a society undergoes during the development process is well illustrated by the figures reported in table 1.1. The table lists changes in average education levels, in the urban-rural structure of the economy, in female labor-force participation, and in family sizes over intervals ranging from one to two decades, from the mid-1970s to the late 1990s. It also includes two measures of economic growth (in GDP per capita and in household survey mean income) and the Gini coefficient for household per capita income. Although the exact initial and final years vary, some general trends emerge. In all economies, the changes achieved on these four fronts in the span of 10 to 20 years were most impressive. The importance of the rural sector declined drastically everywhere, including Indonesia, where it was initially much larger than in the other economies in our sample. The educational level of the population also rose dramatically across all economies. Educational attainment measured by average years of schooling rose by 50 percent in Colombia and by even more in Brazil, Indonesia (urban), and Taiwan (China). (In the latter, educational attainment rose from an already high initial level of six years.) In the Greater Buenos Aires area of Argentina, in Malaysia, and in Mexico, the change was less dramatic. The participation rate of women in the labor force was largely unchanged in Malaysia and increased only slightly in Taiwan, China, but it rose substantially in Indonesia and in the Latin American countries. Average family sizes went down everywhere, falling by a full person or more in Brazil and Colombia.

In terms of economic growth, the disparity of experiences fits neatly into the expected continental lines. The three Asian economies grew so fast since the end of the 1970s that income per capita practically doubled during the 15 or so years under analysis. In the four Latin American countries, growth performance was disappointing. It was close to zero in Argentina and Brazil, positive but small in Mexico, and moderate in Colombia. Taiwan, China, was poorer than both Brazil and Mexico in 1980, but substantially richer in the mid-1990s.

All of those changes are likely to have had strong effects on the distribution of income, because many of them are known to be strongly income selective. Changes in female participation in the labor force or in fertility behavior are certainly not uniform across the population. Moreover, they directly affect per capita income in the households in which they take place. Likewise, per capita growth rates as high as 6 percent a year during 15-year periods are likely to be accompanied by changes in the structure of the economy that have repercussions on income distribution. Nevertheless, the net outcome in terms of the change in the Gini coefficient is far from uniform. It ranges from a decline of 0.4 Gini points in (urban) Brazil to a rise of 8.4 Gini points in (the Greater Buenos Aires area of) Argentina.

However, these changes are not perfectly comparable across the seven economies. For a start, the periods over which each economy was observed differ somewhat. So does the coverage of the survey, particularly for Argentina and Brazil. Nevertheless, it is probably safe to assert that, despite facing broadly similar trends in terms of demographics, education, urbanization, and female participation, the seven economies have experienced very different changes in inequality. How should this observation be interpreted? Can all the differences be attributed to differences in growth rates or in the sectoral composition of output? Did the distributional effects of structural changes tend to compensate one another more in Brazil and Malaysia than in Indonesia and Mexico? Or are the distributional effects of each structural change themselves of smaller size in the first two economies? How is the net result produced in each economy, and why does it differ so much between them? Are changes in the distribution of income associated with changes in the stock of education more important than changes in the returns to skills? Are educational factors more or less important than changes in occupational choices or fertility patterns? Those questions are taken up for each economy in chapters 3 through 9 and are summarized in chapter 10.

Decomposing Changes in Inequality: An Introduction

This study is certainly not the first one in which economists have tried to decompose changes in inequality in order to gain some insight into the processes that underlie them. Because the number of reliable data sets with the required time coverage before World War II was very small, it is probably fair to say that the first well-known empirical study of long-term income distribution dynamics was by Simon Kuznets (1955). Since then, a good number of studies have looked at the determinants of changes in poverty and inequality. The literature is too large to be done justice here, and we do not propose to survey it comprehensively. However, it may be useful to distinguish between two broad approaches to distributional change that are present in the literature. We will refer to the first, which relies primarily on aggregated data, as the *macroeconomic approach*. By contrast, empirical studies relying on fully disaggregated data from household surveys fall under the *microeconomic approach*.

Macroeconomic approaches can be further classified into two groups. The first includes those that use standard regression analysis, relating aggregate poverty or inequality indices as dependent variables to a set of macroeconomic or structural (supposedly) independent variables. There are examples in which the variation occurs on a time series, as in Blejer and Guerrero (1990) and Ferreira and Litchfield (2001), and there are examples in which it occurs in a cross-section, as in Dollar and Kraay (2002), Ravallion (1997), and Ravallion and Chen (1997). These papers were, to a large extent, inspired by an earlier literature related to the empirical Kuznets curve (see, for example, Ahluwalia 1976), which also belongs in this group.

This approach has at least two serious shortcomings. First, concerns about the endogeneity of many right-hand-side variables that are included—as well as about biases arising from others that are not[6]—mean that the regressions can at best be interpreted as (very) reduced-form estimates of the relationship between summary measures of poverty and inequality and a few macroeconomic variables. Second, although single inequality and poverty indices are useful summary statistics, they are informationally restricted and often are not robust to changes in the assumptions underlying their construction (see Atkinson 1970).

The second group of approaches relies on computable general equilibrium models. Once again, there is a long lineage. Some important contributions include Adelman and Robinson (1978); Bourguignon, de Melo, and Suwa (1991); Decaluwé and others (1999); and Lysy and Taylor (1980). Computable general equilibrium models introduce more structure, but they are still essentially macroeconomic in nature and capture the distributional effect of only a limited number of variables, and then only on a limited number of classes or groups. They are also pure simulation models, which rely on rough calibration procedures rather than on time-series or detailed household-level data. These approaches do not capture the most interesting and revealing factors that explain the evolution of individual or household incomes and thus often appear inconclusive. This happens because the inherent diversity of individual situations and the complexity that characterizes the interaction of endowments, human behavior, and market conditions in determining individual incomes require a microeconomic focus.

Of course, in parallel with these macroeconomic strands of the literature on income distribution dynamics there is also an established microeconomic tradition. Its distinguishing feature is that whereas the macroeconomic work relies on aggregated data for countries or regions, the microeconomic work relies on household-level data. The most common microeconomic approach found in the literature is based on decompositions of changes in poverty or inequality measures by population subgroups.[7] In the case of inequality, the change in some scalar measure is decomposed into what is due to changes in the relative mean income of various predetermined groups of individuals or households, what is due to changes in their population weights, and—residually—what is due to changes in the inequality within those groups. When groups are defined by some characteristic of the household or household head, such as location, age, or schooling, the method identifies the contribution of changes in those characteristics to changes in poverty or inequality. The decomposition of changes in the mean log deviation of earnings in the United Kingdom, by Mookherjee and Shorrocks (1982), is the best illustration of this type of work.

The comparison of poverty profiles over time (Huppi and Ravallion 1996) or of poverty probit analyses (Psacharopoulos and others 1993) belong to the same tradition.[8] There are at least four principal limitations to these approaches. First, the analysis again relies on summary measures of inequality and poverty, rather than on the full distribution. Second, the decomposition of changes in inequality or poverty measures often leaves an unexplained residual of a nontrivial magnitude. Third, the decompositions do not easily allow for controls: it is impossible, for instance, to identify the partial share attributable to each factor in a joint decomposition of inequality changes by education, race, and gender subgroups. Finally, they shed no light on whether the contribution of a particular attribute to changes in overall inequality is due to changes in its distribution or due to changes in market returns to it. A large share for education, for instance, might be consistent with large shifts in the distribution of years of schooling, with changes in returns, or—indeed—with various combinations of the two.

An alternative approach, which seeks to address all four of these shortcomings in scalar decompositions, is the counterfactual simulation of entire distributions on the basis of the disaggregated information contained in the household survey data set. This approach was first applied by Almeida dos Reis and Paes de Barros (1991) for Brazil. Juhn, Murphy, and Pierce (1993) use a technique of this kind to study the determinants of the increase in wage inequality in the United States during the 1970s and 1980s. Blau and Khan (1996) use this approach to compare wage distributions across 10 industrial countries. A semiparametric version of this approach is provided by DiNardo, Fortin, and Lemieux (1996) in a study of U.S. wage distribution between 1973 and 1992, which essentially relies on reweighing observations in kernel density estimates of continuous distributions of earnings so as to construct appropriate counterfactual distributions that shed light on the nature of the change in the actual distribution over time.[9]

As in the studies cited in the preceding paragraph, the method proposed and applied in this volume follows in the tradition established by Oaxaca (1973) and Blinder (1973). All of these approaches seek to shed light on what determines differences across income distributions by simulating counterfactual distributions that differ from an observed distribution in a controlled manner. Unlike Blau and Khan (1996); Juhn, Murphy, and Pierce (1993); or, indeed, any of the aforementioned studies, all of which were concerned with wage distributions, the analysis in this book seeks to understand the more complex dynamics of the distribution of *welfare*, proxied by the distribution of (per capita or equivalized) household income. The underlying determinants of this distribution are more complex. In addition to the quantities and prices of individual characteristics that determine earnings rates, household incomes depend also on participation and occupational choices, on demographic trends, and on nonlabor incomes.

As a result, the approach followed here generalizes the counterfactual simulation techniques from the single (earnings) equation model to a system of multiple (nonlinear) equations that is meant to represent mechanisms of household income generation. This system comprises earnings equations, equations for potential household self-employment income, and occupational-choice models that describe how individuals at working age allocate their time between wage work, self-employment, and nonmarket time. In some cases, it also includes equations for determining educational levels and the number of children living in the household.

In each economy, the model is estimated entirely in reduced form, thus avoiding the insurmountable difficulties associated with joint estimation of the participation and earnings equations for each household member. We maintain some strong assumptions about the independence of residuals. Therefore, the estimation results are never interpreted as corresponding to a structural model and no causal inference is drawn. We interpret the parameter estimates generated by these equations only as descriptions of conditional distributions, whose functional forms we maintain hypotheses about. Yet, even in this limited capacity, these estimates help us gain useful insights into the nature of differences across distributions and about the underlying forces behind their evolution over time.

The most important methodological contribution undertaken in this book is to generalize the counterfactual simulation approach to distributional change from earnings to household income distributions. The approach thus applies to problems related to the distribution of total income, rather than only those related to the distribution of earnings. The method can shed light on the evolution of the entire distribution, rather than merely on the path of summary statistics. And it can decompose any change in the incomes of a set of households into its fundamental sources: changes in the amounts of resources at their disposal (reflected in the population or endowments effects), changes in how the markets remunerate those resources (reflected in the price effects), and changes in the decisions made about how to use those resources (reflected in the occupational effects).

Within each such category, this approach also allows us to identify the contributions from *specific* endowments and prices. Thus, we can distinguish the effect of changes in returns to education from those of other "prices," such as the effect of experience or of the gender wage gap. Analogously, we are able to understand the effect of changes in the distribution of education separately from that of changes in demographics. We can then shed some light on how one affects the other, always in terms of understanding how the conditional distributions of those variables have evolved, rather than seeking to establish directions of causation. This is as far as our econometrics allows us to go. But it is farther than we have gone before.

The proposed methodology has some important advantages over others that have been used in the field. First, as we shall see, small changes in aggregate indices of inequality can hide strong countervailing forces. For example, a large reduction in dispersion in the distribution of years of education could be partially offset by the inequality-increasing effect of a rising skill premium. Substantial changes in spatial premiums (such as those evident from wage gaps between urban and rural areas) may be offset by migration and changes in labor-force participation (as in the Indonesian case). A rise in household income inequality arising from increases in the labor-force participation rates of educated women can be partly offset by "progressive" declines in family size (as in the case of Taiwan, China). Methods that rely on decomposing a scalar measure of inequality will gloss over those dynamics. As we show in the subsequent chapters, the evolution of the distribution of income is the result of many different effects—some of them quite large—which may offset one another in whole or in part. Researchers and policymakers may find it useful to disentangle those effects, rather than to focus on a single dimension.

Finally, the approach used here has an additional advantage. Because it analyzes the entire distribution of income, one can assess how different factors affect different parts of the distribution. That assessment can shed light on how different groups (for example, the urban versus the rural poor) are affected by changes in the distribution of assets, changes in the returns to those assets, and changes in how individuals and households choose to use their assets. The next chapter contains a formal presentation of the approach used in this book, which we refer to as generalized Oaxaca-Blinder decompositions.

Notes

1. See, among others, Banerjee and Newman (1993), Galor and Zeira (1993), and Bénabou (2000). For good surveys, see Aghion, Caroli, and Garcia-Penalosa (1999) and Atkinson and Bourguignon (2000).

2. This volume is the result of a five-year multicountry research effort, known as the project on the Microeconomics of Income Distribution Dynamics (MIDD), which was sponsored by the Inter-American Development Bank and the World Bank.

3. A slightly modified version of the argument that follows could just as easily be made for the reverse specification (with inequality explaining growth) or, indeed, for the joint estimation of a two-equation model.

4. Data availability played a role in selecting economies from these two regions. The proposed methodology requires the availability of at least two comparable household surveys, separated by an interval of at least one decade, so that medium- to long-run structural effects of economic development and of changes in the sociodemographic characteristics of the population on the distribution of income may be captured.

5. During the period in which this research project was conducted, a number of other excellent applications of the methodology have been produced. They include Altimir, Beccaria, and Rozada (2001) on Argentina; Bravo and others (2000) on Chile; Dercon (2001) on Ethiopia; Grimm (2002) on Côte d'Ivoire; and Ruprah (2000) on the República Bolivariana de Venezuela.

6. Sometimes only GDP is used as the explanatory variable, as in the Kuznets curve literature.

7. This approach draws on earlier, static, decomposition approaches suggested by Bourguignon (1979), Cowell (1980), and Shorrocks (1980).

8. A related approach decomposes changes in scalar poverty measures into a component attributable to growth in the mean and one attributable to changes in the Lorenz curve (a "redistribution component"; see Datt and Ravallion 1992).

9. An alternative semiparametric approach to the estimation of density functions, which relies on their close relationship to hazard functions, was proposed by Donald, Green, and Paarsch (2000).

References

Adelman, Irma, and Sherman Robinson. 1978. *Income Distribution Policy: A Computable General Equilibrium Model of South Korea*. San Francisco: Stanford University Press.

Aghion, Philippe, Eve Caroli, and Cecilia Garcia-Penalosa. 1999. "Inequality and Economic Growth: The Perspective of New Growth Theory." *Journal of Economic Literature* 37(4): 1615–60.

Ahluwalia, Montek. 1976. "Income Distribution and Development: Some Stylized Facts." *American Economic Review* 66(2): 128–35.

Alesina, Alberto, and Dani Rodrik. 1994. "Distributive Politics and Economic Growth." *Quarterly Journal of Economics* 109: 465–89.

Almeida dos Reis, José, and Ricardo Paes de Barros. 1991. "Wage Inequality and the Distribution of Education: A Study of the Evolution of Regional Differences in Inequality in Metropolitan Brazil." *Journal of Development Economics* 36: 117–43.

Altimir, Oscar, Luis Beccaria, and Martín González Rozada. 2001. "La Evolución de la Distribución del Ingreso Familiar en la Argentina: Un Análisis de Determinantes." *Serie de Estudios en Finanzas Públicas* 7. Maestría en Finanzas Públicas Provinciales y Municipales, Universidad Nacional de La Plata, La Plata Argentina.

Atkinson, Anthony B. 1970. "On the Measurement of Inequality." *Journal of Economic Theory* 2: 244–63.

Atkinson, Anthony B., and François Bourguignon. 2000. "Income Distribution and Economics." In Anthony B. Atkinson and François Bourguignon, eds., *Handbook of Income Distribution*, Vol. 1. Amsterdam: North-Holland.

Banerjee, Abhijit V., and Andrew F. Newman. 1993. "Occupational Choice and the Process of Development." *Journal of Political Economy* 101(2): 274–98.

Bénabou, Roland. 2000. "Unequal Societies: Income Distribution and the Social Contract." *American Economic Review* 90(1): 96–129.

Blau, Francine, and Lawrence Khan. 1996. "International Differences in Male Wage Inequality: Institutions versus Market Forces." *Journal of Political Economy* 104(4): 791–837.

Blejer, Mario, and Isabel Guerrero. 1990. "The Impact of Macroeconomic Policies on Income Distribution: An Empirical Study of the Philippines." *Review of Economics and Statistics* 72(3): 414–23.

Blinder, Alan S. 1973. "Wage Discrimination: Reduced Form and Structural Estimates." *Journal of Human Resources* 8: 436–55.

Bourguignon, François. 1979. "Decomposable Income Inequality Measures." *Econometrica* 47: 901–20.

Bourguignon, François, Jaime de Melo, and Akiko Suwa. 1991. "Modeling the Effects of Adjustment Programs on Income Distribution." *World Development* 19(11): 1527–44.

Bravo, David, Dante Contreras, Tomás Rau, and Sergio Urzúa. 2000. "Income Distribution in Chile, 1990–1998: Learning from Microsimulations." Universidad de Chile, Santiago. Processed.

Cowell, Frank A. 1980. "On the Structure of Additive Inequality Measures." *Review of Economic Studies* 47: 521–31.

Datt, Gaurav, and Martin Ravallion. 1992. "Growth and Redistribution Components of Changes in Poverty Measures." *Journal of Development Economics* 38: 275–95.

Decaluwé, Bernard, André Patry, Luc Savard, and Erik Thorbecke. 1999. "Social Accounting Matrices and General Equilibrium Models in Income Distribution and Poverty Analysis." Cornell University, Ithaca, N.Y. Processed.

Dercon, Stefan. 2001. "Economic Reform, Growth and the Poor: Evidence from Rural Ethiopia." Center for the Study of African Economies, Oxford University, Oxford, U.K. Processed.

DiNardo, John, Nicole Fortin, and Thomas Lemieux. 1996. "Labor Market Institutions and the Distribution of Wages, 1973–1992: A Semiparametric Approach." *Econometrica* 64(5): 1001–44.

Dollar, David, and Aart Kraay. 2002. "Growth *Is* Good for the Poor." *Journal of Economic Growth* 7: 195–225.

Donald, Stephen, David Green, and Harry Paarsch. 2000. "Differences in Wage Distributions between Canada and the United States: An Application of a Flexible Estimator of Distribution Functions in the Presence of Covariates." *Review of Economic Studies* 67: 609–33.

Ferreira, Francisco H. G., and Julie A. Litchfield. 2001. "Education or Inflation?: The Micro and Macroeconomics of the Brazilian Income Distribution during 1981–1995." *Cuadernos de Economía* 38: 209–38.

Forbes, Kristin J. 2000. "A Reassessment of the Relationship between Inequality and Growth." *American Economic Review* 90(4): 869–87.

Galor, Oded, and Joseph Zeira. 1993. "Income Distribution and Macroeconomics." *Review of Economic Studies* 60: 35–52.

Grimm, Michael. 2002. "Macroeconomic Adjustment, Socio-Demographic Change, and the Evolution of Income Distribution in Côte d'Ivoire." World Institute for Development Economics Research, Helsinki. Processed.

Huppi, Monika, and Martin Ravallion. 1996. "The Sectoral Structure of Poverty during an Adjustment Period: Evidence for Indonesia in the Mid-1980s." *World Development* 19: 1653–78.

Juhn, Chinhui, Kevin Murphy, and Brooks Pierce. 1993. "Wage Inequality and the Rise in Returns to Skill." *Journal of Political Economy* 101(3): 410–42.

Kuznets, Simon. 1955. "Economic Growth and Income Inequality." *American Economic Review* 45(1): 1–28.

Lewis, W. Arthur. 1954. "Economic Development with Unlimited Supplies of Labour." *Manchester School* 22: 139–91.

Lysy, Frank, and Lance Taylor. 1980. "The General Equilibrium Model of Income Distribution." In Lance Taylor, Edmar Bacha, Eliana Cardoso, and Frank Lysy, eds., *Models of Growth and Distribution for Brazil.* Oxford, U.K.: Oxford University Press.

Marx, Karl. 1887. *Capital: A Critical Analysis of Capitalist Production,* Vol. 1. London: Sonnenschein. (Republished by St. Leonards, Australia: Allen & Unwin, 1938.)

Mookherjee, Dilip, and Anthony F. Shorrocks. 1982. "A Decomposition Analysis of the Trend in U.K. Income Inequality." *Economic Journal* 92: 886–902.

Oaxaca, Ronald. 1973. "Male-Female Wage Differentials in Urban Labor Markets." *International Economic Review* 14: 673–709.

Psacharopoulos, George, Samuel Morley, Ariel Fiszbein, Haeduck Lee, and William Wood. 1993. "La Pobreza y la Distribución de los Ingresos en América Latina, Historia del Decenio de 1980." Documento Técnico 351S. World Bank.

Ravallion, Martin. 1997. "Can High-Inequality Developing Countries Escape Absolute Poverty?" *Economics Letters* 56: 51–57.

Ravallion, Martin, and Shaohua Chen. 1997. "What Can New Survey Data Tell Us about Recent Changes in Distribution and Poverty?" *World Bank Economic Review* 11(2): 357–82.

Ruprah, Inder. 2000. "Digging a Hole: Income Inequality in Venezuela." Inter-American Development Bank, Washington, D.C. Processed.

Shorrocks, Anthony F. 1980. "The Class of Additively Decomposable Inequality Measures," *Econometrica* 48: 613–25.

Tinbergen, Jan. 1975. *Income Differences: Recent Research.* Oxford, U.K.: North-Holland.

2

Decomposing Changes in the Distribution of Household Incomes: Methodological Aspects

François Bourguignon and Francisco H. G. Ferreira

Many different forces are behind long-run changes in income distributions or, more generally, distributions of economic welfare, within a population. Some of those forces have to do with changes in the distribution of factor endowments and sociodemographic characteristics among economic agents, others with the returns these endowments command in the economy, and others still with modifications in agents' behavior such as labor supply, consumption patterns, or fertility choices. Of course, those forces are not independent of one another. In some cases, they tend to offset one another, whereas in others they could reinforce one another. They are also likely to be affected by exogenous economic shocks as well as by government policies and development strategies. For all of these reasons, it is generally difficult to precisely identify fundamental causes and mechanisms behind the dynamics of income distribution. Yet, extracting information about the nature and magnitude of those forces from observed distributional changes is crucial for an understanding of the development process and the scope of policy intervention in the distributional sphere.

This is a difficult analytical task, and it is tempting to rely on statistical decomposition techniques that are meant to more or less automatically identify the main causes for distributional changes. Such techniques have long been in use in the fields of income and consumption distribution analysis. Largely for computational reasons, however, they have been limited to explaining differences in scalar summary measures of distributions, rather than in the full distributions. In other words, the techniques focused on some specific definition of aggregate social welfare (or inequality) rather than on the distribution of individual welfare. Among the best examples of these techniques are the well-known Oaxaca-Blinder decomposition of differences in mean incomes across population groups with different characteristics (Blinder 1973; Oaxaca 1973) and the variance-like decomposition property of the so-called decomposable summary inequality measures (Bourguignon 1979; Cowell 1980; Shorrocks 1980). In both cases, the underlying logic is that the aggregate mean income (or inequality measure) in a population is the result of the aggregation of various sociodemographic groups or income sources. Thus, changes in the overall mean or inequality measure can be explained by identifying changes in the means and inequality measures within those groups or income sources, and in their weights in the population or in total income.

These early decomposition techniques proved to be extremely useful in several circumstances, and they should still be used as a first step in explaining changes in distributions of some economic attributes. Indeed, the Oaxaca-Blinder approach is still often used to analyze wage discrimination across genders or union status. Likewise, decomposing inequality measures such as the Theil coefficient or the mean logarithmic deviation according to gender, education, or age groups may often be quite informative about the broad structure of inequality in a society. At the same time, there is both a growing need and an increasing computational capacity to work with the entire distribution, rather than merely with its first moment or a few inequality indices. In particular, the focus on poverty reduction, which increasingly drives development policy, requires analysis of the shape of the distribution in the neighborhood of and below the poverty line. In terms of the Oaxaca-Blinder approach, the issue is to know not so much whether mean earnings are lower for women than for men because the former have less average education, as whether the differences are greater or smaller for the bottom part of the earnings distribution. Answering this kind of question requires handling the whole distribution, rather than summary measures. Several techniques for decomposing distributional change, rather than merely changes in individual inequality or poverty measures, have been developed in the past decade or so—in part because of increasing computational capacity.

The technique used to analyze long-run distributional changes in this book belongs to this recent stream of new decomposition methodologies. It is based on a parametric representation of the way in which household income per capita or individual earnings are linked to household or individual sociodemographic characteristics, or *endowments*. From this point of view, it bears great resemblance to the Oaxaca-Blinder approach, except for two points: (a) it deals with the entire distribution, rather than just the means of income or earnings, and (b) the parametric representation of the income-generation process for a household is more complex than the determination of individual earnings, in ways that we shall discuss below. As in the Oaxaca-Blinder method, however, the decomposition of distributional change essentially consists of contrasting representations of the income-generation process (that is, evaluating differences in estimated parameters) for two different distributions (for example, two points in time), on the one hand, and accounting for changes in the joint distribution of endowments, on the other hand. Other methods, which do not rely so much on a parametric representation of individual or household income generation, could also have been applied to the case studies in the chapters that follow.[1] Yet, it turns out that the parametric representation used throughout this volume is actually of inherent interest, because the parameters lend themselves directly to relevant economic interpretations.

This chapter presents this methodology for decomposing observed changes in the (entire) distribution of household income per capita. It opens with a brief survey of decomposition techniques applied to the mean or to summary measures of income inequality. It continues with a general statement of the decomposition techniques that handle the whole distribution, focusing on the parametric method used in this volume. It then shows the detail of the parametric representation of household income-generation processes that, in one way or another, underlies all case studies in this volume. The last section addresses a number of general econometric issues that arise in the estimation of the model.

Decomposing Distributional Change: Scalar Methods

The general problem is that of comparing two distributions of income—or of any other welfare measure[2]—in a population at two points in time, *t* and *t'*. Without too much loss of generality, the two distributions will be represented by their density functions: $f^t(y)$ and $f^{t'}(y)$. The objective is to explain the change from $f^t(y)$ to $f^{t'}(y)$ by a series of elementary changes concerned with changes in the socio-demographic structure of the population, in income disparities across sociodemographic groups or, possibly, in the relative importance and distribution of a particular income source. Before considering this general functional problem, we briefly review simple ways of performing that decomposition when density functions are replaced by some scalar summary index.

The Oaxaca-Blinder Decomposition of Changes in Means

Although it refers to a decomposition of differences in means, rather than in distributions, it is convenient to start this short review with the so-called Oaxaca-Blinder method. Indeed, this method relies on a general principle that will be extensively used later. In addition, dealing with the first moments of the distributions $f^t(y)$ and $f^{t'}(y)$ should provide some indication as to how one could deal with higher order moments and, therefore, with inequality or poverty.

Oaxaca (1973) and Blinder (1973) independently found the following way for comparing the mean earnings of two different populations.[3] Assume that income may satisfactorily be approximated by the following linear model in both periods t and t':

$$(2.1) \qquad \begin{aligned} y_{it} &= X_{it} \cdot \beta_t + u_{it} \\ y_{jt'} &= X_{jt'} \cdot \beta_{t'} + u_{jt'}. \end{aligned}$$

In other words, the income of individual i observed in period t is supposed to depend linearly on a vector of his or her observed characteristics, X_{it}, and on some unobserved characteristics summarized by the residual term, u_{it}. The same relationship holds for individual j observed in period t', who presumably is different from the individual observed in period t. The coefficients β_t and $\beta_{t'}$ simply map individual characteristics, X, into income, y. If the components of X are seen as individual endowments, then the β coefficients may be interpreted as rates of return on those endowments, or as the "prices" of the services associated with them. Given a sample of individual observations at time t and another at time t', these prices may be estimated by ordinary least squares, under the usual assumption that the residual terms are independent of the observed endowments.

Consider now the change in mean earnings or income between periods t and t'. Under the innocuous assumption that the expected value of the residual terms is zero, an elementary transformation leads to the following decomposition of the change in (the cross-sectional) means:

$$(2.2) \qquad \Delta \bar{y} = \bar{y}_{t'} - \bar{y}_t = \beta_t \cdot (\bar{X}_{t'} - \bar{X}_t) + \bar{X}_{t'} \cdot (\beta_{t'} - \beta_t).$$

The change in mean earnings thus appears as the sum of two effects: (a) that of a change in mean endowments at constant prices (that is, the *endowment effect*), and (b) that of a change in prices at constant mean endowments (that is, the *price effect*). In other words, the change in the mean earnings of the population between times t and t' is explained by a change in its mean characteristics (education, age, area of residence, and so on) and by a change in the rates of return to these characteristics. For instance, when the Oaxaca-Blinder decomposition bears on gender differences, the gender gap is decomposed into what is due to (a) the fact that working women and men do not have the same characteristics in terms of education, age, or occupation, and (b) the fact that, at constant characteristics, they are not paid the same rate.

The practical interest of a decomposition such as equation 2.2 is obvious. If economic analysis were able to predict or explain changes in the price system, β, then it would be easy to figure out what such changes may imply for the evolution of mean earnings or incomes. Of course, this decomposition ignores any possible causal relationship between the two sources of change. Yet it is likely that observed changes in prices may be caused at least partly by changes in the sociodemographic structure of the population, and also that changes in prices in turn induce some changes in the sociodemographic structure of the population. For instance, a more educated labor force may lead to narrower wage-skill gaps, and a wider wage-skill gap may be an incentive for part of the population to become more educated.

Three additional points must be noted about the Oaxaca-Blinder decomposition. First, the decomposition identity (equation 2.2) is path dependent. Indeed, an identity similar to equation 2.2 is as follows:

$$\Delta \bar{y} = \bar{y}_{t'} - \bar{y}_t = \beta_{t'} (\bar{X}_{t'} - \bar{X}_t) + \bar{X}_t \cdot (\beta_{t'} - \beta_t).$$

In this case, the endowment effect is evaluated using the prices at period t', whereas the price effect is estimated using the initial mean endowments. There is no reason for this decomposition to give the same estimates of the price and endowment effect as equation 2.2. The path that is used for the decomposition matters.[4]

A second point to be stressed is that different interpretations may be given to the endowment and the price effects identified by the preceding decomposition formula. For instance, the endowment effect may be interpreted as the effect of simply changing the weight of various population subgroups that are predefined by common endowments. The price effect could then be interpreted as the effect of changing the relative mean incomes of these groups. This interpretation may be closer to the definition of the decomposition of distributional changes given at the beginning of this chapter. Note also that the decomposition formula (equation 2.2) may be interpreted simply as the effect on the mean income of changing the importance of various income sources, either through the β coefficients, or through the mean endowments $\bar{X}$. In effect, the decomposition operates through the components $\beta_t^k \bar{X}_t^k$ of the scalar product $\beta_t \bar{X}_t$, which may rather naturally be interpreted as different sources of income.

Finally, the way the Oaxaca-Blinder approach was just presented might give the impression that it has little to do with the analysis of inequality, because it is concerned with means. This impression is not entirely appropriate. Suppose that the decomposition formula (equation 2.2) is applied at time t to the difference in the mean incomes of two population groups A and B—men and women, for instance—rather than being applied to a time difference. Equation 2.2 could then be rewritten as

$$\Delta \bar{y} = \bar{y}_B - \bar{y}_A = \beta_A \cdot (\bar{X}_B - \bar{X}_A) + \bar{X}_B \cdot (\beta_B - \beta_A).$$

This earnings differential represents part of the inequality in the distribution of earnings (at time t): that part which is due to differences between groups A and B. The change in inequality between periods t and t' will therefore include, among other things, the change in the A/B earnings differential. It might thus be decomposed into a change in the difference in endowments between groups A and B and a change in the difference in prices faced by the two groups. This argument simply combines an application of the Oaxaca-Blinder decomposition in a cross-section with an application over time. We will see below that the generalization of the Oaxaca-Blinder method to handle entire distributions, rather than their first-order moments, involves an argument of this type.

Decomposing Changes in Income Inequality Measures

The principle behind the foregoing decomposition may also be applied to higher moments and, in particular, to summary inequality measures. The "decomposable" or Generalized Entropy inequality measures are endowed with very convenient decomposition properties.[5] Suppose that the population of income earners is partitioned into G groups, $g = 1, 2, \ldots, G$, and denote by I_g the inequality measure for group g and by I the inequality for the whole population. These measures satisfy the following general property:

$$(2.3) \quad I = \sum_{g=1}^{G} I_g w(n_g, m_g) + \bar{I}(n_1, \bar{y}_1; n_2, \bar{y}_2; \ldots; n_G, \bar{y}_G) = I_W + I_B$$

where n_g and m_g stand respectively for the population and income shares of group g within the whole population and $\bar{I}(\ldots)$ is the inequality between groups—that is to say, the inequality that would be observed in the population if all incomes were equal within each group g. The distribution of income would thus consist of n_1 times the income $\bar{y}_1$, n_2 times the income $\bar{y}_2$, and so forth. Total inequality, I, thus decomposes into two terms: the mean within-group inequality, where each group g is weighted by a weight, w, which depends on population and income shares, and the between-group inequality, $\bar{I}(\ldots)$.

The preceding property is intuitive because it resembles the well-known decomposition of variances across population subgroups. In the present context, however, we are less interested in the decomposition among groups at a point in time than in that of the change in inequality between two points in time. Differentiating equation 2.3, it follows that the change in overall inequality, ΔI, may be expressed as the sum of the change in within-group inequality, ΔI_W, and the change in between-group inequality, ΔI_B. In turn, both changes may be expressed as linear combinations of changes in within-group inequality measures ΔI_g, and changes in population and income shares, Δn_g and Δm_g.[6]

The mean logarithmic deviation is the simplest of all decomposable measures. Its expression for a population of n individuals i is the following:

$$L = \sum_{i=1}^{n} \frac{1}{n} \text{Log}(\bar{y}/y_i).$$

It is easily shown that the preceding decomposition formula (equation 2.3) writes, in this case

$$L = \sum_{g=1}^{G} n_g L_g + \sum_{g=1}^{G} n_g \text{Log}(\bar{y}/\bar{y}_g) = I_W + I_B.$$

Finally differencing this expression between two periods t and t' yields the following:[7]

$$\Delta L \approx \sum_{g=1}^{G} n_g \left[\frac{\Delta \bar{y}}{\bar{y}} - \frac{\Delta \bar{y}_g}{\bar{y}_g} \right]$$

$$(2.4) \qquad + \sum_{g=1}^{G} \left[L_g + \text{Log}(\bar{y}/\bar{y}_g) \right] \Delta n_g + \sum_{g=1}^{G} n_g \Delta L_g.$$

The total change in inequality is thus expressed as the sum of three types of effects: (a) changes in the relative mean income of the groups, (b) changes in group population weights,[8] and (c) changes in within-group inequality. Analogous expressions can be derived for the other members of the family of decomposable inequality measures.

For practical purposes, this decomposition methodology is implemented as follows. Suppose that the population of earners has been partitioned by educational attainment: no schooling, primary, lower secondary, and so forth. Then, following the preceding decomposition, the change in overall inequality between year t and t' may be analyzed as the sum of (a) the effects of changes in relative earnings by educational level, (b) the effects of changes in the educational structure of the population, and (c) the effects of changes in inequality within educational groups. Thus, the last term is often taken as a kind of residual, corresponding to that part of the change in inequality that is not explained by the change in mean incomes across educational groups and the educational structure of the population.

Of course, the preceding decomposition can be implemented for all possible observed characteristics of individuals in the population and, indeed, for all possible combinations of characteristics. For instance, groups may be defined simultaneously by the education of the household head, his or her age, his or her area of residence, or the number of people in the household. There are numerous applications of this decomposition methodology, starting with the analysis of the evolution of inequality in the United Kingdom by Mookherjee and Shorrocks (1982). One of the reasons for its appeal is its analogy with the Oaxaca-Blinder decomposition: changes in group relative incomes play a role similar to the changes in the price coefficients, β, whereas the change in groups' population weights is another way of representing the changes in the sociodemographic structure of the population, $\overline{X}_{t'} - \overline{X}_t$. There are two basic differences between these two approaches, beyond the fact that one is applied to mean incomes and the other to income inequality. First, the inequality decomposition formula is nonparametric, whereas the Oaxaca-Blinder relies on a linear income model.[9] Second, the inequality decomposition has a residual term—the change in within-group inequality—which is independent of the inputs of the Oaxaca-Blinder decomposition.[10]

This residual is one of the sources of dissatisfaction with the preceding methodology. In empirical applications, it turns out to be an important component of observed change in inequality, even though it does not lend itself to an economic interpretation as easily as the other two components. Another source of dissatisfaction is that it seems somewhat restrictive to analyze changes in distribution through a single summary inequality measure. Of course, this decomposition might be combined with the Oaxaca-Blinder decomposition, thus yielding information on the change in the mean as well as on the disparity of incomes. But that disparity is still summarized by a single index. Using alternative indices belonging to the general class of decomposable inequality measures is always possible but never quite as convincing as looking at differences across the entire distribution.

A final problem with the decomposition of changes in decomposable inequality measures is that it applies to a disaggregation of the population into subgroups, but not to a disaggregation of income by sources. Suppose that the income of individual i may be expressed as the sum of incomes coming from two sources, say, wages (1) and self-employment (2): $y_i = y_{1i} + y_{2i}$.

It may be interesting to decompose the change in the inequality of total income into what is due to the changes in the means and in the inequality of income sources 1 and 2. The preceding decomposition formulas do not work in this case. In particular, it is simply not true that total inequality is the weighted average of the inequality of each income source. The covariance of the two sources within the population is of obvious importance.

Shorrocks (1982) shows the way in which total inequality I_y at a point in time can be decomposed into the inequality coming from the various income sources. In particular, he shows that, for E_2, the Generalized Entropy measure with $\alpha = 2$, it is identically true that

$$(2.5) \qquad E_2 = \sum_j \frac{\text{cov}(y_j, y)}{\sqrt{\text{var}(y_j)\text{var}(y)}} \frac{\overline{y}_j}{\overline{y}} (E_2 \, E_{2j})^{1/2}$$

where $\text{cov}(y_j, y)$ is the covariance between the income source j $(= 1, 2)$ and total income in the population. In other words, the ratio of this covariance and the variance of total income may be interpreted as the percentage contribution of income source j to total inequality, whatever the inequality measure being used.

It turns out that this decomposition is somewhat difficult to use when time changes are considered. Indeed, to analyze how a change in the distribution of an income source—say, source 1—may modify the overall inequality of income, one must first figure out how this change may modify the covariance between that income source and total income. Doing so requires figuring out how the change in the distribution of source 1 may itself modify the covariance between the incomes of sources 1 and 2. In other words, the analyst must not operate only at the level of the marginal distribution of income of one source but at the level of the joint distribution of incomes arising from the various sources. The need to handle this joint distribution may explain why the preceding property of decomposability by income source is seldom used in empirical work on distributional changes.[11]

*Decomposing Changes in Poverty and the Need for
Distributional Analysis*

Poverty measures are scalars that summarize the shape of the distribution of income up to some arbitrary poverty line, z. The simplest poverty measure is the headcount ratio, H, which is simply the value of the cumulative distribution function at the poverty line. Other poverty measures may be defined on the basis of specific axioms. There is an infinity of poverty measures associated with any given poverty line, z, as there is an infinity of inequality measures. Among the properties frequently desired from poverty measures is subgroup decomposability, which simply requires poverty to be additive with respect to a partition of the whole population into two groups. Thus, if P^z is the poverty measure for the whole population when the poverty line is z and if P_j^z measures poverty in group j, the following property should hold:

$$P^z = \sum_j w_j \cdot P_j^z$$

where w_j stands for the demographic weight of group j, as before. Clearly, this property holds for the headcount ratio. In effect, all poverty measures based on the sum of individual income deprivation $(z - y_i)$ caused by poverty, whatever way in which this deprivation is measured, satisfy this property.[12]

Given the linear structure implied by subgroup decomposability, something akin to the Oaxaca-Blinder decomposition principle applies. Differencing the preceding expression with respect to time, we obtain the following:

(2.6) $$\Delta P^z = \sum_j w_j \cdot \Delta P_j^z + \sum_j P_j^z \Delta w_j.$$

In other words, the change in total poverty is decomposed into a component that is due to changes in poverty *within* groups and into a component that is due to changes in the population weights of the groups. If groups are defined by common sociodemographic characteristics, it may be said that the second term corresponds to the endowment effect in the Oaxaca-Blinder decomposition. The first term partly accounts for changes in prices and behavior that may generate changes in the mean income of a group and, therefore, changes in total poverty. But the change in total poverty also partly depends on changes in the distribution of income within groups. This was already the case with the residual term in the decomposition of a change in inequality (see equation 2.4). Unlike in the decomposition of inequality, however, here it is not possible to isolate these two effects. The basic reason is that inequality is defined on relative incomes, and it is therefore independent from the general scale of incomes and from the mean. On the contrary, poverty depends on the distribution of absolute incomes. As a consequence, a change in the general scale of incomes—and therefore in mean income—has a complex effect on poverty, which depends on the shape of the distribution around (and below) the poverty line.

It is, therefore, impossible to have changes in group mean incomes—which we have suggested are analogous to price and possibly behavioral effects—appearing explicitly in a simple way in the decomposition formula for poverty changes, as was the case for decomposable inequality measures. For poverty measurement, changes in mean incomes cannot be straightforwardly disentangled from distributional changes. Thus, poverty changes cannot be decomposed into endowment, price, and behavioral effects without considering the actual distribution within groups, rather than merely some summary poverty measure for each of those groups.[13]

A better understanding of changes in poverty thus requires a more disaggregated approach to distributional dynamics. And poverty is not the only reason to invest in developing such an approach. As indicated earlier, a combination of the standard Oaxaca-Blinder decomposition of changes in means with various inequality decompositions by population subgroup is hardly a direct and effective method to understand disaggregated changes in a distribution of income. The next section proposes a generalization of the Oaxaca-Blinder framework to deal directly with full distributions, rather than just means or other scalar indices.

Decomposing Distributional Change: Nonparametric and Parametric Methods for Entire Distributions

A Simple Generalization of Oaxaca-Blinder: Distributional Counterfactuals

This section offers a general formulation of the way in which the preceding scalar decomposition analysis may be extended to the case of distributional changes. Let $f^t(y)$ and $f^{t'}(y)$ be the density functions of the distribution of income, y, or any other definition of economic welfare, at times t and t'. The objective of the analysis is to identify the factors responsible for the change from the first to the second distribution.

To do so, it seems natural to depart from the joint distributions $\varphi^\tau(y, X)$, where X is a vector of observed individual or household characteristics, such as age, education, occupation, and family size. The superscript τ $(= t, t')$ denotes the period in which this joint distribution is observed. The distribution of household incomes, $f^\tau(y)$, is of course the marginal distribution of the joint distribution $\varphi^\tau(y, X)$:

$$(2.7) \qquad f^\tau(y) = \int \cdots \int_{C(X)} \varphi^\tau(y, X)\, dX$$

where the summation is over the domain $C(X)$ on which X is defined. Denoting $g^\tau(y|X)$, the distribution of income conditional on X, an equivalent expression of the marginal income distribution at time τ is

$$(2.8) \qquad f^\tau(y) = \int \cdots \int_{C(X)} g^\tau(y|X)\, \chi^\tau(X)\, dX$$

where $\chi^\tau(X)$ is the joint distribution of all elements of X at time τ.

Given that elementary decomposition, it is a simple matter to express the observed distributional change from $f^t(\ )$ to $f^{t'}(\ )$ as a function of the change in the two distributions appearing in equation 2.8—that is to say, the distribution of income conditional on characteristics X, $g(y|X)$, and the distribution of these characteristics, $\chi(X)$. To do so, define the following counterfactual experiment:

$$(2.9) \qquad f_g^{t \to t'}(y) = \int \cdots \int_{C(X)} g^{t'}(y|X)\, \chi^t(X)\, dX.$$

This distribution would have been observed at time t if the distribution of income conditional on characteristics X had been that observed in time t'. This counterfactual distribution may be calculated easily once the conditional distributions $g^t(y|X)$ and $g^{t'}(y|X)$, as well as the marginal distribution $\chi^t(X)$, have been identified. Likewise, one may define the counterfactual

$$(2.10) \qquad f_\chi^{t \to t'}(y) = \int \cdots \int_{C(X)} g^t(y|X)\, \chi^{t'}(X)\, dX$$

where, this time, it is the joint distribution of characteristics that has been modified. Note that this latter distribution could also have been obtained starting from the period t' and replacing the conditional income distribution of that period by the one observed in period t. In other words, it is identically the case that, with obvious notations,

(2.11) $f_g^{t \to t'}(y) \equiv f_\chi^{t' \to t}(y)$ and $f_\chi^{t \to t'}(y) \equiv f_g^{t' \to t}(y)$.

On the basis of the definition of these counterfactuals, the observed distributional change $f^{t'}(y) - f^t(y)$ may now be identically decomposed into

(2.12) $f^{t'}(y) - f^t(y) \equiv \left[f_g^{t \to t'}(y) - f^t(y) \right] + \left[f^{t'}(y) - f_g^{t \to t'}(y) \right]$.

As in the Oaxaca-Blinder equation, the observed distributional change is expressed as the sum of a price-behavioral effect and an endowment effect. Indeed, the first term on the right-hand side of equation 2.12 describes the way in which the distribution of income has changed over time because of the change in the distribution conditional on characteristics X. In other words, it shows how the same distribution of characteristics—that of period t—would have resulted in a different income distribution had the conditional distribution $g(y|X)$ been that of period t'. To see that the second term is indeed the effect of the change in the distribution of endowments that took place between times t and t', one can use equation 2.11 and rewrite the preceding decomposition formula as follows:

(2.13) $f^{t'}(y) - f^t(y) = \left[f_g^{t \to t'}(y) - f^t(y) \right] + \left[f^{t'}(y) - f_\chi^{t' \to t}(y) \right]$.

The main difference with respect to the Oaxaca-Blinder approach and the decomposition of scalar inequality measures reviewed earlier is that this decomposition—and the counterfactuals it relies on—refer to full distributions, rather than just to their means. Taking means on equation 2.12 or 2.13 under the parametric assumption that the conditional mean of $g^\tau(y|X)$ may be expressed as $X\beta_\tau$ would actually lead to the Oaxaca-Blinder equation (equation 2.2). More generally, the decomposition formula (equation 2.13) may be applied to any statistic defined on the distribution of income, $f(y)$: mean, summary inequality measures (and not only those which are explicitly decomposable), poverty measures for various poverty lines, and so forth.

The only restrictive property in the preceding decomposition is the path dependence already discussed in connection with the Oaxaca-Blinder equation. In the present framework, this property means that changing the conditional income distribution from the one observed in t to that observed in t' does not have the same effect on the distribution when this is done with the distribution of characteristics X observed in t, as when X is observed in t'. In the present general case, this means that

$$\left[f_g^{t \to t'}(y) - f^t(y) \right] \neq \left[f^{t'}(y) - f_g^{t' \to t}(y) \right].$$

However, the difference is likely to be small when the change in conditional income distributions $g(y \mid X)$ is small.[14]

Extending the Scope of Counterfactuals

In the preceding specification, all the characteristics X were considered on the same footing. But it might be of interest in some instances to decompose further the change in the distribution of these characteristics. For example, one might want to single out the effect of the change in the distribution of schooling or of family size. Doing so simply requires extending the conditioning chain in equation 2.8 and defining new counterfactuals as described below.

For any partition (V, W) of the variables in X, the conditioning chain (equation 2.8) may be rewritten as

$$f^\tau(y) = \int \cdots \int_{C(V, W)} g^\tau(y \mid V, W) h^\tau(V \mid W) \psi^\tau(W) \, dV \, dW$$

where $h^\tau(V \mid W)$ is the distribution of V conditional on W and $\psi^\tau(W)$ the marginal distribution of W. The set of counterfactuals may then be enlarged by modifying the conditional distribution of V. All combinations of the three distributions—$g^{\tau_g}(y \mid V, W)$, $h^{\tau_h}(V \mid W)$, and $\psi^{\tau_\psi}(W)$ with $\tau_g, \tau_h, \tau_\psi = t$ or t'—may be considered as generating a specific counterfactual. Two particular counterfactuals are the actual distributions themselves. They are obtained with the combinations $\tau_g = \tau_h = \tau_\psi = t$ or t'.

Comparing two counterfactuals that differ by only one distribution gives an estimate of the contribution of the change in that particular distribution to the overall distributional change. Of course, there are many paths for evaluating this contribution, with no guarantee that all these paths will generate the same estimate. For instance, the contribution of the change in the distribution of V conditional on W may be evaluated by comparing $f^t(y)$ and the following:

$$f_h^{t \to t'}(y) = \int \cdots \int_{C(V, W)} g^t(y \mid V, W) \, h^{t'}(V \mid W) \, \psi^t(W) \, dV \, dW.$$

But, with obvious notations, it could also be obtained by comparing $f_g^{t \to t'}(y)$ and $f_{g,h}^{t \to t'}(y)$ or $f_h^{t' \to t}(y)$ and $f^{t'}(y)$.

If necessary, a more detailed conditioning breakdown of variables in V could be considered. For instance, it might be of interest to analyze the effect of a change in the distribution of some components of V conditional on the others, thus breaking down $h^t(V\,|\,W)$ into $h_1^\tau(V_1\,|\,V_{-1},\ W)\ h_{-1}^\tau(V_{-1}\,|\,W)$, where V_{-1} stands for the components of V different from V_1. Following the same steps as above, this breakdown opens other counterfactuals and other decomposition paths.[15]

A Parametric Implementation of the Decomposition of Distributional Change

This decomposition analysis may be directly implemented using nonparametric representations—such as kernel density estimates—of the appropriate distributions. With enough observations, it is indeed possible to obtain a nonparametric representation of all the conditional distributions involved in defining counterfactuals. In practical terms, however, this may require a discretization of the distribution of the conditioning variables (V, W) or, in other words, defining groups of individuals with specific combinations of variables V and W. An example of such a use of the general decomposition principle above is provided by DiNardo, Fortin, and Lemieux (1996).[16]

For reasons that have mostly to do with the interpretation of the results of this decomposition, the various studies in this book rely instead on a parametric representation of some of the distributions used for defining counterfactuals. Indeed, dealing with changes in parameters with direct economic meaning, such as the return to education or the age elasticity of labor force participation, makes the discussion of the decomposition results quite fruitful. This section discusses the general principles behind this parametric analysis.

A general parametric representation of the conditional functions $g^\tau(y\,|\,V,\ W)$ and $h^\tau(V\,|\,W)$ relates y and (V, W), on the one hand, and V and W on the other hand, according to some predetermined functional form. These relationships may be denoted as follows:

$$y = G[V,\ W,\ \varepsilon;\ \Omega_\tau]$$

$$V = H[W,\ \eta;\ \Phi_\tau]$$

where Ω_τ and Φ_τ are sets of parameters and ε and η are random variables—η is a vector if V is a vector. These random variables play a role similar to the residual term in standard regressions. They are meant to represent the dispersion of income y or individual characteristics V for given values of individual characteristics (V, W), and W, respectively. They are also assumed to be distributed independently of these characteristics, according to density functions $\pi^\tau(\ )$ and $\mu^\tau(\ )$. Finally, the functions G and H have preimposed functional forms.

With this parameterization, the marginal distribution of income in period τ may be written as follows:

$$f^{\tau}(y) = \int\limits_{G(V, W, \varepsilon; \Omega_{\tau})=y} \pi^{\tau}(\varepsilon)\, d\varepsilon$$

(2.14)
$$\times \left[\int\limits_{H(W, \eta, \Phi_{\tau})=V} \mu^{\tau}(\eta)\, d\eta \right] \Psi^{\tau}(W)\, dV\, dW.$$

Counterfactuals may be generated by modifying some or all of the parameters in sets Ω_{τ} and Φ_{τ}, the distributions $\pi^{\tau}(\ )$ and $\mu^{\tau}(\ )$, or the joint distribution of exogenous characteristics, $\Psi^{\tau}(W)$. These counterfactuals may thus be defined as follows:

$$D[\Psi, \pi, \mu; \Omega, \Phi] = \int\limits_{G(V, W, \varepsilon; \Omega)=y} \pi(\varepsilon)\, d\varepsilon$$

(2.15)
$$\times \left[\int\limits_{H(W, \eta, \Phi)=V} \mu(\eta)\, d\eta \right] \Psi(W)\, dV\, dW$$

where any of the three distributions $\Psi(\ )$, $\mu(\ )$, and $\mu(\ )$, and the two sets of parameters, Ω and Φ can be those observed at time t or t'. For instance, $D[\Psi_{t}, \pi_{t}, \mu_{t}; \Omega_{t'}, \Phi_{t}]$ would correspond to the distribution of income obtained by applying to the population observed at time t, the income model parameters of period t', while keeping constant the distribution of the random residual term, ε, and all that is concerned with the variables V and W. Thus, the contribution of the change in parameters from Ω_{t} to $\Omega_{t'}$ may be measured by the difference between $D[\Psi_{t}, \pi_{t}, \mu_{t}; \Omega_{t'}, \Phi_{t}]$ and $D[\Psi_{t}, \pi_{t}, \mu_{t}; \Omega_{t}, \Phi_{t}]$, which is $f^{t}(y)$. But, of course, other decomposition paths may be used. For instance, the comparison may be performed using the population observed at time t' as a reference, in which case the contribution of the change in the Ω parameters would be given by $D[\Psi_{t'}, \pi_{t'}, \mu_{t'}; \Omega_{t'}, \Phi_{t'}] - D[\Psi_{t'}, \pi_{t'}, \mu_{t'}; \Omega_{t}, \Phi_{t'}]$ (where the notation "$-$" stands for distributional differences). Note that the decomposition may also bear on some subset of the Ω and Φ parameters.

In this parametric framework, the number of decomposition paths may become very large. Thus, the contribution of each individual change in the Ω and Φ parameters, in the distribution of the random or residual terms, $\pi(\ )$ and $\mu(\ )$, and finally in the whole distribution of exogenous characteristics, $\Psi(\ )$, may be evaluated in many different ways. The choice depends on what value is given to the other parameters or the functions used for the other distributions. In general, a single decomposition path is used. But it is important to compare the results with those obtained on different paths to see whether they are very different and, if so, to understand the reasons for the differences.[17]

A Parametric Representation of the Income-Generation Process

This section is devoted to particular applications of the preceding methodology—that is, to a specific set of variables $X = (V, W)$ and some specification of the functions $G(\ )$ and $H(\ )$ above. The actual specifications used in the various chapters in this volume differ somewhat across economies, but they do share a common base, which is described below.

The Simple Case of Individual Earnings

If it were to be applied to the distribution of individual earnings, the preceding methodology would be rather simple. If we ignore for the moment the partition of X into exogenous characteristics (W) and nonexogenous individual characteristics (V), a simple and familiar parametric representation of individual earnings as a function of individual characteristics is given by the following:

$$(2.16) \qquad \text{Log } y = X \cdot \Omega + \varepsilon.$$

In this particular case, the function $G(\ )$ thus writes as follows:

$$G(X, \varepsilon; \Omega) = e^{X \cdot \Omega + \varepsilon}.$$

To obtain estimates for the set of parameters Ω and for the distribution of the random term ε, one may rely on standard econometric techniques. Running a regression on samples of observations i available at time τ,

$$\text{Log } y_i^\tau = X_i^\tau \cdot \Omega_\tau + \varepsilon_i^\tau$$

yields an estimate of the set of parameters Ω_τ, as well as of the distribution $\pi_\tau(\ )$ of the random term. Then, the counterfactuals $D(\ )$ defined earlier in (2.15) can be computed easily. Without the (V, W) distinction, a counterfactual is now defined as $D(\chi, \pi; \Omega)$, where $\chi(W, \eta)$ is the joint distribution of the exogenous components of (V, W). Switching to a discrete representation $\{y_i\}^\tau = (y_1, y_2, \ldots, y_{N_\tau})$ of the distribution at time τ, where N_τ is the number of observations in the sample available at time $\tau = t, t'$, it is identically the case that

$$D(\chi_t, \pi_t, \Omega_t) = \{y_i\}^t.$$

The counterfactual, $D(\chi_t, \pi_t, \Omega_{t'}) = \{y_i\}_{\Omega}^{t \to t'}$, is obtained by computing

$$\text{Log}\,(y_i)_{\Omega}^{t \to t'} = X_i^t \cdot \hat{\Omega}_{t'} + \hat{\varepsilon}_i^t \quad \text{for } i = 1, 2, \ldots, N_t$$

where the notation $\wedge$ stands for ordinary least squares estimates. This counterfactual is thus obtained by simulating the preceding model on the sample of observations available at time t. This simulation shows what would have been the earnings of each individual in the sample if the returns to each observed characteristics had been those observed at time t' rather than the actual returns observed at time t.[18] The returns to the unobserved characteristics that may be behind the residual term $\hat{\varepsilon}_i^t$ are supposed to be unchanged, though. This is equivalent to the evaluation of the price effect for observed characteristics in the Oaxaca-Blinder calculation. The difference is that the evaluation is carried out for every individual in the sample.

The counterfactual on the distribution of the random term $D(\chi_t, \pi_{t'}, \Omega_t) = \{y_i\}_{\pi}^{t \to t'}$ is a little more difficult to construct. Importing the distribution of residuals from time t' to time t requires an operation known as a *rank-preserving transformation*, whereby the residual in the nth percentile (of residuals) at time t is replaced by the residual in the nth percentile at time t', for all n. As this operation is not immediate when the number of observations is not the same in the two samples, an approximate solution is used. It consists of assuming that both distributions of residual terms are the same up to a proportional transformation. An example would be if residuals were normally distributed, with mean zero. The rank-preserving transformation is then equivalent to multiplying the residual observed at time t by the ratio of standard deviations at time t' and t.[19] $D(\chi_t, \pi_{t'}, \Omega_t) = \{y_i\}_{\pi}^{t \to t'}$ is thus defined by

$$\text{Log}\,(y_i)_{\pi}^{t \to t'} = X_i^t \cdot \hat{\Omega}_t + \hat{\varepsilon}_i^t \cdot (\hat{\sigma}_{\varepsilon}^{t'} / \hat{\sigma}_{\varepsilon}^t) \quad \text{for } i = 1, 2, \ldots, N_t.$$

With those counterfactuals at hand, estimates of the contribution to the observed overall distributional change between t and t' of the change in the Ω parameters, in the distribution of residuals (π), and possibly of these two changes taken together may easily be found. The effect of changing the distribution of individual endowments, X, is obtained as the complement of the two previous changes:

$$\{y_i\}^{t'} - D(\chi_t, \pi_{t'}, \Omega_{t'}).$$

This technique is intuitively simple, and a very similar methodology has been in use in the literature on earnings distribution ever since it was introduced by Juhn, Murphy, and Pierce (1993). Things are slightly more complicated when dealing with household incomes. The additional complication arises from the need to take into account behavior related to participation in the labor force or, equivalently, the presence of various potential earners within a household.

A Household Income–Generation Model

Moving from individual earnings to household income per capita requires adding the earnings of the various members of the household and dividing by the total number of persons, or adult equivalents. This computation in turn requires considering not only the earnings of those people who are active but also the participation behavior of all the people of working age. Indeed, one reason the distribution of household income may change over time is that members may change occupation.[20] In an imperfect labor market, moreover, it may also be necessary to take into account the segment of the labor market in which active people work. The model presented below incorporates these various aspects in the specification of the function $G(V, W, \varepsilon; \Omega)$.

The first component of the model is an identity that defines income per capita in a household h, with n_h persons in it:

$$(2.17) \qquad y_h = \frac{1}{n_h} \left[\sum_{i=1}^{n_h} \sum_{j=1}^{J} I_{hi}^{j} y_{hi}^{j} + y_h^{se} + y_{0h} \right].$$

In this expression, *household income* is defined as the aggregation of the earnings y_{hi} across individual members i and activities j, of joint household self-employment income y_h^{se}, and of unearned income such as transfers or capital income, y_{0h}. Individual earnings may come from different activities, $j = 1, 2, \ldots, J$. The variables I_{hi}^{j} are indicator variables that take the value 1 if individual i participates in earning activity j, and 0 otherwise. The set of activities may differ across studies. In studies in which self-employment income is reported at the individual level, this set essentially comprises wage work or self-employment, both full- and part-time, and possibly a combination of part-time wage work and self-employment. In studies in which self-employment income is reported at the household level, being employed in the family business may be taken as an additional activity, $J + 1$, whereas J would include full-time or part-time wage work, possibly combined with part-time work in the family business. Since some of these alternative occupations involve both wage work and self-employment, each occupation in the $J + 1$ set is exclusive of another occupation. It is thus the case that $\sum_{j=1}^{J+1} I_{hi}^j = 0$ or 1, with 0 corresponding to inactivity.

The allocation of individuals across these J or $J + 1$ activities is represented through a multinomial logit model. It is well known (see McFadden 1974) that this model may be specified in the following way:

$$I_{hi}^s = 1 \text{ if } Z_{hi}\Omega^{Ls} + \varepsilon_i^{Ls} > Max(0, Z_{hi}\Omega^{Lj} + \varepsilon_i^{Lj}),$$

(2.18)
$$j = 1, \ldots, J + 1, \forall j \neq s$$
$$I_{hi}^s = 0 \text{ for all } s = 1, \ldots, J + 1 \text{ if } Z_{hi}\Omega^{Ls} + \varepsilon_i^{Ls} \leq 0$$
$$\text{for all } s = 1, \ldots, J + 1$$

where Z_{hi} is a vector of characteristics specific to individual i and household h, Ω^{Ls} are vectors of coefficients, and ε^{Ls} are random variables identically and independently distributed across individuals and occupations according to the law of extreme values. Within a discrete utility-maximizing framework, $Z_{hi}\Omega^{Ls} + \varepsilon_i^{Ls}$ is to be interpreted as the utility associated with occupation s, with ε^{Ls} standing for unobserved utility determinants of occupation s and the utility of inactivity being arbitrarily set to 0.[21] Note, however, that this interpretation in terms of utility-maximizing behavior is not fully justified because occupational choices may actually be constrained by the demand side of the market, as in the case of selective rationing, rather than by individual preferences.

Observed heterogeneity in earnings in each occupation j can be described by a log-linear model reminiscent of the well-known Mincer model:

(2.19) $\log y_{hi}^j = X_{hi}\Omega^{wj} + \sigma^{wj}\varepsilon_{hi}^{wj}$ for $i = 1, \ldots, n_h$

where X_{hi} is a vector of individual characteristics, Ω^{wj} a vector of coefficients, and ε_{hi}^{wj} a random variable supposed to be distributed identically and independently across individuals and occupations, according to the standard normal law. Under those conditions, σ^{wj} is to be interpreted as the unobserved heterogeneity of individual earnings in occupation j. To simplify, earnings functions are often assumed to differ across activities only through the intercepts, so that all components of Ω^{wj} but one are identical across occupations and $\sigma^{wj} = \sigma^w$. Finally, self-employment income at the household level is assumed to be given by

(2.20) $\text{Log } y_h^{se} = \left[Y_h, \sum_i I_{hi}^{se}, \dfrac{\sum I_{hi}^{se} X_{hi}}{\sum I_{hi}^{se}} \right] \cdot \Omega^{se} + \sigma^{se}\varepsilon_h^{se}.$

The first component of the vector in brackets is a set of household characteristics, including available assets in the self-employment activity. The second component is the number of family members involved in that activity, and the third is a vector that corresponds to their average individual characteristics. As before, Ω^{se} is a vector of coefficients, and ε_b^{se} is a random variable distributed as a standard normal. Thus, σ^{se} stands for the unobserved heterogeneity of household-level self-employment income.

The model is now complete. Together, equations 2.17 to 2.20 give a full description of household income–generation behavior and correspond to the function $G(\ )$ discussed earlier. The (V, W) variables are now replaced by the X, Y, and Z characteristics of households and household members. Parameters are all the coefficients included in $(\Omega^{Lj}, \Omega^{wj}, \Omega^{se})$, and random variables are the residual terms in the occupational-choice model, ε^{Lj}; the earning equations, ε^{wj}; and the self-employment function, ε^{se}. The only difference with respect to the general parametric formulation discussed earlier is that the parameterization now extends to the distribution of the random variable terms. These terms are now assumed to be distributed according to some prespecified law, with parameters given by the standard errors $(\sigma^{w}, \sigma^{se})$ in the case of the normal distributions for $(\varepsilon^{wj}, \varepsilon^{se})$. This parameterization of the distribution of random terms introduces some approximation in the decomposition methodology. However, because the normal distribution fits rather well with distributions of (log) earnings or self-employment income, the approximation error is likely to be small.

Econometric estimates of all parameters $(\hat{\Omega}_\tau^{Lj}, \hat{\Omega}_\tau^{wj}, \hat{\Omega}_\tau^{se})$, of the standard errors $(\hat{\sigma}_\tau^{wj}, \hat{\sigma}_\tau^{se})$, and of individual residual terms $(\hat{\varepsilon}_\tau^{L\ddot{y}}, \hat{\varepsilon}_\tau^{w\ddot{y}}, \hat{\varepsilon}_{s\tau}^{se})$ may be obtained on the basis of samples of observations available in t and t'. Then the parametric decomposition technique described in the preceding section may be applied, after substituting the distributions $\pi_\tau(\ )$ and $\mu_\tau(\ )$ by $(\hat{\sigma}_\tau^{wj}, \hat{\sigma}_\tau^{se})$. Typically, the model described in equations 2.17 through 2.20 is evaluated for each household in the sample of period t after substituting the parameters $(\hat{\Omega}_\tau^{Lj}, \hat{\Omega}_\tau^{wj}, \hat{\Omega}_\tau^{se})$, or a subset of them, by their counterpart in period t'. This microsimulation exercise is less simple than the derivation of counterfactual distributions in the case of individual earnings but does not involve any particular difficulty.

Some issues concerning the econometric estimation of the model are discussed in the next section. Yet an important point must be stressed at this stage. The estimates of the earnings functions (equation 2.19) and self-employment functions (equation 2.20) are based on subsamples of individuals and households with nonzero earnings or income in the corresponding activity, which requires controlling for selection biases. The residual terms $(\hat{\varepsilon}_\tau^{wj}, \hat{\varepsilon}_{s\tau}^{se})$ are directly observed only for those individuals or households with nonzero earnings or self-employment income. Simulating the complete household income model (equations 2.17 to 2.20) requires that an estimate be available for *every* random term $(\varepsilon_\tau^{wj}, \varepsilon_{s\tau}^{se})$. For instance, it is possible that individual i in household h who is observed as inactive in period t would become a wage worker when the coefficients of year t', $\hat{\Omega}_{t'}^{Lj}$, are used in the occupational model (equation 2.18). The earnings to be imputed to that individual in this counterfactual experiment are given by equation 2.19. The first part on the right-hand side of that equation is readily evaluated, but some value must be given to the corresponding random term in ε_{hi}^{wj}, because it is not observed. A simple solution consists of drawing that value randomly in a standard normal distribution. In effect, doing so involves drawing from conditional distributions rather than a standard normal distribution because of the obvious endogenous selection of people into the various types of occupations (see below for more detail). Note also that the same remark applies to the residual terms, ε_τ^{Lj}, which are also unobserved. They must be drawn from extreme value distributions in a way that is consistent with observed occupational choices.

The preceding specification of the income-generation model may appear as unnecessarily general. The reason for such a general formulation is that it encompasses different specifications used in the case studies in this book. Each of these specifications is individually simpler than the preceding general model in some aspects and slightly more complicated in others. A simplification common to all case studies is that both the occupational model (equation 2.18) and the individual earnings equation (equation 2.19) are logically defined on household members at working age. Another important simplification is that individual and household self-employment income are never observed simultaneously. Thus, equation 2.20 is irrelevant when self-employment income is observed at the individual level, and equation 2.19 is estimated only for wage employment (rather than allowing for individual self-employment) when self-employment income is registered at the household level. Additional complexity arises from the facts that (a) some studies rely on earnings functions that differ across labor-market segments (defined by gender and by rural and urban areas) and (b) most studies rely on different occupational-choice models for household heads, spouses, and other household members of working age. Those variations do not modify the underlying logic of the income-generation model (2.17–2.20). They were ignored in the preceding discussion for the sake of notational simplicity. At the same time, they show how rich the representation of the income-generation model summarized by the function $G(\ )$ can be.

Before turning to some econometric issues linked to the estimation of the model, we should say a word about the specification adopted for the second stage of decomposition—that is to say, the function $H(\ )$, which relates the set of variables V to those in W and η. Two characteristics are treated as conditional at this second stage: individual education and the number of children in the household. The conditional distribution of the latter variable is represented through a multinomial logit, as in equation 2.18:

$$n_{ch} = m \text{ if } Y_b^D \Phi^{Nm} + \eta_b^{Nm} > Max\left(0, Y_b^D \Phi^{Nj} + \eta_b^{Nj}\right),$$

$$j = 1, \ldots, M, \forall j \neq m$$

(2.21)

$$n_{ch} = 0 \text{ if } Y_b^D \Phi^{Nj} + \eta_b^{Nj} \leq 0 \quad \text{for all } j = 1, \ldots, M$$

where Y_b^D is a subset of household and individual characteristics—essentially the age, the education level, and the region of residence of the household head and of his or her spouse, if present. Here Φ^{Nj} is a vector of coefficients, η_b^{Nj} are independent random variables distributed according to the law of extreme values, and M is some upper limit on the number of children. Likewise the number of years of schooling, X_{bi}^E, of an individual i in household b is related to some simple demographic variables X_{bi}^D such as age, gender, and region of residence, through the same type of multinomial logit specification:

$$X_{bi}^E = s \text{ if } X_{bi}^D \Phi^{Es} + \eta_{bi}^{Es} > Max\left(0, X_{bi}^D \Phi^{Ej} + \eta_{bi}^{Ej}\right),$$

$$j = 1, \ldots, S, \forall j \neq s$$

(2.22)

$$X_{bi}^E = 0 \text{ if } X_{bi}^D \Phi^{Ej} + \eta_b^{Ej} \leq 0 \quad \text{for all } j = 1, \ldots, S$$

where Φ^{Ej} is a matrix of coefficients, η_{bi}^{Ej} a set of independent random variables distributed according to the law of extreme values, and S the maximum number of years of schooling.[22]

The preceding multinomial logit specification is not particularly restrictive. As before, applying the microsimulation methodology to this specification amounts to modifying the distribution of education or family size conditionally on demographic characteristics, by replacing the coefficients estimated for period t with those for period t' in the preceding conditional system. Doing so requires drawing values for the residual variables, η, in a way that is consistent with observed choices. But then, it may readily be seen that this is equivalent to changing the distribution of education or family sizes through simple rank-preserving transformations, conditionally on demographic characteristics.

It is worth concluding the discussion of the income-generation model used in the rest of this book with an important warning on the epistemological nature of this decomposition exercise. It will have been noted that equations 2.21 and 2.22 are not proper

economic models of fertility or schooling. They are purely statistical
models, aimed at representing in a simple way the distribution of
some variable conditionally on others, thus enabling us to perform
the switches required by the methodology for decomposing distributional changes in a manner consistent with the covariance patterns observed in the data. To some extent, the same may be said of
the income-generation model shown in equations 2.17 through
2.20. Earnings or income equations 2.19 and 2.20 might be interpreted as the outcome of the labor market and self-employment
production. In that sense, there is something of an economic model
behind these equations. This injunction is not true, however, of system 2.18, which describes the allocation of individuals across occupations. If this discrete choice specification were to be taken as a
structural model of labor supply, then it would be necessary to
explicitly introduce the wage rate or productivity of self-employment in that specification, as well as to introduce nonlabor income.
Instead, equation 2.18 should be seen as a reduced-form specification. Comparing it at two points in time provides information on
the identity of the individuals who modified their occupation over
time, but not on the reasons they did so.

It would thus be incorrect to rely on counterfactual distributions
where only earnings equations are modified to identify the *total* distributional effect of changes in wages. Only the direct effects can be
captured in this way. Indirect effects that operate through the impact
of these wage changes on labor supply cannot be identified separately from changes in the occupational structure of the labor force.
Without a structural specification of occupational choices, instead
of the reduced form (equation 2.18)[23] and additional economywide
modeling, there unfortunately is no solution to this identification
problem. It is important to keep this "partial equilibrium" nature of
the decomposition methodology in mind when analyzing the results
obtained in the case studies in this book.[24]

Some General Econometric Issues

Estimating the complete household income model (2.17–2.20) in its
general form above would be a formidable undertaking, for several
reasons. First, all the equations of the model clearly should be estimated simultaneously, with nonlinear estimation techniques,
because of the discrete occupational-choice model and because of
the likely correlation among the unobservable terms in the various
equations. In particular, if the allocation of individuals across occupations is in some sense consistent with utility maximization, then
the random term ε^L cannot be considered independent from the

random terms in the earnings and self-employment equations, ε^w and ε^{se}. Indeed, if an individual finds a salaried job with higher earnings than individuals who have the same observable characteristics, he or she is likely to be observed in that job, too. Although extremely intricate, such simultaneous estimation might be manageable—probably under some simplifying assumptions—if every household comprised a single individual. But the obvious correlation across the earnings equations and labor-supply equations of the working-age members of the same household, the number of which varies across households, makes things hopelessly complicated. An additional risk is that the estimates obtained with such a complex econometric specification might not be robust. They might, in particular, show artificially high time variability, thus jeopardizing the decomposition principle shown above.

The microeconometric estimation work undertaken in the case studies reported in this volume relies on a simplified, but possibly more robust, specification, based on the following three principles:

1. Individual earnings functions and household self-employment functions, if applicable, are estimated separately and consistently through the instrumentation of endogenous right-hand-side variables and the usual two-step Heckman correction for selection bias. This standard correction for selection bias allows us to draw the unobserved residual terms, ε^w and ε^{se}, of those individuals with no earnings (or households with no self-employment income) in the appropriate conditional distribution. In particular, it accounts for the fact that the latter should logically expect earnings and self-employment income that are smaller than those who are actually observed in a wage-earning job or a self-employment activity. Yet we do not attempt to link this selection bias correction procedure and the drawing of residuals in the earnings and self-employment income equations to the estimation of the occupational-choice model and to the drawing of residuals in that model.[25] This is unlikely to be a problem if no significant bias is present in the earnings and self-employment equations, as occurs in most cases. It is less satisfactory, of course, when the bias is strongly significant.

2. The simultaneity between household members' labor-supply decisions is taken into account by considering the behavior of household heads and that of the other members sequentially, as conventionally done in much of the labor-supply literature. Thus, the occupational decision of the household head is estimated first with the preceding multinomial logit model and using both the general exogenous characteristics of the household, as well as those of all household members, as explanatory variables. Second, the labor-supply and occupation decision of other members is estimated

conditionally on the decision made by the head of household and possibly on his or her income. In addition, different models were sometimes estimated depending on the position of a person in the family. Indeed, it seems natural that, other things being equal, the spouse does not behave in the same way with respect to labor supply as the daughter of the head of household. The categories for which distinct labor-supply models were estimated include spouses, sons, daughters, and other household members.

3. The drawing of residual terms in the multinomial logit model raises some difficulties. First, none of the error terms is actually observed. What is observed is that the $J + 1$ random terms lie in some region of R^{J+1}, such that all the inequality conditions are satisfied for the observed choice I_{hi} in system 2.18. Specifically, if individual i is observed in occupation 2, rather than in any of the other J occupations ($j \neq 2$) that he or she might have chosen, then the vector of ε_i^L must be such that $Z_{hi}\Omega^{L2} + \varepsilon_i^{L2} > Z_{hi}\Omega^{Lj} + \varepsilon_i^{Lj}, \forall j \neq 2$ and $Z_{hi}\Omega^{L2} + \varepsilon_i^{L2} > 0$. Drawing consistent values for these residual terms essentially consists of independently drawing $J + 1$ values in the law of extreme values and checking whether they satisfy the above condition for the observed I_{hi}, that is, the occupation observed for individual hi. Drawings for which these conditions are not satisfied are discarded, and the operation is repeated until a (single) set of values is drawn such that the conditions in system 2.18 hold.[26]

Finally, combined with the random drawing of residual terms for the potential earnings and self-employment incomes of individuals not observed in such an activity, this procedure for drawing multinomial logit residuals implies that any counterfactual distribution generated by the microsimulation of the model is, in effect, random. This is not too great a problem if the microsimulation relies on a sufficiently large number of observations. For this practical reason, the law of large numbers was supposed to hold in the case studies gathered in this book. If that were not the case, one should repeat each microsimulation a large number of times, so as to obtain a distribution of counterfactual distributions. In the context of the large sample sizes available to the case studies in the chapters that follow, the computation time necessary to generate these Monte Carlo experiments was generally judged excessive. How much the results of single-draw simulations differ from analogous Monte Carlo microsimulations remains an interesting question for further research.

Another concern that is left for future research is perhaps even more basic. Estimates of distributions in this book—whether they are scalar measures or quantile interval means in some curve—are derived from samples and are thus subject to sampling error. Ideally, therefore, one would present confidence intervals for the various statistics and seek to determine their implications for the estimated counterfactual distributions. Recent analytical and software developments in the realm of inference for stochastic dominance may be a promising avenue for further investigation of this important issue (see, for instance, Davidson and Duclos 2000). As microeconomic simulation research evolves, a more rigorous treatment of its statistical inference properties is certain to become necessary.

Notes

1. A powerful semiparametric method for constructing counterfactual distributions that is very similar in spirit to the parametric alternative we use here has been proposed by DiNardo, Fortin, and Lemieux (1996). We return to it later in this chapter.

2. In theory, using income or consumption per capita as a welfare measure should not make any difference for a number of methods discussed in this chapter. Yet the parametric model discussed later is definitely better suited to an income view of welfare. Hence, this chapter generally refers to income distribution or income inequality, rather than to their consumption expenditure counterparts.

3. They were both interested by earning discrimination across individual characteristics such as gender or race. Therefore, the populations they considered were defined by some given sociodemographic characteristic. Conceptually, this is no different than considering two populations at two different points in time, as in what follows.

4. To avoid this problem, some authors use the mean characteristics across periods t and t' to evaluate the price effect and use the time average of prices to evaluate the endowment effect. It will be seen later that such efforts are an application of a more general method to deal with path dependence.

5. For an introduction to decomposable inequality measures, see Cowell (2002) and the references therein.

6. To see this, note that the mean income in group g is such that: $\overline{y}_g = \overline{y} \cdot m_g / n_g$.

7. The approximation in equation 2.4 tends to an equality as the changes become infinitesimally small.

8. Note that the change in population group weights is also present in the change in the overall mean, but this point is overlooked for the sake of simplicity.

9. But, of course, the Oaxaca-Blinder method could also be cast in terms of groups' means and group weights, rather than in terms of a linear income model.

10. Conversely, the inequality decomposition is path independent.

11. Two exceptions are Fields and O'Hara (1996) and Morduch and Sicular (2002). In both cases, however, the authors ignore the preceding

point and the need to handle the joint distribution rather than the marginal distributions of income by sources.

12. The concept of subgroup decomposability was first introduced by Foster, Greer, and Thorbecke (1984). For a discussion of the normative implications of this property, see Sen (1997, appendix).

13. Poverty changes can, of course, be decomposed into a growth component (changes in means) and an inequality component (changes in Lorenz curves). See Datt and Ravallion (1992). But this decomposition is not analogous to a decomposition into price effects, endowment effects, and behavioral changes, because both components are influenced by all three effects.

14. One way to investigate how small these differences are—and to address the problem of path dependence—would be to consider a large number of paths and to estimate the "average" contribution of a particular change over them. Shorrocks (1999) provides a formal definition of the appropriate "averaging" concept, on the basis of Shapley values.

15. A general formulation of these various decomposition paths is given in Bourguignon, Ferreira, and Leite (2002).

16. See also the semiparametric technique proposed by Donald, Green, and Paarsch (2000).

17. An alternative would be to use the Shapley-value approach referred to in note 14.

18. Because the simulation actually bears on micro data rather than aggregate data, this operation is often referred to as *microsimulation*.

19. For situations in which selection into the sample differs across t and t' (say, because participation behavior has changed), an alternative approach exists for generating a counterfactual distribution of residuals. This approach, discussed in Cunha, Heckman, and Navarro (2004), relies on factor analysis (and a number of assumptions) to decompose the variance of residuals into a component due to predictable individual heterogeneity and another due to pure uncertainty (or "luck"). Such a decomposition would enable one to consider estimates of "unobserved" individual fixed effects separately from pure randomness.

20. This change in the population of earners because of changing labor-force participation behavior was only implicit in the preceding analysis of individual earnings. It was simply part of the endowment effect or, in other words, the change in the sociodemographic characteristics of the active population.

21. Ex ante, the probability that individual i of household h takes occupation s is given by the following:

$$P^s\left(Z_{hi}, \Omega^L\right) = \frac{e^{Z_{hi}\Omega^{Ls}}}{1 + \sum_j e^{Z_{hi}\Omega^{Lj}}}$$

whereas the probability of inactivity, $P^0(Z_{hi}, \Omega^L)$, is such that all probabilities sum to unity.

22. The multinomial logit specification is also compatible with schooling being defined by achievement levels, rather than by number of years.

23. The occupational models are not always in pure reduced form. For instance, many case studies model the occupational choice of spouses or secondary household members as a function of the income of the household head, as in much of the standard labor-supply literature. Such studies allow accounting for the typically structural effect of a change in the occupation or earnings of the household head on the occupation of other household members.

24. The same caveat about the partial equilibrium nature of the exercise applies to the original Oaxaca-Blinder decomposition; to the semiparametric approach of DiNardo, Fortin, and Lemieux (1996); and, indeed, to all other approaches previously reviewed.

25. An equivalent to the well-known Heckman two-stage procedure for the correction of selection bias in the case of a dichotomous choice represented by a probit exists with polychotomous choice and the multinomial logit model (see Lee 1983). Yet this method has been shown to be problematic (see Bourguignon, Fournier, and Gurgand 2002; Schmertmann 1994).

26. Specific ε_i^L terms can be obtained as $\varepsilon_i^L = -\log[-\log(x)]$, where x is a random draw in a uniform distribution in $[0, 1]$. An alternative method is proposed in Bourguignon, Fournier, and Gurgand (2001).

References

Blinder, Alan S. 1973. "Wage Discrimination: Reduced Form and Structural Estimates." *Journal of Human Resources* 8(Fall): 436–55.

Bourguignon, François. 1979. "Decomposable Income Inequality Measures." *Econometrica* 47: 901–20.

Bourguignon, François, Francisco Ferreira, and Phillippe Leite. 2002. "Beyond Oaxaca-Blinder: Accounting for Differences in Household Income Distributions across Countries." Policy Research Working Paper 2828. World Bank, Washington, D.C.

Bourguignon, François, Martin Fournier, and Marc Gurgand. 2001. "Fast Development with a Stable Income Distribution: Taiwan, 1979–1994." *Review of Income and Wealth* 47(2): 1–25.

———. 2002. "Selection Bias Correction Based on the Multinomial Logit Model." Working paper. DELTA, Paris.

Cowell, Frank A. 1980. "On the Structure of Additive Inequality Measures." *Review of Economic Studies* 47: 521–31.

———. 2002. "Measurement of Inequality." In Anthony Atkinson and François Bourguignon, eds., *Handbook of Income Distribution*, Vol. 1. Amsterdam: Elsevier.

Cunha, Flávio, James Heckman, and Salvador Navarro. 2004. "Counterfactual Analysis of Inequality and Social Mobility." University of Chicago. Processed.

Datt, Gaurav, and Martin Ravallion. 1992. "Growth and Redistribution Components of Changes in Poverty Measures." *Journal of Development Economics* 38: 275–95.

Davidson, Russell, and Jean-Yves Duclos. 2000. "Statistical Inference for Stochastic Dominance and for the Measurement of Poverty and Inequality." *Econometrica* 68(6): 1435–64.

DiNardo, John, Nicole Fortin, and Thomas Lemieux. 1996. "Labor Market Institutions and the Distribution of Wages, 1973–1992: A Semi-Parametric Approach." *Econometrica* 64(5): 1001–44.

Donald, Stephen, David Green, and Harry Paarsch. 2000. "Differences in Wage Distributions between Canada and the United States: An Application of a Flexible Estimator of Distribution Functions in the Presence of Covariates." *Review of Economic Studies* 67: 609–33.

Fields, Gary, and Jennifer O'Hara. 1996. "Changing Income Inequality in Taiwan: A Decomposition Analysis." Cornell University. Ithaca, New York. Processed.

Foster, James, Joel Greer, and Erik Thorbecke. 1984. "A Class of Decomposable Poverty Measures." *Econometrica* 52: 761–65.

Juhn, Chinhui, Kevin Murphy, and Brooks Pierce. 1993. "Wage Inequality and the Rise in Returns to Skill." *Journal of Political Economy* 101: 410–42.

Lee, Lung-Fei. 1983. "Generalized Econometric Models with Selectivity." *Econometrica* 51: 507–12.

McFadden, Daniel L. 1974. "Conditional Logit Analysis of Qualitative Choice Behavior." In Paul Zarembka, ed., *Frontiers in Econometrics*. New York: Academic Press.

Mookherjee, Dilip, and Anthony Shorrocks. 1982. "A Decomposition Analysis of the Trend in U.K. Income Inequality." *Economic Journal* 92: 886–902.

Morduch, Jonathan, and Terry Sicular. 2002. "Rethinking Inequality Decomposition, with Evidence from Rural China." *Economic Journal* 112: 93–106.

Oaxaca, Ronald. 1973. "Male-Female Wage Differentials in Urban Labor Markets." *International Economic Review* 14: 673–709.

Schmertmann, Carl P. 1994. "Selectivity Bias Correction Methods in Polychotomous Sample Selection Models." *Journal of Econometrics* 60: 101–32.

Sen, Amartya. 1997. *On Economic Inequality*. Oxford, U.K.: Clarendon Press.

Shorrocks, Anthony. 1980. "The Class of Additively Decomposable Inequality Measures." *Econometrica* 48: 613–25.

———. 1982. "Inequality Decomposition by Factor Components." *Econometrica* 50(1): 193–211.

———. 1999. "Decomposition Procedures for Distributional Analysis: A Unified Framework Based on the Shapley Value." University of Essex, Essex, U.K. Processed.

3

Characterization of Inequality Changes through Microeconometric Decompositions: The Case of Greater Buenos Aires

Leonardo Gasparini, Mariana Marchionni, and Walter Sosa Escudero

The main economic variables have oscillated widely in the past two decades in Argentina in association with deep macroeconomic and structural transformations. After reaching a peak of 172 percent monthly in 1989, the inflation rate decreased to less than 1 percent each year in a few years; gross domestic product drastically fell at the end of the 1980s and then grew at unprecedented rates in the first half of the 1990s; unemployment rose steadily from around 5 percent to 14 percent in a short period of time. Income inequality was not an exception in this turbulent period. The Gini coefficient increased from 41.9 to 46.7 between 1986 and 1989, fell to 40.0 toward 1991, and rose steadily in the following seven years, reaching a record level of 47.4 in 1998.[1] In recent economic history, it is difficult to find periods with such marked changes in inequality, both in Argentina and in the rest of the world.

The reasons for these changes in inequality are varied and complex. The main aim of this chapter is to assess the relevance of some forces believed to have affected income inequality in the Greater

Buenos Aires area between 1986 and 1998. More specifically, the microeconometric decomposition methodology proposed in chapter 2 is used to measure the relevance of various factors that appear to have driven changes in inequality. In particular, this methodology is used to identify to what extent changes in (a) returns to education and experience, (b) endowments of unobservable factors and their returns, (c) the wage gap between men and women, (d) labor-market participation and hours of work, and (e) the educational structure of the population contribute to the observed changes in income distribution.

The results presented in this chapter suggest that the observed similarity between the inequality indices of 1986 and 1992 is in fact the consequence of mild forces that operated in different directions but compensated for each other in the aggregate. On the contrary, between 1992 and 1998, nearly all the determinants under study contributed to increased inequality. The dominating forces appear to be the increase in the returns to education; a higher dispersion in the endowments or in the returns to unobservable factors; and the dramatic fall in the hours of work of less skilled, low-income people. Perhaps surprisingly, neither the narrowing of the gender wage gap nor the increase in average education of the population were significant equalizing factors. In addition, the dramatic jump in unemployment in the 1990s does not appear to have had a very significant direct effect on household income inequality.

The rest of this chapter is organized as follows. The basic facts and some issues that might have affected inequality in the past two decades are described first. Next the decomposition methodology implemented to assess the relevance of those factors is presented, and the estimation strategy is explained. The main results of the analysis are then presented. The chapter concludes with some brief final comments.

Income Inequality: Basic Facts and Sources of Changes

Income inequality in Argentina has fluctuated considerably around an increasing trend initiated in the mid-1970s. Figure 3.1 shows the Gini coefficient of equivalent household income between 1985 and 1998 in the Greater Buenos Aires area.[2] After a substantial increase in the late 1980s, inequality plunged in the first two years of the 1990s. A new stage of rising inequality started in 1992 and has not stopped yet. Until 1998, the Greater Buenos Aires area had never experienced the level of income inequality reached in that year, at least since reliable household data sets were available.[3]

For simplicity, this study focused on three years of relative macroeconomic stability separated by equal intervals: 1986, 1992, and 1998. In addition, we restricted the analysis mainly to labor income

Figure 3.1 Gini Coefficient of Equivalent Household Income Distribution in Greater Buenos Aires, 1985–98

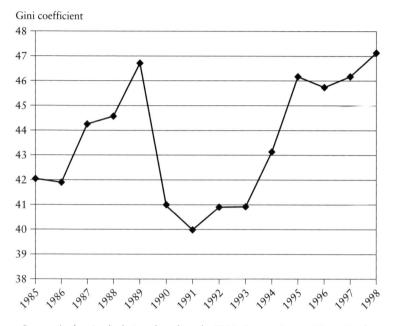

Gini coefficient

Source: Authors' calculations based on the EPH, Greater Buenos Aires, October.

Table 3.1 Distributions of Income in Greater Buenos Aires, Selected Years
(Gini coefficient)

Type of distribution	1986	1992	1998
Earnings	39.4	37.7	44.9
Equivalent household labor income	40.3	41.0	49.5

Source: Authors' calculations based on the EPH, Greater Buenos Aires, October.

(that is, wage earnings and self-employment earnings) for two reasons: (a) the Permanent Household Survey (Encuesta Permanente de Hogares, or EPH) has various deficiencies in capturing capital income, and (b) modeling capital income and retirement payments is not an easy task, especially considering the scarce information contained in the EPH. We also ignored those households whose heads or spouses were older than 65 or received retirement payments.

Table 3.1 shows the basic facts characterized in this chapter. Inequality in individual labor income and in equivalent household labor income, as measured by the Gini, did not change very much between 1986 and 1992; on the contrary, both measures rose dramatically in the next six years.[4,5]

A countless number of factors may have caused the changes in inequality documented in table 3.1. We concentrate on seven: (a) returns to education, (b) the gender wage gap, (c) returns to experience, (d) unobservable factors and their returns, (e) hours of work, (f) employment, and (g) the education of the working-able population. The objective of this chapter is to estimate the sign and the relative magnitude of the effect of those factors on the distribution of earnings and the equivalent household labor income. Although microeconometric decompositions will be used toward that aim, this section begins with an analysis of the basic statistics and regressions to provide some intuitions about the results and to understand the need and usefulness of a microsimulation decomposition technique.

Returns to Education

An increase in the returns to education implies a widening of the wage gap between workers with high levels of education and those with low levels of education. This wider gap, in turn, would imply a more unequal distribution of earnings and probably a more unequal distribution of household income.[6] Table 3.2 shows hourly earnings in real pesos (Arg$) for workers between 14 and 65 years old by educational level. The average wage fell 19 percent between 1986 and 1992 and increased 9.3 percent over the following six years. Changes were not uniform among educational groups. Although in the first period of the analysis the most dramatic drop in hourly earnings was for the *college complete* group, that group enjoyed the greatest increase in wages during the 1992–98 period. Table 3.2 is a first piece of evidence that changes in relative wages

Table 3.2 Hourly Earnings by Educational Level in Greater Buenos Aires, Selected Years

	Means (Arg$ 1998)			Changes (percent)		
Educational level	*1986*	*1992*	*1998*	*1986–92*	*1992–98*	*1986–98*
Primary incomplete	6.6	5.7	5.3	−13.6	−6.8	−19.5
Primary complete	7.7	6.3	5.9	−18.1	−6.0	−23.0
Secondary incomplete	9.2	6.8	6.6	−26.1	−2.8	−28.1
Secondary complete	11.6	9.1	9.1	−21.2	−0.4	−21.5
College incomplete	14.5	11.9	10.6	−17.5	−11.1	−26.7
College complete	24.1	16.3	19.4	−32.3	19.1	−19.4
Total	10.4	8.4	9.2	−19.0	9.3	−11.4

Note: Data cover workers between ages 14 and 65 with valid answers.
Source: Authors' calculations based on the EPH, Greater Buenos Aires, October.

among schooling groups implied a decrease in earnings inequality between 1986 and 1992 and an increase thereafter.

Table 3.3 shows the results of Mincerian log hourly earnings functions, estimated using the Heckman procedure to correct for sample selection. The first three columns refer to household heads (mostly men), the second three columns refer to spouses (nearly all women), and the last three columns refer to other members of the family (roughly half men and half women). Because the EPH does not record years of education, we included dummy variables that capture the maximum educational level achieved. The omitted category is *primary incomplete*. A gender dummy variable, age and age squared, and a dummy variable for youths younger than 18 years old (only relevant for other family members) also were included in the regression. In addition to those variables, the selection equation included marital status, number of children, and a dummy variable that takes the value 1 when the individual attends school. Following Bourguignon, Fournier, and Gurgand (2001), our analysis assumed that labor-market participation choices were made within the household in a sequential fashion. Spouses consider the labor-market status of the head of household when deciding whether to enter the labor market themselves. Other members of the family consider the labor-market status of both the head of household and the spouse before deciding to enter the labor market.

The coefficients of most educational levels are positive, significant, and increasing with the educational level; that is, the returns to education are always positive.[7] For family heads in 1998, an individual who had completed primary school had an hourly wage 18 percent greater than an individual whose primary education was incomplete, if all other factors were constant. The same figures for individuals whose secondary education was incomplete, those who completed secondary school, those whose college education was incomplete, and those who completed college education are 36, 65, 94, and 146 percent, respectively, all with respect to individuals who had not completed primary school. In many cases, returns to education are increasing; that is, the hourly wage gap between educational levels increases with education.[8] For heads of household in 1998, the difference in wages between an individual who had completed primary school and one whose secondary education was incomplete is 18 percent, whereas the difference between an individual at the latter level and one who completed secondary school is 29 percent. The greatest jump is between individuals who did not complete and who completed college: 52 percent.

Figure 3.2 shows predicted hourly earnings for all educational levels. The first panel refers to male household heads and the second

Table 3.3 Log Hourly Earnings Equation Applied to Greater Buenos Aires, Selected Years

Variable	Head of household			Spouse			Other family members		
	1986	1992	1998	1986	1992	1998	1986	1992	1998
Log hourly earnings equation									
Primary complete	0.2150	0.2162	0.1828	0.0393	−0.1731	0.0575	0.0407	0.3349	0.0417
	(5.496)	(4.011)	(2.978)	(0.496)	(−1.695)	(0.462)	(0.441)	(2.884)	(0.287)
Secondary incomplete	0.3994	0.3367	0.3630	0.2241	−0.0243	0.2306	0.2278	0.4361	0.1366
	(9.206)	(5.661)	(5.620)	(2.342)	(−0.211)	(1.848)	(2.400)	(3.795)	(0.953)
Secondary complete	0.6219	0.6229	0.6534	0.5595	0.2652	0.4841	0.4053	0.5726	0.3646
	(12.649)	(10.185)	(9.664)	(6.720)	(2.445)	(3.861)	(3.927)	(4.546)	(2.447)
College incomplete	0.9121	0.9516	0.9382	0.6446	0.5173	0.6579	0.5646	0.7100	0.6699
	(15.469)	(12.713)	(12.714)	(5.210)	(3.666)	(4.347)	(5.289)	(5.919)	(4.592)
College complete	1.3079	1.2607	1.4634	0.8607	0.5764	0.9607	0.7439	0.8109	0.9456
	(22.778)	(18.242)	(20.282)	(7.824)	(4.183)	(5.600)	(5.577)	(5.432)	(5.830)
Male	0.2915	0.1834	0.1675	−0.1865	0.2626	0.2859	0.0454	0.0701	0.1678
	(5.106)	(3.707)	(3.474)	(−0.774)	(1.280)	(1.706)	(0.827)	(1.405)	(3.250)
Age	0.0401	0.0546	0.0452	0.0413	0.0343	0.0454	0.0766	0.0797	0.0846
	(3.969)	(4.882)	(3.951)	(2.120)	(1.533)	(2.028)	(4.351)	(4.267)	(4.138)
Age squared	−0.0004	−0.0006	−0.0004	−0.0005	−0.0004	−0.0005	−0.0009	−0.0009	−0.0011
	(−3.295)	(−4.661)	(−3.155)	(−2.057)	(−1.393)	(−1.813)	(−3.646)	(−3.545)	(−3.735)
Younger than 18							−0.0218	−0.0338	−0.3601
							(−0.250)	(−0.406)	(−2.811)
Constant	0.5599	0.1959	0.2051	1.0778	1.1095	0.6169	0.1849	−0.2793	−0.3190
	(2.400)	(0.806)	(0.792)	(2.554)	(2.283)	(1.178)	(0.577)	(−0.749)	(−0.799)

Selection equation (dep. var. = 1 if hourly earnings > 0)

	(1)	(2)	(3)	(4)	(5)	(6)	(7)	(8)	(9)
Primary complete	0.2931 (2.240)	0.2212 (1.429)	0.3955 (3.052)	−0.3295 (−3.289)	−0.0513 (−0.381)	−0.1975 (−1.346)	0.2137 (1.203)	0.5917 (2.874)	0.2573 (1.126)
Secondary incomplete	0.3494 (2.238)	0.5737 (2.987)	0.4556 (3.234)	−0.1980 (−1.612)	0.0129 (0.083)	0.0398 (0.258)	0.2258 (1.215)	0.8538 (4.015)	0.2308 (1.021)
Secondary complete	0.4875 (2.580)	0.5575 (2.827)	0.5866 (3.736)	−0.0736 (−0.639)	0.1556 (1.066)	0.2299 (1.489)	0.4315 (1.901)	0.7899 (3.296)	0.4376 (1.829)
College incomplete	0.4760 (1.827)	1.0563 (3.318)	0.4125 (2.177)	0.4776 (2.355)	0.5239 (2.433)	0.4153 (2.102)	0.8123 (3.441)	1.5396 (5.794)	0.5657 (2.284)
College complete	1.2176 (3.085)	1.0181 (3.750)	0.8111 (4.537)	0.7033 (4.467)	1.0577 (5.620)	1.3115 (7.588)	0.8274 (2.101)	1.3888 (3.766)	0.8389 (2.752)
Male	0.8594 (5.175)	0.7840 (4.001)	0.6528 (5.263)	1.2982 (2.235)	1.7185 (2.970)	1.3967 (5.353)	0.8164 (8.451)	0.4630 (4.703)	0.5007 (6.182)
Age	0.1099 (3.160)	0.1141 (3.012)	0.1045 (3.748)	0.1288 (4.907)	0.1757 (5.577)	0.1203 (4.279)	0.1960 (5.682)	0.1686 (4.836)	0.2719 (9.111)
Age squared	−0.0014 (−3.541)	−0.0016 (−3.589)	−0.0014 (−4.269)	−0.0017 (−5.117)	−0.0023 (−5.668)	−0.0015 (−4.353)	−0.0029 (−6.385)	−0.0022 (−4.832)	−0.0036 (−8.656)
Married	0.1986 (1.204)	0.1559 (0.841)	0.0588 (0.477)				−0.7813 (−4.386)	−0.4060 (−2.373)	−0.4761 (−3.360)
Children	−0.0087 (−0.202)	−0.0178 (−0.442)	−0.0464 (−1.387)	−0.1929 (−6.496)	−0.1797 (−5.460)	−0.1768 (−5.477)			
Younger than 18							−0.5983 (−3.823)	−0.3063 (−1.925)	−0.5995 (−4.087)
Attending school	−0.8669 (−2.850)	−1.0407 (−3.280)	−0.5569 (−2.509)	−0.3036 (−0.963)	0.3501 (1.040)	0.2020 (0.900)	−1.6477 (−11.458)	−1.7389 (−11.237)	−0.9050 (−7.556)

(Continued on the following page)

Table 3.3 (Continued)

Variable	Head of household			Spouse			Other family members		
	1986	1992	1998	1986	1992	1998	1986	1992	1998
Head of household employed				−0.7922	−0.6382	−0.6148	−0.0351	−0.1624	−0.2210
				(−3.982)	(−3.314)	(−4.386)	(−0.212)	(−1.112)	(−1.951)
Spouse employed							−0.0763	−0.0005	0.0488
							(−0.706)	(−0.005)	(0.547)
Constant	−1.3555	−1.3567	−1.3239	−1.5356	−2.7184	−1.8346	−2.6080	−2.6912	−4.0987
	(−1.892)	(−1.682)	(−2.296)	(−3.015)	(−4.571)	(−3.390)	(−4.233)	(−4.358)	(−8.127)
Number of observations	1,961	1,404	1,967	1,575	1,116	1,413	1,292	1,090	1,631
Chi²	153.77	124.61	148.96	164.62	154.13	303.14	767.13	590.80	861.41
Log likelihood	−1,888.35	−1,368.31	−2,281.71	−1,311.55	998.04	−1,354.19	−841.52	−769.56	−1,191.27
Rho	0.2179	0.6786	0.1247	−0.1691	0.0379	−0.1035	0.1705	0.3726	0.3600
Sigma	0.5562	0.5747	0.6361	0.5603	0.5492	0.6434	0.4848	0.4770	0.5569
Lambda	0.1212	0.3900	0.0793	−0.0948	0.0208	−0.0666	0.0827	0.1777	0.2005

Note: Data represent Heckman maximum likelihood estimation; z values are in parentheses. Data cover all individuals between ages 14 and 65 with valid answers.

Source: Authors' calculations based on the EPH, Greater Buenos Aires, October.

Figure 3.2 Hourly Earnings–Education Profiles for Men
(Heads of Household and Other Family Members), Age 40

A. Heads of household

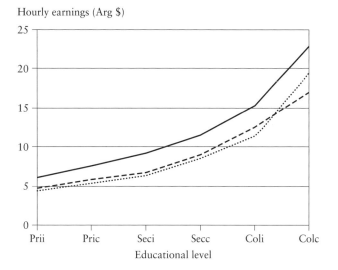

B. Other family members

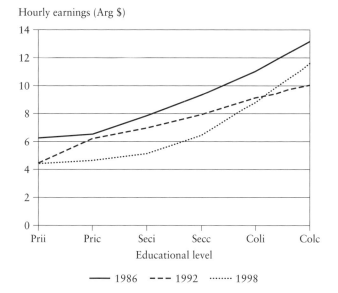

Note: Prii = primary incomplete, Pric = primary complete, Seci = secondary
incomplete, Secc = secondary complete, Coli = college incomplete, Colc = college
complete.

Source: Predicted hourly earnings from models in table 3.3.

to other male household members, both with age kept constant at
40. The wage-education profiles for family heads have a marked
positive slope and are almost parallel everywhere, except for the
substantial increase in the slope between 1992 and 1998 in the
highest educational levels. This situation certainly contributes to
increased earnings inequality among household heads. For other
male family members, the wage-education profile became flatter
between 1986 and 1992 and substantially steeper and more convex
in the following six years. The latter movement could imply a dramatic widening of the earnings gap by educational level.

Figure 3.3 shows the profiles for 40-year-old females. As in the case
of men, the wage-education profiles show a decreasing slope between
1986 and 1992 and an opposite movement between 1992 and 1998.

In summary, the changes in the returns to education appear to have
been mildly inequality reducing between 1986 and 1992 and strongly
inequality increasing in the next six years. Those conclusions are the
most detailed we can draw with basic statistics and regressions. To
get a more complete assessment of the relative significance of these
effects on the income distribution, we need to go beyond this simple

Figure 3.3 Hourly Earnings–Education Profiles for Women
(Spouses), Age 40

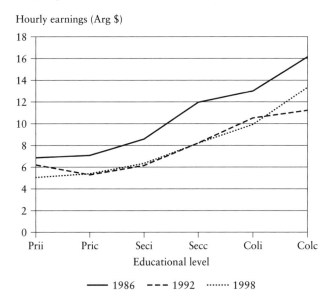

Note: Prii = primary incomplete, Pric = primary complete, Seci = secondary
incomplete, Secc = secondary complete, Coli = college incomplete, Colc = college
complete.

Source: Predicted hourly earnings from models in table 3.3.

analysis. Later sections present a microsimulation methodology that builds from the results of this section and allows a richer analysis.

Gender Wage Gap

Table 3.4 presents mean hourly wages by gender. Wages were higher for males in every year. In 1986, males' hourly wages were on average 16 percent higher than females' hourly wages. The gender gap narrowed to 3 percent in 1998. A conditional analysis also shows a shrinking wage gap for household heads. From table 3.3, the coefficients of the male dummy variable in the regression for household heads are always positive and significant but clearly decrease over time.[9] This narrowing gender wage gap has undoubtedly been an equalizing factor on the earnings distribution.

The effect of the narrowing gender wage gap on the distribution of equivalent household labor income depends on the relative position of working women in that distribution. Two factors play in different directions. On the one hand, female workers are more concentrated in the upper part of the distribution than male workers (partly because of their own labor decisions), and hence a relative wage change in favor of women implies an increase in household income inequality.[10] On the other hand, a proportional wage increase for all women is more relevant in low-income families because women's earnings are a more significant part of total resources in those households than in rich families. An extreme example is the disproportionate number of poor households headed by working women. The total effect of a shrinking gender wage gap on the household income distribution is then ambiguous. We need a more powerful methodology to get a more precise assessment of that effect.

Returns to Experience

Age is used as a proxy for experience in the labor market. The coefficients of age and age squared in the log hourly earnings equation

Table 3.4 Hourly Earnings by Gender in Greater Buenos Aires, Selected Years

Gender	Means (Arg$ 1998)			Changes (percent)		
	1986	1992	1998	1986–92	1992–98	1986–98
Female	9.3	8.1	9.0	−12.6	10.2	−3.7
Male	10.8	8.5	9.3	−21.2	9.0	−14.1
Total	10.4	8.4	9.2	−18.9	9.3	−11.4

Note: Data cover workers between 14 and 65 with valid answers.
Source: Authors' calculations based on the EPH, Greater Buenos Aires, October.

of table 3.3 suggest an inverted U-shaped wage-age profile. The comparison between 1986 and 1998 reveals no major changes in the returns to experience. In contrast, the relevant coefficients did change in subperiods 1986–92 and 1992–98. For instance, between 1992 and 1998, the wage-age profile for heads of household and spouses changed in favor of workers older than 50. Because the mean hourly wage of this group is somewhat lower than the overall mean, in principle we expect a mild equalizing effect on the earnings distribution.[11] Older workers are better located in the distribution of equivalent household income than in the earnings distribution, perhaps because of smaller families; thus, the effect of the change in the returns to experience on that distribution is not clear.[12] The results presented in this chapter help assess the quantitative relevance of those arguments.

Unobservable Factors

Earnings equations allow the estimation of returns to observable factors such as education and experience. The error term usually is interpreted as capturing the joint effect of the endowment of unobservable factors (such as individual ability) and their market value on earnings. In general, the variance of this error term captures the contribution of dispersion in unobservable factors to general inequality. Table 3.3 reports the standard deviation of the error terms of each log hourly earnings equation (labeled as "sigma"). For instance, for household heads, the standard deviation took a value of 0.56 in 1986, 0.57 in 1992, and 0.64 in 1998. The substantial increase between 1992 and 1998 also is present in the spouses' and other members' equations. According to these results, the effect of changes in unobservable factors would have been mildly unequalizing between 1986 and 1992 and substantially unequalizing in the next six-year period.

Hours of Work

During the period under analysis, there has been a slight fall in weekly hours of work: one hour between 1986 and 1992 and less than one-half hour in the next six years. This fall was not uniform across categories of workers. Table 3.5 classifies workers by educational level and records the average hours of work of each group. Although there is not a clear pattern of changes between 1986 and 1992, the 1990s witnessed a dramatic fall in hours of work by workers with low levels of education. This change would have a nonnegligible unequalizing effect on the earnings and income distributions.

Table 3.5 Weekly Hours of Work by Educational Levels in Greater Buenos Aires, Selected Years

	Means (Arg$ 1998)			*Changes (percent)*		
Educational level	*1986*	*1992*	*1998*	*1986–92*	*1992–98*	*1986–98*
Primary incomplete	45.7	45.6	40.2	−0.3	−11.7	−12.0
Primary complete	48.5	46.8	46.5	−3.3	−0.8	−4.1
Secondary incomplete	47.0	47.0	47.5	0.1	1.0	1.1
Secondary complete	46.9	45.1	46.7	−3.9	3.5	−0.5
College incomplete	42.7	41.9	41.8	−1.9	−0.1	−2.0
College complete	42.6	42.3	42.8	−0.5	1.1	0.5
Total	46.5	45.5	45.2	−2.1	−0.8	−2.9

Note: Data cover workers between 14 and 65 with valid answers.
Source: Authors' calculations based on the EPH, Greater Buenos Aires, October.

Figure 3.4 Weekly Hours of Work by Educational Level for Men (Heads of Household), Age 40

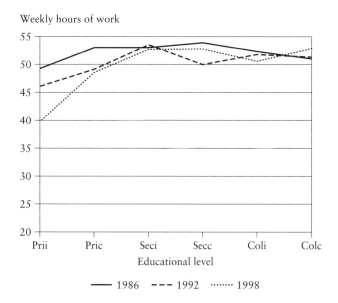

Note: Prii = primary incomplete, Pric = primary complete, Seci = secondary incomplete, Secc = secondary complete, Coli = college incomplete, Colc = college complete.
Source: Predicted weekly hours of work from models in table 3.6.

A conditional analysis yields similar results. Figure 3.4 shows predicted weekly hours of work for male household heads from the Tobit censored data model presented in table 3.6. Although hours of

Table 3.6 Hours of Work Equation for Greater Buenos Aires, Selected Years

Variable	Head of household			Spouse			Other family members		
	1986	1992	1998	1986	1992	1998	1986	1992	1998
Primary complete	3.6994	2.9998	9.1412	−12.8134	−0.8331	−3.7478	9.5376	16.5169	9.4156
	(3.059)	(1.690)	(4.416)	(−3.047)	(−0.158)	(−0.694)	(2.186)	(3.094)	(1.467)
Secondary incomplete	3.6777	7.4547	13.2170	−8.1969	1.6344	5.4827	6.1322	19.4012	9.4008
	(2.722)	(3.780)	(6.057)	(−1.583)	(0.270)	(0.973)	(1.352)	(3.583)	(1.484)
Secondary complete	4.6707	3.7789	13.1584	−1.4443	8.1426	12.0399	8.5914	17.9790	12.4789
	(3.075)	(1.853)	(5.770)	(−0.301)	(1.432)	(2.135)	(1.686)	(3.009)	(1.890)
College incomplete	3.1701	5.7436	10.8928	16.6182	18.4916	20.2824	24.1386	39.7456	21.8096
	(1.552)	(2.149)	(3.979)	(2.095)	(2.277)	(2.858)	(4.185)	(5.859)	(3.152)
College complete	1.7271	5.2378	13.2734	21.8548	32.6159	36.5539	8.2748	23.1498	13.3421
	(0.985)	(2.255)	(5.535)	(3.546)	(4.806)	(6.181)	(1.156)	(3.108)	(1.777)
Male	13.0310	11.0772	15.1987	45.2329	44.9860	43.9907	21.8135	14.8407	15.2718
	(7.291)	(4.845)	(8.093)	(2.677)	(3.380)	(6.512)	(9.650)	(6.134)	(7.018)
Age	1.5803	0.9534	1.3565	5.4816	6.5939	4.4250	4.7870	3.4066	7.5266
	(4.980)	(2.468)	(3.351)	(4.942)	(5.414)	(4.335)	(6.111)	(4.049)	(9.468)
Age squared	−0.0212	−0.0150	−0.0186	−0.0722	−0.0850	−0.0562	−0.0714	−0.0468	−0.1020
	(−5.620)	(−3.248)	(−3.895)	(−5.098)	(−5.455)	(−4.368)	(−6.934)	(−4.130)	(−8.948)
Married	2.7919	3.3768	4.4988	−8.7386	−7.3819	−7.3587	−15.8565	−7.6537	−12.1374
	(1.826)	(1.652)	(2.608)	(−7.070)	(−5.847)	(−6.414)	(−3.813)	(−1.818)	(−3.241)
Children	0.2807	0.0064	−0.4745						
	(0.835)	(0.015)	(−1.036)						
Younger than 18							−18.8104	−14.6823	−23.3702
							(−4.861)	(−3.618)	(−5.426)

Attending school	-14.2282	-16.2041	-13.1575	-13.9652	9.0871	2.5146	-51.2882	-54.3772	-33.9044
	(-4.665)	(-4.315)	(-3.902)	(-1.077)	(0.772)	(0.330)	(-14.003)	(-13.539)	(-10.203)
Head of household employed				-28.5008	-25.8924	-19.6188	-4.0485	-5.6771	-3.6361
				(-3.686)	(-3.669)	(-4.138)	(-1.095)	(-1.619)	(-1.224)
Spouse employed							-3.5146	1.2688	0.0257
							(-1.327)	(0.478)	(0.011)
Constant	3.5987	17.5783	-3.6110	-70.2406	-99.8388	-70.4622	-51.8461	-43.2795	-108.5699
	(0.559)	(2.193)	(-0.435)	(-3.282)	(-4.321)	(-3.570)	(-3.641)	(-2.895)	(-7.913)
Number of observations	1,961	1,404	1,967	1,575	1,116	1,413	1,292	1,090	1,631
Censored	112	97	201	81	705	848	780	609	982
Chi²	279.96	174.00	292.40	143.34	129.49	252.91	877.47	658.90	941.1300
Log likelihood	-8,148.67	-5,880.39	-8,369.46	-3,111.35	-2,502.00	-3,352.46	-2,769.37	-2,602.48	-3,576.4700
Pseudo R²	0.0169	0.0146	0.0172	0.0225	0.0252	0.0363	0.1368	0.1124	0.1163
Sigma	18.2014	19.6320	24.0450	45.6327	42.6309	40.6468	30.5604	31.4037	33.2833

Note: Data represent Tobit maximum likelihood estimation; t ratios are in parentheses. Data cover all individuals between ages 14 and 65 with valid answers.

Source: Authors' calculations based on the EPH, Greater Buenos Aires, October.

work clearly decreased between 1986 and 1998 for the less educated male household heads, changes in hours for the rest of the educational groups were only marginal.

Employment

Household income inequality can change not only because of changes in hours of work but also because of changes on the extensive margin of the labor market. This aspect is particularly interesting in the case of Argentina, because many analysts consider the dramatic jump in the unemployment rate in the 1990s to be the main reason for the increase in inequality.

In table 3.7, adults are grouped according to whether they are employed, unemployed, or out of the labor force (inactive). The percentage of unemployed individuals rose from 2.3 percent in 1986 to 6.5 percent in 1998.[13] The major increase took place between 1992 and 1998. However, the increase in unemployment between 1986 and 1998 was accompanied by a decrease in inactivity of roughly the same magnitude. Despite the jump in the unemployment rate,

Table 3.7 Labor Status by Role in the Household in Greater Buenos Aires, Selected Years

	Proportions by group (percent)		
Labor status	1986	1992	1998
All			
Employed	59.4	60.9	59.5
Unemployed	2.3	3.5	6.5
Inactive	38.3	35.6	34.0
Head			
Employed	94.6	93.1	89.8
Unemployed	2.0	3.1	5.2
Inactive	3.4	3.8	5.0
Spouse			
Employed	31.7	36.8	40.1
Unemployed	1.4	1.7	5.6
Inactive	66.9	61.5	54.3
Other			
Employed	39.6	44.1	39.8
Unemployed	4.0	5.9	8.8
Inactive	56.3	50.0	51.4

Note: Data cover individuals between ages 14 and 65 with valid answers.
Source: Authors' calculations based on the EPH, Greater Buenos Aires, October.

the proportion of working-able people with zero income remained roughly unchanged between 1986 and 1998. Notice that for inequality measures, it is irrelevant whether the individual has zero income because he or she is unemployed or because he or she is not looking for a job. Hence, it is not likely that aggregate changes in labor-market participation played a significant role on inequality changes.[14]

Table 3.7 suggests three different stories in the labor market—for household heads, spouses, and other family members. Some household heads lost or quit their jobs, especially in the period between 1992 and 1998, becoming either unemployed or out of the labor force. By contrast, many of the spouses tried to enter the labor force between 1986 and 1992; most of them found a job, but some of them did not. Other family members were less fortunate; nearly all members of this group who started to look for a job became unemployed (or caused another employed individual to move into the unemployed category).

Education

In Argentina, as in many developing countries, substantial changes in the educational composition of the population have been taking place in recent decades. Table 3.8 presents the proportion of individuals between 14 and 65 years old by level of education. Between 1986 and 1998, there was a strong contraction in the proportion of youths and adults with primary education (both those who completed primary schooling and those who did not). Simultaneously, the share of individuals in all other educational groups increased, particularly in the secondary complete group between 1986 and 1992 and in the college group between 1992 and 1998.

Table 3.8 Composition of Sample by Educational Level in Greater Buenos Aires, Selected Years

Educational level	1986	1992	1998
Primary incomplete	15.4	11.0	7.3
Primary complete	32.0	31.1	25.2
Secondary incomplete	26.0	26.8	30.6
Secondary complete	13.5	15.8	15.2
College incomplete	7.1	8.1	11.7
College complete	6.0	7.3	10.0

Note: Data cover individuals between ages 14 and 65 with valid answers.
Source: Authors' calculations based on the EPH, Greater Buenos Aires, October.

To understand the effects of these changes, one can think of over-all inequality as a function of inequality between educational groups and a weighted average of inequality within educational groups. An increase in the share of a given educational group in the population can increase inequality (a) if the mean income of that group is far from the overall mean (or median) so that inequality between that group and the others grows, and (b) if inequality within that group is high so that the weighted average of inequalities within the group increases. In Argentina, the educational structure has changed in the 1990s in favor of a group with an earnings distribution with a rela-tively high mean and dispersion—the college group. This change feeds the presumption of an unequalizing education effect on the earnings and income distribution, operating through both of the previously mentioned channels.[15] The first channel is linked to Kuznets's (1955) observation: if the highly educated rich are a minority and only some poor children manage to achieve the high-est educational (and income) levels, it is likely that inequality grows as the average education of the population increases, at least until the highly educated group is relatively large. The second channel lies on the convexity of the returns to education, which implies higher wage dispersion for the group of highly educated people.

So far we have analyzed several factors that might have affected inequality. Although we have offered some evidence to argue for each effect, we still do not have a consistent framework to use to confirm the sign of each effect and to assess its quantitative rele-vance. Were changes in the returns to education really an unequal-izing force? Were they really a significant force compared with other factors? The next section presents a framework to tackle these questions.

Methodology

To assess the relevance of the various factors discussed in the previ-ous section on income inequality changes, we adapted the micro-econometric decomposition methodology proposed in chapter 2 to our case.[16]

Let Y_{it} be individual i's labor income at time t, which can be writ-ten as a function F of the vector X_{it} of individual observable characteristics that affect wages and employment, the vector ε_{it} of unobservable characteristics, the vector β_t of parameters that deter-mine market hourly wages, and the vector λ_t of parameters that affect employment outcomes (participation and hours of work).

(3.1) $Y_{it} = F(X_{it}, \varepsilon_{it}, \beta_t, \lambda_t) \qquad i = 1, \ldots, N$

where N is total population. The distribution of individual labor income can be represented as follows:[17]

(3.2) $$D_t = \{Y_{1t}, \ldots, Y_{Nt}\}.$$

We can simulate individual labor incomes by changing one or some arguments in equation 3.1. For instance, the following expression represents labor income that individuals i would have earned in time t if the parameters determining wages had been those of time t, keeping all other things constant:

(3.3) $$Y_{it}(\beta_{t'}) = F(X_{it}, \varepsilon_{it}, \beta_{t'}, \lambda_t) \qquad i = 1, \ldots, N.$$

More generally, we can define $Y_{it}(k_{t'})$, where k is any set of arguments in equation 3.1. Hence, the simulated distribution will be

(3.4) $$D_t(k_{t'}) = \{Y_{1t}(k_{t'}), \ldots, Y_{Nt}(k_{t'})\}.$$

The contribution to the overall change in the distribution of a change in k between t and t', holding all else constant, can be obtained by comparing equations 3.2 and 3.4. Although we can make the comparisons in terms of the whole distributions, in this chapter, we compared inequality indices $I(D)$. Therefore, the effect of a change in argument k on the earnings distribution is given by

(3.5) $$I[D_t(k_{t'})] - I(D_t).$$

As discussed in the previous section, this chapter is devoted to discussing the following effects:

- *Returns to education* ($k = \beta^{ed}$) measures the effect of changes in the parameters that relate education to hourly wages (β^{ed}) on inequality.
- *Gender wage gap* ($k = \beta^{g}$) measures the effect of changes in the parameters that relate gender to hourly wages (β^{g}) on inequality.
- *Returns to experience* ($k = \beta^{ex}$) measures the effect of changes in the parameters that relate experience (or age) to hourly wages (β^{ex}) on inequality.
- *Endowment and returns to unobservable factors* ($k = \varepsilon^{w}$) measures the effect of changes in the unobservable factors and their remunerations affecting hourly wages (ε^{w}) on inequality.
- *Hours of work and employment* ($k = \lambda$) measures the effect of changes in the parameters that determine hours of work and labor-market participation (λ) on inequality.
- *Education* ($k = X^{ed}$) measures the effect of changes in the educational levels of the population (X^{ed}) on inequality.

The previous discussion refers to the distribution of earnings. However, from a social point of view, it is more relevant to study the distribution of household income because a person's utility usually depends not on his or her own earnings but on the household income and the demographic composition of the family. Equivalent household income for each individual in household h in time t is defined as

$$(3.6) \quad Y_{ht}^q = \sum_{j \in ht} (Y_{jt} + Y_{jt}^0) / \left(\sum_{j \in ht} a_{jt} \right)^\theta \qquad h = 1, \dots, H$$

where Y^q stands for equivalent household income, h indexes households, Y^0 is income from other sources, a stands for the equivalent adult of each individual, and θ is a parameter that captures household economies of scale.[18] The distribution of equivalent household income for the population of N individuals can be expressed as follows:

$$(3.7) \qquad\qquad D_t^q = \{ Y_{1t}^q, \dots, Y_{Nt}^q \}.$$

Changing argument k to its value in t' yields the following simulated equivalent household income in year t:

$$(3.8) \quad Y_{ht}^q(k_{t'}) = \sum_{j \in ht} [Y_{jt}(k_{t'}) + Y_{jt}^0] / \left(\sum_{j \in ht} a_{jt} \right)^\theta \qquad h = 1, \dots, H.$$

Hence, the simulated distribution is

$$(3.9) \qquad\qquad D_t^q(k_{t'}) = \{ Y_{1t}^q(k_{t'}), \dots, Y_{Nt}^q(k_{t'}) \}.$$

The effect of a change in argument k, holding all else constant, on equivalent household income inequality is given by

$$(3.10) \qquad\qquad I \left[D_t^q(k_{t'}) \right] - I \left(D_t^q \right).$$

Estimation Strategy

To compute expressions 3.5 and 3.10, we need to estimate parameters β and λ and the residual terms ε. Also, because we do not have panels, we need a mechanism to replicate the structure of observable and unobservable individual characteristics of one year into the population of another year. This section is devoted to explaining the strategies to address these problems.

Estimation of β and λ

Let L_i denote the number of hours worked by person i and w_i be the hourly wage received. Total labor income is given by $Y_i = L_i w_i$. The number of hours of work L_i comes from a utility maximization process that determines optimal participation in the labor market, whereas wages are determined by market forces. The estimation stage specifies models for wages and hours of work, which are used in the simulation stage described earlier.

The econometric specification of the model is similar to the one used by Bourguignon, Fournier, and Gurgand (2001), which corresponds to the reduced form of the labor decisions model originally proposed by Heckman (1974). Heckman shows how it is possible to derive an estimable reduced form starting from a structural system obtained from a utility maximization problem of labor-consumption decisions. Leaving technical details aside, the scheme proposed by Heckman has the following structure. Individuals allocate hours to work and domestic activities (or leisure) to maximize their utility subject to time, wealth, wages, and other constraints. As usual, the solution to this optimization problem can be characterized as demand relations for goods and leisure as functions of the relevant prices. Under general conditions, it is possible to invert these functions to obtain prices and wages as functions of quantities of goods and leisure consumed (or their counterpart, hours of work). In particular, the wages obtained in this fashion (denoted as w^*) are interpreted as marginal valuations of labor, which will be a function of hours of work and other personal characteristics, and represent the minimum wage for which the individual would accept work for a determined number of hours. In equilibrium, if the individual decides to work, the number of hours devoted to labor should equate their marginal value w^* with the wage effectively received. Conversely, a decision not to work is made if the marginal value is greater than the wage offered, given the individual's personal characteristics.

This discussion suggests a way to determine wages demanded by individuals. In parallel it is possible to model market determinants of wages offered (w) as a function of characteristics such as years of education, experience, and age as a standard Mincer equation (Mincer 1974). In equilibrium, it is assumed that the number of hours of work adjusts to make $w = w^*$.

The demand-supply relations discussed so far are structural forms in the sense that they reflect relevant economic behavior in which wages offered and demanded depend on the number of hours of work. Under general conditions, it is possible to derive a reduced form for the equilibrium relations in which wages and hours of work are expressed as functions of the variables taken as exogenous. In this way, the model has two equations—one for wages (w^*) and one for the number of hours of work (L^*)—and both are a function of factors taken as given that affect wages (X_1) and hours (X_2), which may or may not have elements in common. The error terms ε_1 and ε_2 represent unobservable factors that affect the determination of endogenous variables.

According to the characteristics of the problem, we observe positive values of w^* and L^* for a particular individual if and only if the individual actually works. If the person does not work, we only know that the offered wage is smaller than the wage demanded. Consequently, the reduced form model for wages and hours of work is specified as follows:

(3.11) $$w_i^* = X_{1i}\beta + \varepsilon_{1i} \qquad i = 1, \ldots, N$$

(3.12) $$L_i^* = X_{2i}\lambda + \varepsilon_{2i}$$

with

$$w_i = w_i^* \qquad \text{if } L_i^* > 0$$

$$w_i = 0 \qquad \text{if } L_i^* \leq 0$$

$$L_i = L_i^* \qquad \text{if } L_i^* > 0$$

$$L_i = 0 \qquad \text{if } L_i^* \leq 0$$

where w_i and L_i correspond to observed wages and hours of work, respectively. This notation emphasizes that, consistent with the data used for the estimation, observed wages for a nonworking individual are zero.

Following Heckman (1979), for estimation purposes we assume that ε_{1i} and ε_{2i} have a bivariate normal distribution with $E(\varepsilon_{1i}) = E(\varepsilon_{2i}) = 0$, variances σ_{12} and σ_{22}, and correlation coefficient ρ. This particular specification corresponds to the Tobit type III model in Amemiya's (1985) classification.

Even though it is possible to estimate all the parameters using a full information maximum likelihood method, we adopted a limited information approach that has notable computational advantages. If instead of hours of work, we had information only about whether or not the individual works, the model would correspond to the type II model in Amemiya's classification, whose parameters can be estimated on the basis of a simple selectivity model. More specifically, the regression equation would be the wage equation, and the selection equation would be a censored version of the labor supply equation, simply indicating whether or not the individual works. Table 3.3 shows the estimation results of these equations for our case.

Conversely, the hours of work equation corresponds to the Tobit type I model in Amemiya's classification in which the variable is observed only if it is positive. In this case, the parameters of interest could be estimated using a standard censored regression Tobit model (see table 3.6). This strategy is consistent but not fully efficient. In any case, the efficiency loss is not necessarily significant for a small sample.

Unobservable Factors

Unobservable factors that affect wages are modeled as regression error terms of the wage equation 3.11. Their mean is trivially normalized to zero, and their variance is estimated as an extra parameter in the Heckman procedure. To simulate the effect of changes in those unobservable factors between t and t' on inequality, we have rescaled the estimated residuals of the wage equation of year t by $\sigma_{t'}/\sigma_t$, where σ is the estimated standard deviation of the wage equation.[19]

To study employment effects, the decomposition methodology requires simulating earnings for people who do not work. Because we do not observe wages, we cannot apply equations 3.11 and 3.12 to estimate the unobservables. For each individual in that situation, we assigned as an "error term" a random draw from the bivariate normal distribution implicit in the wage-labor supply model (equations 3.11 and 3.12), whose parameters are consistently estimated by the Heckman procedure. Error terms were drawn from the bivariate normal distribution and a prediction (based on observable characteristics, estimated parameters, and sampled errors) was computed for wages and hours worked. If the resulting prediction yields positive hours of work (and the prediction is inconsistent with observed behavior in this group), the error term is sampled again until nonpositive hours of work are predicted.

Individual Characteristics

For the estimation of the education effect, it is necessary to simulate the educational structure of year t' on year t population. Instead of following Bourguignon, Fournier, and Gurgand (2001) and estimating a parametric equation that relates individual educational level to other individual characteristics (age and gender), we apply a rough nonparametric mechanism. We divide the adult population in homogeneous groups by gender and age and then replicate the educational structure of a given cell in year t' into the corresponding cell in year t.

Results

This section reports the results of performing the decompositions described in the methodology using the estimation strategy outlined in the previous section. The objective is to shed light on the quantitative relevance of the various phenomena discussed earlier in this chapter on inequality changes during 1986–98.

Before we show the results, two explanations are in order. First, the decompositions are path dependent. Hence, we report the results using alternatively t and t' as the base year. Second, the simulations are carried out for the whole distribution. To save space, we show only the results for the Gini coefficient. There were not significant variations when other indices were used.[20]

Tables 3.9 to 3.11 show the results both with t and t' as base years. Table 3.12 reports the average of these results.[21] A positive number indicates an unequalizing effect. A large number compared with the other figures in the column suggests a significant effect. For instance, the price effect of education on the earnings distribution in the 1992–98 period (column ii) is 2.9. This finding roughly means that the Gini would have increased 2.9 points if only the returns to education (that is, the coefficients of the educational dummy variables in the wage equation) had changed between those years. The number 2.9 tells us two things: (a) because it is a positive number, it implies that the returns to the education effect increased inequality, and (b) because it is large compared with the other numbers in the column, it indicates that the change in the returns to education was a very significant factor affecting inequality in the distribution of earnings.

The rest of this section is devoted to studying the effects on the earnings and equivalent household labor income distributions of the seven factors that were discussed earlier, with the help of tables 3.9 to 3.12.

Returns to Education

Table 3.12 confirms the presumptions of the earlier section on basic facts and sources for change. Changes in the returns to education had an equalizing effect on the individual labor income distribution between 1986 and 1992 and a strong unequalizing effect over the next six years. The effects on the equivalent income distribution were similar. Over the whole period from 1986 to 1998, changes in the returns to education (in terms of hourly wages) represented an important inequality increasing factor.

Gender Wage Gap

As expected, changes in the gender parameter of the wage equation implied an equalizing effect on the earnings distribution. During the past decade, the gender wage gap has shrunk substantially. Given that women earn less than men, that movement had an unambiguous inequality-decreasing effect on the earnings distribution.

Table 3.9 Decompositions of the Change in the Gini Coefficient: Earnings and Equivalent Household Labor Income in Greater Buenos Aires, 1986–92

Using 1992 coefficients

Indicator	Earnings		Equivalent income	
	Level	Change	Level	Change
1986 observed	39.4		40.3	
1992 observed	37.7	−1.7	41.0	0.7
Effect				
1. Returns to education	38.9	−0.5	39.7	−0.6
2. Gender wage gap	38.4	−1.0	40.4	0.1
3. Returns to experience	41.5	2.1	40.0	−0.3
4. Unobservable factors	39.9	0.5	40.7	0.4
5. Hours of work	39.8	0.4	41.7	1.4
6. Employment	39.4	0.0	40.1	−0.3
7. Education	39.2	−0.2	40.5	0.1
8. Other factors		−3.1		−0.1

Using 1986 coefficients

Indicator	Earnings		Equivalent income	
	Level	Change	Level	Change
1986 observed	39.4	−1.7	40.3	0.7
1992 observed	37.7		41.0	
Effect				
1. Returns to education	39.2	−1.5	42.2	−1.2
2. Gender wage gap	38.8	−1.1	40.9	0.1
3. Returns to experience	36.4	1.3	41.7	−0.7
4. Unobservable factors	37.2	0.5	40.7	0.3
5. Hours of work	38.8	−1.2	40.4	0.6
6. Employment	37.6	0.1	41.0	0.0
7. Education	38.6	−1.0	40.8	0.2
8. Other factors		1.2		1.2

Average changes

Indicator	Earnings	Equivalent income
1986–92 observed	−1.7	0.7
Effect		
1. Returns to education	−1.0	−0.9
2. Gender wage gap	−1.0	0.1
3. Returns to experience	1.7	−0.5
4. Unobservable factors	0.5	0.4
5. Hours of work	−0.4	1.0
6. Employment	0.0	−0.1
7. Education	−0.6	0.2
8. Other factors	−0.9	0.5

Note: The earnings distribution includes those individuals with $Y_{it} > 0$ and $Y_{it}(k_{t'}) > 0$. The equivalent household labor income distribution includes those individuals with $Y_{it}^q \geq 0$ and $Y_{it}^q(k_{t'}) \geq 0$. Nonlabor income is not considered.

Source: Authors' calculations based on the EPH, Greater Buenos Aires, October.

Table 3.10 Decompositions of the Change in the Gini
Coefficient: Earnings and Equivalent Household Labor
Income in Greater Buenos Aires, 1992–98

Using 1998 coefficients

Indicator	Earnings		Equivalent income	
	Level	*Change*	*Level*	*Change*
1992 observed	37.7		41.0	
1998 observed	44.9	7.2	49.5	8.5
Effect				
1. Returns to education	40.8	3.2	43.8	2.7
2. Gender wage gap	37.3	−0.4	41.0	0.0
3. Returns to experience	36.8	−0.9	41.9	0.8
4. Unobservable factors	39.9	2.2	42.8	1.8
5. Hours of work	40.7	3.0	42.9	1.9
6. Employment	37.5	−0.2	41.0	0.0
7. Education	38.2	0.5	41.3	0.2
8. Other factors		−0.2		1.0

Using 1992 coefficients

Indicator	Earnings		Equivalent income	
	Level	*Change*	*Level*	*Change*
1992 observed	37.7	7.2	41.0	8.5
1998 observed	44.9		49.5	
Effect				
1. Returns to education	42.2	2.7	46.5	3.0
2. Gender wage gap	45.3	−0.4	49.6	−0.1
3. Returns to experience	45.9	1.0	48.8	0.7
4. Unobservable factors	43.1	1.8	48.0	1.5
5. Hours of work	43.0	1.9	47.8	1.7
6. Employment	44.8	0.1	49.2	0.3
7. Education	44.8	0.1	48.7	0.8
8. Other factors		2.0		0.6

Average changes

Indicator	Earnings	Equivalent income
1992–98 observed	7.2	8.5
Effect		
1. Returns to education	2.9	2.8
2. Gender wage gap	−0.4	−0.1
3. Returns to experience	−0.9	0.7
4. Unobservable factors	2.0	1.7
5. Hours of work	2.5	1.8
6. Employment	−0.1	0.1
7. Education	0.3	0.5
8. Other factors	0.9	0.8

Note: The earnings distribution includes those individuals with $Y_{it} > 0$ and
$Y_{it}(k_{t'}) > 0$. The equivalent household labor income distribution includes those individuals with $Y_{it}^q \geq 0$ and $Y_{it}^q(k_{t'}) \geq 0$. Nonlabor income is not considered.

Source: Authors' calculations based on the EPH, Greater Buenos Aires, October.

Table 3.11 Decompositions of the Change in the Gini Coefficient: Earnings and Equivalent Household Labor Income in Greater Buenos Aires, 1986–98

Using 1998 coefficients

Indicator	Earnings		Equivalent income	
	Level	Change	Level	Change
1986 observed	39.4		40.3	
1998 observed	44.9	5.5	49.5	9.2
Effect				
1. Returns to education	41.1	1.7	42.0	1.7
2. Gender wage gap	38.1	−1.3	40.5	0.1
3. Returns to experience	39.8	0.4	40.6	0.2
4. Unobservable factors	42.2	2.8	42.7	2.4
5. Hours of work	42.3	3.0	43.5	3.2
6. Employment	39.2	−0.2	40.1	−0.2
7. Education	39.8	0.4	41.2	0.9
8. Other factors		−1.3		0.9

Using 1986 coefficients

Indicator	Earnings		Equivalent income	
	Level	Change	Level	Change
1986 observed	39.4	5.5	40.3	9.2
1998 observed	44.9		49.5	
Effect				
1. Returns to education	43.0	1.9	47.6	1.9
2. Gender wage gap	46.4	−1.5	49.7	−0.2
3. Returns to experience	44.5	0.4	49.2	0.3
4. Unobservable factors	42.7	2.2	47.7	1.8
5. Hours of work	43.5	1.4	46.7	2.8
6. Employment	44.7	0.2	49.4	0.1
7. Education	45.7	−0.8	48.5	1.0
8. Other factors		1.7		1.6

Average changes

Indicator	Earnings	Equivalent income
1986–98 observed	5.5	9.2
Effect		
1. Returns to education	1.8	1.8
2. Gender wage gap	−1.4	0.0
3. Returns to experience	0.4	0.3
4. Unobservable factors	2.5	2.1
5. Hours of work	2.2	3.0
6. Employment	0.0	−0.1
7. Education	−0.2	0.9
8. Other factors	0.2	1.2

Note: The earnings distribution includes those individuals with $Y_{it} > 0$ and $Y_{it}(k_{t'}) > 0$. The equivalent household labor income distribution includes those individuals with $Y_{it}^q \geq 0$ and $Y_{it}^q(k_{t'}) \geq 0$. Nonlabor income is not considered.

Source: Authors' calculations based on the EPH, Greater Buenos Aires, October.

Table 3.12 Decomposition of the Change in the Gini Coefficient: Average Results Changing the Base Year in Greater Buenos Aires, Selected Periods

	Earnings			Equivalent household income		
	1986–92	1992–98	1986–98	1986–92	1992–98	1986–98
Indicator	(i)	(ii)	(iii)	(iv)	(v)	(vi)
Observed	−1.7	7.2	5.5	0.7	8.5	9.2
Effect						
1. Returns to education	−1.0	2.9	1.8	−0.9	2.8	1.8
2. Gender wage gap	−1.0	−0.4	−1.4	0.1	−0.1	0.0
3. Returns to experience	1.7	−0.9	0.4	−0.5	0.7	0.3
4. Unobservable factors	0.5	2.0	2.5	0.4	1.7	2.1
5. Hours of work	−0.4	2.5	2.2	1.0	1.8	3.0
6. Employment	0.0	−0.1	0.0	−0.1	0.1	−0.1
7. Education	−0.6	0.3	−0.2	0.2	0.5	0.9
8. Other factors	−0.9	0.9	0.2	0.5	0.8	1.2

Note: The earnings distribution includes those individuals with $Y_{it} > 0$ and $Y_{it}(k_t) > 0$. The equivalent household labor income distribution includes those individuals with $Y_{it}^q \geq 0$ and $Y_{it}^q(k_t) \geq 0$. Nonlabor income is not considered.

Source: Authors' calculations based on the EPH, Greater Buenos Aires, October.

However, the gender effect becomes negligible in the equivalent household labor income distribution. Earlier, we argued that, on the one hand, the shrinking gender wage gap could increase inequality in the household income distribution because of the concentration of female workers in the upper part of that distribution. On the other hand, however, it could decrease inequality because women's earnings are a more significant part of total resources in low-income households. It appears that these two factors cancel each other out.

Returns to Experience (Age)

The age coefficients in the wage equations of 1986 and 1998 are not substantially different. This fact is translated into a small value for the effect of returns to experience seen in columns iii and vi of table 3.12. Changes were greater in the two subperiods. For instance, the relative increase in earnings for people older than 50 between 1992 and 1998 implies a sizable equalizing effect on the earnings distribution. Instead, the sign of the returns to the experience effect in column v is positive, perhaps because of the different location of the age groups in the earnings and household income distributions, as argued in the section on basic facts and sources for changes.

Unobservables

Changes in endowments and returns to unobservable factors have implied unequalizing changes in wages, which have translated into unequalizing changes in the earnings and equivalent household labor income distributions. These effects were particularly strong in the 1992–98 period. The results of the decompositions suggest that the increase in the dispersion of unobservables was one of the main factors affecting earnings and household inequality over the period under analysis.

Hours of Work

To assess the relevance of changes in hours of work and employment status on inequality, we simulate the distribution in a base year using the parameters of the Tobit employment equations of table 3.6 for a different year. To single out the effect of changes in hours worked, we ignore observations for people who changed labor status between the base year and the simulation (that is, we keep their actual earnings) and change hours of work only for individuals who worked both in the base year and in the simulation. As discussed earlier, the 1990s witnessed a substantial fall in hours of work by low-income workers and an increase in hours of work for the rest. From columns ii and v of table 3.12, it appears that this fact has had a very significant effect on the earnings and household income distributions.

Employment

To assess the effect of changes in individual employment status, we assign zero earnings to people with nonpositive simulated hours of work, whereas people who worked in the simulation are assigned the actual base year earnings.[22]

Unemployment rates skyrocketed in the mid-1990s and have remained very high since then. There is a widespread belief that the increase in unemployment is the main cause of the strong increase in household inequality. Results in column v of table 3.12 suggest that we scale down those conclusions because the employment effect is positive but negligible.[23] Two reasons contribute to reduce the effect of the great increase in unemployment on household inequality. First, during 1992–98, the unemployment rate jumped, but the employment rate did not change much, implying a minor change in the number of individuals without earnings. As stressed earlier, this number, rather than the number of unemployed people, is the relevant number for household inequality. The second point is that the newly unemployed (those who did not work in 1998 but who would have worked given the 1992 parameters) had extremely low individual labor incomes in 1992 (just 10 percent of the rest), but their equivalent household incomes were not far from the median (75 percent of the median). This finding implies that in the simulation using the 1992 parameters, the change in labor status (from unemployed to employed) of some individuals would not have a very strong effect on household inequality because (a) those individuals had very low incomes anyway, and (b) they were not concentrated in the lower tail of the household income distribution.

Education

Argentina has witnessed a dramatic change in the educational composition of its population in the past two decades. According to the results shown in table 3.12, that change had a mild inequality-increasing effect on the earnings and equivalent household income distributions in the 1990s. This result is not surprising given our earlier discussion on sources for change.

Other Factors and Interactions

The last row in table 3.12 is calculated as a residual. It encompasses the effects of interaction terms and of many factors not considered in the analysis. According to table 3.12, these terms are not too large, implying either that the factors not considered in the analysis are not extremely important or that they tend to compensate for each other.

Concluding Remarks

This chapter contributes to a highly discussed topic in Argentina—the increase in income inequality—by using microeconometric decompositions methodology. This technique allows us to assess the relevance of various factors that affected inequality between 1986 and 1998. The results of the chapter suggest that the small change in inequality between 1986 and 1992 is the result of mild forces that compensated for each other. In contrast, between 1992 and 1998, nearly all effects played in the same direction. Changes in the returns to education and experience, in the endowments of unobservable factors and their remunerations, and in hours of work and employment status, as well as the transformation of the educational structure of the population, have all had some role in increasing inequality in Argentina to unprecedented levels. Even the decrease in the wage gap between men and women, which is a potential force for reducing inequality, has not induced a significant decrease in household income inequality.

The increase in the returns to education and unobservable factors and the relative fall in hours of work for unskilled workers are particularly important to characterize the growth in inequality. Perhaps surprisingly, although Argentina witnessed dramatic changes in the gender wage gap, the unemployment rate, and the educational structure, these factors appear to have had only a mild effect on the household income distribution.

Notes

This article is part of a project on income distribution financed by the Convenio Ministerio de Economía de la Provincia de Buenos Aires and the Facultad de Ciencias Económicas de la Universidad Nacional de La Plata. We appreciate the financial support of these institutions. We are grateful to the editors of this volume and seminar participants at the Universidad Nacional de La Plata, Universidad Torcuato Di Tella, Latin American and

Caribbean Economic Association meetings in Rio de Janeiro, meetings of the Asociación Argentina de Economía Política in Córdoba, and Hewlett Foundation Conference at the University of California at Los Angeles for helpful comments and suggestions. We also thank Verónica Fossati and Alvaro Mezza for efficient research assistance. All opinions and remaining errors are the responsibility of the authors.

1. These values correspond to the distribution of the equivalent household income in Greater Buenos Aires. All figures in this chapter were calculated from the Permanent Household Survey (Encuesta Permanente de Hogares, or EPH) for the Greater Buenos Aires area, because data for the rest of urban Argentina are available only from the beginning of the 1990s. Following Buhmann and others (1988), the equivalent household income was obtained by dividing household income by the number of equivalent adults—taken from the National Institute of Statistics and Census (INDEC)—raised to 0.8, a parameter that implies mild household economies of scale.

2. The use of other indices does not change the main conclusions derived from the graph. See Gasparini and Sosa Escudero (2001).

3. These broad trends are also reported by other authors. See Altimir, Beccaria, and González Rozada (2001); Gasparini, Marchionni, and Sosa Escudero (2001); Lee (2000); and Llach and Montoya (1999).

4. All households with valid incomes (including those with no income) were considered in the equivalent household labor income statistics. Ignoring those with zero income did not alter the main results; see our companion paper, Gasparini, Marchionni, and Sosa Escudero (2000). Only workers with positive earnings were included in the individual labor income statistics. Results in table 3.1 are robust to changes in inequality indices (see our companion paper).

5. Gasparini and Sosa Escudero (2001) used bootstrap methods to show that it is possible to reject the null hypothesis that the Gini coefficients of 1986 and 1998 are equal. Although the same is true for the Gini coefficients of 1992 and 1998, one cannot reject the null hypothesis that the Gini coefficients of 1986 and 1992 are equal.

6. Throughout the paper, *wage* refers to hourly labor income earned by wage workers and self-employed workers.

7. We refer to *returns to education* as the change in hourly wages owing to a change in the educational level (and not in years of education). It takes approximately seven years to complete primary school, five or six additional years to complete high school, and approximately five years to complete college.

8. The increasing returns to education could be caused by a selectivity bias in the schooling decision. High-ability people have lower costs of acquiring knowledge and hence are more prone to make a higher human capital investment.

9. Surprisingly, the time pattern is the opposite for other members of the household. However, because the number of working individuals in this group is much smaller than in the head of household group, the global conclusion of a narrowing gender wage gap holds.

10. Although 44 percent of working women are in the highest income quintile of the equivalent household labor income distribution, only 25 percent of men are in that quintile (the Greater Buenos Aires area, 1998). At the other extreme, 6 percent of working women are in the lowest income quintile, whereas 9 percent of men are in that quintile.

11. In 1998, the mean wage for workers between 50 and 60 years old was 86 percent of the overall mean.

12. For instance, although 22 percent of working household heads in their 50s are in the richest quintile of the earnings distribution, 28 percent are in the top quintile of the equivalent household labor income distribution (the Greater Buenos Aires area, 1998). Instead, for working household heads in their 30s, the figures are 36 percent and 28 percent.

13. This implies an unemployment rate of 3.8 percent in 1986 and 9.9 percent in 1998. These figures refer to our restricted sample. The unemployment rates reported by INDEC for the whole country are somewhat higher.

14. Furthermore, there are no signs that the strong increase in unemployment has translated into a disproportionate increase in adults with no income in any of the educational groups. The results of the selection equations in table 3.3 are in line with this conclusion. See Gasparini, Marchionni, and Sosa Escudero (2000) for more information.

15. Between 1986 and 1992, the greatest increase in share was for adults who had completed or not completed secondary school, a group with wages close to the mean and with relative low dispersion; therefore, we expect an equalizing education effect on the earnings distribution.

16. See also Altimir, Beccaria, and González Rozada (2001) and the other chapters in this book.

17. It is typical to restrict this distribution to those individual with $Y_{it} > 0$. We followed that practice in the empirical implementation.

18. In the empirical implementation, we ignore Y_{jt}^0.

19. Under bivariate normal assumptions implicit in the Heckman model, once the correlation between unobservable factors affecting wages and hours worked is kept constant, all remaining effects of unobservable factors on wages come through the variance. Machado and Mata (1998) allowed for heterogeneous behavior of the error term using quintile regression methods.

20. See Gasparini, Marchionni, and Sosa Escudero (2000).

21. According to table 3.12, the observed Gini coefficient of the individual earnings distribution grew 7.2 points between 1992 and 1998. The return to education in column ii is 2.9. This figure is the average of two numbers: (a) the difference between the Gini that results from applying

1998 vector β^{ed} of educational dummy variables to the 1992 distribution and the actual Gini in 1992, and (b) the difference between the actual Gini in 1998 and the Gini that results from applying 1992 vector β^{ed} to the 1998 distribution.

22. Some people did not work in the base year but did work in the simulation. For those individuals, we simulated the base year hours of work and wages using the base year parameters of equations 3.11 and 3.12 and adding error terms obtained by following the procedure described the section on estimation strategy.

23. Naturally, the role of unemployment as the main source of the increase in inequality can be stressed again if it is argued that the fall in the relative wages of the poorest workers was generated by a relative increase in the unemployment rate of that group. However, the evidence on this point is far from conclusive.

References

Altimir, Oscar, Luis Beccaria, and Martín González Rozada. 2001. "La Evolución de la Distribución del Ingreso Familiar en la Argentina: Un Análisis de Determinantes." *Serie de Estudios en Finanzas Públicas 7.* Maestría en Finanzas Públicas Provinciales y Municipales, Universidad Nacional de La Plata, La Plata, Argentina.

Amemiya, Takeshi. 1985. *Advanced Econometrics.* Cambridge, Mass.: Harvard University Press.

Bourguignon, François, Martin Fournier, and Marc Gurgand. 2001. "Fast Development with a Stable Income Distribution: Taiwan, 1979–94." *Review of Income and Wealth* 47(2): 139–63.

Buhmann, Brigitte, Lee Rainwater, Guenther Schmaus, and Timothy Smeeding. 1988. "Equivalence Scales, Well-Being, Inequality and Poverty: Sensitivity Estimates across Ten Countries Using the Luxembourg Income Study Database." *Review of Income and Wealth* 34: 115–42.

Gasparini, Leonardo, and Walter Sosa Escudero. 2001. "Assessing Aggregate Welfare: Growth and Inequality in Argentina." *Cuadernos de Economía (Latin American Journal of Economics)* 38(113): 49–71.

Gasparini, Leonardo, Mariana Marchionni, and Walter Sosa Escudero. 2000. "La Distribución del Ingreso en la Argentina y en la Provincia de Buenos Aires." *Cuadernos de Economía* 49: 1–50.

———. 2001. *La Distribución del Ingreso en la Argentina: Perspectivas y Efectos Sobre el Bienestar.* Buenos Aires: Fundación Arcor.

Heckman, James. 1974. "Shadow Prices, Market Wages, and Labor Supply." *Econometrica* 42: 679–94.

———. 1979. "Sample Selection Bias as a Specification Error." *Econometrica* 47: 153–61.

Kuznets, Simon. 1955. "Economic Growth and Income Inequality." *American Economic Review* 45(1): 1–28.

Lee, Haeduck. 2000. "Poverty and Income Distribution in Argentina. Patterns and Changes." In *Argentina: Poor People in a Rich Country.* Washington, D.C.: World Bank.

Llach, Juan, and Silvia Montoya. 1999. *En Pos de la Equidad. La Pobreza y la Distribución del Ingreso en el Area Metropolitana del Buenos Aires: Diagnóstico y Alternativas de Política.* Buenos Aires: Instituto de Estudios sobre la Realidad Argentina y Latinoamericana.

Machado, José, and José Mata. 1998. "Sources of Increased Inequality." Universidade Nova de Lisboa, Lisbon. Processed.

Mincer, Jacob. 1974. *Schooling, Experience, and Earnings.* New York: Columbia University Press for National Bureau for Economic Research.

4

The Slippery Slope: Explaining the Increase in Extreme Poverty in Urban Brazil, 1976–96

Francisco H. G. Ferreira and
Ricardo Paes de Barros

By both the standards of its own previous growth record during the "Brazilian miracle" years of 1968–73 and those of other leading developing countries thereafter (notably in Asia), the two decades between 1974 and 1994—between the first oil shock and the return of stability with the Real plan—were dismal for Brazil. Primarily, these years were characterized by persistent macroeconomic disequilibrium, the main symptoms of which were stubbornly high and accelerating inflation and a gross domestic product (GDP) time series marked by unusual volatility and a very low positive trend. Figures 4.1 and 4.2 plot annual inflation and GDP per capita growth rates for the 1976–96 period.

The macroeconomic upheaval involved three price and wage freezes (during the Cruzado Plan of 1986, the Bresser Plan of 1987, and the Verão Plan of 1989), all of which were followed by higher inflation rates. Then there was one temporary financial asset freeze (with the Collor Plan of 1990), and finally a successful currency reform followed by the adoption of a nominal anchor in 1994 (the Real Plan). In less than a decade, the national currency changed names four times.[1] Throughout the period, macroeconomic policy was almost without exception characterized by relative fiscal laxity and growing monetary stringency.

Figure 4.1 Macroeconomic Instability in Brazil: Inflation

Inflation rate (percent)

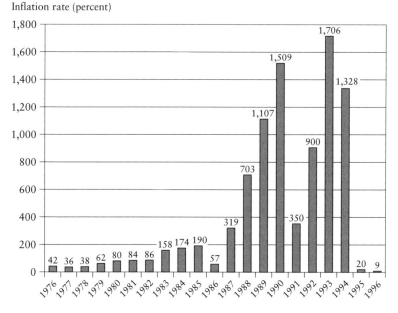

Source: Fundação Getulio Vargas 1999 and Instituto Brasileiro de Geografia e Estatística 1999.

Figure 4.2 Macroeconomic Instability in Brazil: Per Capita GDP

Per capita GDP growth rate (percent)

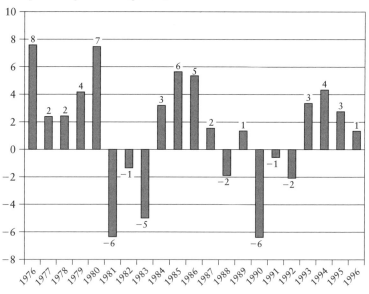

Source: Instituto Brasileiro de Geografia e Estatística 1999.

In addition, substantial structural changes were taking place. Brazil's population grew by 46.6 percent between 1976 and 1996[2] and became more urban (the urbanization rate rose from 68 percent to 77 percent). The average education of those 10 years or older rose from 3.2 to 5.3 effective years of schooling.[3] Open unemployment grew steadily more prevalent. The sectoral composition of the labor force moved away from agriculture and manufacturing and toward the service industries. The degree of formalization of the labor force declined substantially: the proportion of formal workers (wage workers with formal documentation) dropped by nearly half, from just less than 60 percent to just more than 30 percent of all workers (see table 4.1). However, despite the macroeconomic turmoil and continuing structural changes, a casual glance at the headline inequality indicators and poverty incidence measures reported at the bottom of table 4.1 suggests that little changed in the Brazilian urban income distribution between 1976 and 1996.

Nevertheless, as is often the case, casual glances at the data can be misleading. This apparent distributional stability belies a number of powerful, and often countervailing, changes in four realms: the returns to education in the labor markets, the distribution of educational endowments over the population, the pattern of occupational choices, and the demographic structure resulting from household fertility choices. In this chapter, we discuss two puzzles about the evolution of Brazil's urban income distribution in the 1976–96 period and suggest explanations for them.

The first puzzle is posed by the combination of growth in mean incomes and stable or slightly declining inequality on the one hand and rising extreme poverty on the other hand. We argue that this enigma can be explained only by the growth in the size of a group of very poor households, who appear to be effectively excluded both from the labor markets and the system of formal safety nets. This group is trapped in indigence at the very bottom of the urban Brazilian income distribution and contributes to rises in poverty measures, particularly to bottom-sensitive measures like the depth [P(1)] and severity [P(2)] of poverty.[4] This is especially the case when poverty is defined with respect to a low poverty line. E(0) fails to respond to this group because of a rise in the share of families reporting (valid) zero incomes.[5] Other inequality measures, which also fell slightly between 1976 and 1996, compensated for these increases in poverty by declining dispersion further along the distribution. However, the reality of the loss in income to the poorest group of urban households is starkly captured by figure 4.3, which plots the observed (truncated) Pen parades for the four years being studied.[6] The main endogenous channel through which the marginalization

Table 4.1 General Economic Indicators for Brazil,
Selected Years

Economic indicator	1976	1981	1985	1996
Gross national product per capita (in constant 1996 reais)[a]	4,040	4,442	4,540	4,945
Annual inflation rate (percent)[a,b]	42	84	190	9
Open unemployment (percent)[c]	1.82	4.26	3.38	6.95
Average years of schooling[d,e]	3.23	4.01	4.36	5.32
Rate of urbanization[e]	67.8	77.3	77.3	77.0
Self-employed workers (as a percentage of the labor force)[e]	27.03	26.20	26.19	27.21
Percentage of formal employment[e,f]	57.76	37.97	36.41	31.51
Mean (urban) household per capita income (in constant 1996 reais)[e,g]	265.10	239.08	243.15	276.46
Inequality (Gini)[e]	0.595	0.561	0.576	0.591
Inequality (Theil T)[e]	0.760	0.610	0.657	0.694
Poverty incidence (R$30 per month)[e]	0.0681	0.0727	0.0758	0.0922
Poverty incidence (R$60 per month)[e]	0.2209	0.2149	0.2274	0.2176

a. Annual figure is given.

b. Rate shown is for January to December. The 1976 figure is based on the Índice Geral de Preços–Disponibilidade Interna (General Price Index). All other years are based on the Índice Nacional de Preços Consumidor–Real (National Consumer Price Index).

c. Rate is based on the Instituto Brasileiro de Geografia e Estatística (Brazilian Geographical and Statistical Institute) Metropolitan Unemployment Index.

d. Rate is for all individuals 10 years of age or older in urban areas.

e. Rate is calculated from the urban Pesquisa Nacional por Amostra de Domicilios (National Sample Survey) samples by the authors. See appendix 4A.

f. Defined as the number of formal sector (*com carteira*) employees as a fraction of the sum of all wage employees and self-employment workers.

g. Urban only, monthly and spatially deflated.

Source: Authors' calculations.

of this group is captured in our model is a shift in their occupational "decisions" away from either wage or self-employment, toward unemployment or out of the labor force.[7]

Second, the evidence we examine reveals general downward shifts in the earnings-education profile, controlling for age and gender, in both the wage and self-employment sectors over the 20-year data

Figure 4.3 Truncated Pen Parades, 1976–96

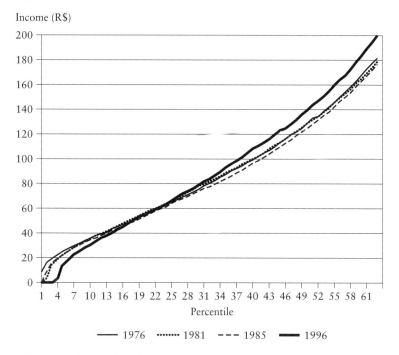

Income (R$)

Percentile

—— 1976 ········ 1981 – – – 1985 ━━ 1996

Source: Authors' calculations.

period, 1976–96 (figure 4.4). Despite a slight convexification of the profile, the magnitude of the shift implies a decline in the (average) rate of return to education for all relevant education levels. Similarly, average returns to experience also fell unambiguously for 0 to 50 years of experience (figure 4.5). The combined effect of changes in these returns—the *price effects*—was an increase in simulated poverty for all measures and for both lines. Simulated inequality also rose, albeit much more mildly. Both effects were exacerbated when the changes (to 1996) of the determinants of labor-force participation decisions also were taken into account. The second puzzle, then, is what forces counterbalance these price and occupational choice effects to explain the observed stability in inequality and "headline poverty."[8] We found that these forces were fundamentally the combination of increased educational endowments, which move workers up along the flattening earnings-education slopes, with an increase in the correlation between family income and family size, caused by a more-than-proportional reduction in dependency ratios and family sizes for the poor. This demographic

Figure 4.4 Plotted Quadratic Returns to Education
(Wage Earners)

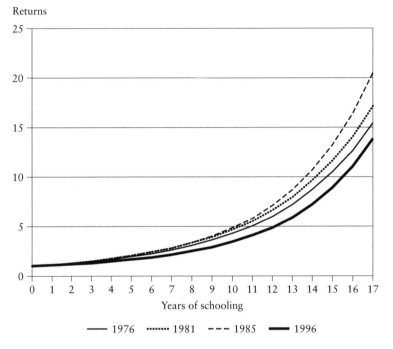

Source: Authors' calculations.

factor had direct effects on per capita income—through a reduction
in the denominator—but also had indirect effects—through participation decisions leading to higher incomes.

Naturally, the coexistence of these two phenomena or puzzles
implies that these last combined educational and demographic
effects did not extend to all of Brazil's poor. At the very bottom,
some of the poor are being cut off from the benefits of greater education and economic growth and remain trapped in indigence.

We address these issues by means of a microsimulation-based
decomposition of distributional changes, which builds on the work
of Almeida dos Reis and Paes de Barros (1991) and of Juhn,
Murphy, and Pierce (1993). The approach, which was described in
chapters 1 and 2 of the book, has two distinguishing features. First,
unlike other dynamic inequality decompositions, such as the
approach proposed by Mookherjee and Shorrocks (1982), it decomposes the effects of changes on an entire distribution rather than
on a scalar summary statistic (such as the mean log deviation).
This approach allows for much greater versatility: within the same

Figure 4.5 Plotted Quadratic Returns to Experience
(Wage Earners)

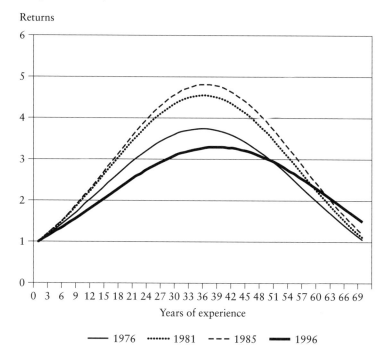

Returns

Years of experience

— 1976 ⋯⋯ 1981 - - - 1985 ━ 1996

Source: Authors' calculations.

framework, a wide range of simulations can be performed to investigate the effects of changes in specific parameters on any number of
inequality or poverty measures (and then for any number of poverty
lines or assumptions about equivalence scales). Second, the evolving
distribution, which it decomposes, is a distribution of household
incomes per capita (with the recipient unit generally being the individual). Therefore, moving beyond pure labor-market studies, the
approach explicitly takes into account the effect of household composition on living standards and participation decisions. As it turns
out, these factors are of great importance for a fuller understanding
of the dynamics at hand.

The remainder of the chapter is organized as follows. The next
section briefly reviews the main findings of the literature on income
distribution in Brazil over the period of study and presents summary
statistics and dominance comparisons for the four observed distributions analyzed: 1976, 1981, 1985, and 1996. The methodology
section outlines how the basic model in chapter 2 of this book was
adapted to the case of Brazil. The section on estimating the model

presents the results of the estimation stage and discusses some of its implications. It is followed by a section presenting the main results of the simulation stage and decomposing the observed changes in poverty and inequality. The chapter then concludes and draws some policy implications.

Income Distribution in Brazil from 1976 to 1996: A Brief Review of the Literature and the Data Set

There is little disagreement in the existing literature about the broad trends in Brazilian inequality since reasonable data first became available in the 1960s. The Gini coefficient rose substantially during the 1960s, from around 0.500 in 1960 to 0.565 in 1970 (see Bonelli and Sedlacek 1989).[9] There was a debate over the causes of this increase, spearheaded by Albert Fishlow (1972) on the one hand and Carlos Langoni (1973) on the other. However, there was general agreement that the 1960s saw substantially increased dispersion in the Brazilian income distribution.[10]

The 1970s displayed a more complex evolution. Income inequality rose between 1970 and 1976, reached a peak in that year, and then fell—both for the distribution of total individual incomes in the economically active population and for the complete distribution of household per capita incomes—from 1977 to 1981. This decline was almost monotonic, except for an upward blip in 1980 (Bonelli and Sedlacek 1989; Hoffman 1989; Ramos 1993). The recession year of 1981 was a local minimum in the inequality series, whether measured by the Gini coefficient or the Theil T index. From 1981, income inequality rose during the recession years of 1982 and 1983. Some authors report small declines in some indices in 1984, but the increase resumed in 1985. In 1986, the year of the Cruzado Plan, a break in the series was caused both by a sudden (if short-lived) decline in inflation and by a large increase in reported household incomes. Stability and economic growth led to a decline in measured inequality, according to all of the authors cited in table 4B.1 in appendix 4B. Thereafter, with the failure of the Cruzado stabilization attempt and the return to stagflation, inequality resumed its upward trend, with the Gini coefficient finishing the decade at 0.606. Table 4B.1 summarizes the findings of this literature, both for per capita household incomes and for the distribution of total individual incomes in the economically active population.

The general trends identified in the existing literature are mirrored in the statistics for the years covered in this chapter: 1976, 1981, 1985, and 1996. The distributions for each of these years were taken from the Pesquisa Nacional por Amostra de Domicílios

(National Sample Survey, or PNAD), run by the Instituto Brasileiro de Geografia e Estatística (Brazilian Geographical and Statistical Institute, or IBGE). Except where otherwise explicitly specified, we deal with distributions for urban areas only, where the welfare concept is total household income per capita (in constant 1996 reais, spatially deflated to adjust for regional differences in the average cost of living), and the unit of analysis is the individual. Details of the PNAD sampling coverage and methodology, sample sizes, definitions of key income variables, spatial and temporal deflation issues, and adjustments with respect to the national accounts baseline are discussed in appendix 4A.

Table 4.2 presents a number of summary statistics for these distributions in addition to the mean, which was provided in table 4.1. The four inequality indices used throughout this chapter are the Gini coefficient and three members of the generalized entropy class

Table 4.2 Basic Distributional Statistics for Different Degrees of Household Economies of Scale

Statistic	1976	1981	1985	1996
Median (1996 R\$)[a]	127.98	124.04	120.83	132.94
Inequality				
Gini, $\theta = 1.0$	0.595	0.561	0.576	0.591
Gini, $\theta = 0.5$	0.566	0.529	0.548	0.567
E(0), $\theta = 1.0$	0.648	0.542	0.588	0.586
E(0), $\theta = 0.5$	0.569	0.472	0.524	0.534
E(1), $\theta = 1.0$	0.760	0.610	0.657	0.694
E(1), $\theta = 0.5$	0.687	0.527	0.580	0.622
E(2), $\theta = 1.0$	2.657	1.191	1.435	1.523
E(2), $\theta = 0.5$	2.254	0.918	1.134	1.242
Poverty, R\$30 per month				
P(0), $\theta = 1.0$	0.0681	0.0727	0.0758	0.0922
P(0), $\theta = 0.5$	0.0713	0.0707	0.0721	0.0847
P(1), $\theta = 1.0$	0.0211	0.0337	0.0326	0.0520
P(1), $\theta = 0.5$	0.0235	0.0315	0.0303	0.0442
P(2), $\theta = 1.0$	0.0105	0.0246	0.0224	0.0434
P(2), $\theta = 0.5$	0.0132	0.0226	0.0204	0.0357
Poverty, R\$60 per month				
P(0), $\theta = 1.0$	0.2209	0.2149	0.2274	0.2176
P(0), $\theta = 0.5$	0.2407	0.2229	0.2382	0.2179
P(1), $\theta = 1.0$	0.0830	0.0879	0.0920	0.1029
P(1), $\theta = 0.5$	0.0901	0.0875	0.0927	0.0960
P(2), $\theta = 1.0$	0.0428	0.0525	0.0534	0.0703
P(2), $\theta = 0.5$	0.0471	0.0508	0.0521	0.0625

a. For urban areas only, and spatially deflated. See appendix 4A.
Source: Authors' calculations.

of inequality indexes, $E(\phi)$. Specifically, we chose $E(0)$, also known as the mean log deviation or the Theil L index; $E(1)$, better known as the Theil T index, and $E(2)$, which is one-half of the square of the coefficient of variation. These indices provide a useful range of sensitivities to different parts of the distribution. $E(0)$ is more sensitive to the bottom of the distribution, whereas $E(2)$ is more sensitive to higher incomes. $E(1)$ is somewhere in between, whereas the Gini places greater weight around the mean.

We also present three poverty indices from the Foster, Greer, and Thorbecke (1984) additively decomposable class $P(\alpha)$. $P(0)$, also known as the headcount index, measures poverty incidence. $P(1)$ is the normalized poverty deficit, and $P(2)$ is an average of squared normalized deficits, thus placing greater weight on incomes furthest from the poverty line. We calculated each of these indices with respect to two poverty lines, representing R\$1 and R\$2 per day, at 1996 prices.[11]

Each of these poverty and inequality indices is presented both for the (individual) distribution of total household incomes per capita and for an equivalized distribution using the Buhmann and others (1988) parametric class of equivalence scales (with $\theta = 0.5$). This method provides a rough test that the trends described are robust to different assumptions about the degree of economies of scale in consumption within households. Although a per capita distribution does not allow for any such economies of scale, taking the square root of family size allows for economies of scale to a rather generous degree. As usual, per capita incomes generate an upper bound for inequality measures, whereas allowing for some extent of local public goods within households raises the income of (predominantly poor) large households and lowers inequality. In the case of the poverty measures, the poverty lines were adjusted as follows: $z^* = z[\mu(n)]^{1-\theta}$, where $\mu(n)$ is the mean household size in the distribution (see Deaton and Paxson 1997).

Table 4.2 also confirms that the evolution of inequality over the period was marked by a decline from 1976 to 1981 and by a subsequent deterioration over the remaining two subperiods. Furthermore, this trend is robust to the choice of equivalence scale, proxied here by two different values for θ, although the inequality levels are always lower when we allow for economies of scale within households. It is also robust to the choice of inequality measure, at least with regard to the inequality increases from 1981 to 1996 and from 1985 to 1996, as the Lorenz dominance results identified in table 4.3 indicate.

The results for poverty are more ambiguous. With respect to the higher poverty line, incidence is effectively unchanged throughout

Table 4.3 Stochastic Dominance Results

	1976	1981	1985	1996
1976			F	
1981				L
1985				L
1996				

Source: Authors' calculations.

the period (and even displays a slight decline for the equivalized distribution). P(1) and P(2), however, showed increases over the period, which become both more pronounced and more robust with respect to θ as the concavity of the poverty measure increases. This trend suggests that depth and severity of poverty, affected mostly by falling incomes at the very bottom of the distribution, were rising.

These results are reflected in table 4.3, in which a letter L (F) in cell (i, j) indicates that the distribution for year i Lorenz dominates (first order stochastically dominates) that for year j. Both 1981 and 1985 display Lorenz dominance over 1996, as suggested earlier. There is only one case of first-order welfare dominance throughout the period, and symptomatically, it is not a case of a later year over an earlier one. Instead, money-metric social welfare was unambiguously higher in 1976 than in 1985. Indeed, all poverty measures reported for both of our lines (and for $\theta = 1.0$) are higher in 1985 than in 1976.[12] This finding is conspicuously not the case for a comparison between 1976 and 1996. Although poverty measures very sensitive to the poorest are higher for 1996, poverty incidence for "higher" lines fall from 1976 to 1996, suggesting a crossing of the distribution functions. Figure 4.3 shows this crossing by plotting the Pen parades [$F^{-1}(y)$], truncated at the 60th percentile for all four years analyzed. Note that although 1976 lies everywhere above 1985, all other pairs cross. In particular, 1976 and 1996 cross somewhere near the 17th percentile.

Before we turn to the model used to decompose changes in the distribution of household incomes, which will shed some light on all of these changes, it is helpful to gather some evidence on the evolution of educational attainment (as measured by average effective years of schooling) and on labor-force participation, for different groups in the Brazilian population, partitioned by gender and ethnicity. Table 4.4 presents these statistics. As seen, there was some progress in average educational attainment in urban Brazil over this period. Average effective years of schooling for all individuals 10 years or older, as reported in table 4.1, rose from 3.2 to 5.3 years.

Table 4.4 Educational and Labor-Force Participation Statistics, by Gender and Race

Statistic	1976	1981	1985	1996
Average years of schooling				
Males	3.32	4.04	4.36	5.20
Females	3.14	3.99	4.37	5.43
Blacks and mixed-race individuals	—	—	—	4.20
Whites	—	—	—	6.16
Asians	—	—	—	8.13
Labor-force participation (percent)				
Males	73.36	74.63	76.04	71.31
Females	28.62	32.87	36.87	42.00
Blacks and mixed-race individuals	—	—	—	55.92
Whites	—	—	—	56.41
Asians	—	—	—	54.88

— Not available.

Notes: Table shows the average effective years of schooling for persons age 10 or older in urban areas. Labor-force participation rates are for urban areas only.

Source: Authors' calculations.

In fact, this piece of good news was vital in preventing a more pronounced increase in poverty. Table 4.4 now reveals that the male-female educational gap has been eliminated, with females 10 years or older being on average slightly more educated than males of the same age. Clearly, this finding must imply a large disparity in favor of girls in recent cohorts. Although a cohort analysis of educational trends is beyond the scope of this chapter,[13] such a rapid reversal may in fact warrant a shift in public policy toward programs aimed at keeping boys in school, without in any way discouraging the growth in schooling of girls. Finally, note the remarkable disparity in educational attainment across ethnic groups, with Asians substantially above average and blacks and those of mixed race below average.

As for labor-force participation, the persistent and substantial increase in female participation from 29 percent to 42 percent over the two decades was partly mitigated by a decline in male participation rates. Those trends notwithstanding, the male-female participation gap remains high, at around 30 percentage points. There is little evidence of differential labor-force participation across ethnic groups.

The Model and the Decomposition Methodology

Let us now turn to the Brazilian version of the general semireduced-form model for household income and labor supply in chapter 2. It is used here to investigate the evolution of the distribution of household incomes per capita over the two decades from the mid-1970s to the mid-1990s. Specifically, we analyzed the distributions of 1976, 1981, 1985, and 1996 and simulated changes between them. As stated earlier, this chapter covers only Brazil's urban areas (which account for some three-quarters of its population). The general model, therefore, collapses to two occupational sectors: wage earners and self-employed workers in urban areas.[14]

Total household income (Y_h) is given by

$$(4.1) \qquad Y_h = \sum_{i=1}^{n} w_i L_i^w + \sum_{i=1}^{n} \pi_i L_i^{se} + Y_{0h}$$

where w_i is the total wage earnings of individual i; L^w is a dummy variable that takes the value 1 if individual i is a wage earner (and 0 otherwise); π_i is the self-employment profit of individual i; L^{se} is a dummy variable that takes the value 1 if individual i is self-employed (and 0 otherwise); and Y_0 is income from any other source, such as transfer income or capital income. Equation 4.1 is not estimated econometrically. It aggregates information on right-hand-side terms 1 (from equations 4.2 and 4.4), 2 (from equations 4.3 and 4.4), and 3 directly from the household data set.

The wage-earnings equation is given as follows:

$$(4.2) \qquad \text{Log } w_i = X_i^P \beta^w + \varepsilon_i^w$$

where $X_i^P = (ed, ed^2, \exp, \exp^2, D_g)$ and ed denotes completed effective years of schooling. Experience (exp) is defined simply as (age − education − 6), because a more desirable definition would require the age when a person first entered employment, a variable that is not available for 1976.[15] D_g is a gender dummy variable, which takes the value of 1 for females and 0 for males; w_i is the monthly earnings of individual i; and ε_i is a residual term that captures any other determinant of earnings, including any unobserved individual characteristics, such as innate talent. This extremely simple specification was chosen to make the simulation stage of the decomposition feasible, as described below. Analogously, the self-employed earnings equation is given as follows:

$$(4.3) \qquad \text{Log } \pi_i = X_i^P \beta^{se} + \varepsilon_i^{se}.$$

Equations 4.2 and 4.3 are estimated using ordinary least squares (OLS). Equation 4.2 is estimated for all employees, whether or not they are heads of household and whether or not they have formal sector documentation (*com* or *sem carteira*). Equation 4.3 is estimated for all self-employed individuals (whether or not they are heads of households). Because the errors ε are unlikely to be independent from the exogenous variables, a sample selection bias correction procedure might be used. However, the standard Heckman procedure for sample selection bias correction requires equally strong assumptions about the orthogonality between the error terms ε and ξ (from the occupational-choice multinomial logit below). The assumptions required to validate OLS estimation of equations 4.2 and 4.3 are not more demanding than those required to validate the results of the Heckman procedure. We assume, therefore, that all errors are independently distributed and do not correct for sample selection bias in the earnings regressions.

We now turn to the labor-force participation model. Because we had a two-sector labor market (segmented into the wage employment and self-employment sectors), labor-force participation and the choice of sector (occupational choice), could be treated in two different ways. One could assume that the choices were sequential, with a participation decision independent from the occupational choice and the latter conditional on the former. That approach, which would be compatible with a sequential probit estimation, was deemed less satisfactory than an approach in which individuals face a single three-way choice, between staying out of the labor force, working as employees, or being self-employed. Such a choice can be estimated by a multinomial logit model. According to that specification, the probability of being in state $s = (0, w, se)$ is given by equation 4.4:

$$(4.4) \qquad P_i^s = \frac{e^{Z_i \gamma_s}}{e^{Z_i \gamma_s} + \sum_{j \neq s} e^{Z_i \gamma_j}} \qquad \text{where } s, j = (0, w, se)$$

where the explanatory variables differ for household heads and other household members, by assumption, as follows. For household heads,

$$Z_1^h = \begin{pmatrix} X_1^P; n_{0-13}, n_{14-65}, n_{>65}, \dfrac{1}{n_{14-65}} \sum_{-1} D_{14-65} ed, \\[2mm] \left[\dfrac{1}{n_{14-65}} \sum_{-1} D_{14-65} ed\right]^2, \dfrac{1}{n_{14-65}} \sum_{-1} D_{14-65} age, \\[2mm] \left[\dfrac{1}{n_{14-65}} \sum_{-1} D_{14-65} age\right]^2, \dfrac{1}{n_{14-65}} \sum_{-1} D_{14-65} D_g, D \end{pmatrix}.$$

Notice that this is essentially a reduced-form model of labor supply, in which own earnings are replaced by the variables that determine them, according to equation 4.2 or 4.3. For other members of the household,

$$
Z_i^b = \begin{pmatrix}
X_i^P;\, n_{0-13},\, n_{14-65},\, n_{>65},\, \dfrac{1}{n_{14-65}}\sum_{-i}D_{14-65}ed, \\[2ex]
\left[\dfrac{1}{n_{14-65}}\sum_{-i}D_{14-65}ed\right]^2,\, \dfrac{1}{n_{14-65}}\sum_{-i}D_{14-65}age, \\[2ex]
\left[\dfrac{1}{n_{14-65}}\sum_{-i}D_{14-65}age\right]^2,\, \dfrac{1}{n_{14-65}}\sum_{-i}D_{14-65}D_g,\, D_1^{se},\, L_1^w w_1,\, D
\end{pmatrix}
$$

where n_{k-m} is the number of persons in the household whose age falls between k and m, D_{14-65} is a dummy variable that takes the value of 1 for individuals whose age is between 14 and 65, D^{se} is a dummy variable for a self-employed head of household, and the penultimate term is the earnings of a wage-earning head. These last two variables establish a direct conduit for the effect of the household head's occupational choice (and possibly income) on the participation decisions of other members. D is a dummy variable that takes the value 1 if there are no individuals age 14 to 65 years in the household. The sums defined over $\{-j\}$ are sums over $\{\forall i \in h | j\}$.

The multinomial logit model in equation 4.4 corresponds to the following discrete choice process:

(4.5) $s = \mathrm{Arg}_j \max \left\{ U_j = Z_i^b \gamma_j + \xi_{\ddot{y}},\; j = (0, w, se) \right\}$

where Z is given above, separately for household heads and other members; the $\xi_{\ddot{y}}$ are random variables with a double exponential density function; and U_j may be interpreted as the utility of alternative j. Once the vector γ_j is estimated by equation 4.4, and a random term ξ is drawn, each individual chooses an occupation j so as to maximize the above utility function.

Once equations 4.2, 4.3, and 4.4 have been estimated, we have two vectors of parameters for each of the four years in our sample ($t \in \{1976, 1981, 1985, 1996\}$): β_t from the earnings equations for both wage earners and the self-employed (including constant terms α_t) and γ_t from the participation equation. In addition, from equation 4.1, we have Y_{0ht} and Y_{ht}. Let $X_{ht} = \{X_i^P, Z_i^b \,|\, \forall i \in h\}$ and $\Omega_{ht} = \{\varepsilon_i^w, \varepsilon_i^{se}, \xi_i^j | i \in h\}$. We can then write the total income of household h at time t as follows:

(4.6) $Y_{ht} = H(X_{ht}, Y_{0ht}, \Omega_{ht}; \beta_t, \gamma_t)$ $h = 1, \ldots, m.$

On the basis of this representation, changes in the distribution of incomes can be decomposed into price effects (β), occupational-choice effects (γ), endowment effects (X, Y_0), and residual effects (Ω), as outlined in chapter 2. Calculating the price and occupational-choice effects is reasonably straightforward once the relevant exogenous parameters have been estimated. Estimating individual endowment effects requires a further step because elements of the X and Y vectors are jointly distributed and a change in the value of any one variable must be understood conditionally on all other observable characteristics.

Specifically, if we are interested in the effect of a change in the distribution of a single specific variable X_k on the distribution of household incomes between times t and t', it is first necessary to identify the distribution of X_k conditional on other relevant characteristics X_{-k} (and possibly other incomes Y_0). This can be done by regressing X_k on X_{-k} at dates t and t', as follows:

$$(4.7) \qquad X_{kit} = X_{-kit}\mu_t + u_{kit}$$

where k is the variable, i is the individual, and t is the date. The vector of residuals u_{kit} represents the effects of unobservable characteristics (assumed to be orthogonal to X_{-k}) on X_k. The vector μ_t is a vector of coefficients capturing the dependency of X_k on the true exogenous variables X_{-k}, at time t. For the sake of simplicity, let us assume that the error terms u are normally distributed with a mean of zero and a common standard deviation σ_t.

The same equation can, of course, be estimated at date t', generating a corresponding vector of coefficients $\mu_{t'}$, and a standard error of the residuals given by $\sigma_{t'}$. We are then ready to simulate the effect of a change in the conditional distribution of X_k from t to t' by replacing the observed values of X_{kit} in the sample observed at time t, with

$$(4.8) \qquad X_{kit}^* = X_{-kit}\mu_{t'} + u_{kit}\frac{\sigma_{t'}}{\sigma_t}.$$

The contribution of the change in the distribution of the variable X_k to the change in the distribution of incomes between t and t' may now be written as follows:

$$(4.9) \qquad \begin{aligned} R_{tt'}^{x^*} &= D[\{X_{kit'}^*, X_{-kit}, Y_{0ht}, \Omega_{ht}\}, \beta_t, \gamma_t] \\ &\quad - D[\{X_{kit}, X_{-kit}, Y_{0ht}, \Omega_{ht}\}, \beta_t, \gamma_t]. \end{aligned}$$

In this study, we perform four regression estimations such as equation 4.7, and hence four simulations such as equation 4.8. The four variables estimated are $X_k = \{n_{0-13}, n_{14-65}, n_{>65}, ed\}$. In the case of the education regression, the vector of explanatory variables X_{-kit} was (1, age, age^2, D_g, regional dummy variables). In the case of the regressions with the numbers of household members in certain age intervals as dependent variables, the vector X_{-kit} was (1, age, age^2, ed, ed^2, regional dummy variables), where age and education are those of the household head. The simulations permitted by these estimations allow us to investigate the effects of the evolution of the distribution of educational attainment and of the demographic structure on the distribution of income. We now turn to the results of the estimation stage of the model.

Estimating the Model

The results of the OLS estimation of equation 4.2 for wage earners (formal and informal) are shown in table 4.5. The static results are not surprising. All variables are significant and have the expected signs. The coefficients on education and its square are positive and significant. The effect of experience (defined as age − education − 6) is positive but concave. The gender dummy variable (female = 1) is negative, significant, and large.

The dynamics are more interesting. Between 1976 and 1996, the earnings-education profile changed shape. After rising in the late 1970s, the linear component fell substantially between 1981 and 1996. Meanwhile, the coefficient of squared years of schooling fell to 1981 but then more than doubled to 1996, ending the period substantially above its initial 1976 value. Overall, the relationship

Table 4.5 Equation 4.2: Wage Earnings Regression for Wage Employees

Variable	1976	1981	1985	1996
Intercept	4.350	4.104	3.877	4.256
	(0.0001)	(0.0001)	(0.0001)	(0.0001)
Education	0.123	0.136	0.129	0.080
	(0.0001)	(0.0001)	(0.0001)	(0.0001)
Education squared (× 100)	0.225	0.181	0.283	0.438
	(0.0001)	(0.0001)	(0.0001)	(0.0001)
Experience	0.075	0.085	0.087	0.062
	(0.0001)	(0.0001)	(0.0001)	(0.0001)
Experience squared (× 100)	−0.105	−0.119	−0.121	−0.080
	(0.0001)	(0.0001)	(0.0001)	(0.0001)
Gender (1 = female)	−0.638	−0.590	−0.635	−0.493
	(0.0001)	(0.0001)	(0.0001)	(0.0001)
R^2	0.525	0.538	0.547	0.474

Note: P-values are in parentheses.
Source: Authors' calculations based on the PNAD.

became more convex, suggesting a steepening of marginal returns to education at high levels. However, plotting the parabola that models the partial earnings–education relationship from equation 4.2, the lowering of the linear term dominates. The profile shifts up from 1976 to 1981 and again to 1985, before falling precipitously (although convexifying) to 1996 (see figure 4.4). The net effect across the entire period was a fall in the cumulative returns to education (from zero to t years) for the entire range. This effect coexisted with increasing marginal returns at high levels of education. The implications for poverty and inequality are clear, with the education price effect leading to an increase in the former and a decline in the latter, all other things being equal.

Returns to experience also increased from 1976 to 1981 and from 1981 to 1985 with a concave pattern and a maximum at around 35 years of experience (see figure 4.5). However, from 1985 to 1996, there was a substantial decline in cumulative returns to experience, even with respect to 1976, until 50 years of experience. The relationship became less concave, and the maximum returns moved up to around 40 years. Over the entire period, the experience price effect was mildly unequalizing (although it contributed to increases in inequality until 1985, which were later reversed) and seriously poverty increasing.

The one piece of good news comes from a reduction in the male-female earnings disparity. Although, when we controlled for both education and experience, female earnings remained substantially lower in all four years (suggesting that some labor-market discrimination may be at work), there was nevertheless a decline in this effect between 1976 and 1996. As we will see from the simulation results, this effect was both mildly equalizing and poverty reducing.

Let us now turn to equation 4.3, which seeks to explain the earnings of the self-employed with the same set of independent variables as equation 4.2. The results are reported in table 4.6. This table reveals that education is also an important determinant of incomes in the self-employment sector. The coefficient on the linear term has a higher value in all years than for wage earners, but the quadratic term is lower. This result implies that, all other things equal, the return to low levels of education might be higher in self-employment than in wage work, but these returns eventually become lower as years of schooling increases. This result will have an effect on occupational choice, estimated through equation 4.4. Dynamically, the same trend was observed as for wage earners: the coefficient on the linear term fell over time, but the relationship became more convex.[16] The coefficients on experience and experience squared follow a similar pattern to that observed for wage earners, as shown in

Table 4.6 Equation 4.3: Total Earnings Regression for the Self-Employed

Variable	1976	1981	1985	1996
Intercept	4.319	4.192	3.853	4.250
	(0.0001)	(0.0001)	(0.0001)	(0.0001)
Education	0.196	0.148	0.165	0.114
	(0.0001)	(0.0001)	(0.0001)	(0.0001)
Education squared ($\times$ 100)	−0.206	0.021	0.012	0.219
	(0.0001)	(0.4892)	(0.6545)	(0.0001)
Experience	0.074	0.079	0.084	0.063
	(0.0001)	(0.0001)	(0.0001)	(0.0001)
Experience squared ($\times$ 100)	−0.101	−0.108	−0.111	−0.082
	(0.0001)	(0.0001)	(0.0001)	(0.0001)
Gender	−1.092	−1.148	−1.131	−0.714
	(0.0001)	(0.0001)	(0.0001)	(0.0001)
R^2	0.431	0.434	0.438	0.336

Note: P-values are in parentheses.
Source: Authors' calculations based on the PNAD.

figure 4.5. Once again, the cumulative return to experience fell over the bulk of the range from 1976 to 1996, contributing to the observed increase in poverty. The effect of being female, all other things equal, is even more markedly negative in this sector than in the wage sector. It also fell from 1976 to 1996, despite a temporary increase in disparity in the 1980s.

A cautionary word is in order before proceeding. All of the estimation results reported in table 4.6 refer to equations with total earnings as dependent variables. The changes in coefficients will, therefore, reflect changes not only in the hourly returns to a given characteristic but also in any supply responses that may have taken place. The analysis is to be understood in this light.

Let us now turn to the estimation of the multinomial logit in equation 4.4. This estimation was made separately for household heads and for others because the set of explanatory variables was slightly different in each case (see the description of vectors Z_1 and Z_i in the previous section).[17]

For household heads, education was not significantly related to the likelihood of choosing to work in the wage sector compared with staying out of the labor force, at any time. In addition, the positive effect of education decreased from 1976 to 1996 to the point where it was no longer statistically significant. The dominant effect on the occupational choices of urban household heads over this period, however, was a substantial decline in the constant term affecting the probability of participating in either productive sector, as opposed to remaining outside the labor force or in unemployment. Because it is captured by the constant, this effect is not related to the educational or experience characteristics of the head of household or to the endowments of his or her household. We interpret it, instead, as the effect of labor-market demand-side conditions, leading to reduced participation in paid work.[18] In the occupational-choice simulations reported in the next section, this effect will be shown to be both unequalizing and immiserizing.

For other members of the household, education did appear to raise the probability of choosing wage work compared with staying out of the labor force, with the relationship changing from concave to convex over the period. It also enhanced the probability of being in self-employment compared with being outside the labor force in both periods, although this relationship remained concave. The number of children in the household significantly discouraged participation in both sectors, although more so in the wage-earning sector. The change in the constant term was much smaller than for household heads, suggesting that negative labor-market conditions hurt primary earners to a greater extent. Consequently, we observed the effect of the occupational choices of other household members on poverty and inequality to be much milder than that of the occupational choices of the heads of households. This finding is in contrast to those in other economies where similar methodologies have been applied. For example, in Taiwan, China, changes in labor-force participation rates of spouses (particularly female spouses) had important consequences for the distribution of incomes (see chapter 9).

The results of the estimation of equation 4.7, with education of individuals 10 years old or older as the dependent variable regressed against the vector (1, age, age^2, D_g, regional dummy variables), are also given in Ferreira and Paes de Barros (1999). Over time, there is a considerable increase in the value of the intercept, which will yield higher predicted values for educational attainment, controlling for age, gender, and regional location. In addition, the gender dummy variable went from large and negative to positive and significant, suggesting that women have more than caught up with men in educational attainment in Brazil over the past 20 years. The effect of individual age is stable, and regional disparities persist, with the South and Southeast ahead of the three central and northern regions.

Regressing the number of household members in the age intervals 0–13, 14–65, and older than 65 years, respectively, on the vector (1, ed, ed^2, age, age^2, regional dummy variables) yields the finding that the schooling of the head of household has a large, negative, and significant effect on the demand for children; hence, as education levels rise, family sizes tend to fall, all other things equal. In addition, some degree of convergence across regions in family size can be inferred, with the positive 1976 regional dummy coefficients for all regions (with respect to the Southeast) declining over time and more than halving in value to 1996.

Simulation Results

After estimating earnings equations for both sectors of the model—wage earners (equation 4.2) and the self-employed (equation 4.3); participation equations for both household heads and other household members (equation 4.4); and endowment equations for the exogenous determination of education and family composition (equation 4.7), we are now in the position to carry out the decompositions described in chapter 1. These simulations, as discussed earlier, are carried out for the entire distribution. The results are summarized in table 4.7, through the evolution of (a) the mean household per capita income $\mu(y)$; (b) four inequality indices—the Gini coefficient, the Theil L index [E(0)], the Theil T index [E(1)], and E(2); and (c) the standard three members of the Foster, Greer, and Thorbecke (1984) class of poverty measures—$P(\alpha)$, $\alpha = 0, 1,$ 2—computed with respect to two monthly poverty lines: an indigence line of R\$30 and a poverty line of R\$60 (both expressed in 1996 São Paulo metropolitan area prices).[19]

Table 4.7 contains a great wealth of information about a large number of simulated economic changes, always by bringing combinations of 1996 coefficients to the 1976 population. To address the two puzzles posed in the introduction to this chapter—namely, the increase in extreme urban poverty between 1976 and 1996 despite (sluggish) growth and (mildly) reducing inequality and the coexistence of a deteriorating labor market with stable headline poverty—we now plot differences in the logarithms of incomes between the simulated distribution of household incomes per capita and that observed for 1976 for a number of the simulations in table 4.7.[20]

Figure 4.6 plots the combined price effects (α and β) separately for wage earners and the self-employed. As can be seen, these effects were negative (that is, they would have implied lower income in 1976) for all percentiles. The losses were greater for wage earners than for the self-employed and, for the latter, were regressive. Those losses are exactly what one would have expected from the downward

Table 4.7 Simulated Poverty and Inequality for 1976, Using 1996 Coefficients

Indicator	Mean income per capita	Inequality				Poverty: z = R$30 per month			Poverty: z = R$60 per month		
		Gini	E(0)	E(1)	E(2)	P(0)	P(1)	P(2)	P(0)	P(1)	P(2)
1976 observed	265.101	0.595	0.648	0.760	2.657	0.0681	0.0211	0.0105	0.2209	0.0830	0.0428
1996 observed	276.460	0.591	0.586	0.694	1.523	0.0922	0.0530	0.0434	0.2176	0.1029	0.0703
Price effects											
α, β for wage earners	218.786	0.598	0.656	0.752	2.161	0.0984	0.0304	0.0141	0.2876	0.1129	0.0596
α, β for self-employed	250.446	0.597	0.658	0.770	2.787	0.0788	0.0250	0.0121	0.2399	0.0932	0.0490
α, β for both	204.071	0.598	0.655	0.754	2.190	0.1114	0.0357	0.0169	0.3084	0.1249	0.0673
α only, for both	233.837	0.601	0.654	0.774	2.691	0.0897	0.0275	0.0129	0.2688	0.1040	0.0545
All β (but no α) for both	216.876	0.593	0.644	0.736	2.055	0.0972	0.0303	0.0143	0.2837	0.1114	0.0590
Education β for both	232.830	0.593	0.639	0.759	2.691	0.0779	0.0234	0.0110	0.2531	0.0953	0.0488
Experience β for both	240.618	0.600	0.654	0.771	2.694	0.0851	0.0265	0.0125	0.2592	0.1000	0.0525
Gender β for both	270.259	0.595	0.649	0.751	2.590	0.0650	0.0191	0.0090	0.2160	0.0797	0.0404

Occupational-choice effects

γ for both sectors (and both heads + others)	260.323	0.609	0.650	0.788	2.633	0.0944	0.0451	0.0331	0.2471	0.1082	0.0671
γ for both sectors (only for other members)	265.643	0.598	0.657	0.757	2.482	0.0721	0.0231	0.0119	0.2274	0.0867	0.0454
γ, α, β for both sectors	202.325	0.610	0.649	0.788	2.401	0.1352	0.0597	0.0402	0.3248	0.1466	0.0902

Demographic patterns

μ_d only, for all	277.028	0.574	0.585	0.704	2.432	0.0365	0.0113	0.0063	0.1711	0.0554	0.0264
$\mu_d, \gamma, \alpha, \beta$, for all	210.995	0.587	0.577	0.727	2.177	0.0931	0.0433	0.0321	0.2724	0.1129	0.0677

Education endowment effects

μ_e only, for all	339.753	0.594	0.650	0.740	2.485	0.0424	0.0136	0.0073	0.1593	0.0567	0.0287
μ_d, μ_e for all	353.248	0.571	0.584	0.688	2.320	0.0225	0.0078	0.0049	0.1131	0.0359	0.0173
$\mu_e, \mu_d, \gamma, \alpha, \beta$, for all	263.676	0.594	0.600	0.727	1.896	0.0735	0.0374	0.0296	0.2204	0.0913	0.0561

Source: Authors' calculations based on the PNAD.

Figure 4.6 Combined Price Effects by Sector

Difference of log incomes

Percentile

━━━ Wage earners ━━━ Self-employment

Source: Authors' calculations.

shifts of the partial earnings-education and earnings-experience profiles, shown in figures 4.4 and 4.5.

In figure 4.7, we adopt a different tack to the price effects by plotting the income differences for each price-effect simulation (for both sectors combined) and then aggregating them. As we would expect from figures 4.4 and 4.5, the returns to education and experience are both immiserizing. The change in partial returns to education alone is mildly equalizing (as can be seen from table 4.7). The change in the partial returns to experience is unequalizing as well as immiserizing. The change in the intercept, calculated at the mean values of the independent variables, was also negative throughout. This change proxies for a "pure growth" effect, capturing the effects on earnings from processes unrelated to education, experience, gender, or the unobserved characteristics of individual workers. It is intended to capture the effects of capital accumulation, managerial and technical innovation, macroeconomic policy conditions, and other factors likely to determine economic growth that are not included explicitly in the Mincer equation. Its negative effect in this

Figure 4.7 Price Effects Separately and for Both
Sectors Combined

Difference of log incomes

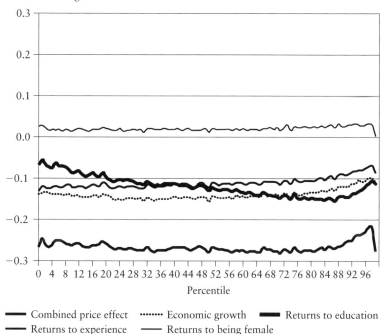

Percentile

■■■ Combined price effect   ⋯⋯⋯ Economic growth   ■■■ Returns to education
─── Returns to experience   ─── Returns to being female

Source: Authors' calculations based on the 1976 and 1996 PNAD.

simulation suggests that these factors were immiserizing in urban
Brazil over the period.

The one piece of good news, once again, comes from the gender
simulation, which reports a poverty-reducing effect as a result of the
decline in male-female earnings differentials captured in tables 4.5
and 4.6. However, this effect was far from being sufficient to offset
the combined negative effects of the other price effects. As the thick
line at the bottom of figure 4.7 indicates, the combined effect of
imposing the 1996 parameters of the two Mincerian equations on
the 1976 population was substantially immiserizing.

Figure 4.8 plots the logarithm of the income differences between
the distribution that arises from imposing the 1996 occupational-
choice parameters (the γ vector from the multinomial logit in
equation 4.4) on the 1976 population and the observed 1976 distribution. It does so both for all individuals (the lower line) and for

Figure 4.8 Occupational-Choice Effects

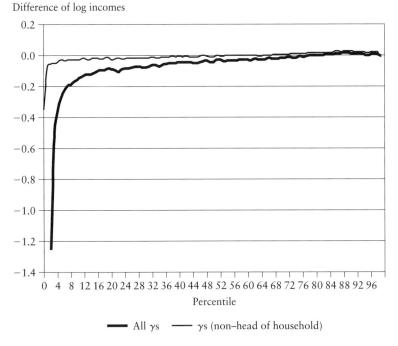

Difference of log incomes

All γs —— γs (non–head of household)

Source: Authors' calculations based on the 1976 and 1996 PNAD.

non–household heads (the upper line). The effect of this simulated change in occupational-choice and labor-force participation behavior is both highly immiserizing and unequalizing, as an inspection of the relevant indices in table 4.7 confirms. It suggests the existence of a group of people who—by voluntarily or involuntarily leaving the labor force, entering unemployment, or being consigned to very ill-remunerated occupations (likely) in the informal sector—are becoming increasingly impoverished.

Combining the negative price and occupational-choice effects provides a sense of the overall effect of Brazil's urban labor-market conditions over this period. This finding is shown graphically in figure 4.9, where the lowest curve plots (a) the differences between the household per capita incomes from a distribution in which all αs, βs, and γs change, and (b) the observed 1976 distribution. It shows the substantially poverty-augmenting (and unequalizing) combined effect of changes in labor-market prices and occupational-choice parameters on the 1976 distribution.

Figure 4.9 The Labor Market: Combining Price and
Occupational-Choice Effects

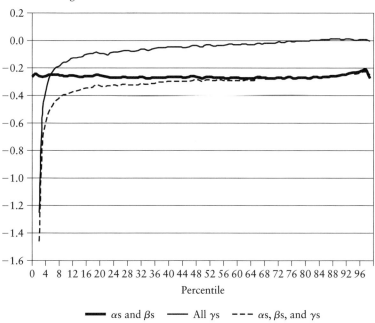

Difference of log incomes

Percentile

■■■ αs and βs   —— All γs   - - - αs, βs, and γs

Source: Authors' calculations based on the 1976 and 1996 PNAD.

At this point, the second puzzle can be stated clearly: given these
labor-market circumstances, what factors can account for the facts
that mean incomes rose, headline poverty did not rise, and inequality appears to have fallen slightly? The first part of the answer is
shown graphically in figure 4.10, where the upper line plots the
differences between the log incomes from a distribution arising from
imposing on the 1976 population the transformation (equation 4.8)
for the demographic structure of the population. The changes in the
parameters μ_d (and in the variance of the residuals in the corresponding regression) have a positive effect on incomes for all percentiles and in an equalizing manner. However, when combined with
a simulation in which the values of all αs, βs, and γs also change, it
can be seen that the positive demographic effect is still overwhelmed.
Nevertheless, it is clear that the reduction in dependency ratios—
and subsequently in family sizes—in urban Brazil over this period
had an important mitigating effect on the distribution of incomes.

Figure 4.10 Demographic Effects

Difference of log incomes

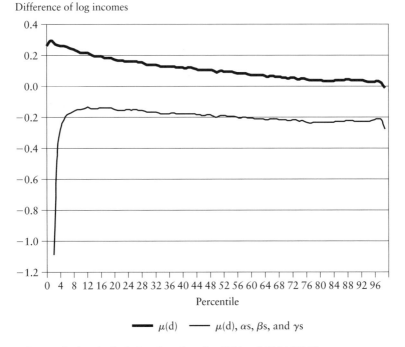

Percentile

μ(d)   —— μ(d), αs, βs, and γs

Source: Authors' calculations based on the 1976 and 1996 PNAD.

One final piece of the puzzle is needed to explain why the deterioration in labor-market conditions did not have a worse effect on poverty. That, as should be evident from the increase in mean years of effective schooling registered in table 4.1, is the rightward shift in the distribution function of education. This effect is shown in figure 4.11, which reveals that gains in educational attainment were particularly pronounced at lower levels of education and thus, presumably, among the poor.

A gain in educational endowments across the income distribution, but particularly among the poor, has both direct and indirect effects on incomes. The direct effects are through equations 4.2 and 4.3, where earnings are positive functions of schooling. The indirect effects are both through the occupational choices that individuals make and through the additional effect that education has on reducing the demand for children and, hence, family size. A simulation of the effect of education is thus quite complex.[21] After it is completed,

Figure 4.11 Shift in the Distribution of Education, 1976–96

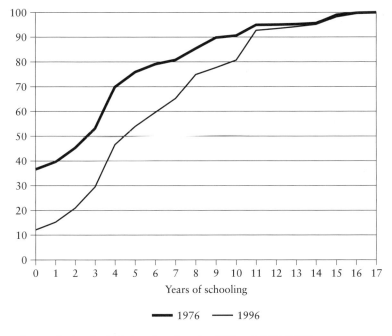

Years of schooling

━━ 1976   ━━ 1996

Source: Authors' calculations based on the 1976 and 1996 PNAD.

one observes, in figure 4.12, a rather flat improvement in log incomes across the distribution (that is, a scaling effect). However, when this effect is again combined with changes in the parameters of the demographic equations, it gains strength and becomes not only more poverty reducing but also mildly equalizing. The bottom line in figure 4.12, in keeping with the pattern, combines both of these effects with the changing αs, βs, and γs. The result is striking: this complex combined simulation suggests that all of these effects, during 20 turbulent years, cancel out almost exactly from the 15th percentile up, hence the small changes in headline poverty. However, from around the 12th percentile down, the simulation suggests a prevalence of the negative occupational-choice (and, to a lesser extent, price) effects, with substantial income losses. These findings account for the rise in indigence captured by the R$30 per month poverty line.

The bottom line in figure 4.12 is, in a sense, the final attempt by this methodology to simulate the various changes that led from the 1976 to the 1996 distribution. Figure 4.13 is a graphical test of the approach. Here the line labeled "1996–76" plots the differences in

Figure 4.12 Education Endowment and Demographic Effects

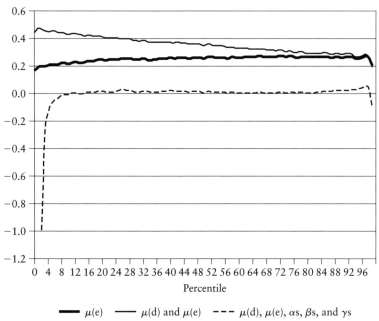

Difference of log incomes

Percentile

━━━ $\mu(e)$ ──── $\mu(d)$ and $\mu(e)$ --- $\mu(d)$, $\mu(e)$, αs, βs, and γs

Source: Authors' calculations based on the 1976 and 1996 PNAD.

actual (log) incomes between the observed 1996 and the observed
1976 distributions. Along with it, we also plotted every (cumulative) stage of our simulations: first, the immiserizing (but roughly
equal) price effects; then these effects combined with the highly
immiserizing occupational-choice effects; then the slightly less bleak
picture arising from a combination of the latter with the parameters
of the family size equations; and, finally, the curve plotting the
differences between the incomes from the simulation with all parameters changing, and observed 1976. As can be seen in figure 4.13,
the last line does not seem to replicate the actual differences badly.
Of course, the point of the exercise is not to replicate the actual
changes perfectly but rather to learn the different effects of different
parameters and possibly to infer any policy implications from them.
However, the success of the last simulation in approximately matching the actual changes does provide some extra confidence in the
methodology and in any lessons we may derive from it.

Figure 4.13 A Complete Decomposition

Difference of log incomes

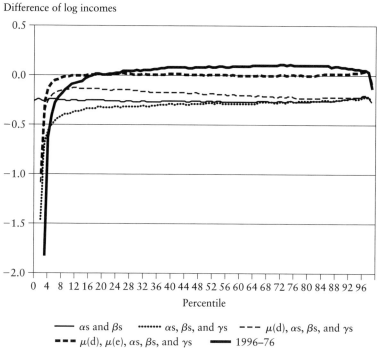

Percentile

——— αs and βs   ········· αs, βs, and γs   – – – μ(d), αs, βs, and γs

■ ■ ■ μ(d), μ(e), αs, βs, and γs   ——— 1996–76

Source: Authors' calculations based on the 1976 and 1996 PNAD.

Conclusions

In the end, does this exercise help improve our understanding of the evolution of Brazil's urban income distribution over this turbulent 20-year period? Although many traditional analysts of income distribution dynamics might have inferred from the small changes in mean income, in various inequality indices, and in poverty incidence that there was little—if anything—to investigate, digging a little deeper has unearthed a wealth of economic factors interacting to determine substantial changes in the environment faced by individuals and families and in their responses.

In particular, we have found that, despite a small fall in measured inequality (although the Lorenz curves cross, as expected) and a small increase in mean income, extreme poverty has increased for sufficiently low poverty lines, or sufficiently high poverty-aversion parameters. This result appears to have been caused by outcomes related to participation decisions and occupational choices, in combination with declines in the labor-market returns to education and experience. These changes were associated with greater unemployment and informality, as one would expect, but more research appears necessary. Although we appear to have identified the existence of a group excluded both from the productive labor markets and from any substantive form of safety net, we have not been able to interpret fully the determinants of their occupational choices. Issues of mobility—exacerbated by the current monthly income nature of the welfare indicator—will also require further understanding in this context. Policy implications appear to lie in the area of self-targeted labor programs or other safety nets, but it would be foolhardy to go into greater detail before the profile of the group that appears to have fallen into extreme poverty in 1996 is better understood.

Second, we have found that, even above the 15th percentile, where urban Brazilians have essentially stayed put, this lack of change was the result of some hard climbing up a slippery slope. These urban Brazilians had to gain an average of two extra years of schooling (still leaving them undereducated for the country's per capita income level) and to substantially reduce fertility in order to counteract falling returns in both the formal labor market and in self-employment.

It may well be, as many now claim, that an investigation of nonmonetary indicators—such as access to services or life expectancy at birth—would lead us to consider the epithet of "a lost decade" too harsh for the 1980s. Unfortunately, we find that if one is sufficiently narrow minded to consider only money-metric welfare, urban Brazil has in fact experienced two, rather than one, lost decades.

Appendix 4A: Data and Methodology

Macroeconomic Data

All macroeconomic indicators reported in this chapter were based on original data from the archives of the IBGE. GDP and GDP per capita figures reported in the introduction came from the series shown in table 4A.1. This series was constructed from the current GDP series (A), which was revised in 1995 and backdated to 1990 and from the old series (B), from 1976 to its final year, 1995. The series reported in table 4A.1 comprises the values of series A from 1990 to 1996 and the values of series B scaled down by a factor of 0.977414 from 1976 to 1989. This factor is the simple average of the ratios A/B over the years 1990–95. The series is expressed in 1996 reais, using the IBGE GDP deflator.

Table 4A.1 Real GDP and GDP Per Capita in Brazil,
1976–1996
(constant 1996 prices)

Year	GDP (reais)	Population	GDP per capita (reais)
1976	434,059,220	107,452,000	4,040
1977	455,477,123	110,117,000	4,136
1978	478,113,823	112,849,000	4,237
1979	510,432,394	115,649,000	4,414
1980	562,395,141	118,563,000	4,743
1981	538,474,976	121,213,000	4,442
1982	542,971,306	123,885,000	4,383
1983	527,054,370	126,573,000	4,164
1984	555,515,747	129,273,000	4,297
1985	599,129,793	131,978,000	4,540
1986	644,002,821	134,653,000	4,783
1987	666,708,887	137,268,000	4,857
1988	666,304,312	139,819,000	4,765
1989	687,391,828	142,307,000	4,830
1990	651,627,236	144,091,000	4,522
1991	658,339,124	146,408,000	4,497
1992	654,759,303	148,684,000	4,404
1993	687,004,026	150,933,000	4,552
1994	727,213,139	153,143,000	4,749
1995	757,918,030	155,319,000	4,880
1996	778,820,353	157,482,000	4,945

Source: Instituto Brasileiro de Geografia e Estatística 1999.

The GDP per capita growth rates plotted in figure 4.1 were derived from this series. Annual inflation and unemployment rates also came from the relevant IBGE series.

The PNAD Data Sets

All of the distributional analyses performed in this chapter were based on four data sets (1976, 1981, 1985, 1996) of Brazil's National Household Survey (Pesquisa Nacional por Amostra de Domicilios, or PNAD), which is fielded annually by the IBGE. For the latter three years, the survey was nationally and regionally representative, except for the rural areas of the North region (except the state of Tocantins). For 1976, rural areas were not surveyed in the North or in the Center-West regions. In this chapter, we were concerned only with urban areas, which are defined by state-level legislative decrees. The urban proportions of the population in each year are given in table 4.1. The PNAD sample sizes, as well as the proportion of missing income values, are given in table 4A.2.

Each PNAD questionnaire contains a range of questions pertaining to both the household and the individuals within the household.

Table 4A.2 PNAD Sample Sizes and Missing or Zero
Income Proportions

Year	Number of households	Number of individuals	Proportion of individuals with missing income	Proportion of individuals whose income is zero
1976	84,660	385,282	0.0052	0.0063
1981	110,151	477,607	0.0073	0.0141
1985	127,128	520,069	0.0073	0.0108
1996	91,621	329,434	0.0291	0.0313

Note: *Income* is total household income per capita.
Source: Authors' calculations based on PNAD.

The household-related questions included regional location, demographic composition, quality of the dwelling, ownership of durables,
and so forth. The individual questions included age, gender, race,
educational attainment, labor-force status, sector of occupation, and
incomes (in both cash and kind) from various sources. The main
variables used in our analysis were those related to incomes, education, demographic structure of the household, and labor-force participation. Tables A.6 to A.9 in Ferreira and Paes de Barros (1999)
summarize the main items in the questionnaire for these variables
and the changes from 1976 to 1996.

Most importantly, the distributions analyzed in this chapter
(except where explicitly otherwise indicated) have, as welfare concept, total household income per capita (regionally deflated). It is
constructed by summing all income sources for each individual
within the household and across all such individuals, except for
lodgers or resident domestic servants. The latter two categories constitute separate households. Total nominal incomes were deflated
spatially to compensate for differences in average cost of living
across various areas in the country, according to the spatial price
index given in table 4A.3.

We assumed, largely because of the lack of earlier comparable
regional price information, that the structure of average regional cost
of living described earlier remained constant over the period. Temporal deflation was undertaken on the basis of the Brazilian consumer
price indices—the Índice Geral de Preços—Disponibilidade Interna
(General Price Index, or IGP-DI) for 1976 and the Índice Nacional
de Preços Consumidor–Real (National Consumer Price Index, or
INPC-R) for the three subsequent years. For 1996, the INPC-R was
upwardly adjusted by 1.2199 to compensate for the actual price
increases that took place in the second half of June 1994 and that
were not computed into the July index, because the latter was already
computed in terms of the unidade real de valor (real value unit). This

Table 4A.3 A Brazilian Spatial Price Index

(São Paulo metropolitan area = 1.0)

PNAD region	Spatial price deflator
Fortaleza metropolitan area	1.014087
Recife metropolitan area	1.072469
Salvador metropolitan area	1.179934
Northeast (other urban areas)	1.032056
Northeast rural	0.953879
Belo Horizonte metropolitan area	0.958839
Rio de Janeiro metropolitan area	1.002163
São Paulo metropolitan area	1.000000
Southeast (other urban areas)	0.904720
Southeast rural	0.889700
Porto Alegre metropolitan area	0.987001
Curitiba metropolitan area	0.987001
South (other urban areas)	0.904720
South rural	0.889700
Belem metropolitan area	1.088830
North (other urban areas)	1.032056
Brasília metropolitan area	1.037915
Center-West (other urban areas)	0.968388

Note: This regional price index is based on the consumption patterns and implicit prices from the 1996 Pesquisa de Padrões de Vida (Living Standard Measurement Survey) for the Northeast and Southeast regions and was extrapolated to the rest of country according to a procedure specified in Ferreira, Lanjouw, and Neri (2003), where the exact derivation of the index is also discussed in detail.

Source: Ferreira, Lanjouw, and Neri 2003.

adjustment is becoming the standard deflation procedure at the Instituto de Pesquisa Econômica Aplicada when comparing incomes across June–July 1994 (see Macrométrica 1994). To center the indices on the first day of the month, which is the reference date for PNAD incomes, the geometric average of the index for a month and for the preceding month were used as that month's deflator. Once again, this procedure is now best practice for price deflation in hyperinflationary periods. Once the deflators were constructed in this way, the values to convert current incomes into 1996 reais were developed, as shown in table 4A.4.

A final possible adjustment to the PNAD data concerns deviations between survey-based welfare indicators (such as mean household income per capita) and national accounts–based prosperity indicators (such as GDP per capita). The international norm is that household survey means are lower than per capita GNP, both because the latter includes the value of public and publicly provided goods and services, which are generally not imputed into the survey indicators, and because of possible underreporting by respondents. Given that the levels of the two series are not expected to match

Table 4A.4 Brazilian Temporal Price Deflators, Selected Years

Year	Value
1976	4.115
1981	49.512
1985	2257.294
1996	1.000

Source: Authors' calculations based on IBGE: IGP-DI and INPC-R.

Table 4A.5 Ratios of GDP Per Capita to PNAD Mean Household Incomes, 1976–96

Year	GDP per capita (A)	Mean PNAD income (B)	(A)/(B)
1976	336.6	190.2	1.770
1981	370.2	187.3	1.976
1985	378.3	188.6	2.005
1996	412.1	233.0	1.769

Source: Authors' calculations based on PNAD and National Accounts data.

exactly, analysts are usually concerned by deviant trends, which may indicate a problem with the survey instrument. Conversely, it may be argued that national accounts data have errors of their own and that many of the "correction" procedures applied to household data rely on reasonably strong assumptions, such as equiproportional underreporting by source.

In deciding whether to adjust the PNAD data with reference to the Brazilian national accounts over this period, we examined the evolution of the ratios of GDP per capita to mean household incomes from the PNAD (for the entire country and without regional price deflation, for comparability). As table 4A.5 shows, these ratios were remarkably stable. In particular, the ratios for the starting and ending points of the period covered, which are of particular importance for our analysis, are almost identical. In this light and because even the disparity with respect to 1981 and 1985 is reasonably small, we judged that the costs of making rough adjustments to the PNAD household incomes on the basis of the national accounts outweighed the benefits.

Appendix 4B: Summary of the Literature

Table 4B.1 shows the evolution of mean income and inequality in Brazil during the period studied and provides a summary of the literature.

Table 4B.1 Evolution of Mean Income and Inequality: A Summary of the Literature

Indicator	1976	1977	1978	1979	1980	1981	1982	1983	1984	1985	1986	1987	1988	1989	1990
Household income per capita															
Bonelli and Sedlacek (1989)															
Gini coefficient	0.561			0.550		0.542		0.549							
Gini coefficient[a]	0.583			0.588		0.584		0.589		0.592					
Hoffman (1989)[b]															
Mean[c]				4.7	4.8	4.6	4.7	3.8	4.0	4.5	5.6				
Gini coefficient				0.588	0.597	0.584	0.587	0.589	0.588	0.592	0.586				
Theil T				0.523	0.536	0.519	0.520	0.523	0.526	0.529	0.519				
Ferreira and Litchfield (1996)															
Mean (1990 US$)						143		126	125	150	213	166	166	196	164
Gini coefficient						0.574		0.584	0.577	0.589	0.581	0.582	0.609	0.618	0.606
Theil T						0.647		0.676	0.653	0.697	0.694	0.710	0.750	0.796	0.745
Total individual income (active population)															
Bonelli and Sedlacek (1989)[d]															
Mean[e]	2241.8			2081.2	2264.0	2040.6		1835.6		2222.1	3112.8				
Gini coefficient	0.589			0.574	0.590	0.562		0.582		0.588	0.577				

(Continued on the following page)

119

Table 4B.1 (Continued)

Indicator	1976	1977	1978	1979	1980	1981	1982	1983	1984	1985	1986	1987	1988	1989	1990
Hoffman (1989)[a,f]															
Mean[g]				340.2		331.2		297.5	293.6	335.7	426.1				
Gini coefficient[h]				0.585		0.572		0.591	0.587	0.599	0.589				
Ramos (1993)[i]															
Mean[j]	85.4	87.5	89.7	93.6		93.4	91.9	86.8	89.2	94.6					
Gini coefficient	0.564	0.543	0.531	0.530		0.514	0.520	0.534	0.536	0.545					
Theil L	0.556	0.511	0.488	0.486		0.457	0.465	0.496	0.498	0.521					
Theil T	0.709	0.607	0.571	0.560		0.513	0.527	0.565	0.558	0.584					

a. Includes those families with zero income.

b. For 1979, excludes the rural areas of the North region and the states of Mato Grosso, Mato Grosso do Sul, and Goiás.

c. Real value, in minimum wages of August 1980, deflated by the Índice do Custo de Vida–Departamento Intersindical de Estatística e Estudos (Cost of Living Index—Inter Trade Union Department of Statistics and Socioeconomic Studies, or ICV-DIEESE).

d. Excludes people with zero income or missing income values.

e. Prices in Cz$1,000 of September 1986. Excludes rural areas in the North region for all years and rural areas of Mato Grosso, Mato Grosso do Sul, and Goiás for 1976 and 1979.

f. Only includes people in the labor force with positive income.

g. In 1,000 cruzeiros of September 1989. Deflators: INPC-IEGE until August 1985; ICV-DIEESE between set/1985 and set/1986.

h. Weighted average of highest and lowest values.

i. For men, ages 18–65, in the labor force in urban areas and working at least 20 hours per week; total income.

j. Base: 1980 = 100.

Source: For Hoffman (1989), the 1979, 1981, 1982, 1983, 1994, 1985, and 1986 PNAD; the 1980 Demographic Census; and Anuário Estatístico 1985 for the years 1979, 1980, 1981, 1982, and 1983. For Bonelli and Sedlacek (1989), the 1976, 1979, 1981, 1983, 1985, and 1986 PNAD and the 1980 Demographic Census. For Lauro Ramos (1993), the 1976, 1977, 1978, 1979, 1981, 1982, 1983, 1984, and 1985 PNAD. For Ferreira and Litchfield (1996), the 1981, 1983, 1984, 1985, 1986, 1987, 1988, 1989, and 1990 PNAD.

Notes

1. The changes were from the cruzeiro to the cruzado in 1986, to the novo cruzado in 1989, back to the cruzeiro in 1990, and to the real in 1994.

2. See table 4A.1 in appendix 4A for a complete population series.

3. Effective years of schooling are based on the last grade completed and are thus net of repetition.

4. All poverty measures reported in this chapter are the $P(\alpha)$ class of decomposable measures from Foster, Greer, and Thorbecke (1984). An increase in α implies an increase in the weight placed on the distance between households' income and the poverty line.

5. $E(\phi)$ denote members of the decomposable generalized entropy class of inequality measures. A lower ϕ means an increased weight placed on distances between poorer people and the mean. $E(0)$, the Theil L index, is particularly sensitive to the poorest people but ignores zero incomes by construction. See Cowell (1995). For the zero incomes in our sample, see appendix 4A, table 4A.2.

6. Pen parades—or quantile functions—are the mathematical inverse of distribution functions; that is, they plot the incomes earned by each person (or group of persons) when these people are ranked by income.

7. The use of terms such as *occupational choice* or *decision* should not be taken to imply an allocation of responsibility. It will become clear when the model is presented that, as usual, these are choices under constraints.

8. By *headline poverty,* we mean poverty incidence computed with respect to the R$60 per month poverty line.

9. Throughout this chapter, this comparison and other comparisons between sample-based statistics are subject to sampling error, and one would ideally like to estimate their level of statistical significance. As discussed in chapter 2, the application of inference procedures to microsimulation-based decompositions remains an item in the agenda for future research.

10. The Fishlow-Langoni debate concerned the importance of education vis-à-vis repressive labor-market policies in determining the high level of Brazilian inequality. See, for example, Fishlow (1972), Langoni (1973), and Bacha and Taylor (1980).

11. At 1996 market exchange rates, this amount was roughly equal to US$1 and US$2. In real terms, this amount would be slightly lower than the conventional poverty lines of purchasing power parities US$1 and US$2 valued at 1985 prices, which the World Bank often uses for international comparisons because of U.S. inflation in the intervening decade.

12. Note that this first-order welfare dominance is not robust to a change in θ to 0.5.

13. See Duryea and Székely (1998) for such an educational cohort analysis of Brazil and other Latin American countries.

14. In Brazil, wage earners include employees with or without formal documentation (*com* or *sem carteira*). The self-employed are own-account workers (*conta própria*).

15. Because education is given by the last grade completed and is thus net of repetition, this definition overestimates the experience of those who repeated grades at school and, hence, biases the experience coefficient downward. The numbers involved are not substantial enough to alter any conclusions on trends.

16. In this case, the relationship actually switched from concave to convex.

17. Space constraints prevent the presentation of the tables reporting these estimations. They are available in Appendix 3 of the working paper version (Ferreira and Paes de Barros 1999).

18. In terms of the occupational-choice framework, these are changes in the constraints with respect to which those choices are made.

19. Table 4.7 and the remaining figures in this chapter refer to the simulation of bringing the coefficients estimated for 1996 on 1976. Similar exercises were conducted for 1981 and 1985 and are reported in Ferreira and Paes de Barros (1999). Likewise, the return simulation of applying the 1976 coefficients on 1996 was conducted, and the directions and broad magnitudes of the changes confirm the results presented here.

20. In computing these differences, we compared the percentiles of the two different distributions described earlier. A different, but equally interesting, exercise is to compare the percentiles of the simulated distribution ranked as in the observed 1976 distribution with that 1976 distribution. These exercises were performed but are not reported because of space constraints. In any case, the plots presented are those that correspond to the summary statistics presented in table 4.7.

21. Note that the different effects are not simply being summed. The effect of greater educational endowments is simulated through every equation in which it appears in the model, thereby affecting fertility choices and occupational statuses, as well as earnings.

References

Almeida dos Reis, José G., and Ricardo Paes de Barros. 1991. "Wage Inequality and the Distribution of Education: A Study of the Evolution of Regional Differences in Inequality in Metropolitan Brazil." *Journal of Development Economics* 36: 117–43.

Bacha, Edmar L., and Lance Taylor. 1980. "Brazilian Income Distribution in the 1960s: Acts, Model Results, and the Controversy." In Lance Taylor, Edmar L. Bacha, Eliana Cardoso, and J. Frank, eds., *Models of*

Growth and Distribution for Brazil. New York: Oxford University Press: 296–342.

Bonelli, Regis, and Guilherme L. Sedlacek. 1989. "Distribuição de Renda: Evolução no Ultimo Quarto de Seculo." In Guilherme L. Sedlacek and Ricardo Paes de Barros, eds., *Mercado de Trabalho e Distribuição de Renda: Uma Coletanea*. Serie Monografica 35. Rio de Janeiro: Instituto de Pequisa Econômica Aplicada.

Buhmann, Brigitte, Lee Rainwater, Guenther Schmaus, and Timothy Smeeding. 1988. "Equivalence Scales, Well-Being, Inequality, and Poverty: Sensitivity Estimates across Ten Countries Using the Luxembourg Income Study Database." *Review of Income and Wealth* 34: 115–42.

Cowell, Frank A. 1995. *Measuring Inequality*, 2nd ed. New York: Harvester Wheatsheaf.

Deaton, Angus, and Christina Paxson. 1997. "Poverty among Children and the Elderly in Developing Countries." Working Paper 179. Princeton University Research Program in Development Studies. Princeton, N.J.

Duryea, Suzanne, and Miguel Székely. 1998. "Labor Markets in Latin America: A Supply-Side Story." Paper prepared for the Inter-American Development Bank and Inter-American Investment Corporation Annual Meeting, Cartagena de Indias, Colombia, March 16–18.

Ferreira, Francisco H. G., and Julie A. Litchfield. 1996. "Growing Apart: Inequality and Poverty Trends in Brazil in the 1980s." Distributional Analysis Research Programme Discussion Paper 23. Suntory and Toyota International Centres for Economics and Related Disciplines, London School of Economics and Political Science.

Ferreira, Francisco H. G., and Ricardo Paes de Barros. 1999. "The Slippery Slope: Explaining the Increase in Extreme Poverty in Urban Brazil, 1976–1996." *Revista de Econometria* 19(2): 211–96.

Ferreira, Francisco H. G., Peter Lanjouw, and Marcelo Neri. 2003. "A Robust Poverty Profile for Brazil Using Multiple Data Sources." *Revista Brasileira de Economia* 57(1): 59–92.

Fishlow, Albert. 1972. "Brazilian Size Distribution of Income." *American Economic Association: Papers and Proceedings 1972*: 391–402.

Foster, James, Joel Greer, and Erik Thorbecke. 1984. "A Class of Decomposable Poverty Measures." *Econometrica* 52: 761–5.

Hoffman, Rodolfo. 1989. "Evolução da Distribuição da Renda no Brasil: Entre Pessoas e Entre Familias, 1979/86." In Guilherme L. Sedlacek and Ricardo Paes de Barros, eds., *Mercado de Trabalho e Distribuição de Renda: Uma Coletanea*. Serie Monografica 35. Rio de Janeiro: Instituto de Pequisa Econômica Aplicada.

Juhn, Chinhui, Kevin Murphy, and Brooks Pierce. 1993. "Wage Inequality and the Rise in Returns to Skill." *Journal of Political Economy* 101(3): 410–42.

Langoni, Carlos Geraldo. 1973. *Distribuição da Renda e Desenvolvimento Econômico do Brasil.* Rio de Janeiro: Expressão e Cultura.

Macrométrica. 1994. "Inflação: Primeiros Meses do Real." *Boletim Mensal Macrométrica* 111 (July–August).

Mookherjee, Dilip, and Anthony F. Shorrocks. 1982. "A Decomposition Analysis of the Trend in U.K. Income Inequality." *Economic Journal* 92: 886–902.

Ramos, Lauro. 1993. *A Distribuição de Rendimentos no Brasil: 1976/85.* Rio de Janeiro: Instituto de Pequisa Econômica Aplicada.

5

The Reversal of Inequality Trends in Colombia, 1978–95: A Combination of Persistent and Fluctuating Forces

Carlos Eduardo Vélez, José Leibovich, Adriana Kugler, César Bouillón, and Jairo Núñez

By the late 1970s, the Colombian economy had completed two decades of consistent reduction in income inequality. For some time, income inequality in Colombia was exemplary of Kuznets's well-known inverted U-shaped curve: after the growing inequality of the first half of the 20th century, substantial reductions in inequality were observed during the 1960s and 1970s as the economy grew. The improvements became marginal during the late 1970s and the 1980s, and income inequality took a U-turn in the late 1980s, completely reversing the equity gains of the two preceding decades.

The rise in national inequality during the 1988–95 period in Colombia was driven by a large increase in inequality in the urban sector, as well as by the simultaneous increase in inequality *between* urban and rural areas. At the same time, Colombia experienced significant changes in the sociodemographic characteristics of the population. Between 1978 and 1995, the most significant changes in those respects were the following: (a) higher educational attainment of the labor force—particularly among women—and greater work experience; (b) a drop in fertility, leading to smaller family size; (c) a decrease in the gender earnings gap; (d) pronounced fluctuations in the structure of wages by educational level; and (e) increased female participation in the labor market. At the same time, the Colombian economy was subjected to major structural reforms and macroeconomic changes that modified key labor-market parameters and affected labor-market performance through different channels. The structural reforms of the early 1990s covered several areas: trade liberalization and trade integration agreements with neighboring countries, liberalization of the capital account, and major changes in labor and social security legislation. The latter increased the relative cost of labor with respect to capital and became a source of difficulty for job creation. In addition, the economy suffered supply shocks linked to major discoveries of oil reserves.

Rural economic activities experienced a marginal shift from agriculture, strictly speaking, and industry to mining and services. In addition, during the late 1970s and early 1980s, agriculture was subjected to a faster process of concentration of land and rural credit. Finally, that sector was hit by a set of negative shocks in the early 1990s: lower tariff protection, real exchange appreciation, lower international prices, drought, and violence.

The purpose of this chapter is to decompose the dynamics of income inequality—urban and rural—so as to measure the specific contribution of some of the preceding factors to changes in income inequality. Within a microsimulation framework based on a reduced-form model of individual earnings and participation in the labor market, we evaluate the following factors:[1] (a) the returns to observable human assets (such as education or experience) and individual characteristics (such as gender, location, or occupational status); (b) the changes in the distribution of these assets and individual characteristics in the population; (c) the changes in labor-force participation and occupational choice behavior; and finally (d) the changes in the overall effect of unobservable earning determinants. This approach is used to decompose the changes in inequality and measure the contribution of each of the preceding factors for the periods 1978–88 and 1988–95 for both individual earnings and household income.

Our findings show that periods of moderate changes in inequality conceal strong counterbalancing effects of equalizing and unequalizing forces. The strongest determinants of individual income distribution dynamics are returns to education, education endowments (that is, how many years of education an individual has), and effects of unobservable factors on earning inequality, in addition to family size and nonlabor income for household income. Some of these factors are persistent, while others are less stable and are strongly dependent on economic conditions. The analysis also shows that the forces that determine changes in the distribution of individual earnings differ in intensity from those that determine changes in the distribution of household income.

A combination of persistent and fluctuating forces characterizes the dynamics of income inequality in the urban sector in Colombia between 1978 and 1995 and explains the reversal that took place in 1988. The persistent forces are linked to demographics and labor supply: the evolution of family behavior—smaller family size and increased labor participation by women—and the growth of educational endowments. The unstable or fluctuating factors tend to respond to changes in the labor demand function—namely, to its labor skills profile. Although the aggregate effect of persistent factors is moderate relative to the effect of fluctuating factors, it is perhaps the best indicator of long-run trends in inequality. Some of these effects are also present, but of much less importance, in the rural sector.

Two of our main findings are contrary to our expectations. First, and intuitively, a greater and more egalitarian education endowment in both urban and rural areas is expected to reduce income inequality. However, according to our decomposition exercise, this intuition held true only in rural areas. Paradoxically, equalization of education endowment led to a deterioration in the income distribution in urban areas in both periods, 1978–88 and 1988–95. This apparent contradiction is explained by the strong convexity of the earnings functions and by the larger interquintile differences in returns to education prevalent in urban areas, with respect to rural areas. Second, increasing female participation in the labor market generated asymmetric effects on per capita income distribution vis-à-vis changes in the per capita labor earnings distribution. The effects were regressive for income distribution and progressive for labor earnings distribution. This surprising discrepancy is easily explained with a simple statistical line of reasoning, which is laid out later in this chapter.

This chapter is divided into four sections. In the first section, we examine the evolution of inequality and poverty indicators for three years: 1978, 1988, and 1995. We examine the changes in some labor-market indicators and in the distribution of sociodemographic characteristics. We also briefly review the main structural reforms and macroeconomic developments that affected labor-market performance. In the second section, we model the income-generating process and provide estimates of parameters that describe the evolution of the structure of earnings and participation behavior. The third section discusses the outcome of the decomposition exercises, which measure the contribution of different factors to the total change in inequality. Finally, we offer some conclusions.

Colombian Income Distribution between 1978 and 1995

The Recent U-Turn in Inequality

Several authors have identified the mid-1960s as the break point in the regressive trend of income distribution during the first half of the 20th century.[2] However, the evolution of the income distribution over the past two decades suggests instead that the regressive trend of the 1960s only presaged a high-water mark. The reduction in inequality was steady from the mid-1960s until the late 1970s. Inequality plateaued from 1978 to 1988 then increased significantly from 1988 to 1995, practically erasing the equity gains of previous decades.[3]

As may be seen in table 5.1, indexes of household income inequality for urban and rural areas are relatively stable from 1978 to 1988 but exhibit opposite tendencies during the 1988–95 period. In urban areas, the Gini coefficient is flat and the Theil index fell a little in the first period. Some reduction of inequality in the upper tail and some increase in the lower tail of the urban distribution are revealed by the simultaneous drop in the transformed coefficient of variation and the increase in the mean log deviation index.

After 1988, urban inequality deteriorated significantly, as indicated by all summary inequality measures reported in table 5.1.[4] In rural areas, the evolution is almost identical between 1978 and 1988: the Gini coefficient and the Theil index deteriorate a little, and the lower and upper tail inequalities show the same rise and decline as in urban areas. From 1988 to 1995, however, rural inequality follows a different path. A clear improvement is noticeable in all inequality indices shown in table 5.1.

This improvement in the rural income distribution was not sufficient to prevent national inequality from rising under the pressure of the increase in the inequality of urban incomes, which represent approximately 80 percent of national household income. It is true that the urban-rural income gap increased after 1988, as urban income per capita nearly doubled between 1978 and 1995 while rural income increased by only 50 percent. However, this evolution is of little importance in explaining the overall worsening of the national distribution of household income. Most of the increase in national inequality after 1988 is explained by changes within urban areas, whereas the limited changes in the national distribution of income during the preceding decade reflect parallel distributional changes within both urban and rural areas.

Table 5.1 Decomposition of Total Inequality between Rural and Urban Areas, Selected Years

	1978			Decomposition		1988			Decomposition		1995			Decomposition	
Indicator	Urban	Rural	Total	Between	Within	Urban	Rural	Total	Between	Within	Urban	Rural	Total	Between	Within
Household inequality															
Gini coefficient	50.2	43.5	53.9			50.2	44.4	54.1			54.4	40.7	56.1		
Mean log deviation, E(0)	38.0	33.8	44.7	8	36	42.5	37.3	49.6	9	40	50.5	30.0	55.8	13	42
Theil, E(1)	52.6	34.6	56.0	8	48	50.3	35.0	55.2	8	47	70.6	29.4	74.7	11	63
Transformed coefficient of variation, E(2)	153.6	60.3	170.4	7	163	105.1	50.5	122.2	7	115	282.7	45.8	331.5	10	321
Population share	57.4	42.6				60.2	39.8				60.7	39.3			
Income share	76.1	23.9				79.0	21.0				82.6	17.4			
Relative income (to the mean)	1.3	0.6				1.3	0.5				1.4	0.4			

	1978		Urban		1988		Urban		1995		Urban	
Indicator	Urban	Rural	Male	Female	Urban	Rural	Male	Female	Urban	Rural	Male	Female
Gini coefficients												
All individuals	47.8	38.5			44.7	39.0			50.3	36.6		
Wage earner			42.1	32.7			39.5	34.3			45.0	39.1
Self-employed			60.8	54.0			53.5	59.0			59.4	57.4

Source: Authors' calculations based on data from DANE, Encuesta Nacional de Hogares.

In view of that relative autonomy of the evolution of urban inequality and rural inequality and their clear contribution to overall inequality, the two sectors are analyzed separately in the rest of this chapter. In urban and rural areas, the inequality of earnings among all employed persons follows a pattern somewhat similar to household inequality. Data from 1978 to 1988 reveal a pronounced decrease in income inequality for all individual urban workers (see the bottom of table 5.1) and stability for rural workers. From 1988 to 1995, earnings inequality for individual rural workers decreases slightly, whereas inequality for urban workers increases quite significantly.

To conclude this short review of the distributional trend in Colombia since 1978, we should mention that, despite fluctuations in income inequality, social welfare in urban Colombia improved substantially and unambiguously both from 1978 to 1988 and from 1988 to 1995. The doubling of income per capita compensated for all changes in income distribution. In rural areas, welfare improvements are unambiguous between 1978 and 1988 but somewhat ambiguous between 1988 and 1995. Vélez and others (2001) find first-order stochastic dominance in both periods in urban areas and during the first period in rural areas as well. However, from 1988 to 1995 in rural areas, second-order stochastic dominance is only satisfied up to the 90th percentile.

Main Forces Driving the Dynamics of Income Distribution

The purpose of this chapter is to identify the forces that shaped the changes of income inequality within urban and rural areas during the 1980s and early 1990s. Before turning to a detailed analysis, we first review the social and demographic developments that may have affected the distribution of income either directly or through the supply of labor. We also assess the simultaneous structural reforms and macroeconomic events that had major impacts on the demand side of the labor market.

EVOLUTION OF THE SOCIODEMOGRAPHIC STRUCTURE OF THE WORKING POPULATION

Greater and More Egalitarian School Attainment.   Urban education levels became higher and more equally distributed throughout the period. The proportion of urban workers who had only completed or had not completed primary education fell by nearly 20 percentage points (see table 5.3), whereas the average number of years of schooling went up from 6.4 to 8.9 years. A more detailed analysis also shows that the increase in educational attainment was greater among women—specifically among younger women, who either caught up with or surpassed men. This general increase in education came with some equalizing of schooling attainment. For instance, the coefficient of variation of the number of years of schooling in the cohort born in 1975 was half what it was four decades earlier. Progress in educational attainment was also observed in the rural population: the average number of years of schooling went up from 2.1 to 3.9 years. Overall, however, the rural sector remained considerably behind the urban sector. As for trends within the urban population, the inequality of educational achievements fell substantially.

Higher Participation in the Labor Force, Particularly by Women. Changes in labor-force participation have been substantial over the period, especially among women. Table 5.2 shows that the average employment rate for women increased from 37.0 to 51.0 percent in urban areas and from 18.6 to 27.5 percent in rural areas. Interestingly, most of this gain in labor-force participation was among female household heads or spouses.

Overall, the share of wage earners in the urban labor force remained relatively constant at about 44 percent. However, the proportion of men employed as wage earners decreased noticeably, suggesting that a higher proportion of women were employed as wage workers. This tendency was still clearer in rural areas, where women entering the labor force tended to concentrate in wage work in commerce and services (López 1998).

Decreasing Fertility Rates. Table 5.3 shows that family size fell in urban areas from 5.1 persons in 1978 to 4.3 in 1988 and 4.1 in 1995. For the average household, this change in size produced, other things being equal, an increase in per capita income of 24 percent, which represents a fourth of the total gain in real earnings per capita for the average Colombian household over the period. This evolution was even more pronounced in rural areas. Overall, the reduction in family size affected all income groups, although in different proportions. Figure 5.1 shows that in urban areas family size fell proportionally more for lower-middle-income households.

MACRO EVENTS AND CHANGES IN DEMAND FOR LABOR

The growth performance of the Colombian economy was satisfactory between 1978 and 1995. Gross domestic product (GDP) per capita grew at an average annual rate of 1.8 percent. But the growth rate was higher by 1 percentage point between 1988 and 1995.[5]

Table 5.2 Labor-Market Indicators in Urban and Rural Areas, Selected Years

	Urban								
	1978			1988			1995		
Indicator	Male	Female	Total	Male	Female	Total	Male	Female	Total
Labor-market statistics									
Average employment rate	88.9	37.0	62.4	88.6	43.3	64.4	90.4	51.0	69.2
Employed by gender	61.4	38.6	100	58.7	41.3	100	56.6	43.4	100
Unemployment rate	6.9	10.3	8.2	7.8	13.9	10.3	6.8	11.4	8.8
Working population by groups									
Percentage of wage earner	64.2	25.6	43.5	59.7	28.9	43.3	56.3	32.8	43.7
Percentage of self-employed	24.0	10.0	16.5	28.3	12.6	19.9	33.4	16.3	24.2
Inactive	11.9	64.4	40.1	12.0	58.5	36.8	10.3	50.9	32.1
Total	100	100	100	100	100	100	100	100	100
Average earnings per month (1995 $Col thousand)	239	150	211	253	182	228	296	206	261
Average wages per hour (1995 $Col thousand)	1.3	0.8		1.2	0.9		1.5	1.2	

	Rural								
	1978			1988			1995		
Indicator	Male	Female	Total	Male	Female	Total	Male	Female	Total
Labor-market statistics									
Average employment rate	76.8	19.6	49.1	79.0	26.5	53.0	76.1	29.6	53.1
Employed by gender	81.4	18.6	100.0	75.6	24.4	100.0	72.5	27.50	100.0
Unemployment rate	1.3	5.4	2.1	2.3	8.9	4.0	2.6	9.70	4.7
Working population by groups									
Percentage of wage earner	46.5	7.6	26.7	47.9	13.7	30.6	46.9	16.5	31.7
Percentage of self-employed	26.4	8.2	17.1	27.2	10.1	18.5	26.0	12.5	19.3
Inactive	27.1	84.2	56.2	24.9	76.2	50.9	27.1	71.1	49.1
Total	100	100	100	100	100	100	100	100	100
Average earnings per month (1995 $Col thousand)	106	68	99	118	86	111	115	86	107

Source: Authors' calculations based on data from DANE, Encuesta Nacional de Hogares.

Table 5.3 Changes in Sociodemographic Characteristics in Urban and Rural Areas, Selected Years

Indicator	Urban			Rural		
	1978	1988	1995	1978	1988	1995
Age structure of the population in working age (percentage)						
12–24	34.9	28.4	23.7	47.2	44.6	40.5
25–34	27.4	32.7	32.7	18.4	20.7	22.1
35–44	18.5	20.9	24.3	15.0	15.8	16.8
45–65	19.1	18	19.2	19.4	18.9	20.6
Education structure in labor force (percentage)						
Illiterate	4.2	2.1	2.1	37.9	22.1	19.8
Primary complete	43.6	32.8	26.8	54.3	60.5	57.8
Secondary incomplete	28.9	28.8	27.4	6.6	13.0	15.8
Secondary complete	11.2	19.8	24.9	1.0	3.6	5.3
Tertiary incomplete	6.3	7.1	8	0.1	0.5	0.8
Tertiary complete	5.8	9.5	10.8	0.1	0.3	0.6
Total	1C0	100	100	100	100	100
Average number of years of education	6.4	7.9	8.9	2.1	3.4	3.9
Household size	5.1	4.3	4.1	5.9	5.1	4.7

Source: Authors' calculations based on data from DANE, Encuesta Nacional de Hogares.

Figure 5.1 Average Household Size by Income Decile in Urban
Colombia, Selected Years

Average household size (persons)

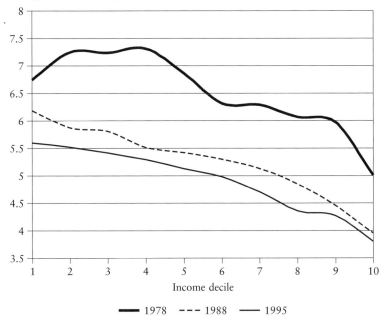

Income decile

━━━ 1978   ---- 1988   ━━━ 1995

Source: Authors' calculations based on data from DANE, Encuesta Nacional de
Hogares.

Labor demand was less dynamic, a change that is likely to have
affected the evolution of income distribution. Employment growth
fell quite significantly after 1990.

Several macroeconomic events and structural reforms during the
early 1990s explain the lack of dynamism of labor demand for less
skilled workers: (a) exchange rate appreciation and labor legislation
reforms in the early 1990s that increased the relative cost of labor
relative to capital; (b) a tendency of domestic industry to invest in
more capital-intensive technology, as exposure to international competition rose because of tariff reductions and regional trade integration; and (c) a gradual shift of productive activities toward more
capital-intensive activities, as production shifted from agriculture
and industry to mining and services. The substantial rise in payroll
taxation in the 1990s also slowed down the demand for unskilled
labor and the generation of wage-earning jobs,[6] despite the labor
reform of 1990 (Ley 50), which reduced labor costs by diminishing
the expected value of the cost of dismissals (*cesantías*). Only one

factor helped reinforce the demand for low-skilled labor: the five-fold increase in construction activity in the early 1990s, closely related to exchange rate appreciation, which derived from unprecedented capital inflows.[7]

On the agricultural side, the first half of the 1990s was characterized by a set of negative circumstances and policy measures that produced a major reduction in output. The removal of import controls, the lowering of tariffs, the appreciation of the exchange rate, low international prices, scarce credit, frequent drought, and increasing violence all contributed to a substantial agricultural decline (Jaramillo 1998). Changes in rural credit and land ownership should have had more direct effects on the distribution of income. The 1974–84 decade witnessed an increase in the concentration of land ownership (Lorente, Salazar, and Gallo 1994). However, this trend reversed in the subsequent decade, when the Gini coefficient of land ownership went down from 0.61 to 0.59. The same egalitarian evolution occurred in the credit market. Until 1984, credit and interest rate subsidies were concentrated among large-scale producers. But a shift occurred between 1984 and 1993. The controls over interest rates gradually crumbled, and credit tended to deconcentrate (Gutiérrez 1995).

Determinants of Household Income: 1978, 1988, and 1995

The explanation of the dynamics of income distribution relies on some representation of household income–generating behavior in the various periods under analysis. Household income is modeled as the outcome of two interrelated process: (a) the determination of labor earnings as a function of observed and unobserved individual characteristics and (b) the individual decision to participate to the labor force as a wage worker or a self-employed worker and the probability of being employed.[8] This section presents the main results of the estimation of earning and occupational choice equations. It also highlights the most prominent changes in underlying individual or market behavior that are likely to have led to changes in the distribution of income during the 1978–95 period.

Urban and rural earnings are modeled independently. In each case, four separate Mincer earning equations are estimated for the logarithm of self-employed workers' and wage workers' earnings and for each gender. Explanatory variables are the number of years of schooling, potential labor experience, location. Both schooling and experience include quadratic terms that control for heterogeneity in results by levels of schooling or experience. For urban areas, equations for men are estimated by ordinary least squares (OLS), and a two-stage Heckman selection-bias correction is used for women. For rural areas, the Heckman correction is applied to wage earners of both genders; OLS is used for self-employed workers because the selection bias failed to be significant.

Occupational choice behavior is estimated as a multinomial logit model with three possible situations: (a) self-employed, (b) wage earner, and (c) inactive. This model is estimated separately for household heads, spouses, and other members of the household—with gender dummy variables included in each case. The same occupational model is used for all individuals of working age in rural areas. Explanatory variables include the variables likely to affect potential individual earnings—schooling, experience, region, and gender. These variables describe the earning and domestic production capacity of all other household members—that is, household composition summarized by number of household members by gender and age group, average schooling, and average experience.

Changes in the Earnings Equations

The eight panels of tables 5.4 and 5.5 show the individual regressions for log earnings of male and female wage earners and self-employed workers in urban and rural areas for the three years considered in this analysis.

For all years and for all occupational situations, the coefficients have the expected sign and are generally highly significant. The positive estimate of the quadratic term for education reveals that the marginal rate of return to schooling increases with schooling within all groups—except for male, rural, self-employed workers in 1995—and the reverse is true of experience, as predicted by the Mincerian model.

Figures 5.2 and 5.3 show how the changes in parameter estimates for schooling affected wage differentials across schooling levels for urban male and female wage and self-employed workers. Changes in returns to schooling clearly contributed to flattening the earnings-schooling profile of men between 1978 and 1988 and, therefore, to equalizing the earnings distribution. Indeed, the relative income of low-educated workers increased much more than that of those with more education. No change took place for self-employed women, whereas middle-educated wage-earning women seemed to lose in comparison with those women of other educational levels. The evolution of income distribution was radically different between 1988 and 1995. For men, relative incomes increased at both the lower and

Table 5.4 Earnings Equations of Wage and Self-Employed Male and Female Urban Workers, Selected Years

Variable	Male wage earners (ordinary least squares)			Male self-employed workers (ordinary least squares)		
	1978	1988	1995	1978	1988	1995
Constant	9.0234*	9.5537*	9.8234*	8.4609*	8.9284*	9.3611*
Schooling	0.0474*	0.0027	−0.0379*	0.1232*	0.0901*	0.0321*
Schooling squared	0.0046*	0.0055*	0.0075*	0.0007	0.0024*	0.0051*
Experience	0.0727*	0.0541*	0.0476*	0.0867*	0.0561*	0.0536*
Experience squared	−0.0011*	−0.0007*	−0.0007*	−0.0013*	−0.0007*	−0.0007*
Residual variance	0.5142	0.457	0.5211	0.885	0.7913	0.8156
Number of observations	2,234	9,762	8,534	834	4,635	5,059
R^2	0.4774	0.4659	0.3983	0.2818	0.3216	0.3029

Variable	Female wage earners (Heckman correction)			Female self-employed workers (Heckman correction)		
	1978	1988	1995	1978	1988	1995
Constant	9.2313*	9.3672*	9.4141*	8.2978*	8.3962*	8.8958*
Schooling	0.0267†	0.0383*	−0.0015	0.0361	0.0457**	0.0254
Schooling squared	0.0049*	0.0034*	0.0062*	0.0068**	0.0063*	0.0061*
Experience	0.0399*	0.0416*	0.0337*	0.0342**	0.0461*	0.0448*
Experience squared	−0.0007*	−0.0006*	−0.0006*	−0.0004†	−0.0006*	−0.0006*
Residual variance	0.4587	0.458	0.4934	0.8905	0.9159	0.9127
Number of observations	4,046	18,676	17,621	4,046	18,676	11,837
Chi²	774*	3229*	3,082*	201*	792*	844*

Note: Regional dummy variables are omitted from the table. *Indicates significance at the 1 percent level or better, **indicates significance at the 5 percent level, and †indicates significance at the 10 percent level.
Source: Authors' calculations.

Table 5.5 Earnings Equations of Wage and Self-Employed
Male and Female Rural Workers, Selected Years

Variable	Male wage earners (Heckman correction)		Male self-employed workers (ordinary least squares)	
	1988	1995	1988	1995
Constant	10.4208*	10.7522*	9.2593*	9.2058*
School	0.0221*	−0.0050	0.0749*	0.0738*
School squared	0.0021*	0.0042*	0.0005	−0.0005
Age	0.0668*	0.0474*	0.0656*	0.0730*
Age squared	−0.0008*	−0.0005*	−0.0006*	−0.0007*
Atlantic	−0.3041*	−0.2729*	−0.0335	−0.0317
Oriental	−0.2324*	−0.0454*	−0.2765*	−0.2297*
Central	−0.2345*	−0.2016*	0.0583	−0.2490*
Model chi²	1,237.2	1,970.0	n.a.	n.a.
Adjusted R²	n.a.	n.a.	0.1243	0.1180
Number of observations	4,438	4,691	2,515	2,604

Variable	Female wage earners (Heckman correction)		Female self-employed (ordinary least squares)	
	1988	1995	1988	1995
Constant	9.8676*	10.0758*	10.5254*	10.0828*
School	0.0800*	0.0527*	0.0636*	0.0647*
School squared	0.0015	0.0021*	0.0014	0.0035*
Age	0.0576*	0.0508*	0.0040	0.0186*
Age squared	−0.0005*	−0.0005*	0.0000	−0.0001
Atlantic	−0.2306*	−0.1884*	−0.1274	0.1923*
Oriental	−0.1947*	0.0025	−0.5907*	−0.0297
Central	−0.1825*	−0.1305*	−0.1065	−0.0722
Model chi²	n.a.	n.a.	1,028.6	1,081.3
Adjusted R²	0.4211	0.3877	n.a.	n.a.
Number of observations	1,300	1,645	965	1,246

*Significant at the 5 percent level.
n.a. Not applicable.
Source: Authors' calculation based on DANE, Encuesta Nacional de Hogares.

the upper end of the distribution of schooling, with a priori ambiguous effects on inequality. The same was observed for female wage workers, as in the previous period, whereas the evolution was unambiguously equalizing for female self-employed workers.

This evolution of earning differential with respect to education is broadly consistent with the macroeconomic factors that affected the labor market through the early 1990s: capital deepening and a complementary demand for skilled workers at the top of the distribution, and construction boom and a demand for unskilled workers at the bottom.

Figure 5.2 Change in Income from Changes of Returns to Education, Relative to Workers Who Have Completed Secondary Education: Male and Female Wage Earners in Urban Colombia, Selected Periods

Percent change in relative income

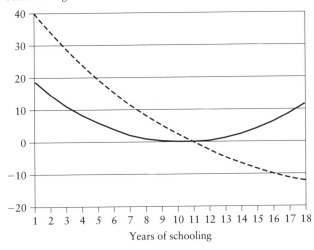

Years of schooling

Percent change in relative income

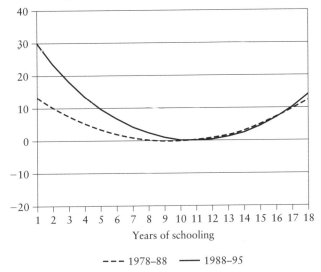

Years of schooling

--- 1978–88 ——— 1988–95

Source: Authors' calculations.

Figure 5.3 Change in Income from Changes of Returns to Education, Relative to Workers Who Have Completed Secondary Education: Male and Female Self-Employed Workers in Urban Colombia, Selected Periods

Percent change in relative income

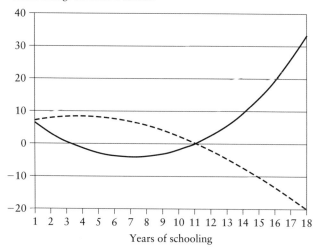

Years of schooling

Percent change in relative income

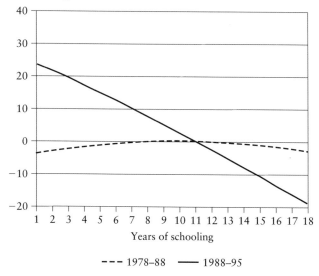

Years of schooling

--- 1978–88　——— 1988–95

Source: Authors' calculations.

Compared with returns to education in the urban labor market, returns in rural areas behaved similarly but showed more heterogeneity over time and across labor groups (table 5.5). Returns to education increased with years of schooling attained, except for self-employed male workers in 1988 and 1995. As in the urban case, the convexity of the earnings equation with respect to years of schooling decreased from 1978 to 1988 and increased again after.

The variance in the residuals of the earnings equations represents the joint dispersion across earners of the rewards for unobserved skills, as well as measurement error and transitory components of earnings.[9] Table 5.4 shows a reduction in that variance between 1978 and 1988 and an increase between 1988 and 1995 for all male urban earners, whereas changes are somewhat limited for female urban earners. Observed changes in that variance seem large enough to affect the inequality of individual earnings and that of household incomes.[10]

It is clear from tables 5.4 and 5.5 that shifts in earning differentials across gender and occupational groups depend on the characteristics of earners. For example, for otherwise equal men and women who have 8 years of schooling and 10 years of experience in urban areas, we would expect to find a small increase in the male-female wage differential but a large drop in the differential between men (wage or self-employed workers) and self-employed women. Most of the resulting substantial drop in the male-female earnings gap actually took place between 1988 and 1995. In the rural sector, equal men and women who have three years of schooling will likely exhibit a continuous substantial drop in the earning differential between male self-employed workers and male wage workers but an increasing gender wage differential in favor of men.

Changes related to experience are of limited amplitude. Regional differences declined for all groups between 1978 and 1988 but did the opposite during the 1990s.[11]

Changes in Participation and Occupational Choice Behavior

Occupational choices are modeled as a multinomial logit. Three choices are considered: inactivity, wage work, and self-employment. Dependent variables include all characteristics of individuals as well as summary characteristics for the household they belong to. The estimation is made independently for household heads, spouses, and other male and other female adult members. The main features of occupational choice behavior within those groups of individuals and their evolution over time are summarized in the following paragraphs.

URBAN

Labor-force participation displays the usual features (see table 5.6). Higher levels of education increase the probability of being employed, in particular for spouses.[12] Participation decreases with experience or age for household heads and spouses, but it tends to increase for other household members. Spouse participation is particularly sensitive to demographics and household potential income. It falls with the number of children in the household and with the average human capital endowment (education and experience) of other household members. The latter effect is quite strong.[13]

From 1978 to 1988, changes in the average participation rate are insignificant among male household heads. Changes are substantially positive for spouses and female household heads and negative for other household members. All these findings are in full agreement with the aggregate evolution shown in table 5.3. More interestingly, this evolution was not neutral with respect to education, but the bias depends on the group being considered. Married women's participation increased more among the least educated (see figure 5.4), whereas participation declined relatively more for the least-educated, secondary, male household members. From 1988 to 1995, participation kept increasing for all women, with the same bias toward the least educated. Other male household members also saw a tilt in participation in favor of the least skilled. As in the preceding period, changes in participation among household heads were negligible.

The negative impact of family size on female participation in the labor force shifted over time too. It ended up concentrating among spouses in households with very young children, but most of that evolution took place between 1978 and 1988 (see figure 5.4). With respect to the effect of the characteristics of other household members on spouse participation, figure 5.4 shows an interesting evolution. It would seem that the increase in spouse participation tended to concentrate first in households that had a relatively higher potential income, as summarized by the average educational level of nonspouse members. But between 1988 and 1995, that increase concentrated more among less educated households. This feature will prove important.

Concerning the choice between wage work and self-employment, estimates conform to what is observed elsewhere. Wage work tends to be more common for younger and more educated individuals. The effect of education tends to be more pronounced among spouses and other household members than among heads of household.[14] The education gradient for wage employment became positive and significant for household heads in 1995 also. Over time, two

Table 5.6 Marginal Effect of Selected Variables on Occupational Choice among Wage Earners, Self-Employed Workers, and Inactive Individuals for Urban Heads of Household, Spouses, and Other Household Members, and All Rural Workers, Selected Years

Urban household heads

Variable	Self-employed			Inactive		
	1978	1988	1995	1978	1988	1995
Constant (percent)	−33.8*	−23.5*	−2.2*	−16.9*	−19.7*	−20.4*
Schooling (percent)	−0.1	−0.2	−0.9*	0.2	−0.1**	−0.2*
Experience (percent)	1.2*	0.9*	0.7*	0.0	0.1	0.2**
Gender (female) (percent)	−13.8†	−13.0*	−14.7*	15.6*	12.8*	11.3*
Children under 2 (percent)	4.1	0.8	−1.0	−3.7	−1.0	0.0
Children 2–5 (percent)	1.7	0.9	1.1	0.1	−0.6	0.0
Children 6–13 (percent)	0.9	0.8	2.6*	−0.9	−1.1*	−0.9†
Number of observations	2,587	12,657	12,104	2,587	12,657	12,104
Pseudo R^2	0.1812	0.1418	0.1364	0.1812	0.1418	0.1364

Urban spouses

Variable	Self-employed			Inactive		
	1978	1988	1995	1978	1988	1995
Constant (percent)	−13.1	−19.6*	−22.4**	23.6*	28.2*	26.8*
Schooling (percent)	0.3	0.7*	0.7*	−1.5†	−2.6*	−3.2*
Experience (percent)	0.2	0.3*	0.3	0.0*	−0.3*	−0.2*
Children under 2 (percent)	−3.2	−2.0*	−2.8**	4.8	7.9*	10.3*
Children 2–5 (percent)	−0.7	0.4*	−0.5**	2.4*	2.1*	4.2*
Children 6–13 (percent)	−0.3	0.2*	1.8*	1.3*	0.8**	−0.8
Number of observations	1,931	9,586	9,233	1,931	9,586	9,233
Pseudo R^2	0.0909	0.0907	0.0898	0.0909	0.0907	0.0898

144

Urban other family members

Variable	Self-employed			Inactive		
	1978	1988	1995	1978	1988	1995
Constant (percent)	−10.0	−15.1*	−10.0**	−3.2*	3.4*	−7.3*
Schooling (percent)	0.0	0.2*	0.0*	−3.2†	−3.0*	−2.8*
Experience (percent)	0.4	0.5*	0.6	−0.1*	−0.1*	0.0*
Gender (female) (percent)	−9.8†	−11.9*	−7.9†	34.5*	28.5*	23.2*
Female* children under 2 (percent)	−2.8	−1.1*	−1.4**	17.3	15.1*	12.8*
Female* children 2–5 (percent)	6.1	−2.0*	0.5**	−0.6*	5.2*	5.5*
Female* children 6–13 (percent)	−0.2	0.7*	0.4*	4.2*	1.6**	1.8
Number of observations	3,009	12,787	11,437	3,009	12,787	11,437
Pseudo R²	0.1432	0.1185	0.1219	0.1432	0.1185	0.1219

All rural workers

Variable	Wage earner			Inactive		
	1978	1988	1995	1978	1988	1995
Schooling (percent)	0.9†	0.4*	0.7*	−1.6†	−0.9**	−1.5†
Age (percent)	1.4*	1.0*	0.8*	−2.0*	−1.9*	−1.8*
Number of observations	13,084	18,781	19,992	13,084	18,781	19,992
Pseudo R²	0.394	0.3419	0.3277	0.394	0.3419	0.3277

Note: The excluded categories are wage earners for urban and self-employed persons for rural. Significance indicators of Multinomial Logit Estimators * at the 1 percent level, ** at the 5 percent level, and † at the 10 percent level. Some variables used in the model are not included in the table.
Urban: Average educational level of the household, average years of experience, number of other males between 14 and 65 years old, number of other females between 14 and 65 years old, number of other males older than 65, number of other females older than 65. *Rural:* Population less than 2 years old, population between 3 and 5 years old, population between 6 and 9 years old, males between 18 and 65 years old, female between 18 and 66 years old, males older than 65, females older than 65, average educational level of household, average age of household, three regional dummy variables, females, household heads, and spouses.

Source: Authors' calculations based on DANE, Encuesta Nacional de Hogares.

Figure 5.4 Probability of Being Employed or a Wage Earner
in Urban Colombia according to Various Individual or
Household Characteristics, Various Groups of Household
Members, Selected Years

A. Spouses

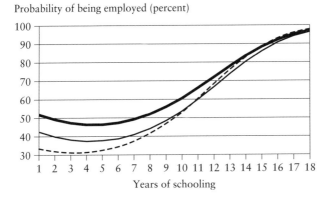

Probability of being employed (percent)

Years of schooling

B. Spouses

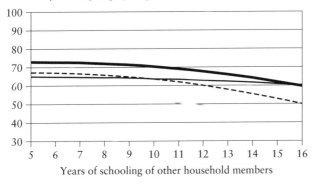

Probability of being employed (percent)

Years of schooling of other household members

C. Other females

Probability of being employed (percent)

Years of schooling

--- 1978 ——— 1988 ━━━ 1995

Figure 5.4 (Continued)

D. Spouses (completed high school)

Probability of being employed (percent)

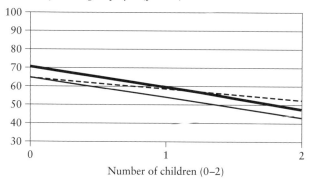

Number of children (0–2)

E. Male heads of household

Probability of being a wage earner if employed (percent)

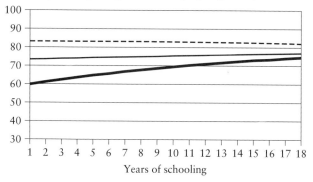

Years of schooling

F. Other males (completed high school)

Probability of being a wage earner if employed (percent)

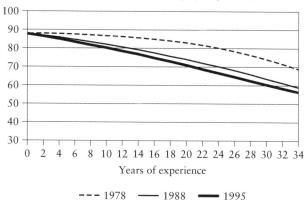

Years of experience

--- 1978 —— 1988 ▬▬ 1995

Source: Authors' calculations.

evolutions are noticeable. First, all male workers moved somewhat away from wage work. Female workers did the same, to a smaller extent, during 1978–88, but spouses and female heads of household went back to wage work in substantial numbers after 1988. Second, the choice between wage work and self-employment tended to become more sensitive to differentials in age and education.

RURAL

The main features of occupational choice behavior in rural areas are similar to what is observed in urban areas. Labor-force participation tends to increase with education and age in every period. Wage work tends to increase with years of schooling and decrease with age. Over time, the most noticeable changes are the increase in female participation with a bias toward wage work. However, female participation rates remain very limited. Another noticeable evolution is that, with time, the sensitivity of wage work to education tends to concentrate more in higher educational levels.

Summary

The main noticeable features of the evolution of individual earnings determinants and occupational-choice behavior are the following:

• A reduction in the convexity of earnings with respect to schooling for most workers during the 1980s, followed by an increase in that convexity—especially for women—during the 1990s.

• A decrease in the dispersion of the rewards for unobserved skills or unobserved earning determinants among male workers between 1978 and 1988 and an increase in the dispersion of these rewards between 1988 and 1995 for all workers, except self-employed women.

• A reduction in earnings differentials by gender and between wage workers and self-employed workers during the 1980s, and an increase in differentials during the 1990s.

• A continuous increase in female participation, more pronounced in urban than in rural areas, as well as among spouses and female household heads. This evolution was differentiated by individual and household characteristics. Overall female participation increased more among less educated people in urban areas.

• The shift from wage work to self-employment among urban male workers was more pronounced among the least skilled men. The same evolution took place among women between 1978 and 1988 but it reversed thereafter.

Understanding Income Distribution Dynamics in Colombia: Factor Decomposition by Microsimulations, 1978–88 and 1988–95

We now move one step further and decompose the evolution of inequality by isolating its dynamic response to changes in skill prices, in structural parameters of participation and occupational choice, and in skill endowments over time. We follow the framework established in chapter 2. This section presents the results of the decomposition of the changes in the distribution of both individual labor earnings and household per capita income for the periods 1978–88 and 1988–95. For reasons discussed at the end of this section, the analysis focuses mostly on urban areas.

The decomposition methodology consists of various steps. First, the changes in the distribution of individual labor earnings are decomposed into changes that are due to (a) changes in returns to observable human assets—education and experience—and regional location premia; (b) changes in the residual variance of earnings equations, or returns to unobserved productive characteristics; and (c) structural changes in labor-force participation and occupational choice. Remaining unexplained changes in earnings may be attributed to changes in the sociodemographic structure of the population—that is, in the distribution of individual endowments. Among these changes, we single out the paradoxical effect of the equalization of the educational endowment. Finally, we apply the same methodology to observed changes in the inequality of household income per capita and explain the reason for divergences with the results obtained with individual earnings. In the household case, we also examine the role of changes in family size.

Urban Areas

Persistent and fluctuating forces are behind the reversal of the inequality trend in urban areas.

INDIVIDUAL LABOR EARNINGS

During the 1978–88 period, income inequality among individual workers fell markedly. The Gini coefficient lost 3.1 points, from 47.8 to 44.7. The decomposition of the change in inequality shown in table 5.7 allows us to identify four major equalizing forces, partially counterbalanced by two unequalizing factors. The equalizing forces are (a) changes in returns to education, (b) a drop in the variance of the residual term in the male earnings equation, (c) a squeeze

Table 5.7 Decomposition Income Distribution Changes for Households and Individual Workers in Urban and Rural Colombia: Changes in the Gini Coefficient, Selected Periods

(Gini points)

Indicator	Change Gini	Returns						Total	Endowments		
		Education	Experience	Regions	Constant	Partici-pation	Residual variance		Education	Family size	Nonlabor income
Urban											
1978–88											
All individual workers	-3.1	-2.3	-0.7	0.0	-0.8	0.8	-2.4	2.3	3.0	n.a.	n.a.
Households	0.0	-1.9	0.1	0.1	-0.2	0.7	-1.5	2.4	2.3	-0.6	-0.9
1988–95											
All individual workers	5.5	0.0	-0.1	0.0	0.0	0.6	2.5	2.5	1.2	n.a.	n.a.
Households	4.2	-0.1	0.1	0.1	0.4	-0.4	1.1	2.9	0.8	-0.4	0.4
Persistent (P) and fluctuating (F) factors		F/P	P		F	P/F	F		P	P	F
Rural											
1988–95											
All individual workers	-2.4	-1.2	-1.3	-1.1	n.a.	-0.9	-1.8	-0.4	-1.3	n.a.	n.a.
Households	-3.7	-0.1	0.1	-0.2	n.a.	-0.4	-0.6	n.a.	-0.4	-0.7	n.a.

n.a. Not applicable.
Source: Authors' calculations.

in earnings differentials between gender and type of occupation (self-employment versus wage work), and (d) changes in returns to experience. The unequalizing factors are (a) the change in the distribution of educational endowments and (b) the shift in labor-force participation behavior. In the aggregate, equalizing forces dominate, and the change in inequality is negative.[15]

This evolution reversed between 1988 and 1995. The Gini coefficient rose from 44.7 to 50.3, completely erasing the gains in inequality experienced during the previous decade. Some of the preceding forces played similar roles during this period.[16] Most equalizing forces remained inoperative or even reversed direction, as with the variance in the residual term, whereas unequalizing factors remained present (table 5.7). Most of the increase in inequality during this period is explained by three regressive forces: (a) the larger variance of the residual term in the earnings equation, (b) the expansion of education endowments in the working population, and (c) the change in occupational choice behavior.

We now analyze in more detail all the factors that had some influence on the evolution of the earnings distribution during one period or the other.

Returns to Education. As seen in the preceding section (in figure 5.2 and table 5.4), changes in returns to education were strongly equalizing during the period 1978–88, especially among male earners. By itself, this evolution explains a reduction of 2.3 points in the Gini coefficient of individual earnings. From 1988 to 1995, changes in returns to education were without effect on the level of earning inequality, as measured by the Gini coefficient. However, this neutrality hides important counterbalancing adjustments at both tails of the schooling range. For practically all groups of urban earners, a simultaneous rise in the relative earnings of both the least and the most skilled workers took place, with the exception only of self-employed women, as shown in figure 5.2. These counterbalancing forces resulted in no change in the Gini coefficient for the universe of all earners. But such a change in the distribution is essentially ambiguous rather than truly neutral. Some other measures of inequality could have shown a rise while still others would have shown a drop in inequality.[17]

Residual Variance. The fluctuation in residual variance shown in table 5.2, mostly for male wages, affected income inequality accordingly. It brought a reduction in the Gini coefficient of 2.4 points for all workers for the period 1978–88 and the opposite evolution in the subsequent period. By definition, it is impossible to identify what is behind this phenomenon. It might be an economic phenomenon—for instance, an increase in the relative return to the specific talent of people at the bottom of the distribution. But it also simply might be noise in the data. In the latter case, the overall drop in the Gini coefficient between 1978 and 1988 could be thought to be largely artificial, because it is much influenced by the residual variance. However, that would not be the case for the increase in the Gini observed in the following period, as may be seen in table 5.7.

Experience.   The substantial drop in the returns to experience of male wage workers shown by earning equations (see table 5.4) as well as the flattening of earning profiles with respect to age, contributed to a 0.7 point fall in the Gini coefficient. Returns to experience kept falling—and earning profiles kept flattening—in the second period, but at a much slower pace. As a result, their effect on inequality was small.

Earning Differentials across Labor-Market Segments.   The preceding effects were evaluated by modifying the coefficients of the earning functions in table 5.4 so as to leave mean earnings constant in the various labor-market segments defined by gender and occupational status.[18] Doing so indeed isolates the change in the slope of the earning function from changes in mean earnings. Modifying intercepts so as to obtain the new mean earnings, without changing the slope coefficients, enables the identification of the distributional effect of changes in earning differentials across labor-market segments. Between 1978 and 1988, the mean relative earnings of the various groups of earners became less differentiated. The (real) mean earnings of self-employed males—the highest of all four groups of workers—fell by 9 percent, while the two lowest mean earnings, those of female wage earners and self-employed workers, increased by 6 and 40 percent, respectively (see table 5.8). This situation caused a moderate drop—0.8 points—in the Gini coefficient for all individual earnings. After 1988, the gender gap widened again while the occupational-status gap continued to narrow. In terms of overall distribution, these two movements canceled each other. Overall, it turned out that the equalizing effect of the increase in the relative earnings of self-employed women canceled the two other unequalizing evolutions.

Participation and Occupational Choice.   The participation and occupational-choice effect is also a large unequalizing factor for individual earners in both periods. It explains 0.8 additional Gini points from 1978 to 1988 and 0.6 additional points from 1988 to 1995. Structural changes in participation involve both changes from

Table 5.8 Mean Income: Effect of Change in the Constant of the Earnings Equation
(percent)

Type of worker	1988–95	1978–88	Relative income, 1988[a]
Male wage earners	0	3	1.00
Male self-employed workers	7	−9	1.20
Female wage earners	−13	6	0.80
Female self-employed workers	61	40	0.68

a. Relative to wage earners' average.
Source: Authors' simulations and calculations.

Table 5.9 Simulated Changes in Participation and Occupational Choice in Urban Colombia, Selected Periods
(percentage of the employed)

Indicator	1978–88			1988–95		
	All	Male	Female	All	Male	Female
Occupational choice						
Self-employment into wage earning	0.9	0.6	0.3	0.4	0.2	0.2
Wage earning into self-employment	4.0	3.2	0.8	3.8	3.0	0.8
Participation	1.7	−0.4	2.1	5.0	0.8	4.2

Source: Authors' simulations and calculations.

inactivity to activity and changes in occupational status from wage work to self-employment (and vice versa). To describe the distributional effect of these phenomena, we can consider the percentiles of the original distribution of earnings where entries and exits from a particular occupational group take place.[19] From 1978 to 1988, the two most significant changes in participation and occupational choices (table 5.9) are (a) a 4 percent shift of the labor force—mostly men—from wage work to self-employment that is partially compensated by a 1 percent move in the opposite direction and (b) a 2 percent increase in the participation of women when changes in sociodemographic characteristics are not taken into account, as is the case here.

It may be seen in figure 5.5 that the shift from wage work to self-employment among male workers has an unequalizing effect on the distribution. Entries exceed exits at the two extremes of the distribution, thus producing a kind of mean preserving spread. Things are more ambiguous for women participation. If it were not for the left-side hump in the curve, the net entry of women into the labor force would be similar to a mean preserving squeeze in the

Figure 5.5 Simulated Occupational-Choice and Participation Changes in Percentage Points by Percentile of Earnings for Urban Males and Females, 1978–88

A. Change from wage earning to self-employment in males

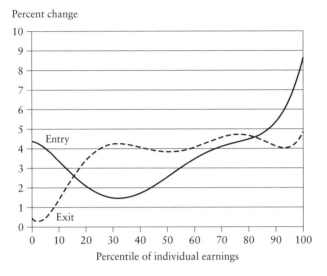

Percent change

B. Participation change (net entries) in females

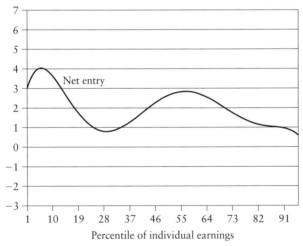

Percent change

Source: Authors' calculations.

distribution, entries being more numerous at the middle than at the extremes. However, the hump on the left side of the distribution contributes to an increase in the Gini coefficient. Overall, it turns out that the Gini is little affected by the increase in female participation in the labor force. The evolution between 1988 and 1995 is very similar to that for the shift from wage work to self-employment. The inequality-enhancing effect of the increase in female participation is more unequalizing than before (see figure 5.6). Altogether, however, these two effects result in an increase in the Gini coefficient for the whole earnings distribution slightly lower than in the preceding period.

The key structural changes behind the evolution just described are rather evident. First, the inequality of the distribution of earnings of self-employed workers is much larger than that of wage earners. The shift from wage work to self-employment thus tends to increase inequality, as shown in panel A of figure 5.5 and panel A of figure 5.6. This effect is possibly reinforced by the selectivity of that shift and, in particular, by the increasing likelihood for older cohorts and the least educated (figure 5.4) to be self-employed. Second, two phenomena are at play in the distributional impact of change in female participation. On the one hand, the increase in participation tended to be more pronounced among the least educated. On the other hand, that increase was higher in well-educated households during the period 1978–88 and among least-educated households in 1988–95. The latter phenomenon explains the difference in the shape of the curves shown in figures 5.5 and 5.6. Altogether the effects of changes in returns and in participation and occupation behavior explain a drop of 5.4 points in the Gini coefficient between 1978 and 1988 and a rise of 3.1 points between 1988 and 1995. The difference from actual changes points to a strongly unequalizing effect of "endowments"—that is, the change in the sociodemographic structure of the population—of 2.5 and 2.3 points of the Gini coefficient, respectively. The nature of the phenomena behind this residual of the decomposition analysis will be taken up below in connection with household income inequality.

HOUSEHOLD INCOME INEQUALITY: THE ROLE OF
STRUCTURAL PARAMETERS

From 1978 to 1988, the dynamics of urban household income inequality and of individual income inequality are quite dissimilar. Lower inequality of individual labor earnings coincides with unchanged household inequality (tables 5.1 and 5.7). It may be seen in table 5.7 that most of that difference is explained by the much

Figure 5.6 Simulated Occupational-Choice and Participation Changes in Percentage Points by Percentile of Earnings for Urban Males and Females, 1988–95

A. Change from wage earning to self-employment in males

Percent change

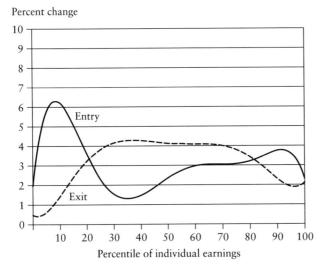

Percentile of individual earnings

B. Participation change (net entries) in females

Percent change

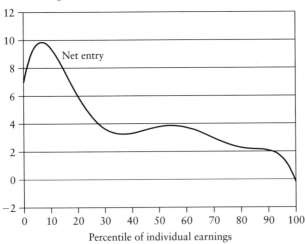

Percentile of individual earnings

Source: Authors' calculations.

lesser equalizing role of changes in earning equations (returns and residual variance) for household income than for individual labor earnings. During the 1988–95 period, the distributions of both household income and individual earnings become substantially more unequal, this evolution being slightly less pronounced for household income. Table 5.7 shows that the difference comes essentially from differences in the effect of changes in occupational choice behavior, residual variance, and earning differentials across labor-market segments. These various differences between changes in household income and individual earnings distributions are now taken up in turn.

Participation and Occupational Choice. It turns out that female participation explains the discrepancy between household and individual distribution dynamics from 1988 to 1995. Although the occupation and participation effect was unequalizing for individual earnings, the same changes in the coefficients of the occupational model are equalizing at the household level: –0.4 versus 0.6. Figure 5.7,

Figure 5.7 Changes in Employment Rate by Income Percentile, Females in Urban Colombia, Selected Periods

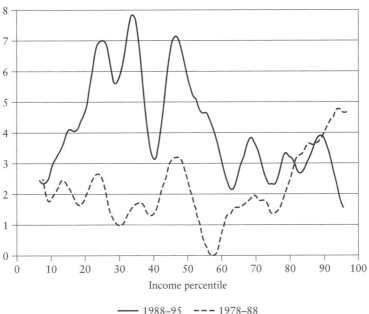

Percent change

Income percentile

—— 1988–95   - - - 1978–88

Source: Authors' calculations.

which shows the mean change in employment by percentiles of the household income distribution, helps clarify what is going on. In both periods, female participation increased more for the least educated (see figure 5.4). This would explain why net gains in employment are higher for the bottom half of the distribution of household income than for the top half. However, another feature of the change in participation behavior must be taken into account: participation between 1978 and 1988 tended to increase more in richer households, as suggested by the average educational level of nonspouse adult members between 1978 and 1988, and the reverse being true afterward. As a consequence, the equalizing effect of increased relative female participation among the least skilled is counterbalanced by the household income effect in 1978–88—that is, the upward-sloping right end of the curve in figure 5.7. In fact, it is reinforced by the household income effect in 1988–95, leading to a drop in inequality. It has been shown above that the same phenomena increased the number of low-earning participants in the labor force and contributed to an increase in the Gini coefficient for individual earnings.

Earning Differentials across Labor-Market Segments.   From 1978 to 1988, the shift in relative earnings associated with the constant term was much less equalizing at the household level (–0.2 versus –0.8 for individuals). Gender gap reductions benefit female wage earners who are in the upper lower half and at the middle of the individual earnings distribution but more than proportionally belong to middle- to high-income households. It is the case, therefore that closing the gender gap tends to make the distribution of individual earnings more equal but the distribution of household income less equal. This effect dominates for the distribution of household income during the period 1988–95. Note, however, that the change in the differential of earnings between wage earners and self-employed workers is likely to have less effect at the household level because of some diversification of household members in terms of occupational status.

Experience.   During the 1978–88 interval, the equalizing effect of changes in returns to experience at the individual level is not visible at the household level. While the Gini coefficient for individuals fell by 0.7 points, the change is insignificant for households. It even increased by 0.1 points. The explanation for this discrepancy is similar to that for the preceding one. Experienced workers tend to be in the upper half of the individual earnings distribution, so that a drop in their relative earnings contributes to more equality. However, they also happened to be spread fairly uniformly in the distribution of household income. Therefore their relative earning gains do not contribute to a reduction in inequality at the household level.

Residual Variance.   Finally, we note that the sign of the effect of the change in the residual term of the earning functions is the same for household income as for individual earnings, but the absolute value is smaller. That simply reflects diversification within the households caused by the presence of multiple earners. As it was assumed that the residual term was not correlated within households, increasing its variance leads to a larger increase in inequality at the individual level than at the household level.

ENDOWMENT EFFECT: EDUCATION, FAMILY SIZE, AND NONLABOR INCOME

We now come to the endowment effect. In table 5.7, the endowment effect is found essentially as the residual of the returns and the occupational-choice effects with respect to actual changes in the Gini coefficient. However, it is also possible to simulate directly the impact on the distribution of individual earnings or household income of a change in the distribution of specific sociodemographic variables. This simulation is done simply by importing from year 1988 to year 1978 the education level of individuals or the size of household, conditionally on the gender, the age, and the region of residence of individuals or household heads. The same is done for the years 1988 and 1995 to evaluate the education and family size endowment effect in table 5.7.

A somewhat unexpected result is that changes in educational endowments have a substantially regressive impact on both household and individual income inequality. The Gini coefficient would thus have increased by 2.3 and 3.0 points, respectively, if schooling levels had been distributed in 1978 like those observed in 1988, and by 1.2 and 0.8 if 1988 schooling levels had been those of 1995 (table 5.7). This effect is surprising because, as we saw in the first section, the distribution of educational endowments among urban as well as rural workers became less unequal as the new cohorts entering the labor force were on average more educated and less differentiated in terms of years of schooling.

One would expect that more equality in education would lead to a reduction in income inequality. However, a simple argument shows that this is true only if the relative returns to an additional year of schooling are constant across schooling levels. As emphasized above, this situation is not the case in Colombia. In effect, earning equations show that the earning profile is convex with respect to education. Hence, the most educated workers benefit proportionally more from an additional year of schooling than the less educated workers. This finding is true for wage earners and self-employed workers, as well as across gender. Moreover, as shown above, this convexity tended to increase over time.[20]

To show that the convexity of the (log) earnings with respect to schooling is responsible for the rise in inequality attributed to the expansion of education, consider the following simplified framework. Two individuals ($i = 1, 2$) have different marginal rates of return to education, r_i, this rate being higher for the most educated individual ($r_1 < r_2$). Define inequality by the ratio of incomes Y_2 / Y_1. If both individuals experience an increase in schooling, ΔS_i, the proportional rise in labor income α_i is by definition equal to

$$(5.1) \qquad \alpha_i = r_i \Delta S_i, \quad i = 1, 2.$$

For inequality to remain constant, changes in schooling should be such that both individuals have the same percentage change in income, $\alpha = \alpha_1 = \alpha_2$, that is,

$$(5.2) \qquad r_1 \Delta S_1 = \alpha = r_2 \Delta S_2.$$

Therefore, since individual 1 has a lower rate of return to education than individual 2, the increase in education for the latter must be smaller than for the former. That is, the ratio of changes in schooling should be inversely related to the ratio of rates of return:

$$(5.3) \qquad \Delta S_1 = \Delta S_2 (r_2/r_1) > \Delta S_2$$

since it was assumed that $(r_2/r_1) > 1$.

It follows that if marginal rates of return are increasing with the level of schooling, changes in schooling will generally increase income inequality, unless they are sufficiently progressive—that is, smaller in absolute value for more educated people. Consider for instance a progressive change in educational endowments: $\Delta S_2 < \Delta S_1$, such that

$$(5.4) \qquad (r_1/r_2) < \Delta S_2/\Delta S_1 < 1.$$

Income inequality will increase even though inequality in schooling may decrease.

The Colombian urban labor market illustrates this situation. The marginal rate of return to education for a college graduate is nearly twice the rate for an individual with average education, and the ratio between the two has increased by 10 percent from 1978 to 1995. As a result, egalitarian changes in educational endowments that are required to prevent income inequality from increasing as a consequence of the expansion of education are becoming more difficult to attain.

Family Size. Average family size in urban areas fell from 5.1 to 4.3 persons between 1978 and 1988 and produced an equalizing effect of 0.6 points in the Gini coefficient. Nearly half of that change is explained by the reduction in the average number of children younger than 13 per household. This number fell from 1.77 to 1.33. The number of children in urban households is modeled as a function of the education and age of the household head and his or her spouse, plus some regional dummy variables.[21] The simulation behind the family size figure in table 5.7 is based on the change in these coefficients between 1978, 1988, and 1995. In effect, approximately 75 percent of the observed change may be attributed to changes in coefficients, the remainder being caused by changes in the age and education structure of the population of household heads and their spouses. Average family size did shrink at a slower pace from 1988 to 1995. The average number of children per household only declined by one-tenth. However, the equalizing effect remained strong, with 0.4 points of the Gini coefficient.

Nonlabor Income. During both periods, changes in the distribution of nonlabor income contributed to some increase in income inequality among urban Colombian households. In the first period, the share of nonlabor income (taken to be fully exogenous in our decomposition analysis) increased by almost 5 percentage points of total income. Together with changes in its distribution and its correlation with labor income determinants, this change caused an increase in per capita income inequality of 0.8 Gini points. Between 1988 and 1995, the share of nonlabor income remained unchanged, but its distribution became more unequal and its correlation with labor income rose, producing an additional 0.6 point rise in the Gini coefficient.

In summary, the decomposition methodology used in this study was successful in identifying the main factors behind the reversal of inequality trends in urban Colombia and the causes for observed discrepancies between individual earnings and household incomes. Concerning the former, the factors to be highlighted are the changes in returns to education and experience (1978–88), the residual variance, and the earning gaps between labor-market segments. Discrepancies between individual and household income distribution dynamics are explained mainly by the features of changes in female participation and changes in the gender gap.

Most of the effects discussed earlier, except perhaps those linked to female participation, may be considered the result of fluctuations in the economic environment and, therefore, potentially reversible, rather than the result of persistent forces. The same is not true of the endowment effects. Changes in the educational structure of the population are a major component of these effects, for both individual earnings and household incomes. These changes proved to be consistently and substantially unequalizing. Another persistent force is related to the evolution of fertility. The decline in family size proved to be consistently equalizing. Finally, increasing female participation in the labor force should probably also be included among persistent forces, even though it affected the inequality of household incomes in a different way in the two periods.

Rural Areas

During the two decades covered by this decomposition exercise, the distribution of income in rural areas experienced an inequality path depicted as an inverted U. The increase in income inequality during the 1978–88 period was reversed in the 1988–95 period, with the Gini coefficient falling then by 2.4 points for individuals and 3.7 points for households. Overall, income inequality decreased because the improvements of the later period more than compensated for the inequality increase of the initial period.

The decomposition methodology produced results that were found less satisfactory than for urban areas. The reason is essentially that important income determinants such as the land cultivated by farmers were unobserved. As a consequence, earnings equations had little explanatory power, especially for male self-employed workers, and were very unstable (see table 5.5). This instability, possibly linked with the lower quality of the data in 1978, made it practically impossible to apply the microsimulation methodology to the 1978–88 period. Results were better for the 1988–95 period, even though they must be evaluated with much care. We thus limit our discussion to that second period.

The decomposition exercise suggests that all observable factors— returns, occupational choice, and endowments—contributed to equalizing the distribution of individual earnings and household income in rural areas between 1988 and 1995. For individual earnings, factors ranked by equalizing power are (as shown in table 5.7) the reduction of the variance of the residual term of earning equations, the change in returns to human assets (education and age), the changes in the distribution of years of schooling, and finally changes in the structural parameters of occupational choice.

At the household level, all these factors produced similar effects, but the order of importance is somewhat different. The reduction in family size (−0.7 points in the Gini coefficient) is now the dominant factor. Then come the changes in occupational-choice parameters, the change in the distribution of years of schooling, the smaller variance of the residual term in the earnings equation, and the changes in returns to human assets. Concerning the last factor, the difference between individual earnings and household income is rather large. That these effects are practically negligible for households can be explained only by a rather large degree of diversification of individual characteristics and occupations within households. For instance, if there are old and young workers within a household, the individual effect of experience is neutralized. The same may be true of years of schooling and even of regional disparities if those disparities go in opposite directions, depending on the type of occupation.

Compared with urban areas, income dynamics in rural areas show both similarities and discrepancies. Similar results are observed in the case of equalizing changes in returns to education and experience, as well as in the reduction in family size. The three cases of discrepancies are linked to regional disparities (which were without effect in the urban case), to participation and occupational choice (progressive instead of regressive for individual workers); and to the equalizing effect of education. The net inflow of workers into the labor force was tilted toward low-wage groups and was larger for women. These events generated major improvements in earnings for the poorest 30 percent of the population and produced a drop in the Gini coefficient for individual workers and households of 0.9 and 0.4 points, respectively.

The most interesting discrepancy is, of course, the difference in the effects of educational expansion. In the line of argument above, the explanation is to be found in differences between urban and rural areas in the profile of marginal returns to schooling. Returns to education are higher and the earnings functions are more convex in urban areas.[22] Consequently, interquartile (first to third) differences in returns by levels of education and skill wage premiums are much higher in urban areas. According to the analysis above, maintaining the interquartile inequality of earnings requires the change in educational endowments to be equalizing in both cases but more progressive in urban areas, which have larger differences in marginal returns to schooling. In other words, it is possible to find educational policies that produce opposite effects on urban and rural income inequality. According to our calculations, an egalitarian educational policy that provides to the third quartile in the distribution of education half the additional years of education provided to the first quartile will reduce inequality of earnings in rural areas by 1.2 percent. But the same policy will increase inequality of earnings by 2.6 percent in urban areas.

Conclusions

The methodology used here permitted the identification of the main factors that influenced the evolution of the Colombian distribution of income over the past two decades or so. They include (a) the structure of earnings with respect to education, age, occupational status, gender, and region (in the rural sector only); (b) the variance of unobserved individual earning determinants; (c) labor-force participation behavior, most noticeably among women; (d) the structure of the population by educational level; and (e) the structure of the household population by family size. These factors matter for the distribution of both individual earnings and household income, but they have different weights depending on the perspective that is adopted. Discrepancies between the two perspectives (individual earnings versus household earnings) are associated mainly with the increase in female participation in the labor force and the decreasing gender gap.

The nature of the factors responsible for the evolution of inequality in Colombia is not surprising. Several of those factors were already emphasized in purely static decompositions of inequality.[23] However, static decomposition analysis may conceivably be orthogonal to dynamic decomposition analysis. The present study permitted the identification of those factors that were of importance in the evolution of inequality. In addition, it enabled a precise distinction among various aspects of a given factor. When considering education as an important source of inequality, it was shown for Colombia how different could be the effect of changing the returns to education and that of changing the educational structure of the population.

We have clearly listed in this chapter the factors that were responsible for the evolution of inequality of individual earnings and household income during the 1978–88 and the 1988–95 periods. We shall not repeat the list here. Instead, it seems more interesting to use the temporal dimension of our analysis to try to distinguish which factors are associated with the long-run structural development of the economy and which factors reflect transitory phenomena that may be reversed and—in some instances—actually have been reversed during the period under scrutiny. Four persistent and five fluctuating factors may thus be identified (table 5.7). The most persistent effects are essentially associated with the demographic structure of the population and with labor-supply behavior. On the demographic side, the persistent factors are obviously the expansion—as well as the equalization—of educational endowments and the reduction in family size that results from the drop in fertility. On the labor-supply side, the dominant structural factor is, of course, the rise of female participation in the labor force. The effect of educational expansion was shown to be strongly unequalizing in urban areas and equalizing in rural areas because of the different structure of earnings with respect to education. The effect of the drop in fertility is always equalizing. Finally, the increase in the female labor supply has always been unequalizing for individual earnings. In a first stage, it has been unequalizing for household income too, when it took place predominantly in the upper part of the household income distribution. It then became equalizing. If it remains so in the future, then one can see that the overall effect on inequality of all these structural factors, which are intimately linked to the development process, is a priori ambiguous. It has actually been positive, most probably even when the rural sector is taken into account, over the past two decades. To make it negative would clearly require a durable change in the structure of returns to education.

Fluctuating factors include returns to human assets (possibly with the exception of experience) and the variance of the effect of unobserved earning determinants. In both periods, the aggregate effect of these fluctuating factors was stronger than that of the persistent factors, making them the dominant determinant of observed changes in income inequality. The erratic behavior of these major determinants of the dynamics of income inequality reveals the significant difficulties of any attempt to predict the evolution of income inequality, at least in urban areas but also most probably at the national level. However, if it may be expected that fluctuations will tend to cancel each other out in the long run, the joint effect of persistent factors becomes the best available predictor of long-run trends in inequality.[24]

If this study has shed some light on the factors responsible for the dynamics of income distribution of Colombia, the decomposition methodology on which it relies is essentially descriptive. True, some effects unveiled by this methodology are far from simple and were rather unexpected. But it remains the case that this methodology does not include any true economic modeling. To a large extent, what have been discussed here are essentially facts. It remains to relate these facts to some basic economic scenario. The way to do so is obvious for some of the factors. For instance, it is tempting to relate the evolution of the structure of marginal returns to schooling to the evolution of trade variables or to skill-biased technological change (see, for instance, Cárdenas and Gutiérrez 1996; Núñez and Sanchez 1998a; Santamaría 2000). More generally, one would also like to link the skill gap to the evolution of the supply of skilled labor—that is, to the change in the educational structure of the population and to differential labor-supply behavior. According to the most comprehensive evidence, the rise in skill premiums in Colombia is mostly linked to the sluggish supply of highly skilled workers in the past two decades.[25] But, furthermore, the change in educational structure—including the labor supply— may be endogenous to the skills gap itself. Starting from this single parameter, the skills gap, one sees that practically all the factors discussed in this chapter are interrelated within some kind of general equilibrium model. For instance, according to Robbins (1998), the dramatic change in educational attainment, labor-force participation, and fertility rates among Colombian women has been determined largely by the increasing opportunity cost of women's time. That is, the value of labor-market opportunities associated with larger gross national product per capita has shifted the equilibrium of the Colombian family toward fewer and more educated children.

It is probably too soon to start building the economic model that would integrate the various factors that this chapter identified as crucial in explaining the evolution of the distribution of income in Colombia. Yet relying on a single factor such as the wage-skill gap— as is often done in the literature on the economic determinants of inequality—appears extremely restrictive in view of the much richer representation of income distribution changes given in this chapter. There surely is some middle way between these two extreme routes, and it is to be hoped that the facts unveiled by our analysis will be useful in exploring it.

Appendix: Data Sources

Urban Data

SURVEYS

The household surveys used for this chapter are Encuesta de Hogares (EH) 19 from June 1978, EH 61 from September 1988, and EH 89 from September 1995, all from Departamento Nacional de Estadística (National Department of Statistics, or DANE), Colombia. To maintain comparability over the years of the study, we represent the urban area by the largest seven cities, or what is called *urbano tradicional*. Thus we excluded medium and small urban areas (*resto urbano*) from the surveys of 1978 and 1995. The remaining group of cities is what we call *urban Colombia*. Those cities—Barranquilla, Bucaramanga, Bogotá, Manizales, Medellín, Cali, and Pasto—account for 67 percent of the urban population (average over 1978–98) and are very heterogeneous in terms of location and socioeconomic characteristics.[26]

TOP CODING AND NONINFORMANTS

We were concerned about the integrity of the data, which led us to decide to introduce as little "noise" as possible. We did not impute earnings to noninformants, nor did we correct for the top-coding problem present in the Encuestas Nacional de Hogares (National Household Surveys). Regarding noninformants, our decision was to delete them. That is, we discarded all households that reported total income of zero or did not report at all (missing). In addition, we deleted all households in which at least one member was employed at the time of the survey but did not report income. Those adjustments meant the deletion of nearly 20 percent of the original number of households in the sample. To account for this reduction in the number of observations, we scaled the sampling weights up, by dividing the sample into 42 city-strata cells (42 = 7 cities times 6 strata), and multiplying the original sampling weights by the ratio of the pre- to postdeletion numbers of weighted observations.

PRICE DEFLATORS

All income sources in the three household surveys were deflated with Colombian consumer price indexes (CPIs), provided by DANE. For each city, we applied its own CPI, to take into account the differences in regional prices. The base month and year is December 1988.

Rural Data

We used rural household surveys for the years 1988 and 1995. These surveys are carried out by DANE. The sizes of the surveyed samples were, respectively, 18,781 and 19,992 (5,603 and 6,020 households). These samples were drawn from the four most populated regions in the country (Atlantic, Oriental, Central, and Pacific). The relevant information was taken only from households whose income was obtained by labor activities; thus, all other income sources were considered exogenous.

We made the following adjustments and corrections of the surveys:

• In the two surveys, households were removed from the analysis mainly for two reasons: the head of the household did not report labor income, in spite of being employed, and the proportion of the noninformants was more than 50 percent of the employed population.

• Households with no income were removed.

• Outliers were removed.

• The factor of expansion was calculated again, taking into account the *territorios nacionales* as well as the households that were eliminated on the basis of criteria formerly outlined.

Notes

1. The methodology for the decomposition analysis is discussed in chapter 2.

2. Berry and Urrutia (1976), Londoño (1995), Ocampo (1992), Reyes (1987), and Urrutia (1984) all give evidence of significant distributional improvements during the 1970s (Misión de Empleo 1986). Ocampo and others (1998) explain this evolution by (a) the reduction of the rural labor-force surplus because of fast migration in the 1950s; (b) the fast pace of capital accumulation and modernization in the rural sector; and (c) larger, better-targeted investments in education and health delivered through the "Frente Nacional" (1958–74, a period in which the Liberal and Conservative parties agreed to have alternate access to the presidency). See Selowsky (1979) and Vélez (1996) for an in-depth analysis of these expenditures.

3. The choice of the years 1978, 1988, and 1995, which is justified by the availability and comparability of distribution data, is also justified for the long-run economic comparison. In those three years, economic activity was almost at the peak of the business cycle. Growth was close to or higher than 4 percent, and unemployment was low, between 8 and 10 percent.

4. Figures in table 5.1 confirm the results of previous studies that examined the changes in urban income inequality. For example, Núñez and Sánchez (1998b) find a decrease in the Gini coefficient from 0.47 in 1976 to 0.41 in 1982 and an increase to 0.48 in 1995. Similarly, Núñez and Sánchez (1998a) find a decrease in the variance of the log wage from 0.65 in 1976 to 0.59 in 1986 and an increase to 0.64 in 1996. See Ocampo and others (1998) as well.

5. Cycles were not completely absent. The economy went through a moderate recession period during the first half of the 1980s. In the second half of the 1980s, macroeconomic policy kept the exchange rate competitive and the public deficit moderate. Interest rates fell, and some trade restrictions

were lifted. Nontraditional exports grew at a high pace. After a low level of activity in 1991, the economy recovered in 1994 and 1995, possibly because of trade liberalization.

6. Payroll contributions increased an impressive 13 percentage points— up to 13.5 percent for pensions and 12 percent for health insurance. This increase came on top of preexisting payroll taxes of 9 percent, which were earmarked for labor-training and social welfare programs. In summary, including remunerated annual leave and "semester premia," the reforms of 1993 lifted total payroll contributions to 59.4 percent for regular workers. Cárdenas and Gutiérrez (1996) show the increasing complementarity of skilled labor and capital in the Colombian manufacturing industry.

7. In addition to the liberation of the capital account in 1993, major discoveries of oil reserves resulted in a jump in oil exports revenues and contributed to expectations of exchange rate appreciation in the second half of the 1990s. See Cárdenas and Vélez (1987).

8. For detailed model specifications, see chapter 2.

9. This variance may also reflect differences in working time. In imperfectly competitive labor markets, it may also reflect heterogeneity on the demand side of the market.

10. Less inequitable access to land and credit should be associated with lower residual variance of rural labor earnings.

11. The difference between the largest regional premium and the largest regional penalty declined throughout the period for male and female wage earners and for self-employed male workers. For example, the difference fell from 10.9 and 16.3 percent between 1978 and 1988 to 4.4 and 2.7 percent from 1988 to 1995 for male and female wage earners.

12. As usual, the participation of household heads is uniformly high, above 98 percent.

13. A 17 percent drop in participation was associated in 1978 with a drop in the average education of other household members from college to primary levels.

14. Ten years of schooling represent an increase of 10 percent in the probability of being a wage earner, assuming that the person is employed.

15. Note that this aggregate evolution masks divergent evolutions across gender groups. From 1978 to 1988, there was a reduction in inequality among male workers, but a significant increase in inequality among female workers.

16. This decomposition at the individual level is also consistent with the profile established for the different groups of workers; in fact, during that period, both groups of male workers and female wage workers experienced a significant rise in inequality. Simultaneously, however, self-employed women exhibit opposite inequality tendencies. Thus, the consistent behavior among male and female wage earners and their larger mass within the labor force provides the dominant effect observed at the aggregate level.

17. As an illustration, it may be noted that, despite very similar evolutions of the returns to education across gender, the Gini coefficient increased for women and did not change for men.

18. This modification requires changing both the coefficients of the schooling variables and the intercept; see chapter 2.

19. Note, however, that there need not be a direct relationship between the earning level of those who exit a particular occupational group and those who enter it. Indeed, the microsimulation methodology used in this book describes changes in cross-sections of individuals, not the job history of particular individuals.

20. Fortunately, separate simulations of change in the mean educational endowment and change in the distribution of education reveal the equalizing effect of the latter and the dominant regressive effect of the former. Hence, endowment equalization alone has an income-equalizing effect, as expected.

21. Using quadratic and cubic terms for education and age.

22. This situation is consistent with the various studies that have shown evidence of a strong rural-urban labor-market segmentation in Colombia. See Jaramillo and Nupia (1998); Jaramillo, Romero, and Nupia (2000); and Urrutia (1993).

23. Using household survey data, Musgrove (1986) and Medina and Moreno (1995) find that the education of heads of household is the main explanatory factor of inequality, followed by family size, age of heads of household, economic sector, and gender of heads of household. The entropy measure decomposition by Bernal and others (1997) reiterates the key role of education. Even time-series studies (Bernal and others 1997) have identified the regressive effects of unemployment and slow growth on income inequality. Finally Sánchez and Núñez (2000), a very important study on cross-municipal differences in economic development, finds that human capital endowments explain 44 percent of inequality across municipalities—especially for college graduates, at 28 percent—while infrastructure differences account for 22 percent of the total.

24. Notice that these findings are relatively free of business-cycle effects because the three cutoff years correspond to levels of minimum unemployment.

25. According to Santamaría's (2000) estimates, the elasticity of high skill premium to supply is approximately –0.5. His findings support the technology hypothesis: no links to trade openness were found. And they are consistent with international literature that identified this as a worldwide phenomenon: Juhn, Murphy, and Pierce (1993) and Mincer (1996) showed that the growing skill bias in the demand for labor started in the United States in the 1970s and Murphy, Riddell, and Romer (1998) are able to explain its evolution using a cross-country model.

26. In the 1978 survey, the coding of the metropolitan areas changed, and thus we resorted to other methods—mainly demographic—to identify

the seven cities. Although we are confident of the outcome of this exercise, the outcome is not 100 percent exact.

References

Bernal, Raquel, Mauricio Cárdenas, Jairo Núñez, and Fabio Sánchez. 1997. "Macroeconomic Performance and Inequality in Colombia, 1976–1996." *Archivos de Macroeconomía.* Documento 72, Departamento Nacional de Planeación, Bogotá.

Berry, Albert, and Miguel Urrutia. 1976. *Income Distribution in Colombia.* New Haven, Conn.: Yale University Press.

Cárdenas, Mauricio, and Catalina Gutiérrez. 1996. "Efficiency and Equity Effects of Structural Reform: The Case of Colombia." Fedesarrollo, Bogotá. Processed.

Cárdenas, Mauricio, and Carlos Eduardo Vélez. 1987. "Evolución y Determinantes de la Pobreza en Colombia." In José Antonio Ocampo and Manuel Ramírez, eds., *El Problema Laboral Colombiano: Informes Especiales de la Misión de Empleo.* Bogotá: Controloría General de la República, Departamento Nacional de Planeación, and Servicio Nacional de Aprendizaje.

Gutiérrez, Catalina. 1995. "El Crédito Agropecuario en Colombia, Comportamiento del Mercado y Crédito por Usuarios," Tesis PEG, Universidad de los Andes, Bogotá.

Jaramillo, Carlos Felipe. 1998. *Liberalization, Crisis and Change in Colombian Agriculture.* Boulder, Colo.: Westview Press.

Jaramillo, Carlos Felipe, and Oskar Andrés Nupia. 1998. "Salarios Rurales, Agricultura e Integración: Una Evaluación de Cambios Recientes en el Mercado Laboral Rural." Documentos Centro de Estudios sobre Desarrollo Económico (July). Universidad de los Andes, Bogotá.

Jaramillo, Carlos Felipe, Carmen Astrid Romero, and Oskar Andrés Nupia. 2000. "Integración en el Mercado Laboral Colombiano: 1945–1998." Documentos CEDE, Centro de Estudios sobre Desarrollo Económico (August). Universidad de los Andes, Bogotá.

Juhn, Chinhui, Kevin M. Murphy, and Brooks Pierce. 1993. "Wage Inequality and the Rise in Returns to Skill." *Journal of Political Economy* 101(3): 410–42.

Londoño, Juan Luis. 1995. *Distribución del Ingreso y Desarrollo Económico: Colombia en el Siglo XX.* Santafé de Bogotá: Tercer Mundo Editores.

López, Hugo. 1998. "El Empleo en Colombia 1998: Situación Actual y Desafíos Futuros." CIDE and Departamento Nacional de Planeación, November. Processed.

Lorente, Luis, Armando Salazar, and Angela Gallo. 1994. "Distribución de la Propiedad Rural en Colombia." In *Transformaciones en la Estructura*

Agraria," Minagricultura, 80 Años. Tercer Mundo Editores, Banco Ganadero, Caja Agraria, and Vecol (Empresa Colombiana de Productos Veterinarios). Bogotá.

Medina, Carlos Alberto, and Hernando Moreno. 1995. "Desigualdad en la Distribución del Ingreso Urbano en Colombia: Un Análisis de Descomposición del Coeficiente Gini." *Coyuntura Social* 12: 61–74.

Mincer, Jacob. 1996. "Changes in Wage Inequality, 1970–1990." NBER Working Paper W5823. National Bureau of Economic Research, Cambridge, Mass.

Misión de Empleo. 1986. "El Problema Laboral Colombiano: Diagnóstico, Perspectivas y Políticas." *Economía Colombiana* 10.

Murphy, Kevin M., W. Craig Riddell, and Paul M. Romer. 1998. "Wages, Skills, and Technology in the United States and Canada." NBER Working Paper No. W6638. National Bureau of Economic Research, Cambridge, Mass.

Musgrove, Philip. 1986. "Desigualdad en la Distribución del Ingreso en Diez Ciudades Sudamericanas: Descomposición e Interpretación del Coeficiente de Gini." *Cuadernos de Economía* 23: 201–27.

Núñez, Jairo A., and Fabio J. Sanchez. 1998a. "Descomposición de la Desigualdad del Ingreso Laboral Urbano en Colombia: 1976–1997." *Archivos de Macroeconomia.* Documento 86, Junio, Departamento Nacional de Planeación, Bogotá.

———. 1998b. "Educación y Salarios Relativos en Colombia 1976–1995: Determinantes, Evolución e Implicaciones para la Distribución del Ingreso." *Archivos de Macroeconomía.* Documento 74, January, Departamento Nacional de Planeación, Bogotá.

Ocampo, José Antonio. 1992. "Reforma del Estado y Desarrollo Económico y Social en Colombia." *Analisis Politico* 17.

Ocampo, José Antonio, Maria J. Perez, Camilo Tovar, and Francisco J. Lasso. 1998. "Macroeconomia, Ajuste Estructural y Equidad en Colombia: 1978–1996." In Enrique Ganuza, Lance Taylor, and Samuel Morley, eds., *Política Macroeconomíca y Pobreza en America Latina y el Caribe.* Santiago: PNUD-CEPAL-BID.

Reyes, Alvaro. 1987. "Tendencias del Empleo y la Distribución del Ingreso." In José Antonio Ocampo and Manuel Ramírez. *El Problema Laboral Colombiano: Informes Especiales de la Misión de Empleo.* Bogotá: Servicio Nacional de Aprendizaje.

Robbins, Donald J. 1998. "The Determinants of Human Capital Accumulation in Colombia, with Implications for Trade and Growth Theory." *Archivos de Macroeconomía.* Documento 91, July, Departamento Nacional de Planeación, Bogotá.

Sánchez, Fabio J., and Jairo A. Núñez. 2000. "Geography and Economic Development in Colombia: A Municipal Approach." Research Network Working Paper R-408. Inter-American Development Bank, Washington, D.C.

Santamaría, Mauricio. 2000. "External Trade, Skill, Technology and the Recent Increase of Income Inequality in Colombia." Ph.D. diss. Georgetown University, Washington, D.C. Processed.

Selowsky, Marcelo. 1979. *Who Benefits from Government Expenditure? A Case Study of Colombia*. New York: Oxford University Press and World Bank.

Urrutia, Miguel. 1984. *Los de Arriba y los de Abajo*. Santafé de Bogotá: Fedesarrollo and CEREC.

———. 1993. "Twenty-Five Years of Economic Growth and Social Progress, 1960–1985." In Miguel Urrutia, ed., *Long-Term Trends in Latin American Development*. Washington, D.C.: Inter-American Development Bank.

Vélez, Carlos Eduardo. 1996. *Gasto Social y Desigualdad: Logros y Extravíos*. Bogotá: Departamento Nacional de Planeación.

Vélez, Carlos Eduardo, Mauricio Santamaría, Benedicte de la Brière, and Natalia Millan. 2001. "Inequality, Poverty, and Welfare in Urban Colombia: An Overview of the Last Two Decades." Washington, D.C.: World Bank. Processed.

6

The Evolution of Income Distribution during Indonesia's Fast Growth, 1980–96

Vivi Alatas and François Bourguignon

Like several other countries in Southeast Asia, Indonesia has been growing extremely fast over the past two decades. From the beginning of the 1980s until the recent economic crisis in 1997, the average annual growth rate has been more than 7 percent for gross domestic product (GDP) and 4.5 percent for GDP per capita. In 16 years, household standards of living doubled. At the same time, the structure of the economy changed substantially. The manufacturing and service sectors gained relative importance compared with the traditional agriculture sector, and the urbanization rate increased from approximately 25 percent in 1980 to 36 percent in 1996. Sociodemographic structures also changed. Most noticeable during this period were the dramatic increases in the average educational level of the population and drops in both fertility levels and family size.

It might be expected that such changes would have some effect on the distribution of income, yet available summary measures of inequality do not show such an evolution. Per capita consumption expenditures seem to have equalized slightly since the early 1980s, but the inequality of both household income per capita and individual wage income increased. However, with the possible exception of wages, these changes in inequality appear to be rather moderate—not more than 1 or 2 points for the Gini coefficient. This moderate change strongly contrasts with the big changes that occurred during the same period in both the economic and the sociodemographic structures. Furthermore, this evolution is also quite different from the very discernible increase in inequality observed in neighboring South-Asian "tigers" such as Malaysia and Thailand, which went through the same accelerated growth process (Ahuja and others 1997).

This chapter attempts to shed light on the various forces that might have affected the distribution of income in Indonesia from the beginning of the 1980s until the 1997 crisis. It also looks at how these forces might have offset each other to produce only moderate changes in the distribution of income. Specifically, this chapter seeks to identify the contributions of three sets of phenomena: (a) changes in the structure of earnings in both the formal and the informal labor markets; (b) changes in occupational choice, particularly the choices between family work, self-employment, and wage work; and (c) changes in the sociodemographic structure of the population. This analysis is only partial, because we do not seek to understand how the three forces may have interacted with one another and with the demand side of the labor market. Yet we believe this kind of analysis is a necessary first step toward a more general appraisal of the relationship between the process of economic development in Indonesia and the distribution of income.

This chapter is part of a wider multicountry project on the dynamics of income distribution in the course of economic development. It shares with other studies a common methodology that decomposes observed changes in the distribution of income into components corresponding to the three economic forces listed above. For a statement on this methodology, see chapter 2 and Bourguignon, Fournier, and Gurgand (1998).

Until now, relatively little has been done to understand the mechanisms behind the evolution of income distribution in Indonesia. Previous papers have focused on the evolution of the distribution of consumption expenditures per capita and the socioeconomic structure of poverty (see in particular Hill and Weiderman 1994; Ravallion and Bidani 1994; Ravallion and Huppi 1991). Some studies published in the early 1980s considered more specifically the distribution of income.[1] These studies, however, are mostly descriptive, and many of them focus on the period that preceded the acceleration of economic growth and structural change. More analytical studies of the distribution of income include applied general equilibrium modeling of the macroeconomic adjustment episode of the 1980s (see, for example, Thorbecke 1991). Such studies are purely static because they do not use the microeconomic information available on changes in the distribution of income.

Cameron (1998) published a study based on the methodology for decomposing changes in the distribution, as proposed by DiNardo, Fortin, and Lemieux (1996). With such a methodology, Cameron was able to measure the distributional effects of changes in the age structure of the population, the drop in the GDP share of agriculture, or the increased educational level of the labor force. The period studied, however, is rather short (1984–90) so the effects under study are of limited amplitude. This decomposition methodology remains merely descriptive. By relying more on in-depth microeconomic modeling of the structure of wages and occupational choice, we believe we can go a little further in understanding the forces that might have contributed to changes in the distribution of income in Indonesia. Our period of analysis (1980–96) is also much longer, thus allowing for more pronounced structural effects.

The first section of this chapter provides general background on how the distribution of income in Indonesia evolved, as well as ways in which related aggregate economic and sociodemographic characteristics also evolved. The second part discusses the decomposition methodology used to analyze the various changes. The third section is devoted to the distributive effects of the evolution of the structure of labor incomes in the wage labor market, as well as in the self-employment farm and nonfarm sectors. This section is followed by the distributive effects of changes in individual and family occupational-choice behavior, with particular emphasis on choices between wage work, family work, and self-employment. The final section provides a general decomposition of the change in the income distribution into the preceding effects and a residual that summarizes the effects of the changes in the sociodemographic structure of the population on the distribution. A special analysis is provided to show the effect of the changes in the geographical and educational structures of the population.

Overview of the Evolution of Income Distribution

This section discusses the available evidence on the evolution of the distribution of income and of the sociodemographic structure of the population between 1980 and 1996. The information provided is based on the Susenas (national socioeconomic) survey for 1980 and the Susenas survey complemented by the savings and income survey for 1996. The discussion aims to identify some of the general factors that may have influenced the evolution of the distribution of household income during this period.

Table 6.1 Evolution of Mean Household Income, 1980–96
(1996 Rp thousands)

Income definition	1980	1996	*1980–96 annual growth rate (percent)*
Mean household income	170	340	4.4
Mean household income from economic activity	154	307	4.4
Wage income	88	150	3.4
Farm income	32	60	4.0
Nonfarm self-employment income	34	96	6.7
Mean household income per capita	32.5	72.2	5.1
Mean household income from economic activity by an active household member	78	166	4.8

Source: Authors' estimates from Saving and Investment Survey 1996, Susenas 1980 and 1996.

As previously mentioned, income per capita has grown quickly since 1980. The mean real household income has doubled, whereas disposable income per capita has multiplied by 2.2. As seen in table 6.1, various sources of income did not grow at the same rate. In particular, wage income lagged behind other income sources. Wage income represented 57 percent of the total income from economic activity in 1980 but less than 50 percent in 1996. The same is true, but to a lesser extent, of farm income. The lion's share in the increase of household income during the 1980s and early 1990s went to the nonfarm income of the self-employed and small entrepreneurs. The increase represented, on average, one-fifth of total household income in 1980 and a little less than one-third in 1996. Because these various types of income have very different distributions, this evolution may be a potentially powerful source of change in the overall distribution of household income. Actually, as nonfarm self-employment income is likely to be more unequally distributed than wage income, this change in the structure of income by source should have contributed to an increase in inequality.

The evolution of the occupational structure of the population at working age shown in table 6.2 largely confirms the preceding analysis. The dominant feature in table 6.2 is the growth of the urban population. The urban population at working age—taken here to be people 12 years old and older—increased from 21 percent to 34 percent in 1996, a relative increase of 75 percent. This change in the relative size of the urban population was more or less proportional across occupations, with inactivity and wage employment lagging somewhat behind self-employment. The migration process behind

Table 6.2 Evolution of the Socioeconomic Structure of the
Population, 1980–96
(percent)

Variable	1980	1996
Age structure (population at working age)		
12 to 24	48.2	42
25 to 65	50	53.2
More than 65	1.9	4.8
Educational structure (population at working age = 100)		
No education	23.7	13.3
Primary school not completed	39.1	28.7
Primary school completed	24.6	31.7
Secondary school (low)	7.9	12.2
Secondary school (high)	4.1	11.8
University	0.5	2.4
Occupation (population at working age = 100)		
Rural		
Inactive	23.0	18.5
Pure wage earners	16.4	9.4
Self-employed and family workers	30.7	29.6
Mixed activity[a]	8.8	8.3
Total	79.0	65.8
Urban		
Inactive	9.0	13.5
Pure wage earners	7.2	11.0
Self-employed and family workers	4.3	8.0
Mixed activity[a]	0.6	1.7
Total	21.0	34.2
Average household size (persons)		
Rural	4.7	4.2
Urban	5.3	4.5

a. Individuals reporting wage work and some other activity.
Source: Authors' estimates from Saving and Investment Survey 1996, Susenas
1980 and 1996.

the decline in the rural population had a strong occupational bias. In
net terms, inactivity and pure wage employment were the main factors that fed the migration process. In comparison, the self-employed
remained relatively as numerous in the rural areas as before. Because
the absolute number of farmers did not increase much during
1980–96, the expanding occupation in the rural sector has also been
nonfarm self-employment. In summary, the dominant feature in the
evolution of Indonesia's occupational structure during the fast growth
period was a powerful migration process away from inactivity and
wage work in the rural sector toward nonfarm self-employment in
the rural sector and, more importantly, both wage work and self-
employment in the urban sector. Presumably, the highest propensity

to migrate toward cities was among landless workers.[2] This evolution
is consistent with that of the structure of income shown in table 6.1.
The share of wages in total income tended to fall, whereas nonfarm
self-employment income increased substantially.

The second major feature of the evolution (described in table 6.2)
was the dramatic increase in the educational level of the population
at working age. In 1980, almost two-thirds of the population had not
completed primary school. Sixteen years later, this proportion was
down to 40 percent. Simultaneously, the share of the population with
some secondary education went up from 12.5 percent to 26.4 percent. Overall, the average number of years of schooling in the working age population increased from 4 years to 5.5 years, a 40 percent
increase. In addition, even though longer schooling would mean
lower employment participation of the youngest, this evolution has
not increased the overall inactivity rate of the population at working
age. On the contrary, the inactivity rate went down from 29 percent
to 28 percent in the rural sector and from 42.7 percent to 39.5 percent in the urban sector. Therefore, activity substantially increased in
the population above school age. All these changes—longer schooling, a more educated labor force, changes in activity rates—are potentially powerful factors affecting change in the distribution of income.

Table 6.3 summarizes the evolution of the distribution of income.
The top of the table refers to the distribution of household income per

Table 6.3 Evolution of the Personal Distribution of Income,
1980–96

	1980	1996
Household income per capita (household members)		
Shares (percent) of		
Poorest 10 percent	2.4	2.5
Poorest 20 percent	6.2	6.4
Poorest 40 percent	17.3	17.0
Richest 20 percent	45.2	47.3
Richest 10 percent	29.6	32.0
Richest 5 percent	19.0	21.4
Summary inequality measures		
Gini coefficient	0.384	0.402
Theil index	0.272	0.314
Mean logarithmic deviation	0.253	0.273
Wage income (individual wage earners)		
Summary inequality measures		
Gini coefficient	0.492	0.512
Theil index	0.433	0.476
Mean logarithmic deviation	0.455	0.563

Source: Authors' estimates from Saving and Investment Survey 1996, Susenas
1980 and 1996.

capita, with households weighted by the number of their members. This distribution is equivalent to the distribution of individual income, where each individual in the population, either adult or child, was given the income per capita of the household to which he or she belonged. The distribution appears to be slightly more unequal in 1996 than in 1980. This proposition is true using the usual summary inequality measures of the Gini coefficient and the Theil index, but it is not true in the sense of Lorenz dominance. Some redistribution took place between 1980 and 1996 from the middle toward both ends of the distribution. The redistribution toward the bottom, however, is very limited, so most summary inequality measures, except those close to a Rawlsian criterion, will actually point to increasing inequality. Relative poverty, as measured by the ratio between the income of the 10, 20, or 40 percent poorest persons and the mean income of the population, changed little during this period.[3] This result agrees with the available literature. Ravallion and Huppi (1991) made a similar observation with expenditure data for the post-1982 adjustment period, as did Cameron (1998) working with per capita income data in 1984 and 1990.

That relative poverty remained almost constant means that absolute poverty has dramatically declined. With the mean income per adult equivalent more than doubling over the period and almost constant shares of the poorest groups in society, the absolute income of these groups also doubled, resulting in a fast decline in absolute poverty. The amplitude of that decline depends on the definition used for the poverty limit. Because the definition of poverty is usually cast in terms of consumption expenditures rather than income, we shall not consider it further here. More generally, despite the increase in relative inequality, the distribution of absolute household income per capita in 1980 is unambiguously dominated in terms of social welfare by that of 1996 in the sense that the mean absolute income of all groups in society is higher in the latter year.[4]

On the whole, the available data suggest moderate changes and possibly some stability in income distribution. This finding contrasts with the very strong changes observed in the structure of the economy and the sociodemographic structure of the population. The rest of this chapter attempts to explain this apparent contradiction.

Decomposing the Changes in the Distribution of Income by Economic Sources

Our decomposition methodology is based on the concept of a household income function. The income y_{it} of household i observed at time t is assumed to depend through a function denoted Y( ) on four sets of arguments: its observable sociodemographic characteristics or those of its members (x), unobservable characteristics (ε), the set of prices or rates at which these characteristics are remunerated in the labor market (β), and a set of parameters defining the participation and occupational choice behavior of its members (λ):

$$(6.1) \qquad\qquad y_{it} = Y(x_{it}, \varepsilon_{it}; \beta_t; \lambda_t).$$

The overall distribution of household income at time t, vector D_t, may then be expressed as a (vector) function of the distribution of observable and unobservable household characteristics at date t, the price vector β_t, and the vector of behavioral parameters λ_t. Let $H(\ )$ be that function:

$$(6.2) \qquad\qquad D_t = H(\{x_{it}, \varepsilon_{it}\}, \beta_t, \lambda_t)$$

where $\{\ \}$ refers to the distribution of the corresponding variable in the population. With this representation of the overall distribution of income, it is easy to identify the effects of each argument of the function $H(\ )$ on the change in the distribution of income. We may thus distinguish the following:

Price or earnings effect

$$(6.3) \quad B_{tt'}(\lambda_t) = H(\{x_{it}, \varepsilon_{it}\}, \beta_{t'}, \lambda_t) - H(\{x_{it}, \varepsilon_{it}\}, \beta_t, \lambda_t).$$

Occupational-choice effect

$$(6.4) \quad L_{tt'}(\beta_t) = H(\{x_{it}, \varepsilon_{it}\}, \beta_t, \lambda_{t'}) - H(\{x_{it}, \varepsilon_{it}\}, \beta_t, \lambda_t).$$

Population effect

$$(6.5) \quad P_{tt'} = H(\{x_{it'}, \varepsilon_{it'}\}, \beta_t, \lambda_t) - H(\{x_{it}, \varepsilon_{it}\}, \beta_t, \lambda_t).$$

Thus, the population effect P is obtained by comparing the distribution at date t and the hypothetical distribution obtained by simulating on the population observed at date t' the remuneration structure and the behavioral parameters of period t. Likewise, the effect of the change in prices is obtained by comparing the initial distribution and the hypothetical distribution obtained by simulating on the population observed at date t the remuneration structure observed at date t'. A symmetric definition applies to the occupational-choice effect. However, one must keep in mind that the evaluation of a change in any subset of the coefficients (β, λ) depends on the value that is selected for the complementary subset. For example, one may evaluate the occupational-choice effect using the characteristics of the population at time t and the structure of earnings at time t, β_t, as shown in equation 6.4. But one could also evaluate the occupational choice using the earnings structure of year t', $\beta_{t'}$, or any arbitrary set of coefficients β, as implied by the arguments of $B_{tt'}$ and $L_{tt'}$ on the left-hand side of equations (6.4) and (6.5).

With the previous notations, the population effect is simply obtained as a residual of all the others. If $C_{tt'}$ is the overall change in the distribution between t and t', then it comes as an identity that:

$$(6.6) \qquad C_{tt'} = B_{tt'}(\lambda_t) + L_{tt'}(\beta_{t'}) + P_{t't}$$

where $P_{t't}$ is the population effect evaluated with the price structure and the occupational behavior of t', rather than t. It is important to keep in mind that the order in which a decomposition 6.6 is made may matter. In other words, it is generally the case that $P_{tt'} \neq P_{t't}$, the same being true of the price and the occupational effects B and L. Evaluating all these effects using the sample observed at time t as a reference, as in equations 6.3 through 6.5, does not necessarily lead to the same decomposition of the actual change in inequality $C_{tt'}$ as if the sample observed at time t' had been chosen as a reference. In other words, a decomposition such as 6.6 of the overall change in the distribution of income is *path dependent*. This path dependence is more pronounced when the structure of the population, described by $\{x_i, \varepsilon_i\}$, differs very much between the initial and terminal period t and t'. We shall see that this is indeed the case for Indonesia.

The household income function $Y(\ )$ used in the case of Indonesia may be summarized by the following set of equations:

$$(6.7) \qquad \mathrm{Log}\, w_{mi}^t = X_{mi}^t \cdot \beta^t + u_{mi}^t \quad i = 1, \ldots k_m$$

$$(6.8) \quad L_{mi}^t = Ind[X_{mi}^t \cdot \lambda_{1X}^t + Z_{mi}^t \cdot \lambda_{1Z}^t + v_{mi}^t] \quad i = 1, \ldots k_m$$

$$(6.9) \quad L_{mi}^{At} = Ind[X_{mi}^t \cdot \lambda_{2X}^t + Z_{mi}^t \cdot \lambda_{2Z}^t + v_{mi}^{At}] \quad i = 1, \ldots k_m$$

$$(6.10) \quad L_{mi}^{NAt} = Ind[X_{mi}^t \cdot \lambda_{3X}^t + Z_{mi}^t \cdot \lambda_{3Z}^t + v_{mi}^{At}] \quad i = 1, \ldots k_m$$

$$(6.11) \qquad y_m^t = \sum_{i=1}^{k_m} L_{mi}^t \cdot w_{mi}^t + \Pi_A^t \left[Z_m^{Tt}, \sum_{i=1}^{k_m} L_{mi}^{At}, s_A^t; \beta_A^t \right]$$

$$+ \Pi_{NA}^t \left[Z_m^{Tt}, \sum_{i=1}^{k_m} L_{mi}^{NAt}, s_{NA}^t; \beta_{NA}^t \right] + y_{0m}^t.$$

The first equation expresses the (log) wage of member i of household m as a function of personal characteristics, X. In the following equations, L_{mi}^t, L_{mi}^{At}, and L_{mi}^{NAt} stand respectively for the labor supplied by member i as a wage worker outside the family business, the labor supplied on the family farm—when the family has access to land— and the labor supplied on the family (nonfarm) business. The notation *Ind* corresponds to the 0/1 indicator function. In other words, labor supply in each of these three categories is essentially a discrete yes or no variable that depends on the characteristics X of the individual who is considered and those of the household Z to which the individual belongs. The reason for modeling labor supply as an index function, taking the value 0 or 1 according to whether an individual supplies labor or not in a given occupation, is that working time is not observed. Variables included in X are the standard individual human capital variables. Household characteristics Z include the productive assets available in the household—in particular cultivable land—and, for family members other than the head of household, some characteristics of the household head, including labor-supply choice. The set of labor-supply parameters λ thus comprises three subsets. There is a set of coefficients λ_1 describing wage labor supply, another set λ_2 describing the supply of labor to the family farm, and another set λ_3 for nonfarm business. In addition, these three sets are different when one considers the head of household or another family member.

In theory, these three discrete labor-supply functions should be estimated simultaneously with some kind of multinomial probit, where the random terms v_i, which stand for unobserved determinants, would be assumed to be correlated with each other. In simpler terms, these three functions were estimated under the form of a multinomial logit, where the endogenous discrete occupational-choice variable could take only four possible values: (i) inactive, (ii) pure wage worker, (iii) pure self-employed or family worker, or (iv) mixed activity (that is, part-time wage work and self-employment or family work).

The last equation of the model, 6.11, defines *total household income* as the sum of the wage income of those members supplying wage labor (k_m in the number of persons at working age) profit from farm activity, and profit from nonfarm activity, with $\Pi_A(\ )$ and $\Pi_{NA}(\ )$ as the corresponding profit functions. Finally, y_0 stands for income from (mostly private) transfers or from financial wealth and is considered exogenous. Because of the nature of the data, profit from farm or nonfarm self-employment is defined at the household level. Only wage incomes are observed on an individual basis in Susenas; all other incomes are reported at the level of the household. The main arguments of the farm and nonfarm profit functions are the number of household members involved in the family business and the productive assets owned or operated by the household, a variable that is included in the set Z. These functions depend on sets of parameters, β_A^t and β_{NA}^t, which are to be estimated for the two years included in the analysis.

The variables u in the wage equation, v in the (discrete) labor supply equations, and s in the profit functions stand for the usual residual terms in the corresponding econometric estimation procedure. We shall also interpret them as fixed effects at the individual or household level, representing the influence on income and occupational choice behavior of some unobserved variables, or possibly measurement errors. Their variance is also a factor to be considered in simulating the evolution of the distribution of household income. A problem with these terms is that they are not observed for individuals who are not working as wage earners or for households not engaged in self-employment activity. They also are not observed for occupational choices. All these stochastic terms must be generated by drawing randomly in the appropriate distribution conditionally on the occupational choice that is observed. The detail of this procedure is discussed in chapter 2.

Changes in Income Functions and Their Effect on the Distribution of Household Income

We begin our analysis with the evolution of the structure of individual wages. To describe that evolution, we use a conventional Mincerian specification of the earning function (equation 6.7) and we study how the parameters of that function changed over time. The explanatory variables of the earning function comprise the number of years of schooling and its square; job experience (as conventionally measured by age − years of schooling − 6) and its square; a dummy variable for part-time work;[5] a dummy variable for people living in Java, which is the largest island of Indonesia but also among its poorest as of 1980; and a constant.[6] This calculation is made separately for male and female workers and for the urban and the rural sectors. We are thus assuming some market segmentation between men and women and across geographic areas. This hypothesis apparently fits the data. As seen in table 6.4, individual earning functions are indeed significantly different for men and for women, both in cities and in rural areas. In particular, returns to education are considerably higher for women than for men in cities, and returns on education are lower in the rural section than in the urban sector for both men and women in 1980.

Our main interest lies in the changes in the structure of earnings and therefore the changes in the coefficients of earning equations

Table 6.4 Individual Wage Functions by Gender and Area, 1980–96

Function	Urban males		Urban females		Rural males		Rural females	
	1980	1996	1980	1996	1980	1996	1980	1996
Schooling	0.0777	0.0313	0.1503	0.1287	0.0598	0.0955	0.0017	0.0385
	0.0035	*0.0132*	*0.0066*	*0.0199*	*0.0046*	*0.0160*	*0.0076*	*0.0235*
Schooling squared	0.0012	0.0035	−0.0006	−0.0004	0.0032	0.0016	0.0089	0.0070
	0.0002	*0.0007*	*0.0004*	*0.0011*	*0.0003*	*0.0010*	*0.0006*	*0.0016*
Experience	0.0722	0.0854	0.0489	0.0526	0.0523	0.0730	0.0219	0.0293
	0.0013	*0.0037*	*0.0024*	*0.0061*	*0.0015*	*0.0045*	*0.0023*	*0.0068*
Experience squared	−0.0010	−0.0012	−0.0006	−0.0008	−0.0007	−0.0010	−0.0003	−0.0004
	0.0000	*0.0001*	*0.0000*	*0.0001*	*0.0000*	*0.0001*	*0.0000*	*0.0001*
Part-time work	−0.2773	−0.4454	−0.1724	−0.3691	−0.3622	−0.7651	−0.3284	−0.7060
	0.0171	*0.0403*	*0.0471*	*0.0822*	*0.0128*	*0.0388*	*0.0212*	*0.0658*
Jakarta (dummy)	−0.1265	0.1159	−0.2228	0.1525				
	0.0152	*0.0473*	*0.0304*	*0.0808*				
Java (outside Jakarta)	−0.2807	−0.1846	−0.3169	−0.1134	−0.3960	−0.0790	−0.5713	−0.2834
	0.0106	*0.0318*	*0.0216*	*0.0531*	*0.0121*	*0.0375*	*0.0202*	*0.0643*
Constant	10.4397	10.8596	9.7630	10.3288	10.5229	10.4495	10.4318	10.3409
	0.0221	*0.0775*	*0.0396*	*0.1147*	*0.0259*	*0.0886*	*0.0397*	*0.1402*
Number of observations	15,380	2,302	4,694	1,030	15,080	2,520	6,846	1,023
R^2	0.414	0.385	0.343	0.371	0.311	0.306	0.299	0.340
Root of mean square error	0.578	0.691	0.650	0.772	0.707	0.924	0.726	0.957
Average rate of return to schooling								
At schooling = 5	0.084	0.049	0.147	0.126	0.076	0.104	0.046	0.073
At schooling = 8	0.088	0.059	0.145	0.125	0.086	0.108	0.073	0.094

Note: Dependent variable is log wage; ordinary least squares estimates. Standard errors are in italics.

Source: Authors' estimates from Saving and Investment Survey 1996, Susenas 1980 and 1996.

between 1980 and 1996. From that point of view, there are four salient features in table 6.4. These are described in the following paragraphs.

First, the return to education fell in the urban sector, especially for male workers, whereas it increased in the rural sector. However, the significance of the latter evolution is not clear, because estimates in 1996 are not as precise as in 1980. Note also that the drop in the rate of return to education for urban male workers is less pronounced for the highest skills, because the convexity of their earnings with respect to education increased over time.

Second, part-time wage work represented a greater disadvantage in 1996 than it did in 1980. This result may be interpreted as a change in labor supply. The working hours of those reporting wage work as one out of at least two activities are shorter in 1996 than in 1980. Individuals reporting wage work as well as self-employment or family work were earning between 25 and 30 percent less than pure wage earners in 1980. In 1996, this proportion was 35 percent in the urban sector and 50 percent in the rural sector.

Third, the disadvantage of working in Java declined substantially between 1980 and 1996. This drop is still more pronounced for wage workers in Jakarta. There the earning differential with respect to the rest of the country (outside Java) went from negative 10 to negative 20 percent, to approximately positive 15 percent.

Fourth, the dispersion of earnings because of unobserved wage determinants—or possibly transitory wage components—increased between 1980 and 1996. This increase, however, is more important in the rural sector, possibly reflecting more heterogeneity in working time among individuals employed as wage workers in plantations or in rural industries.

These patterns in the evolution of the structure of wages—and in particular the change in regional earning differentials—seem to fit what is known of the general evolution of the labor market in Indonesia during the period under analysis. Examples of the general analysis of the evolution of the labor market can be found in Manning (1998), and the analyses on regional imbalances can be seen in Hill and Weidemann (1991).

Table 6.5 shows the estimates of household profit functions for farm activities, nonfarm activities, and both activities—that is, households involved simultaneously in farm and nonfarm businesses. The specification used is similar to the wage functions. The dependent variable is the logarithm of profits, whereas the main argument is the logarithm of the number of household members who report that they are working in the family business.[7] Data problems prevented us from using a finer definition of the household

Table 6.5 Household Profit Functions in Farm and Nonfarm Activities, 1980–96

Function	Nonfarm profits		Farm profits		Profits from both activities	
	1980	1996	1980	1996	1980	1996
Number of household members involved in business	1.1496	1.0922	0.4586	0.6210	0.5342	0.5619
	0.0691	0.1538	0.0443	0.0708	0.0518	0.0855
Schooling (head)	0.0656	0.0507	0.0863	0.0685	0.0487	0.0914
	0.0072	0.0176	0.0080	0.0128	0.0102	0.0170
Schooling squared (head)	0.0004	−0.0009	−0.0069	−0.0040	0.0012	−0.0036
	0.0005	0.0011	0.0007	0.0010	0.0010	0.0013
Experience (head)	0.0066	0.0154	0.0036	0.0072	0.0096	0.0112
	0.0030	0.0060	0.0032	0.0049	0.0040	0.0064
Experience squared (head)	−0.0002	−0.0003	0.0000	−0.0001	−0.0002	−0.0002
	0.0000	0.0001	0.0000	0.0001	0.0001	0.0001
Jakarta (dummy)	−0.3484	0.3897				
	0.0374	0.0981				
Java (dummy)	−0.5400	−0.2161	−0.4867	−0.3579	−0.3830	−0.0993
	0.0205	0.0433	0.0219	0.0333	0.0278	0.0418
Fishing and forestry			1.0572	0.6166	0.4281	0.3390
			0.0581	0.0695	0.0749	0.0985
Land: less than 0.5 hectare			—	—	—	—
Land: from 0.5 to 1 hectare			0.5953	0.2775	0.1502	0.0990
			0.0277	0.0417	0.0325	0.0529
Land: from 1 to 2 hectares			0.8678	0.4197	0.2843	0.2606
			0.0315	0.0543	0.0386	0.0776
Land: more than 2 hectares			1.0740	0.5933	0.4361	0.4721
			0.0406	0.0892	0.0531	0.1344
Constant	11.6725	11.8601	10.5055	11.2764	11.5369	11.6334
	0.0596	0.1254	0.0667	0.0996	0.0836	0.1311
Number of observations	8,011	2,098	11,398	3,041	3,630	1,254
R^2	0.2143	0.1010	0.2833	0.1666	0.2622	0.1298
Root of mean square error	0.8494	0.9520	1.0412	0.8560	0.7069	0.6994
Average rate of return to schooling						
At schooling = 5	0.0679	0.0463	0.0517	0.0483	0.0549	0.0736
At schooling = 8	0.0692	0.0437	0.0310	0.0362	0.0587	0.0629

Note: Dependent variable is log profit, OLS estimates. Standard errors are in italics.
Source: Authors' estimates from Saving and Investment Survey 1996, Susenas 1980 and 1996.

labor input, and in particular from making a distinction between the number of hours worked of individuals reporting themselves mainly as a family worker, of those reporting farm or nonfarm business as their only self-employment activity, and of those reporting some wage work in addition to their primary employment. We decided to count the latter as half a full-time person contributing to the family output; this determination, however, was arbitrary. Actually, the model that is estimated is a kind of reduced-form model in which the size of the pool of individuals on which the family can draw to do nonwage market work is the main explanatory variable. For the same reason (that is, the nonobservability of hours of work in different activities), it has not been possible to distinguish the human capital of household members according to their degree of involvement in the family business. Instead, we have used the human capital characteristics of the head of household, who is most often the main operator of the business.

Other explanatory variables in the household profit functions include a dummy variable for the Java island (as in the wage equations) and (in the form of size dummy variables) a dummy variable for those households having access to land whose surface they cultivate. Agricultural households with the smallest plots (less than 0.5 hectare) are taken as a reference. Agricultural activity also includes fishing and forestry. Households involved in fishing and forestry do not work any land, but they may own productive assets under the form of a boat or fishing nets, which might give them an advantage over small farmers. Productive assets other than land are not observed. This explains the limited number of variables used in the profit functions appearing in table 6.5, in particular for nonfarm activity. It must also be stressed that there is no way to distinguish in the data sources the labor input associated with farm or nonfarm work for households reporting both activities. Thus, it was not possible to use these households simultaneously with pure farmers or self-employed people working purely in nonfarm activities in the estimation of the corresponding profit functions. As a consequence, a special profit equation was run for those households. We tried to control for selection into that group using the standard Heckman two-stage procedure. Possibly because of the lack of proper instruments, the correction for selection proved insignificant.

Several interesting features appear in the estimation results summarized in table 6.5. First, it is somewhat reassuring that the number of household members employed—full time or part time—in a family business is a highly significant and rather stable determinant of household profit from self-employment. As explained before, however, this variable does not precisely measure the household labor input; thus, not much can be inferred from the corresponding coefficients.[8] Second, it is also reassuring to find that the level of education for the head of household—and presumably for those working with him—has a positive influence on self-employment income. The drop in the rate of return to education for nonfarm profits seems to be consistent with what was observed for male workers in the urban wage-labor market. The increase observed for both activities is less expected and contrasts somewhat with the stability observed for pure farm profits. Another feature consistent with the evolution observed in the wage-labor market is the fall in the disadvantage of living in Java for nonfarm profits and profits from both farm and nonfarm activities. In fact, the coefficient for the Jakarta dummy variable in the nonfarm profit equation suggests a true economic boom in that part of the country during the period under analysis.

The returns to land size in the farm profit function declined substantially. Other things being equal, profits in larger farms and in both fishing and forestry fell relative to profits in the smallest farms. This suggests that the rent on land declined between 1980 and 1996. Various phenomena, however, may be behind this change in the observed structure of farm incomes. The intercept term in the farm income equation in table 6.5 shows a considerable increase between 1980 and 1996. Because the coefficients associated with variables other than land did not change much, this increase essentially means that very small farmers benefited more from changes in prices and possibly productivity than did large farmers, perhaps because price changes or technical progress was biased in favor of their particular output mix. This result appears very clearly in the simulation of price effects on typical households that is reported in table 6.6. The drop in the relative return to land is not observed at all among households involved in both farm and nonfarm activities. In other words, farmers who were also involved in nonfarm activities, possibly because of lower returns to land, and those who got involved in farming during the period under analysis, did not benefit from the same favorable evolution of prices or productivity as pure farmers did. This may be precisely the reason they went into both activities.

A last feature to be stressed in the estimation results shown in table 6.5 is the substantial loss of explanatory power of the three econometric models between 1980 and 1996. Compared with wage equations, the R^2 statistic is rather low for 1980 and still lower for 1996. In 1996, it amounted to 10 percent for nonfarm profits—versus 21 percent in 1980—and approximately 15 percent for farm profits and profits from both activities. Interestingly enough, however, the variance of the residual terms of these various regressions falls in the case of pure farmers, remains constant for both activities, and increases only slightly in the case of nonfarm profits. Therefore, conventional variables explain less about household self-employment income, but at the same time the overall variance of income from both activities went down substantially. This evolution is the opposite of what was found for individual wages.

Before evaluating the distributive effects of the changes just discussed, we can focus on the various price effects shown in table 6.6. On the basis of the regressions just discussed, table 6.6 shows the evolution of various representative individual or household incomes while maintaining the characteristics of income recipients constant. Table 6.6 shows a rather high variability in the evolution of particular types of incomes, whether differences are seen among geographic locations, education, gender, self-employment income source, and so on. Such a picture undoubtedly corresponds to what may be seen as an economy undergoing a period of exceptionally fast growth. At the same time, this picture seems to contradict the observation that income distribution became only slightly more unequal between 1980 and 1996 in Indonesia.

We now evaluate more precisely the effect of the change in the coefficients of wage and profit functions—what we have called price changes—on the distribution of income. We begin with the change in the structure of individual earnings. As in table 6.6, we replace the income of all individual wage earners in the 1980 sample by the value obtained using the function estimated for 1996. More precisely, in the earning equation (6.7), we replace the vector of coefficients β estimated for 1980 with the coefficients estimated for 1996, keeping the residual term constant. We do so only for those individuals observed as wage earners in 1980. The result of the substitution for the inequality of the distribution of individual earnings is shown in the rows b to k in the left-hand part of table 6.7 for three frequently used inequality measures: the Gini coefficient and Theil's two entropy measures, with $E(0)$ being the mean logarithmic deviation. The right-hand part of that table reports the results of the symmetric exercise. Starting from the sample observed in 1996, we apply the earning functions estimated for 1980 and evaluate the corresponding changes in the distribution of individual earnings.

The overall price effect in table 6.7 is obtained by modifying all the coefficients β at the same time. It is also interesting to evaluate the effect of a change in only a subset of these coefficients, possibly a single coefficient at a time. For example, one may want to evaluate only the effect of the change in the rate of return to education or to experience. This evaluation can be done using an arbitrary individual or household as a reference. Changing only the β associated with education is equivalent to assuming that an individual with zero schooling would have seen no change in his or her wage. The results shown in tables 6.7 and 6.8 assume that the mean wage or mean self-employment income is maintained constant when we do partial simulations.

The left-hand side of table 6.7 shows that four factors contributed to an increase in the inequality of individual earnings during the

Table 6.6 Simulated Evolution of Typical Incomes: Price Effect

Type of income	Percentage increase from 1980 to 1996		Percentage increase in mean from 1980 to 1996 because of price effect
Wages			
Urban male, 35 years old, 5 years of schooling, working full time		All urban males	54
Non-Java	50		
Java (outside Jakarta)	65		
Jakarta	91		
Urban male, 35 years old, 10 years of schooling, working full time			
Non-Java	29		
Java (outside Jakarta)	42		
Jakarta	64		
Urban female, 35 years old, 5 years of schooling, working full time		All urban females	73
Non-Java	52		
Java (outside Jakarta)	86		
Jakarta	121		
Rural male, 35 years old, 5 years of schooling, working full time		All rural males	46
Non-Java	44		
Java	98		

Rural female, 35 years old, 5 years of schooling, working full time		All rural females 28
Non-Java	20	
Java	60	
Self-employment income		
Nonfarm profits, 1.5 family members working, 40-year-old head of household with 5 years of schooling		Nonfarm profits 52
Non-Java	22	
Java (outside Jakarta)	69	
Jakarta	155	
Farm profits, 0.5 to 1 hectare, 1.5 family members working, 40-year-old head of household with 5 years of schooling		Farm profits 89
Non-Java	67	
Java	91	
Farm profits, more than 2 hectares, 1.5 family members working, 40-year-old head of household with 5 years of schooling		
Non-Java	42	
Java	62	
Income from both activities, smallest plot, 1.5 family members working, 40-year-old head of household with 5 years of schooling		Income from both activities 52
Non-Java	20	
Java	60	

Table 6.7 Decomposition of Changes in the Distribution of Individual Earnings

	Change 1980 to 1996	Gini (percent)	E(0) (percent)	E(1) (percent)	Change 1996 to 1980	Gini (percent)	E(0) (percent)	E(1) (percent)
a	Initial values (1980)	49.24	45.51	43.32	Initial values (1996)	51.26	56.31	47.66
b	Overall price effect	0.87	2.15	2.74	Overall price effect	−0.51	−5.22	−2.83
c	Return to education	0.32	0.68	0.54	Return to education	0.14	0.11	0.08
d	Male urban	−0.25	−0.40	−0.48	Male urban	0.14	0.30	0.04
e	Male rural	0.55	0.98	1.00	Male rural	−0.16	−0.47	−0.23
f	Female urban	−0.15	−0.32	−0.24	Female urban	0.21	0.54	0.34
g	Female rural	0.16	0.42	0.25	Female rural	−0.05	−0.26	−0.08
h	Return to experience	0.51	1.03	1.00	Return to experience	−0.47	−0.91	−0.95
i	Java differential	−0.92	−2.02	−1.23	Java differential	0.90	1.95	1.36
j	Differential growth rates of mean wage in main wage-worker groups	1.09	2.39	2.12	Differential growth rates of mean wage in main wage-worker groups	−0.54	−1.70	−1.21
k	Nonobservable factors' variance	4.17	11.58	8.92	Nonobservable factors' variance	−2.55	−8.41	−5.59
l	Total price + residual variance effect	5.13	13.81	11.76	Total price + residual variance effect	−2.40	−10.24	−6.33
m	Labor supply and occupational choice	0.65	0.94	1.68	Labor supply and occupational choice	2.45	4.93	4.09
n	Actual change in inequality (1996–80)	2.02	10.80	4.35	Actual change in inequality (1980–96)	−2.02	−10.80	−4.35
o	Population effect (base 1996)[a]	−3.76	−3.94	−9.10	Population effect (base 1980)[a]	−2.07	−5.49	−2.11

a. The population effect is defined according to identity (6.6) in the text. The base year refers to the structure of earnings and occupational preferences used in evaluating the distributional effects of the change in the sociodemographic structure of the population.

Source: Authors' estimates from Saving and Investment Survey 1996, Susenas 1980 and 1996.

194

period under analysis, whereas a single factor contributed to a leveling off of individual earnings. Overall, changes in the rates of return to education and to experience have been unequalizing. As mentioned above and, in the case of education, as illustrated in table 6.7, these overall effects correspond to various phenomena that were not necessarily convergent. The drop in the rate of return to education in the urban sector contributed to some equalizing of the distribution, whereas the opposite was true of the increase in the rate of return to education in the rural sector. When all wage workers are put together, including part-time workers, the second effect (the increase in the return to education in the rural sector) is dominant, because the poorest wage workers become still poorer. Indeed, as indicated above, changes in earning function coefficients are simulated while the mean earning or income of the corresponding group of workers remains constant. Under these conditions, the observed increase in the rate of return to the education of rural workers necessarily impoverishes those workers with the lowest level of schooling and increases inequality. All these effects appear clearly in rows *d*, *e*, and *f* of table 6.7, but none of them is really very strong. Stronger unequalizing effects are linked to changes in the structure of wages that cannot be associated with human capital variables. The first one is linked to the segmentation of the labor market and, more precisely, to the male-female and urban-rural segmentation (row *j*). The main point is that the urban-rural wage differential tended to increase for constant population characteristics between 1980 and 1996. Using the average characteristics of wage workers in 1980, the urban-rural gap increased by 18 percentage points, as shown in table 6.6. Even though the male-female differential fell somewhat—by 5 percentage points with the 1980 average individual characteristics but asymmetrically in the urban and the rural sectors—the widening urban-rural wage gap resulted in a strong increase in overall earning inequality. A stronger unequalizing factor resulted from the generalized increase in the variance of the residuals of the earning equations that corresponds to an increase in the heterogeneity of unobserved earning determinants, including working hours, especially for part-time workers. With a 4 point increase in the Gini coefficient, this is definitely a major phenomenon, the nature of which is still to be identified. In particular, it cannot be ruled out that measurement errors are partly driving this evolution.

In front of all these unequalizing forces, a single factor contributed to equalizing individual earnings: the reduction in the initial relative disadvantage suffered by individual earners living on the Java island compared with the rest of the country. Overall, changes in the structure of earnings observed among broadly defined groups of individual earners—male-female, urban-rural, Java–non-Java—thus tended to compensate each other, as may be seen by adding rows *i* and *j*.

Comparing the left- and right-hand sides of table 6.7, we see that the preceding conclusions are qualitatively robust with respect to the path followed in performing the decomposition. Applying the earning functions of 1980 to the 1996 sample yields effects with the opposite sign to those just analyzed.

Interestingly, the picture looks quite different when one switches to household income—see table 6.8. There are two reasons for this. On the one hand, household income includes self-employment income from farming or nonfarming activities in addition to wage income. On the other hand, household income generally combines all these income sources.

Several differences appear when comparing the decomposition of price effects in the left-hand side of tables 6.7 and 6.8. First, the overall contribution of educational returns to change in household income inequality is much more moderate, as a result of the equalizing effect of the drop in the rate of return to schooling in the non-farm profit function. The effect of a lower educational return for both wage (male) workers and those with nonfarm profits now almost fully compensates for the effect of the increase in the return to schooling among rural wage workers. It is also noticeable that changes in the rate of return to education in the earning equations have less effect on the inequality of household incomes than on individual earnings. This result reflects the fact that wage income represents on average only half the total household income.

Second, the change in the return to experience in earning and profit functions now contributes substantially to equalizing household income. This result is the opposite of what was observed for individual earnings. Associated with the fact that the return to experience tends to increase is the fact that older people involved in self-employment activities were in households located at the bottom part of the distribution.

Third, the drop in the Java–non-Java differential is still equalizing but less strongly so than for individual earners, perhaps because, as seen in table 6.5, the differential changed only very moderately for pure farm incomes.

Fourth, the contribution of differences in growth rates of the main income sources reinforces the effect of urban-rural and male-female differentials on the inequality of individual earnings in table 6.7. These growth rates appear in the right-hand side of table 6.6. Their overall effect on the distribution is more modest than for wage workers because they tend to offset each other when combined within household income. It turns out that the major equalizing factor is the increase of pure farm incomes relatively to other income sources.

Overall, the effect of changes in prices on the distribution of household income is in the opposite direction and larger in absolute value than it is for wage workers. It amounts to a drop of approximately 1 point in the Gini coefficient. This equalizing of the distribution is primarily because of the drop in the differential rate of return on land size, the change in the experience or age structure of earnings and self-employment incomes, and the Java–non-Java differential.

The overall effect of the change in the variance of unobserved income determinants is unequalizing, as it is for individual earners, but to a lesser extent. This situation reflects the drop in the unexplained heterogeneity of farm incomes, as shown in table 6.5. The overall increase in inequality remains quite substantial, though. It more than compensates the equalizing role of the pure price effects.

In summary, changes in the structure of individual earnings and self-employment incomes from the perspective of 1980 had an overall unequalizing effect on household incomes (see row p in table 6.8). The total effect resulted mostly from an increase in the unexplained heterogeneity of wages and, to a lesser extent, the nonfarm self-employment incomes (see row o), which overcompensated the equalizing effect of the drop in the Java–non-Java differential (row m), of the drop in the differential return to land (row k), and of the change in the experience or age structure of earnings and self-employment incomes (row l). In addition, aggregate price changes, such as the change in urban-rural or male-female wage differentials or in relative agricultural profits versus other activities, each had some effect on the distribution but tended to offset each other (see row n).

For household income, as for individual earnings, the picture is only slightly different when one uses 1996 rather than 1980 as the starting point of the decomposition methodology. Comparing both sides of table 6.8, one can see that, as expected, the sign of the effects is simply reversed, and their intensity is slightly modified. The change in intensity is because the structure of the population with respect to the characteristics of interest in the present decomposition is substantially different in the initial and terminal years. In a single instance, the difference is large enough to produce a contradiction between the two sides of the table. In row n of table 6.8, the effect of the differences in the growth rates of the various income sources is (a) a minor increase in inequality when applying the 1996 price structure to the 1980 population and (b) a very substantial increase in inequality when going in the opposite direction.

The reason for that apparent contradiction appears clearly in table 6.9, which shows the structures of the 1980 and 1996 samples

Table 6.8 Decomposition of Changes in the Distribution of Household Income Per Capita

	Change 1980 to 1996	Gini	E(0)	E(1)	Change 1996 to 1980	Gini	E(0)	E(1)
a	Initial values (1980)	38.44	25.30	27.25	Initial values (1996)	40.22	27.25	31.32
b	Overall price effect	-0.93	-0.99	-1.19	Overall price effect	1.65	2.76	2.13
c	Education	0.10	0.30	0.09	Education	1.54	2.64	3.96
d	Male urban	-0.08	0.01	-0.09	Male urban	0.21	0.71	0.24
e	Male rural	0.22	0.44	0.26	Male rural	0.06	0.50	0.16
f	Female urban	-0.06	0.04	-0.09	Female urban	0.31	0.84	0.49
g	Female rural	0.07	0.21	0.09	Female rural	0.10	0.56	0.20
h	Pure farm profit	0.05	0.06	0.09	Pure farm profit	-0.10	-0.14	-0.14
i	Mixed activity	-0.04	-0.05	-0.08	Mixed activity	0.10	0.13	0.13
j	Nonfarm profit	-0.40	-0.53	-0.82	Nonfarm profit	1.28	1.86	3.56
k	Land return	-0.31	-0.43	-0.26	Land return	0.18	0.37	0.12
l	Experience	-0.67	-0.86	-1.24	Experience	0.12	0.39	-0.57
m	Java differential	-0.25	-0.13	0.06	Java differential	0.37	0.52	-0.76
n	Differential growth rates in main income sources	0.34	0.66	-0.03	Differential growth rates in main income sources	3.44	5.80	5.37
o	Nonobservable factors' variance	2.04	3.28	3.73	Nonobservable factors' variance	-1.72	-1.94	-3.54

	(base 1996)			(base 1980)			
p	Price + residual variance effect	1.39	2.64	3.58	Price + residual variance effect	0.23	0.44	-0.35
q	Labor supply and occupational choice	4.68	6.79	7.99	Labor supply and occupational choice	2.38	4.13	2.51
r	Price + residual variance + labor supply effect	6.50	11.65	10.47	Price + residual variance + labor supply effect	2.54	9.10	2.79
s	Actual change in inequality (1996–80)	1.78	1.95	4.06	Actual change in inequality (1980–96)	-1.78	-1.95	-4.06
t	Population effect (base 1996)[a]	-4.72	-9.70	-6.41	Population effect (base 1980)[a]	-4.32	-11.05	-6.85
u	Rural-urban structure of the population (base 1996)	1.19	1.61	2.08	Rural-urban structure of the population (base 1980)	-0.71	-0.91	-1.19
v					Education effect (base 1980)	-1.33	-2.46	-2.38
w					Education effects without changes in occupations (base 1980)	-0.85	-1.61	-0.75

a. The population effect is defined according to identity (6.6) in the text. The base year refers to the structure of earnings and occupational preferences used in evaluating the distributional effects of the change in the sociodemographic structure of the population.

Source: Authors' estimates from Saving and Investment Survey 1996, Susenas 1980 and 1996.

Table 6.9 Mean and Dispersion of Household Incomes
according to Some Characteristics of Heads of Households

	1980			1996		
Characteristic	*Weight*	*Mean*	*Standard deviation*	*Weight*	*Mean*	*Standard deviation*
Urban	20.7	153.2	158.1	33.3	144.0	146.2
Rural	79.3	86.2	72.3	66.7	78.0	56.6
Male	87.5	104.8	102.8	88.3	104.0	100.1
Female	12.4	66.1	69.3	11.7	69.7	95.3
Pure wage worker	31.8	101.1	104.5	26.4	123.1	106.1
Pure self-employed	43.1	103.9	103.5	45.7	92.8	101.6
Pure farm	25.3	90.9	73.3	20.4	66.7	45.5
Farm and nonfarm	8.3	105.1	94.8	11.0	89.2	62.3
Nonfarm	9.4	137.7	158.3	14.3	133.1	158.4
Wage worker and self-employed	17.6	91.4	81.5	18.0	81.9	61.9
Pure farm	14.3	84.1	58.3	11.8	68.3	45.6
Farm and nonfarm	2.0	108.2	85.9	3.1	92.6	58.9
Nonfarm	1.3	144.5	192.2	3.0	123.8	95.8
Inactive						
Total	100	100	100	100	100	100

Source: Authors' estimates from Saving and Investment Survey 1996, Susenas
1980 and 1996.

with respect to some simple characteristics of the heads of household. The relative growth of farm income with respect to urban wages or nonfarm income naturally should have a different effect when applied to samples in which the proportion of farmers and wage workers and their relative incomes are noticeably different. There are fewer heads of household who are pure wage workers in 1996 than in 1980, and their mean household income is higher. Approximately the same proportion are pure farmers between the two years of interest, but their mean income now is lower, because their characteristics are different since the price effect was going in the opposite direction. Applying the same changes in the relative income of these two groups to these two samples leads to distinct overall effects on income inequality. Farmers were poorest in 1996, but the price effect has been the largest for farmers. In 1980, farmers were close to the overall mean income in the population. Thus, the price effect can only be much stronger when starting from 1996 than when starting from 1980. There is a difference between the mean incomes reported in table 6.9 and the growth rates shown in row n in the decomposition in table 6.8. The mean income in table 6.9 incorporates changes both in the mean characteristics of the people who receive the corresponding incomes and in the mean of the various income sources for fixed characteristics. The decomposition in table 6.8 takes only the latter into account.

Changes in Occupational-Choice Behavior and Its Effect on Household Income Distribution

Occupational-choice behavior is modeled as a multinomial logit model with personal and household sociodemographic characteristics as explanatory variables. Distinct models are estimated for household heads, spouses, and other household members, as well as for the urban and the rural sectors for each of these groups. Rather than reporting the coefficients of this model, we show in table 6.10 the semielasticity of the probability of making a specific occupational choice with respect to selected variables. These variables include schooling, experience, number of children, availability of cultivable land (owned or rented) for all individuals, and a few characteristics of the heads of household for other family members. The wage is zero for heads of household who are not employed as wage workers. Therefore, elasticities with respect to that variable reflect both the usual income effects of the occupational choice of secondary household members and the effect on their choice of being in a household where the head is either inactive or self-employed.

The first interesting feature of these elasticities is the drastic increase of the role of accessibility to land in explaining the occupational choices of rural heads of household and their spouses. In 1980, it was certainly the case that household heads and spouses that had access to some land worked less frequently as pure wage workers (thus leaving the cultivation of available land to other household members) than as self-employed. The semielasticity of the corresponding choice with respect to the access to land dummy variable is negative in the case of pure wage workers and positive in the case of the self-employed. In 1996, the size of these elasticities increased considerably, thus indicating that outside employment as a pure wage worker was much less frequent and self-employment on the farm was much more frequent for household heads and spouses on farms. In other words, a clear increase in specialization took place within rural households. For practical purposes, only the heads of households or their spouses who had no access to land chose to be pure wage workers in 1996, whereas there was more flexibility in 1980. Consequently, other household members' occupational choices became less dependent on whether they lived in households with access to land.

Two other features of the evolution of occupational-choice behavior are notable in table 6.10 and both are concerned with household secondary members. First, the sensitivity of wage work to schooling changed for spouses and other members. For spouses, it declined in the urban sector and increased substantially in the rural sector; it increased in both sectors for other members. This

Table 6.10 Occupational-Choice Behavior, 1980–96

(derivative of the (Log) probability of being in various occupations with respect to selected variables[a])

Variable	Household head (1980) Urban	Household head (1980) Rural	Spouse (1980) Urban	Spouse (1980) Rural	Other (1980) Urban	Other (1980) Rural	Household head (1996) Urban	Household head (1996) Rural	Spouse (1996) Urban	Spouse (1996) Rural	Other (1996) Urban	Other (1996) Rural
Inactivity												
Schooling	−0.051	−0.122	−0.054	0.015	−0.066	−0.107	−0.031	−0.045	−0.007	−0.048	−0.100	−0.062
Experience	0.103	0.053	−0.012	−0.012	−0.035	−0.047	0.069	0.078	−0.015	−0.009	−0.049	−0.051
Children	−0.076	−0.059	0.030	0.030	0.034	0.051	−0.012	−0.033	0.114	0.057	0.053	0.018
Access to land		−2.149		−0.660		−0.681		2.040		2.651		0.266
Head's schooling			0.013	0.003	0.007	0.038			0.012	0.018	0.037	0.018
Head's experience			0.004	0.007	0.001	0.001			0.007	0.006	0.005	0.000
Head's wage			0.118	0.313	0.113	0.319			0.104	0.081	0.109	0.055
Wage work												
Schooling	0.037	−0.029	0.148	−0.069	0.039	0.061	0.033	0.026	−0.039	0.124	0.131	0.094
Experience	−0.013	−0.014	0.037	0.006	0.006	0.021	−0.017	−0.021	−0.009	0.014	0.045	0.038
Children	0.006	−0.020	−0.124	−0.082	−0.049	−0.020	−0.015	−0.016	−0.125	−0.092	−0.027	−0.053
Access to land		−3.151		−2.287		−1.572		−13.963		−14.694		−0.279
Head's schooling			−0.100	−0.104	−0.010	−0.050			−0.028	−0.091	−0.039	−0.018
Head's experience			−0.030	−0.003	0.001	0.000			0.003	−0.027	−0.002	0.000
Head's wage			−0.057	0.020	0.097	0.117			0.103	0.024	0.064	0.049

Self-employment												
Schooling	-0.097	0.032	0.025	0.026	0.032	0.044	-0.019	-0.085	0.000	-0.036	0.054	0.050
Experience	0.001	0.006	0.024	0.016	0.009	-0.008	0.004	0.000	0.017	0.009	0.012	0.031
Children	-0.009	-0.025	-0.037	0.006	0.015	-0.029	-0.016	0.011	-0.067	-0.073	-0.028	0.097
Access to land		1.577		1.677		1.667		14.538		3.539		1.381
Head's schooling		0.019		0.038		0.010		0.006		0.017		-0.004
Head's experience		0.009		-0.008		-0.002		-0.009		0.015		0.001
Head's wage		-0.462		-0.339		-0.317		-0.077		-0.206		-0.246
Mixed activity												
Schooling	-0.006	-0.012	0.175	0.003	0.012	0.113	0.002	0.049	0.064	0.139	0.111	-0.015
Experience	-0.012	-0.017	0.101	-0.002	0.046	0.049	-0.024	-0.015	0.018	0.059	0.061	0.068
Children	0.074	0.092	-0.006	-0.110	0.010	-0.042	0.050	0.078	-0.101	-0.252	-0.153	-0.113
Access to land		1.527		0.635		1.472		15.343		-4.654		-5.935
Head's schooling		-0.142		-0.022		-0.028		-0.068		-0.047		0.022
Head's experience		-0.066		0.006		0.010		0.011		-0.076		-0.006
Head's wage		-0.190		-0.620		-0.566		-0.375		-0.429		-0.359

a. Schooling and experience in years, access to land as a dummy variable, head's wage in 100,000 Rupiahs.
Source: Authors' estimates from Saving and Investment Survey 1996, Susenas 1980 and 1996.

finding suggests that wage work may have been of a different nature in 1996 than in 1980 in both the urban and the rural sectors.

Second, occupational choices of spouses and other members generally became less dependent on the characteristics of heads of household, particularly their labor-force status or wage. In 1980, secondary members in households in which the head was a wage worker tended to be either inactive or pure wage workers. In 1996, that relationship virtually disappeared.

Table 6.10 shows changes in the sensitivity of occupational choice to some selected variables but provides nothing about changes in that behavior independent of personal or household characteristics—that is, changes common to all households. The result of all these changes taken together appears in table 6.11, which shows the simulated changes in occupational-choice status of the whole population. This simulation resulted from applying the occupational-choice behavior of one year to the observations of the other year. The simulation exercise is similar to what was done in the preceding section. Individual characteristics are kept constant, and the 1996 model describing occupational choice is applied to the 1980 sample and vice-versa. As shown in table 6.11, which very much resembles a conventional mobility matrix, the change in occupational-choice behavior between 1980 and 1996 was rather drastic. Indeed, without changes in the sociodemographic structure of the population, a major shift would have taken place in the shares of the various occupations. In net terms, approximately 9 percent of the whole population would have switched from pure wage work to self-employment. Moreover, because access to land is considered exogenous, this additional self-employment would have been only in nonfarm activities. Among the changes in occupational-choice behavior analyzed above in connection with individual or household characteristics, only the much higher sensitivity to a household's access to land can explain that evolution. Other changes were not strong enough for such an occupational reallocation to take place.

This simulated evolution goes in the direction actually observed, as emphasized in table 6.2. The magnitude of the simulated evolution, however, is much bigger. To understand this apparent overshooting, keep in mind that the occupational-choice model discussed above, which is behind the simulation in table 6.11, is a reduced-form model that may hide complex equilibrating mechanisms in the labor market. In other words, simulated changes may not reflect a modification of individual *preferences* for one occupation over another but may indicate equilibrating mechanisms for other labor markets or phenomena that led people with given characteristics to modify their occupations.

Table 6.11 Simulated Changes in Occupational Choices, Whole Population

	Simulated with 1996 occupational-choice behavior				
		Pure wage worker	Self-employed worker	Mixed activity	Total
Observed 1980 status	Inactive				
Inactive	83.6	1.1	13.5	1.8	32.0
Pure wage worker	8.5	61.5	24.0	6.1	23.6
Self-employed worker	6.1	0.8	92.1	1.1	35.0
Mixed activity	5.3	1.1	12.2	81.4	9.4
Total	31.4	15.2	43.4	10.0	100.0
	Simulated with 1980 occupational-choice behavior				
		Pure wage worker	Self-employed worker	Mixed activity	Total
Observed 1996 status	Inactive				
Inactive	84.3	8.6	5.8	1.3	32.0
Pure wage worker	3.0	94.8	1.8	0.4	20.3
Self-employed worker	9.6	14.8	72.7	2.9	37.7
Mixed activity	5.7	15.5	3.0	75.8	10.0
Total	31.8	29.2	29.9	9.1	100.0
	Simulated 1980 with 1996 schooling structure				
		Pure wage worker	Self-employed worker	Mixed activity	Total
Observed 1980 status	Inactive				
Inactive	86.15	10.07	3.12	0.65	31.98
Pure wage worker	8.20	85.64	5.18	0.98	23.56
Self-employed worker	4.80	8.16	83.81	3.22	35.03
Mixed activity	4.69	2.53	5.69	87.08	9.43
Total	40.66	35.17	20.48	3.69	100

Source: Authors' estimates from Saving and Investment Survey 1996, Susenas 1980 and 1996.

A major hypothesis suggested by this study is that the migration from rural to urban areas is probably the dominant phenomenon behind the observed changes in occupational-choice behavior. The decomposition of the mobility matrix into rural and urban areas in table 6.12 shows that the switch from wage work to self-employment occurs in both sectors but on a much larger scale in the rural sector. There, the share of individuals who chose to be employed as pure wage workers is nearly divided in two between 1980 and 1996. It is indeed difficult not to relate such a dramatic evolution to the very strong net migration flow out of the rural sector that was noted earlier. As was seen in table 6.2, the rural sector lost 17 percent of its share of the total population of working-age people between 1980

Table 6.12 Simulated Changes in Occupational Choices, Rural and Urban Population

	Simulated with 1996 occupational-choice behavior				
Urban: observed 1980 status	Inactive	Pure wage worker	Self-employed worker	Mixed activity	Total
Inactive	88.5	2.0	7.7	1.8	42.7
Pure wage worker	7.9	78.3	10.7	3.1	34.0
Self-employed	6.5	2.4	89.4	1.6	20.6
Mixed activity	2.3	0.7	4.1	92.9	2.8
Total	41.9	28.0	25.4	4.7	100.0

	Simulated with 1996 occupational-choice behavior				
Rural: observed 1980 status	Inactive	Pure wage worker	Self-employed worker	Mixed activity	Total
Inactive	81.7	0.7	15.8	1.7	29.1
Pure wage worker	8.7	54.1	29.8	7.4	20.8
Self-employed	6.0	0.5	92.5	1.0	38.9
Mixed activity	5.5	1.1	12.8	80.6	11.2
Total	28.6	11.8	48.2	11.4	100.0

	Simulated with 1980 occupational-choice behavior				
Urban: observed 1996 status	Inactive	Pure wage worker	Self-employed worker	Mixed activity	Total
Inactive	85.3	9.7	4.8	0.3	39.6
Pure wage worker	3.8	93.8	2.2	0.1	32.1
Self-employed	9.5	14.6	75.7	0.3	23.4
Mixed activity	11.7	25.2	5.9	57.2	4.9
Total	37.8	38.6	20.6	3.0	100.0

	Simulated with 1980 occupational-choice behavior				
Rural: observed 1996 status	Inactive	Pure wage worker	Self-employed worker	Mixed activity	Total
Inactive	83.6	7.8	6.5	2.1	28.1
Pure wage worker	2.0	96.0	1.3	0.7	14.2
Self-employed	9.6	14.9	71.9	3.5	45.1
Mixed activity	4.5	13.5	2.4	79.6	12.6
Total	28.7	24.3	34.7	12.3	100.0

Source: Authors' estimates from Saving and Investment Survey 1996, Susenas 1980 and 1996.

and 1996. In absolute terms, the population in rural areas increased at an annual rate of 1.3 percent, whereas the total population grew at 2.4 percent a year. Taking as a reference the hypothetical case in which both the rural and urban populations would have grown at the same natural rate of 2.4 percent, we calculate that this migration must have represented an outflow equal to approximately 16 percent of the rural population at working age. Assuming that farmers—and to a lesser extent individuals self-employed in nonfarm activities—were the last to migrate to cities, such an outflow could easily explain a drastic fall in the proportion of wage workers in the rural labor force.

In the absence of panel data during the 1980–96 period and without information in 1980 or 1996 Susenas on the migration status of surveyed individuals, it is unfortunately impossible to give direct evidence on the preceding hypothesis. However, an interesting contribution of the present study is the suggestion that this phenomenon is very important in explaining changes in the Indonesian distribution of income.

At the same time, the likely importance of migration raises some problems for the interpretation to be given to the occupational-choice effects shown in tables 6.11 and 6.12, as well as in tables 6.7 and 6.8. Our methodology for estimating these effects implicitly assumes that individuals observed in 1980 and in 1996 are homogeneous after we control for their observed characteristics. In other words, we assume that unobserved characteristics are distributed in the same way at the two dates. Instead, let us suppose that there was some unobserved characteristic that caused people who chose to be pure wage workers in 1980 to migrate at a higher rate to cities between 1980 and 1996. In that case, the methodology used in this chapter will consider as a change in occupational preference what actually may be the selectivity of the migration process with respect to an unobserved variable that affects occupational choice. If that variable were observed, no change in occupational-choice behavior would be detected, and migration would have an effect only on the sociodemographic structure of the population. The inobservability of migration or its determinants in our database leads to an identification problem. Part of the distributional effects attributed to changes in occupational-choice behavior may simply be spurious because of the size of selective migration in Indonesia.

If migration is the explanation of the change in occupational-choice behavior identified by our methodology, how are we to explain the simulated predicted fall in the urban proportion of wage workers shown in table 6.12? There are many simple explanations behind this fall. First, the drop in the proportion of urban wage workers is consistent with a rapid growth in their absolute number. In fact, we may compute that the absolute number of wage workers more than doubled despite their lower share in the urban population. In addition to this very vigorous expansion, it is likely that opportunities for self-employment also boomed. A second explanation of the fall in the proportion of urban wage workers is the fast increase in nonfarm profits relative to wages in Java and, more particularly, in Jakarta (see table 6.6). In the case of the urban sector, it is therefore possible that a structural occupational-choice model taking explicitly into account the structure of relative earnings would succeed in explaining the drop in the proportion of wage workers. In sum, a consistent explanation of the changes in the coefficients of the multilogit model describing occupational choices in 1980 and 1996 is available. It has to do with a major change in the structure of the Indonesian economy driven, on the one hand, by rural-urban migrations and, on the other hand, by booming self-employment opportunities in the urban sector. In other words, the observed changes in coefficients are not to be attributed uniquely to an exogenous modification of preferences among various occupations, as suggested by the logical structure of the multilogit model. Market mechanisms responsible for population movements are hidden behind those changes, but the unavailability of the appropriate data prevents us from explicitly identifying these mechanisms and measuring their effects.

The changes in the multilogit coefficients whose interpretation is ambiguous, combined with strong changes in the structure of the population, result in much more moderate *actual* changes in the occupational structure of the labor force. By comparing the last columns of the first two matrices in table 6.11, we see that the actual change in the proportion of pure wage workers in the population at working age between 1980 and 1996 was considerably smaller than the simulated change under the assumption of modified occupational-choice behavior and constant sociodemographic structure of the population. With the preceding interpretation of the changes in occupational-choice coefficients in mind, we now look at the effect of simulating these changes on the distribution of household income. The results appear in row m of table 6.7 and row q of table 6.8. As expected, the effect of that change on the distribution of earnings among wage workers is moderate, because most of the phenomenon under analysis is concerned with the allocation of the labor force between wage work and self-employment. The effect on the distribution of household income is much more substantial. Unchecked by the changes in the sociodemographic structure of the population, the change in occupational-choice behavior would have caused a major increase in the inequality of the distribution. The explanation for this increase is rather simple. If all could be analyzed in terms of household groups defined by the occupational status of the head of household, as shown in table 6.9, the change being considered here would be equivalent to shifting a substantial proportion of the pure wage workers—a group with average income and average income dispersion—to nonfarm self-employment—a group with the highest mean income and the largest income dispersion.[9,10] Such a change necessarily increases inequality. Given the size of the initial occupational shift, the resulting increase in inequality is substantial. Table 6.8 shows that it amounts to more than 4 points in the Gini coefficient.

Interestingly, the same increase in inequality is obtained, although to a much lesser extent, when applying the occupational-choice behavior estimated for 1980 to the 1996 sample. The reason for this apparently contradictory path dependence of the decomposition methodology is the same as what was seen in the previous section. Referring again to table 6.9, we see that in 1996 wage workers were relatively richer than the rest of the population in comparison with the case in 1980, especially in the urban sector. The reverse shift from self-employed to wage worker implied by the change in occupational-choice coefficients thus implies again an increase in inequality.

The Distributive Effect of Changes in the Sociodemographic Structure

As explained earlier, the effect of changes in the sociodemographic structure on income distribution is obtained as the difference between the actual change in the distribution and what is explained altogether by the effects of changes in prices, unobserved heterogeneity, and occupational-choice behavior. Tables 6.7 (row o) and 6.8 (row t) show that the resulting effect is quite substantial, amounting to a drop of 4 to 5 points in the Gini coefficient and more for the other inequality measures shown there.

The importance of population effects is the counterpart of the high, and possibly artificial, occupational-choice effect discussed in the preceding section. Overall population effects in tables 6.7 and 6.8 are essentially obtained as residuals of the decomposition method. Thus, these effects necessarily include the opposite of the effect of occupational-choice behavior. If there is an identification problem for this effect, the same identification problem must be present in the opposite direction when we try to identify the population effect. Hence, the estimated overall population effects in tables 6.7 and 6.8 must be considered with some caution.

Instead of computing population effects residually with the identification problem just discussed, one may want to simulate directly the effects of changing the sociodemographic structure of the population with respect to some particular characteristic. For example, what has been the effect on the income distribution of the change in the structure of the population with respect to characteristics such as education, age, geographical location, family composition, or the distribution of land? Isolating the effect of changes in the socio-demographic structure along each of these variables is difficult. There is no simple way to fully account for the correlation of one individual attribute, such as age or geographical location, with the other attributes of a person or to account for the correlation of individual attributes across various members of a household. It is possible, however, to get some idea of the potential importance of some of these effects by trying to simulate the effect of changes in the marginal distribution of some of these characteristics while considering the distribution of other characteristics conditionally on the characteristic under study as given.

In view of the potentially crucial role of rural-urban migration in explaining the evolution of the distribution of income and of the structure of occupation, it seemed of interest to try to isolate the rural-urban effect with a simple method. Row u in table 6.8 shows the effect of changing the rural-urban structure of the 1980 population to replicate that of 1996. The limitation of this experiment, however, is that the full sociodemographic and income structures of the population remain unchanged within the rural and the urban sectors. As in DiNardo, Fortin, and Lemieux (1996), this computation is done by simply reweighting all observations in the sample by two constant factors, one for the urban sector and the other for the rural sector. Therefore, everything is as if representative rurals were emigrating to cities and immediately becoming representative urbans. Under this very strong assumption, the result in table 6.8 shows that rural urban migrations would have contributed to making the distribution of income more unequal, whether one uses 1980 or 1996 as the base year. It is not clear, however, whether this result would still hold if the unobserved selectivity of migration could be taken into account. We now consider the effects of changing the structure of schooling within the population. Starting from the 1980 sample with 1980 earning, self-employment, and occupational-choice functions, we modify the distribution of schooling in the population to make the distribution identical to that observed in 1996. This modification is made in a very simple way using a *rank-preserving replication* of the distribution of schooling in one year for the other year within population groups defined by gender, age, and area of residence. According to that transformation, the most educated woman between the ages of 35 and 40 in an urban area in 1980 is given the schooling of the most educated woman between the ages of 35 and 40 in an urban area in 1996; the same would be true for the second most educated woman and so on. After the schooling of the 1980 sample has been modified in this way, individual and household incomes can then be recomputed using the earning and self-employment functions of 1980 as well as the occupational-choice models. In this simulation, we take precautions for children who may now be predicted to still be in school. If they were initially active in some occupation, they must be withdrawn from the labor force.[11] We shall see that this modification is of some importance in the results below.

As shown in table 6.8, this simulation suggests that the progress of schooling in the Indonesian population actually had an unequalizing effect on the distribution of household incomes. This result may seem surprising at first. Indeed, it is generally the case that an increase in the average level of schooling of a population comes with a drop in the inequality in schooling levels. The distribution of income should then become more equal too. Clearly, the last part of this argument relies on the implicit assumption that schooling is remunerated at a common rate throughout the economy. This assumption certainly did not hold true in Indonesia, neither in 1980 nor in 1996. On the one hand, we have seen that individual earnings tended to be convex functions of the level of schooling, the convexity coefficient being generally strongly significant, except for urban women. Self-employment incomes also exhibit some convexity with respect to the education of the heads of household. On the other hand, the returns to schooling are higher in some population subgroups than in others. In particular, they are higher for urban wage workers than for rural wage workers. They also are higher in wage work than in self-employment and, for the latter, they are higher for nonfarm than for farm activities (see the bottom rows of tables 6.4 and 6.5). Under these conditions, it may not be the case that a higher mean and a lower variance of the number of years of schooling lead to a more equal distribution of income. For example, the convexity of the earning function for male wage workers implies that an additional year of schooling will mean a higher relative gain of income for those who initially had a higher level of schooling. If one were to think of the progress of schooling as everybody going to school for an additional year, this convexity of the return to schooling would clearly be unequalizing. Likewise, an equal average increment in the level of schooling in the urban and rural sectors would lead to a bigger relative income gain in the urban sector, and, therefore, to more inequality. The results appearing in the last row of table 6.8 suggest that a similar background may indeed have occurred in Indonesia. Even without any change in occupational choices, the relative income gains permitted by the switch from the 1980 to the 1996 structure of schooling within the population would have contributed to an increase in inequality slightly less than 1 point in the Gini coefficient. Of course, this is a partial effect because it is implicitly assumed that the increase in the supply of educated workers would not have modified returns to schooling, however, tables 6.4 and 6.5 indicate that the structure of the returns to schooling in 1996 was not very different from that of 1980.

The second effect of the change in the educational structure of the population goes through induced changes in occupational choices. As previously mentioned, the increase in the average schooling of the population results in an increasing number of individuals choosing wage work over other occupational status. The last matrix in table 6.11 shows how this effect goes in the opposite direction to that of the change in occupational preferences and how it amounts to a little less than half of that change. The difference between the last two rows of table 6.8 indicates that this schooling-induced change in occupational choices contributed to an increase in income inequality. Two effects are behind this finding. On the one hand, it is possible that changes of occupation caused by the increase in schooling occurred more frequently in the upper half of the distribution and led individuals from self-employment to better-paid wage work. On the other hand, the labor-supply effect of longer schooling may have had negative income effects on poor families (particularly when a child withdrew from the labor force to go to school according to the mechanism described above). Hence, the overall increase in schooling in low income families would probably not have taken place in Indonesia without the general autonomous increase in income that was observed between 1980 and 1996. Without it, poor families could not have afforded sending their children to school for additional years.

Another interesting result of this simulation of a change in the educational structure of the population is the contribution of that evolution to the mean income of the population. Under the assumption of constant returns to education and constant occupational-choice behavior, this contribution was approximately one-fifth of the overall growth in income per capita between 1980 and 1996—a rather sizable effect. The overall contribution of the population effect to the relative increase in household income is shown in figure 6.1.

Conclusion: The Main Forces toward More Inequality or Less Inequality

What has been the evolution of the distribution of income in Indonesia between 1980 and 1996, and what were the main economic and social forces behind that evolution?

Concerning the overall evolution, data at our disposal suggest that the inequality of the distribution of household income per capita has increased moderately under the period under analysis,

Figure 6.1 Summary Decomposition of Changes in the
Equivalized Household Distribution of Income

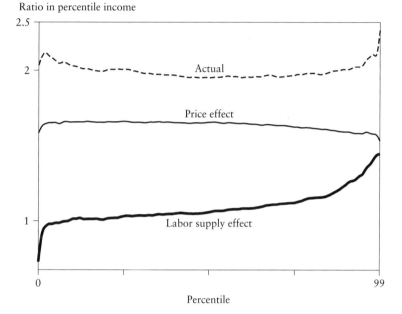

Ratio in percentile income

with a transfer from the middle of the distribution toward the top.
However, this evolution seems to have been the result of several
forces in the opposite direction. Concerning the relative structure of
wages and self-employment income, the most significant equalizing
forces for household income have been the drop in the return to the
relative size of land in agriculture; the drop in the Java–non-Java
income differential, and in some cases a reversal of that differential;
and the fall in the relative return to experience in self-employment
activities. Changes in educational returns had mixed effects. The
same is true for changes in the structure of income by main sources.
Overall, however, these price effects have been equalizing. If the
characteristics of households and household members had remained
the same and occupational choices had not changed, then the distribution of household income would have become more equal, with
the opposite being true of the distribution of individual earnings
among wage workers.

A force working in the direction of more inequality is the increase
in the variance of the residuals of the various earning and self-
employment income functions, which may correspond to an increase
in the unobserved heterogeneity of individual earnings and self-
employment incomes (outside agriculture). This finding considerably

reinforces the observed unequalizing price effect observed among individual wage earners, and it more than offsets observed equalizing price effects for the distribution of household income.

Two other major forces may have had counterveiling effects on inequality: the estimated changes in occupational-choice behavior and the related changes in the sociodemographic structure of the population. The former tended to shift individuals away from wage work into nonfarm self-employment, both in the urban and in the rural sectors, but more strongly in rural areas. Using the 1980 sample as a reference, this shift had a strong unequalizing effect on the distribution. The effect of changes in the sociodemographic structure of the population went in the opposite direction. These changes also explain how the occupational structure of the labor force changed less than what would have been implied by pure occupational-choice behavior.

These two components of the change in the distribution of income are represented in a synthetic way in figure 6.1. This figure shows the change in the mean real income of the various percentiles of the distribution of equivalized household income between 1980 and 1996. The change is decomposed into three parts: the price effect; the occupational-choice effect; and the population effect, which is defined as a residual of the two former effects in comparison with the total effect. The main lessons of the decomposition exercise are pretty clear. The price effect, which is responsible on average for a 55 percent increase in real income, is mildly equalizing, with the upper third of the distribution gaining less than the bottom, except for the very first percentiles. The occupational-choice effect represents on average a much lower increase in real income—a few percentage points—and it is strongly unequalizing. Households in figure 6.1 have been reranked so that the occupational effect must not be interpreted as if the bottom percentiles of the 1980 distribution had lost real income and the top percentiles had gained real income. Instead, those households that lost very much because of this change in labor supply became poorer than the first 1980 percentiles, whereas the same is true of those who gained very much. The difference between the actual changes and the sum of the two preceding curves corresponds to the population effect. It is clearly equalizing because of the increase in the actual real income of the bottom percentiles and because the increase in the income of the top part of the distribution is already accounted for by the occupational effect.

The discussion in the preceding sections has shown that there is some ambiguity about the interpretation to be given to the preceding decomposition and, in particular, to the occupational-choice effect. A hypothesis that has been discussed in some detail is that this effect or the population effect is strongly influenced by the important rural-urban migration that took place in Indonesia during the period under analysis. The estimation of the occupational-choice effect relies very much on the assumption that there is no unobservable variable that could explain both the choice of being a pure wage worker in 1980 and the subsequent migration later on. If such a variable had been available, the occupational-choice model could have led to very limited differences between 1980 and 1996 and, therefore, to a much flatter curve for the occupational-choice effect shown in figure 6.1. As a result, the population effect would have been much closer to the difference between the actual and the price effect curves in figure 6.1—that is, an ambiguous evolution favoring both the poorest and the richest percentiles. It is thus possible that the decomposition shown in figure 6.1 tends to substantially overestimate both the occupational-choice and the population effects. Identifying the exact role of rural-urban migrations is left for further work based on an appropriate longitudinal database.

Among the changes in the sociodemographic structure of the population, some emphasis was put on the role of the change in the relative weights of the urban and rural sectors and in the educational structure of the population. A simple simulation exercise has shown that, under the assumption of no change in the sociodemographic and income structures of the urban and rural sectors, urbanization had contributed to equalizing the distribution of incomes. Conversely, under the assumption of a constant structure of wages and self-employment incomes, the change in the educational structure of the Indonesian population had an unequalizing effect on household incomes. This somewhat unexpected result is explained, on the one hand, by the heterogeneity of the rate of return to education across sectors and occupations, as well as increasing marginal returns in some cases, and, on the other hand, by the negative effect of longer schooling on the income of families with potentially actively employed children. The counterfactual exercise undertaken for Indonesia thus seems to contradict the view that educational progress necessarily improves the distribution of income.

Notes

1. Most of these studies were published in the *Bulletin of Indonesian Economic Studies*. See, for example, Hughes and Islam (1981), Papanek (1985), Sigit (1985), and Sundrum (1979).

2. Only panel data would permit analysis of this issue in detail. Unfortunately, such data are not available.

3. These ratios are the shares appearing in table 6.3 for the corresponding bottom quantiles of the distribution, divided respectively by 10, 20, and 40.

4. In fact there is first–order stochastic dominance of 1996 over 1980; that is, the cumulative distribution function of (real) income in 1996 is everywhere below that of 1980. Note that there is no contradiction between this statement and the fact noted before that there is no Lorenz dominance between the two distributions. The Lorenz dominance concept relates to income relative to the mean criterion, whereas stochastic dominance refers to absolute income and takes into account the effect of the drastic change in the mean on social welfare.

5. Hours of work are not reported in the survey. The part-time dummy variable used here refers to individuals who report another activity on top of being a wage worker—for example, "mixed activity" in table 6.2. Instrumenting this variable led to excessive instability of the corresponding coefficient between 1980 and 1996 and was therefore abandoned.

6. As the stochastic terms in labor-supply equations and the wage function may not be independent, it might seem necessary to correct the estimation of wage equations for the resulting selection bias. Attempts at doing so yielded insignificant changes in the coefficients. The correction procedure was thus abandoned.

7. Of course, this variable is instrumented so as to account for its obvious endogeneity. Instruments essentially are the variables entering the occupational-choice models, as seen in the following section.

8. Yet it is interesting that, as could be expected, nonfarm profit functions suggest constant marginal returns to labor, whereas the marginal product of labor is strongly decreasing in farm activity.

9. This statement is true for both the urban and the rural sectors.

10. Note, however, that things are a little more complicated than suggested by this simple argument, because, unlike what is implicitly assumed in table 6.9, the structure of household income by sources is also changing in our experiment, conditionally on the occupation of the household head. Indeed, the great variety of income sources within households is what motivates much of the analysis in this chapter.

11. This change is more difficult to make in the opposite direction, going from 1996 to 1980, because children in school were excluded from the estimation of the occupational-choice model. For this reason, only the education effect with base 1980 appears in table 6.8.

References

Ahuja, Vinod, Benu Bidani, Francisco Ferreira, and Michael Walton. 1997. *Everyone's Miracle? Revisiting Poverty and Inequality in East Asia.* Washington, D.C.: World Bank.

Bourguignon, François, Martin Fournier, and Marc Gurgand. 1998. "Distribution, Development, and Education: Taiwan, 1979–1994." Processed.

Cameron, Lisa. 1998. "Income Inequality in Java: Relating the Increases to the Changing Age, Educational and Industrial Structure." University of Melbourne, Melbourne, Australia. Processed.

DiNardo, John, Nicole Fortin, and Thomas Lemieux. 1996. "Labor Market Institutions and the Distribution of Wages, 1973–1992: A Semiparametric Approach," *Econometrica*, 64(5): 1001–44.

Hill, Hal, and Anna Weidemann. 1991. "Regional Development in Indonesia: Patterns and Issues." In Hal Hill, ed., *Unity and Diversity: Regional Economic Development in Indonesia since 1970*. Oxford, U.K.: Oxford University Press.

Hughes, G. A., and Iyanatul Islam. 1981. "Inequality in Indonesia: A Decomposition Analysis." *Bulletin of Indonesian Economic Studies* 17(2): 42–71.

Manning, Chris. 1998. *Indonesian Labour in Transition: An East Asian Success Story?* Cambridge, U.K.: Cambridge University Press.

Papanek, Gustav. 1985. "Agricultural Income Distribution and Employment in the 1970s." *Bulletin of Indonesian Economic Studies* 21(2): 24–50.

Ravallion, Martin, and Benu Bidani. 1994. "How Robust Is a Poverty Profile?" *World Bank Economic Review* 8(1): 75–102.

Ravallion, Martin, and Monika Huppi. 1991. "Measuring Changes in Poverty: A Methodological Case Study of Indonesia during an Adjustment Period." *World Bank Economic Review* 5(1): 57–82.

Sigit, Hananto. 1985. "Income Distribution and Household Characteristics." *Bulletin of Indonesian Economic Studies* 21(3): 51–68.

Sundrum, R. M. 1979. "Income Distribution, 1970–76." *Bulletin of Indonesian Economic Studies* 15(1): 137–41.

Thorbecke, Erik. 1991. "Adjustment, Growth, and Income Distribution in Indonesia." *World Development* 19(11): 1595–614.

Uppal, Jogindar. 1986. "Income Distribution and Poverty in Indonesia." *Journal of Economic Development* 11(2): 177–96.

7

The Microeconomics of Changing Income Distribution in Malaysia

Gary S. Fields and Sergei Soares

The Facts and the Questions Asked

The Malaysian income distribution has exhibited major changes over the 24 years from 1973 to 1997 for which data are available. Real average per capita income increased by 2.5 times, the absolute poverty rate fell from more than 50 percent of the population to less than 8 percent, income inequality decreased, and ethnic disparities narrowed (World Bank, n.d.). This record has caused Malaysia to be cited as a successful case of growth with redistribution (Ahuja and others 1997).

Within this overall period, however, both the growth and the distribution experience were uneven. Economic growth was much slower in the 1984–89 period—just a 1.6 percent average annual increase in real gross domestic product (GDP) per capita. Also, income inequality exhibited two distinct phases. The first phase, from 1973 to 1989, was marked by falling income inequality. This decline was reversed, however, from 1989 to 1997, during which time income inequality rose. But because the changes in inequality in both periods were modest relative to the magnitude of economic growth, poverty in Malaysia fell continuously, albeit at a slower rate during the slow growth years of the 1980s.

This study uses data from Malaysia's Household Income and Expenditure Surveys to quantify the importance of different factors in accounting for the changes in Malaysia's income distribution between 1984 and 1989 and between 1989 and 1997. These particular years were chosen because 1997 is the year of the most recent available survey, 1984 is the year of the earliest survey comparable with the 1997 survey,[1] and 1989 is important for three reasons:

1. Income inequality fell until 1989 and rose thereafter.
2. Economic growth was slow in 1984–89 and rapid in 1989–97.
3. The closest year to the beginning of Malaysia's National Development Policy, which placed heightened emphasis on the eradication of hardcore poverty, is 1989.

The analysis is therefore divided into these two periods so that we can assess the factors responsible for the falling inequality in the first period and for the rising inequality in the second. We shall also look at the factors accounting for rising mean income and falling poverty in the two periods. All data are expressed in constant 1997 ringgit.

Two aspects of the income distribution are examined here, and each is measured both nonparametrically and parametrically. The two aspects are location and inequality.

The locational aspect gauges the level of income. The location of any given income distribution is depicted using a quantile function, also called a *Pen Parade*: $y = \Gamma^{-1}(p)$ (that is, the income amount corresponding to the household at the pth position in the income distribution). Locational differences are depicted nonparametrically by comparing quantile functions. We also present two summary measures of locational differences: differences in means and differences in poverty headcount ratios.

The inequality aspect tells us how dispersed a given income distribution is. The inequality of any given income distribution is depicted by a Lorenz curve, and nonparametric inequality comparisons may be made by comparing these curves. In addition to Lorenz curves, two summary measures of inequality are used: Gini coefficients and Theil indices.

The location of the distribution, which is measured nonparametrically by a quantile function, gives the income amount in real Malaysian ringgit for households at each percentile of the per capita income distribution. These quantile functions are shown in figure 7.1. In the 1989–97 period, there was a clear upward movement, which means that, at every part of the income distribution, incomes grew. For the 1984–89 period, though, the quantile curve comparisons are

Figure 7.1 Changing Quantile Functions
(household per capita monthly income in constant 1997 ringgit)

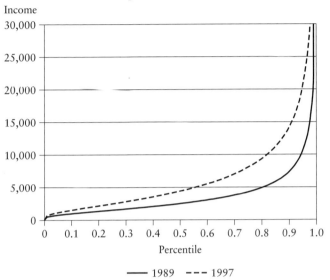

A. Actual quantile functions, 1989 and 1997

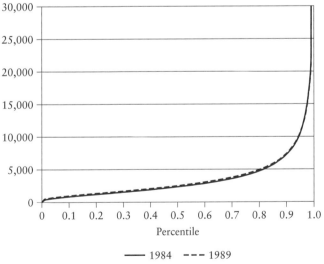

B. Actual quantile functions, 1984 and 1989

Source: Authors' calculations.

Figure 7.2 Differences in Quantile Functions
(household per capita monthly income in constant 1997 ringgit)

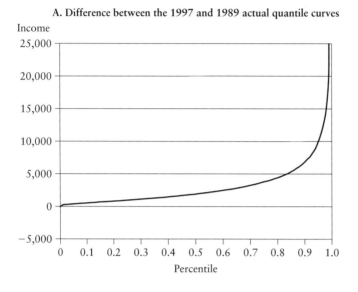

A. Difference between the 1997 and 1989 actual quantile curves

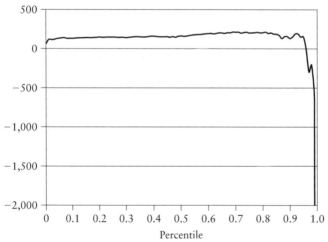

B. Difference between the 1989 and 1984 actual quantile curves

Source: Authors' calculations.

much less clear from visual inspection—per capita income among
the households in the Household Income and Expenditure Surveys
grew at only half a percent per year during that period—and so the
levels curves in figure 7.1 are supplemented by the difference curves
shown in figure 7.2. At each centile of the income distribution, these

Table 7.1 Location of Actual Distribution of Per Capita Household Income, 1984 and 1989, 1989 and 1997

Indicator	Mean (ringgit, except change)	Poverty headcount (percent)
1984 and 1989		
Actual value, 1984	3,637.76	37.9
Actual value, 1989	3,752.74	33.7
Actual change (percentage)	+3.2	−11.1
1989 and 1997		
Actual valuc, 1989	3,752.74	33.7
Actual value, 1997	7,070.29	14.4
Actual change (percentage)	+88.4	−57.3

difference curves display the amount by which that centile's income rose or fell between the base year and the final year. We see in panel A of figure 7.2 that the differences are all positive, which is another way of establishing that incomes were higher at every position in the income distribution in 1997 than in 1989.[2] This finding is not the case, however, for the earlier period: although incomes rose throughout most of the income distribution between 1984 and 1989, they fell in the richest three centiles, according to these data.

To supplement these dominance comparisons, we calculated two measures of location—the mean income and the poverty headcount ratio—for each of the two periods.[3] These measures show that incomes were generally rising in both periods, as shown in table 7.1.

In summary, although incomes in the 1984–89 period did not become uniformly higher, the two most commonly used locational measures—the mean income and the poverty headcount ratio (namely, the fraction of people below a fixed real income amount)—show a shift toward higher incomes overall.

The second aspect of the income distribution studied here is the inequality aspect. This aspect is measured nonparametrically by a Lorenz curve, which depicts the cumulative percentage of income received by each cumulative percentage of households, ordered from lowest income to highest. The 45-degree line represents a perfectly equal distribution of income. Therefore, when one Lorenz curve lies closer to the 45-degree line than another, a phenomenon that is termed *Lorenz dominance*, the first income distribution is more equal than the second. This finding means that, as shown by Atkinson (1970) and others, any inequality index obeying the principle of transfers will show lower inequality for the dominant distribution relative to the dominated one. Figures 7.3 and 7.4 depict a dominance relationship in both periods: household income inequality fell in Malaysia from 1984 to 1989 and rose from 1989 to 1997. As a consequence of Lorenz dominance, the Gini coefficient

Figure 7.3 Changing Lorenz Curves

A. Actual Lorenz curves, 1989 and 1997

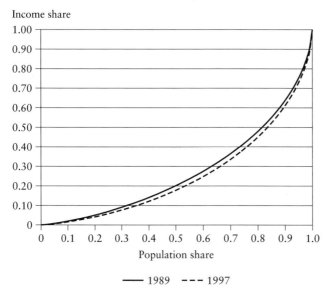

B. Actual Lorenz functions, 1984 and 1989

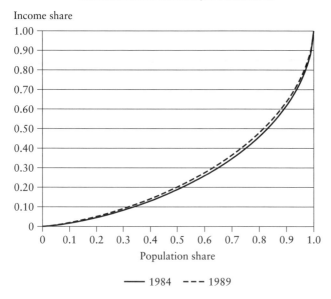

Source: Authors' calculations.

Figure 7.4 Differences in Lorenz Curves

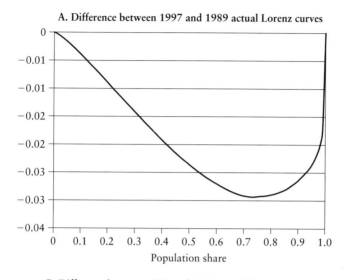

A. Difference between 1997 and 1989 actual Lorenz curves

Population share

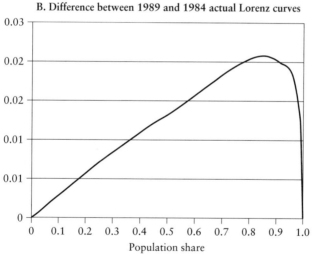

B. Difference between 1989 and 1984 actual Lorenz curves

Population share

Source: Authors' calculations.

and the Theil index also exhibit falling inequality in the first period and rising inequality in the second, as shown in table 7.2.

These, then, are the basic distributional changes to be explained, about which we ask the following questions:

• Which factors contributed how much to the increase in household income levels and the fall in absolute poverty in the 1984–89 and 1989–97 periods?

Table 7.2 Inequality of Actual Distribution of Per Capita
Household Income, Selected Periods

Indicator	Gini coefficient	Theil index
1984 and 1989		
Actual value, 1984	0.4856	0.4753
Actual value, 1989	0.4610	0.4161
Actual change (percentage)	−5.1	−12.5
1989 and 1997		
Actual value, 1989	0.4610	0.4161
Actual value, 1997	0.4993	0.5051
Actual change (percentage)	+8.3	+21.4

• Which factors contributed how much to the falling income
inequality from 1984 to 1989 and the rising income inequality from
1989 to 1997?

The factors to be examined are changes in households' demographic characteristics, their productive assets, individuals' decisions
about labor-force participation, their opportunities for working in
various occupational positions, and the structure of returns to various characteristics in wage employment and self-employment.
Because of lack of data, we have not been able in this study to investigate the ethnic dimension of changing income distribution. This
question of vital national interest remains to be explored.

The relative weights of the various factors are quantified using
logistic and linear regressions combined in various ways to simulate
counterfactual distributions of income. The basis is a two-equation
model: the first equation estimates the determinants of occupational
position, and the second estimates the determinants of earnings conditional on being in a given occupational position. The simulations
then involve replacing one year's coefficients or determinants by
those from the other year and gauging how different the distributions are. The second section of the chapter details the overall
methodology. The third section presents the results of the estimation
phase. The fourth section then gives the simulation methodology
and results. Conclusions are summarized in the last section.

Methodology

The analysis proceeds by representing the actual income distributions,
deriving the simulated income distributions, and comparing the ability of the several simulated distributions to fit the actual changes in
location and inequality in the 1984–89 and 1989–97 periods.

The Actual Income Distributions

Let $Y_{h\tau}$ represent the income of household h at time τ. Household income is the sum of labor earnings in wage employment, labor earnings in self-employment, and other income, summed over all members, all at time τ:

$$Y_{h\tau} = \Sigma_{i\epsilon h} Y_{i\tau}.$$

Household income depends on the demographic makeup of the household, the characteristics of various household members, the productive assets household members own, and the returns these productive assets earn in wage employment and in self-employment.[4] This function may be formalized thus:

$$Y_{h\tau} = H_\tau\left(X_{h\tau}^D, X_{h\tau}^H, Y_{h\tau}^O, \Omega_{h\tau}; \beta_\tau, \lambda_\tau\right)$$

where

$Y_{h\tau}$ = income of household h at time τ

H_τ = income-generating function at time τ

$X_{h\tau}^D$ = vector of demographic characteristics of household h at time τ

$X_{h\tau}^H$ = productive assets owned by household h at time τ

$Y_{h\tau}^O$ = other income received by household h at time τ

$\Omega_{h\tau} \equiv [(\varepsilon_i^w), (\varepsilon_i^{se}), (\eta_i^w), (\eta_i^{se})]$ = unobserved residuals in the equations determining household members' labor earnings in wage employment (ε_i^w), labor earnings in self-employment (ε_i^{se}), participation in wage employment (η_i^w), and participation in self-employment (η_i^{se})

$\beta_\tau = (\beta_\tau^w, \beta_\tau^{se})$ = regression coefficients in the wage and self-employment equation

$\lambda_\tau = (\lambda_\tau^w, \lambda_\tau^{se})$ = multinomial logit coefficients in the wage employment and self-employment participation equations.

Next, we shall aggregate the observations on each household into an overall economywide income distribution. Let X_τ^D, X_τ^H, Y_τ^O, and Ω_τ be vectors denoting the corresponding random variables in the population as a whole. Given the regression coefficients β_τ and the logit coefficients λ_τ, the actual distribution of household incomes at time τ can be written as

$$D_\tau = D\left[X_\tau^D, X_\tau^H, Y_\tau^O, \Omega_\tau; \beta_\tau, \lambda_\tau\right].$$

Next, the X_τ^D and X_τ^H factors are regrouped into two overlapping sets: those characteristics that enter into the determination of labor earnings (X_τ) and those that enter into the determination of occupational position (Z_τ). Thus, the distribution of household incomes at time τ may be rewritten as follows:

$$D_\tau = D[X_\tau, Z_\tau, Y_\tau^O, \Omega_\tau; \beta_\tau, \lambda_\tau].$$

Finally, these relationships are parameterized using two basic equations: (a) a system of occupational-position equations, which determines the likelihood that a given person will be a wage employee, self-employed, or a nonearner (either an unpaid family worker or economically inactive); and (b) an earnings equation, which predicts the individual's earnings within that occupational category. Specifically:

$$\text{Prob}(i = \text{self-employed worker})_\tau = \Lambda(\lambda_{j=1\tau} Z_{ij\tau} + \eta_{ij\tau})$$
$$\text{Prob}(i = \text{wage employee})_\tau = \Lambda(\lambda_{j=2\tau} Z_{ij\tau} + \eta_{ij\tau})$$

and

$$\ln Y_{ij\tau} = \beta_{j\tau} X_{ij\tau} + \varepsilon_{ij\tau}$$

where

$\Lambda(.)$ is the logistic function

$\lambda_{j\tau}$ is a set of logit coefficients determining occupational position (wage employee, self-employed worker, or nonearner) of individual i at time τ

$Z_{ij\tau}$ is a set of determinants of occupational position
$\eta_{ij\tau}$ are the residuals in the occupation equation

$\ln Y_{ij\tau}$ is the logarithm of labor income of individual i in occupational position j at time τ

$\beta_{j\tau}$ is a set of linear regression coefficients
$X_{ij\tau}$ is a set of determinants of labor income
$\varepsilon_{ij\tau}$ are the residuals in the earnings equation.

The Simulated Income Distributions

To simulate the contributions of groups of explanatory factors to the change in the economywide distribution between one year t and another t', the year t' values are substituted in place of the year t values in

$$D_\tau = D[X_\tau, Z_\tau, Y_\tau^O, \Omega_\tau; \beta_\tau, \lambda_\tau]$$

holding the other values constant when possible. Five such simulations are performed:

1. The *effect of changing the whole reward structure* is defined as the change in the income distribution that would be realized if the year t' values of β are used instead of the year t values:

$$B_{tt'} \equiv D[X_t, Z_t, Y_t^O, \Omega_t; \beta_{t'}, \lambda_t] - D[X_t, Z_t, Y_t^O, \Omega_t; \beta_t, \lambda_t].$$

2. Similarly, the *effect of changing the whole occupational-position structure* is estimated by using the year t' values of λ rather than the year t values:

$$O_{tt'} \equiv D[X_t, Z_t, Y_t^O, \Omega_t; \beta_t, \lambda_{t'}] - D[X_t, Z_t, Y_t^O, \Omega_t; \beta_t, \lambda_t].$$

3. The *effect of changing the whole population structure* is defined as the income distribution that results when the Xs and Zs in year t are replaced by those in year t':

$$P_{tt'} = D[X_{t'}, Z_{t'}, Y_{t'}^O, \Omega_{t'}; \beta_t, \lambda_t] - D[X_t, Z_t, Y_t^O, \Omega_t; \beta_t, \lambda_t]^5.$$

It may be noted that the counterfactual distribution used in describing the change in population structure from t to t' is the same one used in describing the change of both the reward and occupational structures from t' to t. What makes the two expressions different is the reference distribution with which the counterfactual is compared.

4. We may be interested also in the *effect of a change in the returns* to the kth characteristic alone. This calculation is made by replacing β_k in year t by its value in year t', while simultaneously keeping average income constant. Obviously, such a change is meaningful only for analyzing inequality changes.[6]

5. Finally, we can also find the *effect of changes in the quantities* of a single characteristic, such as education. Our way of estimating the population effect of the kth characteristic alone is to assign to the individual at the pth position in the education distribution for that gender category in year t the number of years of education at that position in t', holding the Zs and all other Xs constant. The contribution of this change to the change in the income distribution between year t and year t' may then be expressed as the population structure effect of the kth characteristic:

$$P_{k,tt'} \equiv D[X_{kt'}, X_{-t}, Z_t, Y_t^O, \Omega_t; \beta_t, \lambda_t] \\ - D[X_{kt}, X_{-t}, Z_t, Y_t^O, \Omega_t; \beta_t, \lambda_t]$$

where the changed factor is denoted X_k and the others are denoted X_-.

Comparing the Five Simulations

The final step is to compare the simulations and thereby determine the relative importance for income distribution change of the five simulated factors: the change in the whole reward structure, the change in the whole occupational-position structure, the change in the whole population structure, the change in the returns to education, and the change in the quantities of education.

As described earlier, two aspects of income distribution change are of interest: the locational aspect and the inequality aspect. For each of those aspects, we seek to determine how important different factors are in accounting for the change in income distribution between one year and another. In many cases, we are able to make unambiguous ordinal statements.

We turn now to a more detailed presentation of the implementation of these methods and the empirical results.

Estimation Results in the Case of Malaysia

Estimating the Determinants of Occupational Position

At any given time τ, each individual is classified into one and only one occupational position: wage employee, self-employed worker, or nonearner (which includes those in unpaid family work and the economically inactive).[7] A three-way multinomial logit equation was then run in which the occupational position of individual i at time τ is expressed as a function of the individual's characteristics:

$$\text{Prob}(i = \text{self-employed worker})\tau = \Lambda(\lambda_{j=1\tau} Z_{ij\tau} + \eta_{ij\tau})$$
$$\text{Prob}(i = \text{wage employee})\tau = \Lambda(\lambda_{j=2\tau} Z_{ij\tau} + \eta_{ij\tau}).$$

In each year, occupational-position equations are estimated separately for men and women and for household heads and other members of the household.

For heads of households, the $Z_{ij\tau}$ include (a) the individual's own characteristics—an education spline[8] and an age quartic—and (b) the average characteristics of other family members—their mean education entered as a quadratic; their mean age, also entered as a quadratic; the fraction of family members who are female; family size; the household dependency ratio; and the location (rural or urban). For family members other than heads of households, the $Z_{ij\tau}$ includes everything that is included for the head, plus the head's own characteristics, plus the head's actual occupational position.[9,10] Because average characteristics of family members other than the head of household appear here as well and include the individual whose occupational choice is being estimated, this step may possibly have introduced multicollinearity, but the analysis of the standard errors does not suggest that this happened.

The residuals, $\eta_{ij\tau}$, are interpreted as representing unobserved determinants of occupational choice.

Tables 7.3 through 7.6 report these estimations, respectively, for male heads of household, female heads of household, male family members who are not heads of household, and female family members who are not heads of household in each of the three years. To

Table 7.3 Occupational-Position Equations for Male Heads of Household

Wage employee	1984		1989		1997	
	Coefficient	z value	Coefficient	z value	Coefficient	z value
Primary education spline	0.00209	1.85	−0.00172	−1.59	0.00023	0.16
Secondary education spline	0.00156	0.75	0.00002	0.01	0.00086	0.47
Higher education spline	0.00886	1.00	0.01027	1.60	0.00499	0.73
Age	1.85300	13.55	2.05609	15.10	2.25254	12.44
Age squared	−0.04661	−10.80	−0.05336	−12.37	−0.05687	−9.84
Age cubed	0.00044	7.64	0.00053	9.15	0.00054	6.99
Age quartic	−1.40E-06	−5.12	−1.80E-06	−6.51	−1.76E-06	−4.70
Other household members' mean education	0.0058	2.03	0.0054	2.07	−0.0020	−0.64
Other household members' mean education squared	−0.0001	−2.77	−0.0001	−3.19	0.0000	−0.86
Other household members' mean age	−0.0512	−4.89	−0.0298	−3.12	−0.0282	−2.25
Other household members' mean age squared	0.0005	3.75	0.0002	1.90	0.0001	0.71
Dependency ratio	−0.0177	−0.11	0.0851	0.55	−0.1769	−0.91
Number of people in household	−0.1067	−10.47	−0.0754	−7.53	−0.0955	−6.44
Percentage of members who are female	0.2236	2.17	0.0351	0.38	0.1298	1.11
Rural	0.2097	4.27	0.1781	4.06	0.3048	5.29
Constant	−18.8505	−12.54	−21.2167	−14.16	−23.4937	−11.90

(Continued on the following page)

Table 7.3 (Continued)

Self-employed worker	1984 Coefficient	z value	1989 Coefficient	z value	1997 Coefficient	z value
Primary education spline	−0.00784	−7.37	−0.01292	−12.96	−0.00685	−5.19
Secondary education spline	−0.01653	−7.76	−0.01983	−11.78	−0.01131	−6.08
Higher education spline	−0.03074	−3.13	−0.03154	−4.31	−0.02269	−3.11
Age	2.55979	17.94	2.47911	17.70	2.92113	15.55
Age squared	−0.06916	−15.80	−0.06795	−15.73	−0.07652	−13.38
Age cubed	0.00075	13.33	0.00075	13.39	0.00080	10.99
Age quartic	−2.92E-06	−11.22	−2.99E-06	−11.41	−3.00E-06	−8.95
Other household members' mean education	0.0033	1.20	0.0018	0.72	−0.0026	−0.88
Other household members' mean education squared	−0.0001	−2.97	0.0000	−2.05	0.0000	−1.15
Other household members' mean age	−0.0063	−0.64	0.0167	1.86	0.0082	0.69
Other household members' mean age squared	0.0001	1.00	−0.0001	−0.99	−0.0001	−1.14
Dependency ratio	0.5001	3.16	0.8968	5.95	0.3859	2.01
Number of people in household	−0.0551	−5.75	−0.0317	−3.37	−0.0468	−3.26
Percentage of members who are female	0.1324	1.31	0.0128	0.14	0.2271	1.96
Rural	0.6887	14.52	0.7778	18.35	0.9409	16.87
Constant	−28.4668	−17.63	−27.4292	−17.31	−34.1626	−15.86
N	39,056		45,182		30,386	
Log likelihood	−26,928.0		−31,803.0		−20,019.8	
Pseudo R^2	0.2432		0.2473		0.2677	

Source: Authors' calculations.

Table 7.4 Occupational-Position Equations for Female Heads of Household

Wage employee	1984 Coefficient	z value	1989 Coefficient	z value	1997 Coefficient	z value
Primary education spline	−0.00973	−5.49	−0.00501	−2.85	−0.00241	−1.11
Secondary education spline	0.02970	9.55	0.02027	7.83	0.01852	6.98
Higher education spline	0.03715	2.31	0.05905	4.48	0.02561	2.40
Age	0.02401	0.14	0.19955	0.96	0.15186	0.71
Age squared	0.00534	0.98	0.00155	0.22	0.00277	0.39
Age cubed	−0.00017	−2.26	−0.00014	−1.44	−0.00015	−1.56
Age quartic	1.11E-06	3.21	1.11E-06	2.24	1.15E-06	2.39
Other household members' mean education	0.0198	4.87	0.0203	4.96	0.0300	6.60
Other household members' mean education squared	−0.0002	−5.24	−0.0002	−5.36	−0.0002	−6.68
Other household members' mean age	0.0466	3.43	0.0467	3.64	0.0314	2.18
Other household members' mean age squared	−0.0005	−2.83	−0.0006	−3.20	−0.0002	−0.99
Dependency ratio	−0.1694	−0.92	−0.5716	−3.01	−0.8949	−3.98
Number of people in household	−0.1825	−9.51	−0.1721	−8.79	−0.1742	−7.51
Percentage of members who are female	0.2976	2.69	0.2356	2.16	0.3042	2.45
Rural	0.1950	2.60	0.2327	3.15	0.2189	2.46
Constant	−2.2106	−1.19	−4.5755	−2.08	−4.0615	−1.78

(Continued on the following page)

Table 7.4 (Continued)

Self-employed worker	1984 Coefficient	z value	1989 Coefficient	z value	1997 Coefficient	z value
Primary education spline	−0.01473	−8.54	−0.0125563	−7.90	−0.0065768	−3.18
Secondary education spline	−0.01093	−2.11	−0.00921	−2.59	−0.00266	−0.79
Higher education spline	−0.00060	−0.02	−0.00769	−0.28	−0.04939	−2.00
Age	0.56572	2.29	0.50710	2.29	0.70626	2.07
Age squared	−0.01294	−1.65	−0.00850	−1.24	−0.01318	−1.24
Age cubed	0.00012	1.10	0.00002	0.21	0.00007	0.51
Age quartic	−4.15E-07	−0.79	0.00000	0.55	0.00000	−0.03
Other household members' mean education	0.0088	2.26	1.11E-02	2.99	1.66E-02	3.40
Other household members' mean education squared	−0.0001	−2.47	−0.0001	−3.79	−0.0001	−3.75
Other household members' mean age	−0.0028	−0.23	0.7374	10.73	0.7776	8.50
Other household members' mean age squared	0.0001	0.77	−0.0001	−0.94	−0.0002	−0.92
Dependency ratio	0.2932	1.69	−0.3764	−2.23	−0.1466	−0.62
Number of people in household	−0.0879	−5.61	−0.1361	−8.39	−0.1269	−5.49
Percentage of members who are female	0.0759	0.74	0.2165	2.23	0.4565	3.52
Rural	0.9015	12.57	−8.3824	−3.28	−12.5866	−3.21
Constant	−8.6442	−3.13	0.0127	1.10	0.0165	1.03
N	6,092		6,697		4,406	
Log likelihood	−5,218.1		−5,585.9		−3,587.9	
Pseudo R^2	0.1721		0.184		0.2055	

Source: Authors' calculations.

Table 7.5 Occupational-Position Equations for Male Family Members Who Are Not Heads of Household

Wage employee	1984		1989		1997	
	Coefficient	z value	Coefficient	z value	Coefficient	z value
Primary education spline	0.0215	15.122	0.0252	17.551	0.0328	14.663
Secondary education spline	−0.0239	−22.444	−0.0164	−15.999	−0.0155	−9.623
Higher education spline	−0.0325	−8.03	−0.0314	−8.797	−0.0688	−17.592
Age	2.75251	29.475	2.17816	22.931	3.68268	25.588
Age squared	−0.08989	−22.814	−0.06682	−16.524	−0.12529	−20.111
Age cubed	0.00123	17.958	0.00086	12.079	0.00181	16.129
Age quartic	−6.13E-06	−14.79	−4.12E-06	−9.378	−9.61E-06	−13.507
Household head's primary education spline	0.0506	2.044	0.0469	2.001	0.1448	3.308
Household head's secondary education spline	0.0054	0.217	0.0068	0.29	−0.0471	−1.083
Household head's higher education spline	−0.0048	−6.545	−0.0062	−9.174	−0.0077	−8.521
Wage worker household head	0.1625	3.424	0.1153	2.627	0.2851	4.464
Self-employed household head	−0.7603	−16.817	−0.9299	−22.506	−0.7843	−12.143
Age of household head	−0.0660	−8.736	−0.0895	−12.207	−0.0625	−6.241
Age squared of household head	0.0006	7.826	0.0008	10.989	0.0006	5.535
Other household members' mean education	−0.00023	−0.081	−0.00059	−0.214	0.00428	1.068
Other household members' mean education squared	−0.00002	−0.935	−0.00003	−1.469	−0.00006	−2.457
Other household members' mean age	−0.07876	−7.265	−0.05666	−5.294	−0.07109	−4.847
Other household members' mean age squared	0.00083	4.933	0.00043	2.62	0.00057	2.692
Dependency ratio	−1.2429	−9.202	−1.2657	−9.436	−1.2411	−6.652
Number of people in household	0.0100	1.706	0.0104	1.762	−0.0077	−0.804
Percentage of members who are female	−0.2789	−3.348	−0.3057	−3.922	−0.0820	−0.751
Rural	−0.3841	−11.922	−0.3295	−10.78	−0.2632	−5.875
Constant	−23.9567	−30.015	−19.3282	−23.764	−33.5582	−27.788

(Continued on the following page)

Table 7.5 (Continued)

Self-employed worker	1984 Coefficient	1984 z value	1989 Coefficient	1989 z value	1997 Coefficient	1997 z value
Primary education spline	0.0201	10.738	0.0204	11.339	0.0293	9.957
Secondary education spline	−0.0302	−17.497	−0.0207	−13.671	−0.0179	−7.706
Higher education spline	−0.0687	−5.921	−0.0598	−7.539	−0.0717	−8.789
Age	2.54996	19.639	1.91709	17.629	2.92895	16.84
Age squared	−0.07722	−15.453	−0.05372	−12.849	−0.08694	−13.245
Age cubed	0.00099	12.4	0.00063	9.463	0.00108	10.472
Age quartic	−4.61E-06	−10.35	−2.67E-06	−7.282	−4.84E-06	−8.497
Household head's primary education spline	−0.0570	−1.379	0.0649	2.012	−0.0300	−0.409
Household head's secondary education spline	0.0550	1.308	−0.0315	−0.963	0.0908	1.234
Household head's higher education spline	−0.0038	−2.707	−0.0079	−6.428	−0.0045	−2.767
Wage worker household head	−0.8832	−10.61	−0.8465	−11.366	−0.7113	−6.497
Self-employed household head	−0.5235	−7.951	−0.5649	−9.792	−0.4950	−5.442
Age of household head	−0.0820	−6.87	−0.0849	−7.542	−0.0275	−1.689
Age squared of household head	0.0008	6.713	0.0008	7.622	0.0003	2.304
Other household members' mean education	−0.00825	−1.874	−0.01007	−2.53	−0.00808	−1.362
Other household members' mean education squared	−0.00001	−0.334	0.00004	1.192	−0.00001	−0.344
Other household members' mean age	−0.08399	−5.505	−0.08254	−5.717	−0.08332	−3.923
Other household members' mean age squared	0.00091	4.46	0.00078	3.947	0.00061	2.18
Dependency ratio	−1.0785	−4.679	−0.7329	−3.463	−1.2544	−3.882
Number of people in household	0.0356	4.264	0.0114	1.386	−0.0031	−0.215
Percentage of members who are female	−0.2687	−1.951	−0.2391	−1.979	−0.1369	−0.776
Rural	−0.0521	−0.975	0.0808	1.663	0.1826	2.551
Constant	−24.6899	−20.094	−19.0942	−18.229	−31.4272	−18.593
N	30,125		32,968		19,490	
Log likelihood	−19,951.4		−23,187.6		−11,519.0	
Pseudo R^2	0.2747		0.2503		0.3348	

Source: Authors' calculations.

236

Table 7.6 Occupational-Position Equations for Female Family Members Who Are Not Heads of Household

Wage employee	1984 Coefficient	1984 z value	1989 Coefficient	1989 z value	1997 Coefficient	1997 z value
Primary education spline	−0.0034	−5.15	−0.0004	−0.515	0.0025	2.608
Secondary education spline	0.0148	21.578	0.0177	27.184	0.0145	18.966
Higher education spline	0.0352	11.57	0.0295	12.001	0.0158	6.955
Age	1.67491	21.484	1.34996	17.853	1.79105	19.422
Age squared	−0.05940	−17.943	−0.04448	−13.924	−0.06019	−15.47
Age cubed	0.00088	14.984	0.00062	10.88	0.00085	12.306
Age quartic	−4.85E-06	−13.01	−3.24E-06	−9.053	−4.49E-06	−10.266
Household head's primary education spline	0.0336	1.855	0.0335	1.696	0.0196	0.694
Household head's secondary education spline	−0.0430	−2.397	−0.0417	−2.135	−0.0483	−1.734
Household head's higher education spline	−0.0008	−1.935	−0.0008	−2.012	−0.0005	−0.961
Wage worker household head	0.0470	1.327	−0.0060	−0.18	0.1607	3.794
Self-employed household head	−0.9105	−25.628	−0.9937	−29.633	−0.5769	−13.338
Age of household head	0.0036	0.684	−0.0100	−1.911	−0.0277	−4.492
Age squared of household head	−0.0001	−1.231	0.0001	0.949	0.0002	3.944
Other household members' mean education	0.01834	11.382	0.01828	11.258	0.03353	17.162
Other household members' mean education squared	−0.00012	−10.332	−0.00013	−11.859	−0.00022	−17.519
Other household members' mean age	0.08659	13.269	0.08062	13.131	0.09172	13.007
Other household members' mean age squared	−0.00118	−10.882	−0.00102	−10.444	−0.00111	−10.473
Dependency ratio	−0.6548	−7.317	−0.8010	−8.917	−0.7536	−7.3
Number of people in household	0.0140	3.474	0.0261	6.271	0.0231	4.156
Percentage of members who are female	0.3826	7.316	0.3845	7.796	0.3698	6.512
Rural	−0.1427	−6.725	−0.1744	−8.705	−0.2280	−9.238
Constant	−19.0756	−26.816	−16.6686	−23.933	−21.2268	−25.008

(Continued on the following page)

Table 7.6 (Continued)

Self-employed worker	1984		1989		1997	
	Coefficient	z value	Coefficient	z value	Coefficient	z value
Primary education spline	−0.0030	−3.101	−0.0035	−3.728	−0.0014	−1.071
Secondary education spline	−0.0087	−5.187	−0.0049	−3.504	0.0009	0.595
Higher education spline	−0.0168	−1.271	−0.0129	−1.395	−0.0221	−3.138
Age	0.85015	7.456	0.89822	7.694	1.36133	7.955
Age squared	−0.02173	−5.244	−0.02240	−5.351	−0.03713	−6.081
Age cubed	0.00024	3.796	0.00024	3.837	0.00044	4.769
Age quartic	−1.06E-06	−3.065	−1.06E-06	−3.094	−2.01E-06	−4.006
Household head's primary education spline	−0.0162	−0.59	−0.0037	−0.128	0.0466	1.149
Household head's secondary education spline	−0.0018	−0.064	−0.0124	−0.43	−0.0637	−1.588
Household head's higher education spline	−0.0066	−7.242	−0.0046	−5.618	−0.0038	−3.898
Wage worker household head	−0.3586	−5.653	−0.3779	−6.381	−0.1490	−1.868
Self-employed household head	−0.6048	−10.202	−0.6650	−12.062	−0.3167	−4.147
Age of household head	−0.0280	−2.918	−0.0124	−1.249	0.0018	0.132
Age squared of household head	0.0002	2.469	0.0001	1.378	0.0000	0.211
Other household members' mean education	0.01515	5.574	0.01529	5.816	0.00990	3.118
Other household members' mean education squared	−0.00011	−3.976	−0.00011	−4.82	−0.00005	−2.135
Other household members' mean age	0.01740	1.936	0.00867	0.978	0.02605	2.264
Other household members' mean age squared	0.00000	0	0.00002	0.192	−0.00024	−1.641
Dependency ratio	0.5484	3.773	0.3783	2.604	0.6152	3.407
Number of people in household	−0.0427	−5.441	−0.0363	−4.602	−0.0309	−2.708
Percentage of members who are female	0.1892	2.08	0.2735	3.173	0.2785	2.631
Rural	0.2726	6.954	0.1193	3.191	0.1100	2.397
Constant	−13.3864	−11.164	−14.7904	−11.845	−20.9209	−11.358
N	66,748		76,409		48,010	
Log likelihood	−42,365.3		−46,667.0		−31,708.8	
Pseudo R^2	0.1451		0.1603		0.1706	

Source: Authors' calculations.

briefly summarize the results variable by variable:

- Education behaves quite inconsistently. More schooling sometimes increases the likelihood of being a wage employee and sometimes lowers the likelihood. On the whole, more schooling decreases the likelihood of being a self-employed worker.
- The age quartic is consistently statistically significant for males and for female family members who are not heads of household.[11]
- On the whole, the likelihood of being a wage employee is an inverted U-shaped function of the education of other household members. The effect of others' education on the likelihood of being a self-employed worker shows no consistent pattern or sign.
- A higher dependency ratio, when statistically significant, reduces the likelihood of being a worker of either type.
- Rural residency exhibits inconsistent effects: sometimes positive, sometimes negative, sometimes insignificant.
- For the most part, the household head's education and occupational position has no statistically significant effect on the occupational position of other members of the household. However, one consistently strong relationship is found: if household heads are self-employed, the likelihood of other family members being either wage employees or self-employed workers reduces and, therefore, the likelihood of such family members being nonearners increases.
- The percentage of household members who are female exhibits no consistent relationship with occupational position.

Overall, these equations explain at most 33 percent of the variation in occupational position—more typically, about 25 percent. Because we have not done well in predicting occupational positions from the observed Zs, we expect that the changes in the λs would not explain much of the change in income distribution—a result borne out below.

Estimating the Earnings Conditional on Working in Occupational Position j

Let $\ln Y_{ij\tau}$ denote the log earnings of individual i if he or she works in sector j at time τ. Mincerian earnings functions are run separately for each sex and occupational position in each year:

$$\ln Y_{ij\tau} = \beta_{j\tau} X_{ij\tau} + \varepsilon_{ij\tau}.$$

$X_{ij\tau}$ includes, for each individual, an education spline, an age quartic, the state or territory of residence, and the occupation.[12] The estimation method is least squares weighted by survey sampling weights.

The results are reported in tables 7.7 through 7.10. In sum, given all of the past work on earnings determination in Malaysia, the

Table 7.7 Earnings Functions for Male Wage Earners

Indicator	1984		1989		1997	
	Coefficient	t-statistic	Coefficient	t-statistic	Coefficient	t-statistic
Personal characteristics						
Primary education spline	0.0389	0.0001905	0.0373	0.0001922	0.0361	0.0002724
Secondary education spline	0.0624	0.0001717	0.0623	0.0001512	0.0623	0.0001894
Higher education spline	0.2316	0.0007179	0.1841	0.0005963	0.1883	0.0006319
Age	0.28416	0.0153997	0.16584	0.0138697	0.18552	0.0210321
Age squared	−0.00642	0.0005932	−0.00203	0.0005257	−0.00388	0.0008202
Age cubed	0.00006	0.00000957	0.00000	0.00000835	0.00004	0.0000135
Age quartic	−2.36E-07	5.47E-08	1.14E-07	4.71E-08	−1.67E-07	7.93E-08
Occupation type controls[a]						
Administrative	0.6418	0.0180555	0.6344	0.0156284	0.5910	0.0159054
Clerical	−0.1411	0.013193	−0.1460	0.0116656	−0.2395	0.0136742
Sales	−0.1914	0.0151369	−0.2449	0.0135295	−0.2025	0.0160976
Service	−0.2094	0.0133601	−0.2311	0.0117256	−0.2988	0.0138895
Agricultural	−0.5126	0.013968	−0.5117	0.0124101	−0.5087	0.0157854
Transport	−0.2186	0.0122767	−0.2762	0.0107799	−0.2266	0.0117937
State and territory controls[b]						
Kedah	−0.3195	0.0131683	−0.2945	0.0120095	−0.3911	0.0146376
Kelantan	−0.3686	0.0144275	−0.3878	0.0131978	−0.5808	0.017606
Malacca	−0.1000	0.0172556	−0.1212	0.0155574	−0.1521	0.0183993
Negeri Sembilan	−0.0254	0.0150409	−0.0507	0.0148235	−0.0977	0.0177568
Pahang	−0.0224	0.0140924	−0.0482	0.0127214	−0.1961	0.0161556

Penang	−0.1685	0.0124166	−0.1309	0.0113615	−0.1667	0.0141379
Perak	−0.0861	0.011218	−0.1569	0.0102817	−0.1796	0.0128203
Perlis	−0.2334	0.0269607	−0.2267	0.0252113	−0.3898	0.0356908
Selangor	0.0687	0.0104173	0.0028	0.0091038	−0.0062	0.0109967
Terengganu	−0.2344	0.0158872	−0.2484	0.0151346	−0.4515	0.0179932
Sabah	0.1780	0.0124087	0.0873	0.0110471	−0.3425	0.0134478
Sarawak	0.1458	0.0128018	0.0996	0.010382	−0.1750	0.0136306
Kuala Lumpur Federal Territory	0.0469	0.0116526	0.0147	0.0107884	0.0968	0.0133574
Labuan Federal Territory	0.3142	0.0408939	0.2288	0.0416833	−0.2285	0.0510746
Rural	−0.1195	0.0060626	−0.0816	0.0054616	−0.1360	0.0069082
Constant	4.8462	0.1421178	5.9796	0.1305984	6.5495	0.1926577
N	42,212		43,462		31,037	
R^2	0.4954		0.5268		0.5269	

a. Professional is the omitted category for type of occupation dummy variables. Agricultural is the omitted category for industry dummy variables.

b. Johor is the omitted category for state dummy variables.

Source: Authors' calculations.

Table 7.8 Earnings Functions for Female Wage Earners

Indicator	1984		1989		1997	
	Coefficient	t-statistic	Coefficient	t-statistic	Coefficient	t-statistic
Personal characteristics						
Primary education spline	0.0502	0.0003053	0.0466	0.000272	0.0311	0.0003927
Secondary education spline	0.0704	0.0003449	0.0682	0.0002629	0.0756	0.0003156
Higher education spline	0.2326	0.0011348	0.2123	0.0008219	0.2086	0.0008438
Age	0.19257	0.0244384	0.00263	0.0238335	0.0973	0.0268184
Age squared	−0.00413	0.0009452	0.00319	0.0009475	−0.00127	0.0010287
Age cubed	0.00003	0.0000152	−0.00008	0.0000158	0.00000	0.0000165
Age quartic	−7.19E-08	8.61E-08	5.33E-07	9.37E-08	4.39E-08	9.36E-08
Occupation type controls[a]						
Administrative	0.5346	0.0521472	0.5470	0.0376302	0.5078	0.0273037
Clerical	−0.0917	0.0177607	−0.0719	0.0139077	0.0168	0.0154189
Sales	−0.3621	0.0254899	−0.3847	0.0196092	−0.1791	0.0218852
Service	−0.4284	0.0217624	−0.4186	0.0166567	−0.3273	0.0194526
Agricultural	−0.5801	0.023592	−0.5453	0.0194627	−0.5893	0.028392
Transport	−0.4067	0.0203835	−0.3991	0.0155248	−0.1772	0.0173669
State and territory controls[b]						
Kedah	−0.3575	0.0217858	−0.3202	0.0184167	−0.3000	0.0215843
Kelantan	−0.3967	0.0282192	−0.3777	0.0214635	−0.5953	0.0274921
Malacca	0.0426	0.0277971	−0.0954	0.0215031	−0.0862	0.0263248
Negeri Sembilan	0.0526	0.0242397	−0.0309	0.0214229	−0.0878	0.0257788

Pahang	−0.0408	0.0246622	−0.1224	0.0204205	−0.2123	0.0267125
Penang	−0.0262	0.0199427	0.0375	0.0156935	−0.1145	0.0194869
Perak	−0.1108	0.0185593	−0.2310	0.0152549	−0.1606	0.0191274
Perlis	−0.3763	0.056986	−0.3087	0.0422209	−0.4496	0.0531267
Selangor	0.1340	0.0169423	0.0666	0.0131163	0.0458	0.0160888
Terengganu	−0.3847	0.032457	−0.5049	0.0270794	−0.5387	0.0302347
Sabah	0.1897	0.0231272	0.0788	0.0188336	−0.2162	0.021585
Sarawak	0.0115	0.0241385	−0.0823	0.0171885	−0.2471	0.0215064
Kuala Lumpur Federal Territory	0.1267	0.0187183	0.0483	0.0155756	0.1510	0.018729
Labuan Federal Territory	0.3133	0.0948176	0.0827	0.0842317	−0.1052	0.0972086
Rural	−0.0968	0.010786	−0.0787	0.0082683	−0.1307	0.0106025
Constant	5.7326	0.2234147	7.5171	0.2140876	7.1942	0.2490198
N	19,518		21,361		16,458	
R^2	0.4566		0.5206		0.4838	

a. Professional is the omitted category for type of occupation dummy variables. Agricultural is the omitted category for industry dummy variables.
b. Johor is the omitted category for state dummy variables.
Source: Authors' calculations.

Table 7.9 Earnings Functions for Male Self-Employed Workers

Indicator	1984		1989		1997	
	Coefficient	t-statistic	Coefficient	t-statistic	Coefficient	t-statistic
Personal characteristics						
Primary education spline	0.0457	0.0003598	0.0382	0.0002983	0.0302	0.0004276
Secondary education spline	0.0345	0.0005819	0.0081	0.000418	0.0331	0.00049
Higher education spline	0.3080	0.0040602	0.2716	0.0028335	0.2269	0.0023625
Age	0.22692	0.0365089	0.18452	0.0298886	0.08582	0.0417171
Age squared	-0.00442	0.0012065	-0.00312	0.0010029	-0.00010	0.0013409
Age cubed	0.00003	0.0000168	0.00001	0.0000142	-0.00003	0.0000183
Age quartic	-5.23E-03	8.43E-08	3.34E-08	7.22E-08	1.97E-07	8.94E-08
Occupation type controls[a]						
Administrative	0.7193	0.0755071	0.5252	0.058264	0.6405	0.0609656
Clerical	0.1450	0.1655865	-0.1977	0.1536284	-0.2662	0.1832357
Sales	0.2060	0.0685357	0.1295	0.0514717	0.1104	0.0561268
Service	0.2399	0.0740804	0.2028	0.0574954	0.2022	0.0623777
Agricultural	-0.5708	0.0685861	-0.6016	0.0514621	-0.6660	0.0574319
Transport	-0.0530	0.0698278	-0.1305	0.0527441	-0.1289	0.0578391
State and territory controls[b]						
Kedah	-0.5506	0.0301611	-0.4238	0.0243937	-0.4177	0.031252
Kelantan	-0.7094	0.0324645	-0.5582	0.0256289	-0.8000	0.032281

	Coefficient	SE	Coefficient	SE	Coefficient	SE
Malacca	−0.3005	0.0501995	−0.3475	0.0410869	−0.3181	0.0542258
Negeri Sembilan	−0.0753	0.043619	−0.0391	0.0327049	−0.1309	0.0415467
Pahang	0.1768	0.0333628	0.1363	0.0252698	−0.1363	0.0339798
Penang	−0.4545	0.0356298	−0.3051	0.0304199	−0.2203	0.0403336
Perak	−0.3209	0.028331	−0.3400	0.0232337	−0.1953	0.0309794
Perlis	−0.6057	0.0577062	−0.3310	0.0498519	−0.3992	0.0631633
Selangor	−0.1017	0.0335816	−0.1466	0.0264077	−0.1205	0.0323531
Terengganu	−0.5005	0.0370056	−0.5494	0.0290478	−0.7039	0.0406846
Sabah	−0.1784	0.034745	−0.2077	0.0255397	−0.4927	0.0328248
Sarawak	−0.3089	0.0302265	−0.1176	0.0220151	−0.3287	0.0311621
Kuala Lumpur Federal Territory	0.0784	0.0401453	−0.0700	0.0359767	0.0114	0.0413027
Labuan Federal Territory	0.1450	0.175511	−0.0366	0.1528962	−0.1279	0.1469839
Rural	−0.1983	0.018096	−0.1309	0.0147298	−0.1871	0.0190435
Constant	5.5721	0.3987639	6.1301	0.3205579	7.6345	0.4664547
N	14,760		18,153		10,296	
R^2	0.4024		0.3591		0.4774	

a. Professional is the omitted category for type of occupation dummy variables. Agricultural is the omitted category for industry dummy variables.
b. Johor is the omitted category for state dummy variables.
Source: Authors' calculations.

245

Table 7.10 Earnings Functions for Female Self-Employed Workers

Indicator	1984 Coefficient	1984 t-statistic	1989 Coefficient	1989 t-statistic	1997 Coefficient	1997 t-statistic
Personal characteristics						
Primary education spline	0.0271	0.0007504	0.0261	0.0006077	0.0369	0.0008634
Secondary education spline	0.0429	0.001525	0.0258	0.0010613	0.0360	0.0010827
Higher education spline	0.4955	0.0135178	0.5051	0.0081062	0.4509	0.006585
Age	−0.06235	0.0820761	−0.12307	0.0737428	−0.13394	0.0897577
Age squared	0.00385	0.0027932	0.00550	0.0024562	0.00543	0.0028281
Age cubed	−0.00007	0.0000402	−0.00009	0.0000347	−0.00008	0.0000377
Age quartic	3.85E-07	2.07E-07	4.38E-07	0.000000176	3.61E-07	0.00000018
Occupation type controls[a]						
Administrative	0.6477	0.253743	0.9640	0.2015068	1.3937	0.1734257
Clerical	0.5204	0.8695833	0.3858	0.4428975	−0.6466	0.479348
Sales	0.5587	0.1116119	0.6119	0.0878289	0.3323	0.1010374
Service	0.3763	0.114728	0.4224	0.0913222	−0.2267	0.1028117
Agricultural	−0.3495	0.1099618	−0.1088	0.0884907	−0.4034	0.1043874
Transport	−0.3703	0.1117319	−0.1466	0.0888045	−0.4564	0.1030985
State and territory controls[b]						
Kedah	−0.3476	0.0680422	−0.2078	0.0528805	−0.2666	0.0760583
Kelantan	−0.5907	0.058756	−0.3795	0.049004	−0.4668	0.0657163
Malacca	−0.1279	0.0976855	−0.2759	0.0894252	0.0038	0.1140702
Negeri Sembilan	0.1023	0.0909417	0.1481	0.0684099	−0.0169	0.0952677

Pahang	0.0898	0.0796982	0.1735	0.0625389	0.0013	0.0890748
Penang	−0.3133	0.0850171	0.0225	0.0771066	−0.1303	0.0863604
Perak	−0.4626	0.0588165	−0.2652	0.049564	−0.1247	0.0708262
Perlis	−0.7558	0.1743062	−0.1521	0.1119044	−0.1429	0.15133
Selangor	0.0248	0.0774129	0.1454	0.0592302	−0.0927	0.0716125
Terengganu	−0.4968	0.0710387	−0.3404	0.0602639	−0.4435	0.0898252
Sabah	−0.0934	0.0739025	0.1433	0.0620403	−0.1166	0.0797324
Sarawak	−0.2545	0.064145	−0.0310	0.0502364	−0.1980	0.0715687
Kuala Lumpur Federal Territory	0.1785	0.0984459	0.0617	0.0787426	0.2634	0.0877873
Labuan Federal Territory	0.0449	0.4972773	0.3628	0.3519849	−0.0330	0.5882578
Rural	−0.2921	0.0351709	−0.2845	0.029582	−0.2148	0.0381521
Constant	8.0816	0.8626305	8.6192	0.7928124	9.3229	1.02006
N	4,740		5,238		3,361	
R^2	0.2624		0.253		0.2743	

a. Professional is the omitted category for type of occupation dummy variables. Agricultural is the omitted category for industry dummy variables.
b. Johor is the omitted category for state dummy variables.
Source: Authors' calculations.

following findings are hardly surprising, other things being equal:

- Education raises earnings.
- The quartic polynomial in age is statistically significant.
- Workers in administrative jobs earn more than professionals, while those in other occupations earn less than professionals.
- Nonagricultural workers earn more than agricultural workers.
- Workers in the Kuala Lumpur Federal Territory and in Johor earn more than workers in other states.

The overall fit of these models is quite good. For male and female wage earners, half or more of the variance in log earnings is explained by these variables. For self-employed workers the fit is poorer, which is not surprising given the variability in work hours and in complementary resources among self-employed workers.

Simulating the Role of Various Factors in Explaining the Changing Per Capita Household Income Distribution in Malaysia

The next step is to proceed from estimation to simulation.

Description of the Simulations

The simulations proceed from a change in labor earnings of individuals, to a change in the income of the household, to a change in the overall household income distribution. In the Malaysian data, labor earnings from wage employment or self-employment are assigned to given individuals. The simulations change these amounts. Any other income received by the individual, such as transfer income, is assumed to be invariant with respect to any of the simulated changes and is not modeled.

More specifically, the income of household h in a reference year t is the sum of the incomes of each of the household members:

(7.1) $$Y_{ht} = \Sigma_{i\varepsilon h} Y_{it}.$$

Household member i is found in occupational position j (wage employment, self-employment, or nonearner) according to the logit equations

(7.2) $\text{Prob}(i = \text{self-employed worker})\tau = \Lambda(\lambda_{j=1\tau} Z_{ij\tau} + \eta_{ij\tau})$

and

$$\text{Prob}(i = \text{wage employee})\tau = \Lambda(\lambda_{j=2\tau} Z_{ij\tau} + \eta_{ij\tau}).$$

Third, the earnings of individual i in occupational position j at time t is a function of a set of income determinants X:

$$(7.3) \qquad \ln Y_{ijt} = \beta_{jt} X_{ijt} + \varepsilon_{ijt}.$$

Five simulations are performed by substituting some of the values for a comparison year t' into equations 7.1 to 7.3 in place of the base year (t) values.

SIMULATION 1: THE EFFECT OF CHANGING THE WHOLE REWARD STRUCTURE

For the reward structure as a whole, change all βs, including the constant, from their year t values to their year t' values:

$$\ln Y_{ijt}^{i} = \beta_{jt'} X_{ijt} + \varepsilon_{ijt}.$$

Everybody keeps the same occupational category; only the rewards within the category are changed. The residual ε_{ijt} is found by estimating the original wage equation and comparing its prediction with the observed wage. Our interpretation is that the residual represents unobserved determinants of labor income. Consistent with this interpretation, we assign a price to these characteristics, which is the variance of the residuals. So whenever we change β_{jt} to $\beta_{jt'}$, we also multiply the residuals by the ratio of their variances in t and t'.

SIMULATION 2: THE EFFECT OF CHANGING THE WHOLE OCCUPATIONAL-POSITION STRUCTURE

In the occupational-position equation, change all λs from their year t values to their year t' values:

$$\text{Prob}(i = \text{self-employed worker})_{t}^{ii} = \Lambda(\lambda_{j=1t'} Z_{ijt} + \eta_{ijt})$$

$$\text{Prob}(i = \text{wage employee})_{t}^{ii} = \Lambda(\lambda_{j=2t'} Z_{ijt} + \eta_{ijt}).$$

The residuals (the η_{ijt}) cannot be uniquely identified from the original estimating equation (equation 7.2), so they must be assigned. The residuals in the occupational-position equation are not as easy to determine as the residuals in the earnings equation. Where the former are uniquely identified by the difference between observed and predicted earnings, the latter must be drawn from an inverse hyperbolic secant, which is the distribution consistent with the multinomial logit occupational-position equation. However, not just any random draw is acceptable, as residuals must be consistent with observed choices. Individual i's choice obeys the following rules:

• If $\lambda_{j=1t'} Z_{ijt} + \eta_{ijt} > \lambda_{j=2t'} Z_{ijt} + \eta_{ijt}$ and $\lambda_{j=1t'} Z_{ijt} + \eta_{ijt} > 0$, then individual i is a self-employed worker.

- If $\lambda_{j=2t'} Z_{ijt} + \eta_{ijt} > \lambda_{j=1t'} Z_{ijt} + \eta_{ijt}$ and $\lambda_{j=2t'} Z_{ijt} + \eta_{ijt} > 0$, then individual i is a wage earner.
- If both $\lambda_{j=2t'} Z_{ijt} + \eta_{ijt} < 0$ and $\lambda_{j=1t'} Z_{ijt} + \eta_{ijt} < 0$, then individual i is either inactive or an unpaid family worker.

Note that only the λs change in these expressions. The Zs, and more significantly, the η_{ijt} residuals, remain the same. Hence, the residual drawn must be coherent with the three conditions above to be in accordance with the occupational choice observed. An easy way to ensure this coherence is to draw the residuals randomly from the inverse hyperbolic secant and to check whether they are coherent with observed Zs and choices and estimated λ. For those individuals whose drawn residuals are incoherent, we then redraw them and check again, keeping the drawn residuals for those individuals whose Zs, λs, and ηs were coherent with their observed choices. We keep redrawing previously incoherent residuals until no more individuals are left with incoherent Zs, λs, and ηs. Generally, a few dozen draws are necessary.

One final comment on individuals observed in inactivity but simulated as wage earners or self-employed workers: because these individuals were observed in inactivity, they have no wage residual associated with them that can be used in the construction of their counterfactual earnings. In this case, new residuals are drawn from normal distributions with zero mean variance equal to the observed variance of the observed residuals of wage earners or self-employed workers.

SIMULATION 3: THE EFFECT OF CHANGING THE WHOLE
POPULATION STRUCTURE

For the population structure as a whole, the third simulation changes all Xs and all Zs from their year t values to their year t' values:

$$\text{Prob}(i = \text{self-employed worker})^{iii} = \Lambda(\lambda_{j=1t} Z_{ijt'} + \eta_{ijt'})$$
$$\text{Prob}(i = \text{wage employee})^{iii} = \Lambda(\lambda_{j=2t} Z_{ijt'} + \eta_{ijt'})$$
$$\ln Y_{ijt}^{iii} = \beta_{jt} X_{ijt'} + \varepsilon_{ijt'}.$$

Note that residuals and other income are considered part of X and Z. This third simulation puts some people into new occupational categories, and it changes the incomes within occupational categories for others.

SIMULATION 4: THE EFFECT OF A CHANGE IN THE PRICE OF
EDUCATION ALONE

For the price effect of education alone, the question is what would happen if the gain in income for an extra year of education were to be changed from the year t to the year t' values, while keeping all other βs constant. This simulation changes only the coefficients on the education spline, using base year values for the coefficients on the other Xs and adjusting the constant so that the regression line rotates through the mean:

$$\ln Y_{ijt}^{iv} = \beta_{ed,ijt'}\, X_{ed,ijt} + \beta_{non\text{-}ed,ijt}\, X_{non\text{-}ed,ijt} + \varepsilon_{ijt}.$$

By construction, this simulation has no effect on levels, so only its effect on inequality will be looked at.

SIMULATION 5: THE EFFECT OF A CHANGE IN THE QUANTITY OF EDUCATION ALONE

For the population effect of education alone, the individual at the kth position in the education distribution for that gender and age category in year t is assigned the number of years of education at that position in t', holding all other Xs and the Zs constant:

$$\ln Y_{ijt}^{v} = \beta_{ed,ijt}\, X_{ed,ijt'} + \beta_{non\text{-}ed,ijt}\, X_{non\text{-}ed,ijt} + \varepsilon_{ijt}.$$

This operation is a rank-preserving transformation of the quantity of education each individual possesses. Earnings within an occupational category are then reestimated with the new, generally higher, years of education substituted in place of the original ones.[13]

Assessing the Effects

The relative effects of the five simulations on the location and inequality of the Malaysian income distribution are assessed both parametrically and nonparametrically. For location, quantile curves are compared as well as specific statistics—the mean income and the poverty rate. For inequality, comparisons are made of Lorenz curves and of two inequality measures—the Gini coefficient and the Theil index.

We look first at the 1984–89 period and then at the 1989–97 period. For each period, there are two sets of simulations: the A set takes the earlier year as t and the later year as t', whereas the B set does the reverse.

A criterion is needed for deciding when one effect is more important than another. We shall say that an explanatory factor contributes more to the increase (or decrease) in the dependent variable (location as measured by quantile functions, means, and poverty headcounts; inequality as measured by Lorenz curves, Gini coefficients, and Theil indexes), the more positive (or more negative) the change in the explanatory factor. In cases where all simulations go part of the way toward explaining an observed change, the ordering

rule is simple: the larger the effect, the more important the explanatory factor. However, some simulated effects may be larger than the
observed change, and others may be negative. In these cases, the
preceding ranking criterion would be that the most important
explanatory factor is the one that goes furthest in the same direction
as the observed change, even to the point of overshooting.

Results for the 1984–89 Period

Focusing first on the location of the income distribution, we find, as
noted earlier, that per capita incomes grew by only half a percent a
year between 1984 and 1989. Accordingly, the plots of the actual
1984 and 1989 distributions barely diverge, and the simulation
graphs in levels can hardly be distinguished from the actual distributions (figures 7.5 and 7.6). The changes in the actual quantile
function between 1984 and 1989, depicted in figures 7.7 and 7.8,
are no more informative: no simulated effect lies everywhere
between the zero line and the plus curve, nor does any simulated
effect always lie above the actual change. Thus, no one factor can be
judged to be more important nonparametrically than any other in
explaining locational changes between 1984 and 1989. Accordingly, we turn our attention to the two location indices: the mean
and the poverty headcount.

The results for the two indices are presented in tables 7.11 and
7.12. We see that the modest increase in the mean income is well
accounted for by the increase in mean education (simulation 5).
Indeed, at this time, the population was becoming better educated
(table 7.13). According to our estimates, this increase in mean education accounted for 86 to 87 percent of the increase in mean
income. The changes in the whole population structure, including
not only years of education but all other factors as well, accounted
for 145 to 251 percent of the increase in the mean. In other words,
the actual mean did not increase by as much as the changing population structure would have implied, because other factors were
operating to drive the mean downward. The other simulated
changes, by contrast, exhibited either small effects (simulation 1) or
unstable effects (simulations 2 and 3) on the mean. As for the change
in the poverty rate, the change in the population structure accounts
almost exactly for the change (100 to 104 percent). By contrast, the
other factors (the changing reward structure and the changing occupational structure) perform poorly.

We turn now to the inequality aspect of the changing income
distribution. Malaysia experienced an unambiguous decrease in
inequality from 1984 to 1989, as measured by the Lorenz curves

Figure 7.5 Household Quantile Curves: 1984 Baseline
(household per capita monthly income in constant 1997 ringgit)

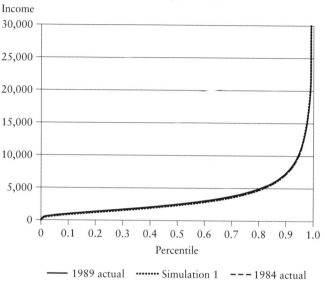

A. 1989 βs; 1984 Xs

—— 1989 actual   ⋯⋯ Simulation 1   − − − 1984 actual

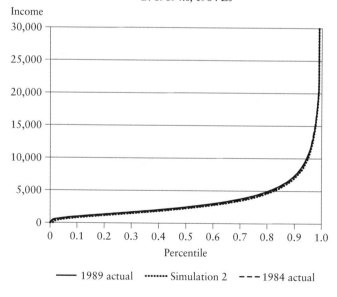

B. 1989 λs; 1984 Zs

—— 1989 actual   ⋯⋯ Simulation 2   − − − 1984 actual

(*Continued on the following page*)

Figure 7.5 (Continued)

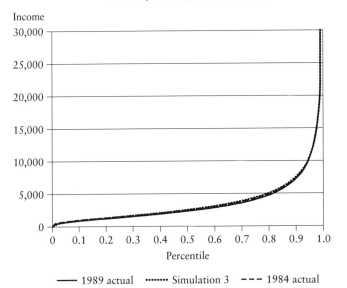

C. 1984 βs and λs; 1989 Xs and Zs

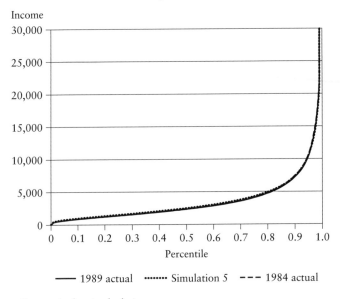

D. 1989 education quantities; 1984 other Xs and βs

Source: Authors' calculations.

Figure 7.6 Household Quantile Curves: 1989 Baseline
(household per capita monthly income in constant 1997 ringgit)

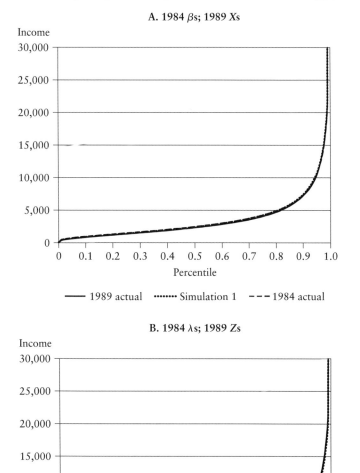

A. 1984 βs; 1989 Xs

—— 1989 actual   •••••• Simulation 1   – – – 1984 actual

B. 1984 λs; 1989 Zs

—— 1989 actual   •••••• Simulation 2   – – – 1984 actual

(Continued on the following page)

Figure 7.6 (Continued)

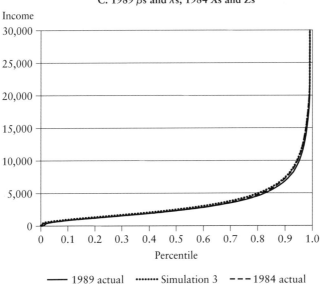

C. 1989 βs and λs; 1984 Xs and Zs

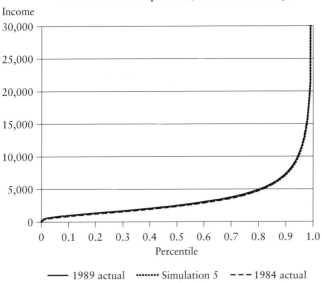

D. 1984 education quantities; 1989 other Xs and βs

Source: Authors' calculations.

Figure 7.7 Quantile Curves: Simulated Values Minus 1984
Actual Values

(household per capita monthly income in constant 1997 ringgit)

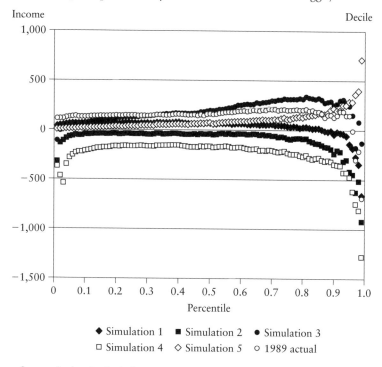

♦ Simulation 1   ■ Simulation 2   ● Simulation 3
□ Simulation 4   ◇ Simulation 5   ○ 1989 actual

Source: Authors' calculations.

of per capita household income (panels B of figures 7.3 and 7.4).
To gauge the relative importance of these five factors, we plotted
the differences between the actual Lorenz curve and each of the
simulated ones in figures 7.9 and 7.10.[14] We see that simulations 1
and 3 fit the actual change most closely, followed by simulations 2
and 5, and lastly by simulation 4. For the B set of simulations, simulations 1 and 3 also come the closest. Thus, in both sets of simulations, the falling inequality in the 1984–89 period is best accounted
for by changes in the reward structure and in the population structure, of which a key component was the falling returns to education,
particularly higher education (see data for the higher education
spline" in tables 7.7 to 7.10).

A word of explanation is also in order regarding simulation 4,
the results of which appear somewhat paradoxical. During the
1984–89 period, the estimated coefficients of the wage equations
shown in tables 7.6 to 7.10 indicate that the earnings education

Figure 7.8 Quantile Curves: Simulated Values Minus
1989 Actual Values

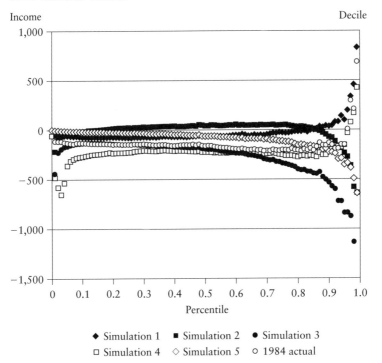

Source: Authors' calculations.

profile became less steep for all gender and occupation categories. In
view of this development, why does substituting the 1989 prices of
education into the 1984 distribution increase inequality, as seen
both by Gini and Theil summary measures and in terms of Lorenz
dominance?

The answer, essentially, is the aggregation of the four gender and
occupational-position groups into families and then into an overall
distribution. We examined the Theil and Gini coefficients for each
of the four groups separately—wage-earning men, wage-earning
women, self-employed men, and self-employed women. The summary measures are shown in table 7.14. As expected from the regression coefficients, the earnings inequality of simulation 4 within each
one of these groups was less than that observed in the original data.
Because the average income of each group had been adjusted to
remain constant, the increase in inequality could not be attributed
to inequality between the groups. This finding can be seen by noting
that the observed Theil coefficient for the economically active

Table 7.11 Distribution of Per Capita Household Income, Substituting 1989 Values into 1984 Distribution

| | *Location* | | | *Inequality* | |
| | | | | | |
Indicator	*Mean*	*Poverty headcount (percent)*		*Gini*	*Theil*
Actual value, 1984	3,637.76	37.9		0.4856	0.4753
Actual value, 1989	3,752.74	33.7		0.4610	0.4161
Actual change (as a percentage of total change)	3.2	−11.1		−5.1	−12.5
Simulated change (absolute value)					
Simulation 1	3,650.23	35.9		0.4710	0.4415
Simulation 2	3,529.35	38.9		0.4871	0.4761
Simulation 3	3,804.83	33.7		0.4708	0.4408
Simulation 4	—	—		0.5078	0.5152
Simulation 5	3,738.16	36.4		0.4851	0.4731
Simulated change (as a percentage of total change)					
Simulation 1	10.8	46.6		59.5	57.1
Simulation 2	−94.3	−23.7		−6.0	−1.4
Simulation 3	145.3	100.1		60.0	58.2
Simulation 4	—	—		−90.3	−67.4
Simulation 5	87.3	35.2		2.2	3.7

—Not available.
Source: Authors' calculations.

Table 7.12 Distribution of Per Capita Household Income, Substituting 1984 Values into 1989 Distribution

Indicator	Location		Inequality	
	Mean	Poverty headcount (percent)	Gini	Theil
Actual value, 1989	3,752.74	33.7	0.4610	0.4161
Actual value, 1984	3,637.76	37.9	0.4856	0.4753
Actual change (as a percentage of total change)	−3.1	12.5	5.3	14.2
Simulated change (absolute value)				
Simulation 1	3,740.57	35.5	0.4753	0.4445
Simulation 2	3,739.95	32.8	0.4577	0.4183
Simulation 3	3,463.74	38.1	0.4725	0.4429
Simulation 4	—	—	0.5024	0.5007
Simulation 5	3,654.20	34.8	0.4593	0.4138
Simulated change (as a percentage of total change)				
Simulation 1	10.6	44.1	58.2	48.0
Simulation 2	11.1	−20.0	−13.2	3.7
Simulation 3	251.3	104.3	46.9	45.3
Simulation 4	—	—	168.2	142.8
Simulation 5	85.7	26.6	−7.0	−3.8

—Not available.
Source: Authors' calculations.

Table 7.13 Rising Educational Attainments in Malaysia, 1984–97

(percentage of population age 14 and above)

Indicator	1984	1989	1997
School level			
Primary	35.96	33.22	26.78
Junior high	21.18	22.92	21.36
Senior high	17.87	20.61	28.74
University	4.84	6.21	11.19
Religious education only	20.15	17.94	11.93
Total	100	100	100
Average years of schooling, excluding religious education			
Men	7.07	7.50	8.61
Women	5.60	6.25	7.60
All	6.32	6.86	8.10
Average years of schooling including religious education			
Men	8.03	8.35	9.27
Women	7.80	8.20	9.12
All	7.92	8.28	9.20

Source: Milanovic (1999).

population was 0.483 in 1984, whereas when 1989 education prices are substituted in, it falls to 0.460.

One possibility is that, once nonlabor income was added in, some correlation between simulation 4 losers and winners and nonlabor income would lead to the results observed, but this possibility proves not to be the case. Inclusion of nonlabor income, as shown in table 7.13, does not change the results: simulation 4 results still decrease the 1984 level of inequality. The Theil index for the economically active population falls from 0.487 to 0.467.

So if Theil indices fall for the economically active population when education prices are substituted into the 1984 distribution, then why do they rise for per capita family income? The reason is that, when individuals are aggregated into families, the correlation between simulation losers and winners (remember that the simulation changes returns to only one characteristic, education) and pairing and family size leads to increased family income inequality per capita.

Results for the 1989–97 Period

Between 1989 and 1997, the two principal distributional facts are (a) that the economy became richer at all centiles of the income

Figure 7.9 Lorenz Curves: Simulated Values Minus 1984
Actual Values

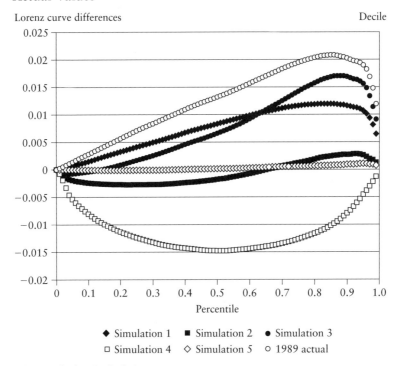

Source: Authors' calculations.

distribution (see panels A of figures 7.1 and 7.2) and (b) that the
income distribution became unambiguously more unequal (see
panels A of figures 7.3 and 7.4). Analysis of the same five simulations as in the earlier period suggests the following explanations.

First, as regards the location of the income distribution, the two
simulations that perform the best are simulation 3 (changing the
whole population structure) and simulation 1 (changing the whole
reward structure). We can see this outcome in three ways: (a) by
comparing the several panels of figures 7.11 and 7.12; (b) by comparing the five simulated quantile differences with the actual quantile difference (figures 7.13 and 7.14); and (c) by comparing the five
simulated changes in mean and poverty headcount ratio to the actual
changes (tables 7.15 and 7.16). In this period, the educational level
of the population was increasing—even more so than in the earlier
period (table 7.13)—but these increased educational attainments
account for only a modest amount of the total change.

If not education, then what explains the large increases in average
income from 1989 to 1997? In part, a generalized increase in base

Figure 7.10 Lorenz Curves: Simulated Values Minus 1989
Actual Values

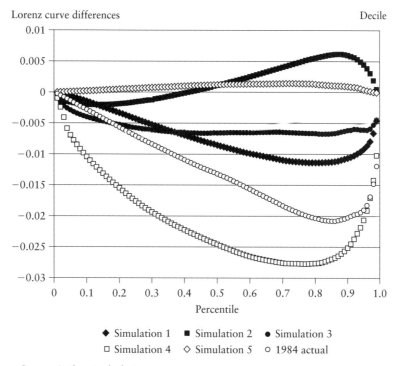

Source: Authors' calculations.

income: the constant in the wage equation increases from 1989 to
1997 for all occupational categories, except wage-earning women.
For wage-earning men and self-employed women, who together
account for about 55 percent of the population with positive income,
the increase in the constant is around 0.5 logarithmic units, meaning
an increase in ringgit of about 75 percent. For self-employed men
(about 15 percent of those with positive incomes), the log change is
1.5, leading to an increase in ringgit by a factor of almost 3.

Another explanation is that there is one dimension of occupational determination that we did not model: the decrease in agricultural occupation. For all years and all modeled occupational
categories, there is a very strong negative premium associated with
having an agricultural occupation. Other things being equal, working in agriculture reduces earnings by about 60 percent. From 1984
to 1989, the percentage of employed individuals in agriculture
remained stable at 32 percent, but from 1989 to 1997, it fell by
almost half to 17 percent. This change alone may have increased
average incomes by about 10 percent.

Table 7.14 Actual and Simulated Inequality for Disaggregated Gender and Occupational-Position Groups

Theil T for wage income by sex and activity category

Indicator	Wage-earning men	Wage-earning women	Self-employed men	Self-employed women	All groups
Observed, 1984	0.369	0.308	0.710	0.645	0.483
1989 βs, 1984 others	0.348	0.297	0.680	0.638	0.460
Observed, 1989	0.351	0.295	0.472	0.525	0.409
1984 βs, 1989 others	0.373	0.306	0.508	0.537	0.433

Gini coefficient for wage income by sex and activity category

Indicator	Wage-earning men	Wage-earning women	Self-employed men	Self-employed women
Observed, 1984	0.423	0.414	0.565	0.568
1989 βs, 1984 others	0.414	0.408	0.555	0.565
Observed, 1989	0.415	0.407	0.485	0.520
1984 βs, 1989 others	0.425	0.414	0.499	0.524

Theil T for all income (wage income + other income)

Indicator	Wage-earning men	Wage-earning women	Self-employed men	Self-employed women	All groups
Observed, 1984	0.388	0.311	0.630	0.550	0.487
1989 βs, 1984 others	0.370	0.301	0.603	0.545	0.467
Observed 1989	0.362	0.300	0.412	0.458	0.405
1984 βs, 1989 others	0.381	0.310	0.442	0.466	0.427

Gini coefficient for all income (wage income + other income)

Indicator	Wage-earning men	Wage-earning women	Self-employed men	Self-employed women
Observed, 1984	0.432	0.415	0.532	0.530
1989 βs, 1984 others	0.424	0.409	0.523	0.528
Observed 1989	0.422	0.409	0.451	0.491
1984 βs, 1989 others	0.431	0.415	0.463	0.494

Source: Authors' calculations.

Figure 7.11 Household Quantile Curves: 1989 Baseline

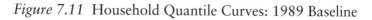

A. 1997 βs; 1989 Xs

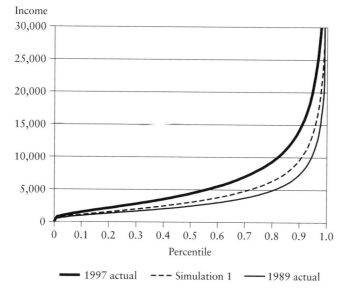

B. 1997 λs; 1989 Zs

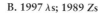

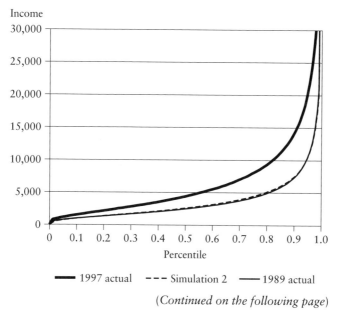

(*Continued on the following page*)

Figure 7.11 (*Continued*)

C. 1989 βs and λs; 1997 Xs and Zs

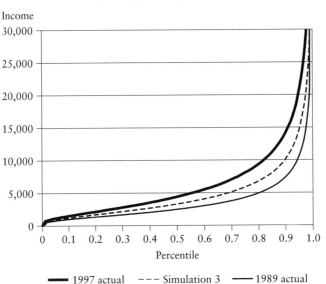

D. 1997 education quantities; 1989 other Xs and βs

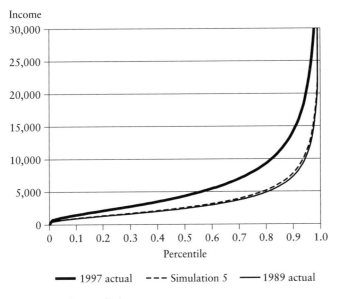

Source: Authors' calculations.

Figure 7.12 Household Quantile Curves: 1997 Baseline

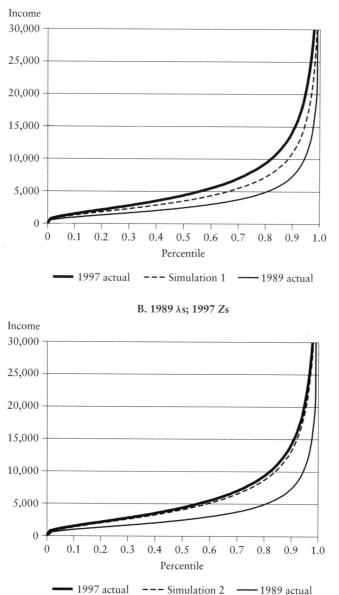

A. 1989 βs; 1997 Xs

B. 1989 λs; 1997 Zs

(*Continued on the following page*)

Figure 7.12 (*Continued*)

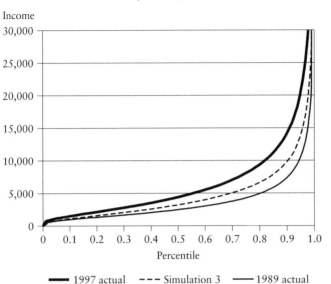

C. 1997 βs and λs; 1989 Xs and Zs

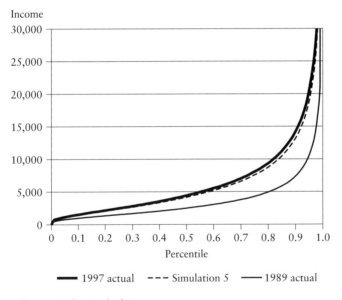

D. 1989 education quantities; 1997 other Xs and βs

Source: Authors' calculations.

Figure 7.13 Quantile Curves: Simulated Values Minus 1989 Actual Values

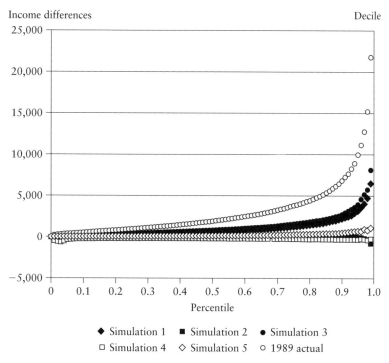

Source: Authors' calculations.

We turn finally to the causes of increased income inequality in Malaysia in the 1989–97 period. Simulation 3 exhibits the largest effect in both the A and B sets of simulations. From this result, we conclude that the increase in inequality in the 1989–97 period is best accounted for by changes in population structure. On the other hand, the factor estimated to be the next largest in the A set of simulations, simulation 4, works in the opposite direction in the B set. The same aggregation issues discussed in detail for the 1984–89 period probably were at work in the 1989–97 period. Next in importance, the factors that exhibit consistent effects (simulation 1 and simulation 5) are also the ones whose effects are small. Interestingly, the very small contribution of education's quantity effect in Malaysia is the exact opposite of what was found in Taiwan, China. There, the increased equality of years of education was the major factor that lowered income inequality (see chapter 9).

Figure 7.14 Quantile Curves: Simulated Values Minus 1997
Actual Values

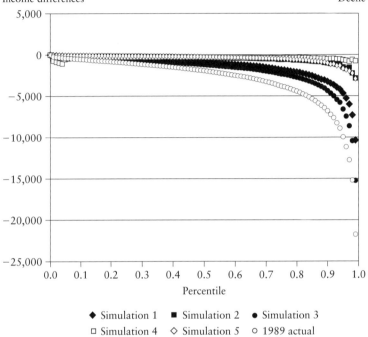

Source: Authors' calculations.

Conclusion

This chapter set out to answer the questions of

• Which factors contributed how much to the increase in household income levels and the fall in absolute poverty in the 1984–89
and 1989–97 periods?

• Which factors contributed how much to the falling income
inequality from 1984 to 1989 and the rising income inequality from
1989 to 1997?

Our analysis of the microeconomics of changing income distribution in Malaysia reveals the following:

• In the earlier period, the modest increase in mean income and
the modest reduction in the poverty headcount ratio are accounted
for by the changing population structure.

Table 7.15 Distribution of Per Capita Household Income, Substituting 1997 Values into 1989 Distribution

Indicator	Location		Poverty headcount (percent)	Inequality	
	Mean			Gini	Theil
Actual value, 1989	3,752.74		33.7	0.4610	0.4161
Actual value, 1997	7,070.29		14.4	0.4993	0.5051
Actual change (as a percentage of total change)	88.4		−57.3	8.3	21.4
Simulated change (absolute value)					
Simulation 1	4,768.10		26.0	0.4802	0.4495
Simulation 2	3,796.67		32.1	0.4548	0.3938
Simulation 3	5,252.83		22.4	0.4963	0.6095
Simulation 4	—		—	0.4960	0.4836
Simulation 5	3,973.48		31.3	0.4634	0.4188
Simulated change (as a percentage of total change)					
Simulation 1	983.1		280.7	21.9	43.5
Simulation 2	138.2		136.5	125.0	137.6
Simulation 3	1404.7		366.7	−43.4	−226.4
Simulation 4	—		—	−42.1	−13.9
Simulation 5	292.0		156.0	90.2	95.3

—Not available.
Source: Authors' calculations.

Table 7.16 Distribution of Per Capita Household Income, Substituting 1989 Values into 1997 Distribution

	Location		Inequality	
Indicator	Mean	Poverty headcount (percent)	Gini	Theil
Actual value, 1997	7,070.29	14.4	0.4993	0.5051
Actual value, 1989	3,752.74	33.7	0.4610	0.4161
Actual change (as a percentage of total change)	−46.9	134.3	−7.7	−17.6
Simulated change (absolute value)				
Simulation 1	5,529.86	19.8	0.4822	0.4708
Simulation 2	6,761.98	16.8	0.5177	0.6778
Simulation 3	4,878.73	24.7	0.4774	0.4362
Simulation 4	—	—	0.5258	0.5607
Simulation 5	6,607.18	15.7	0.4942	0.4962
Simulated change (as a percentage of total change)				
Simulation 1	−52.0	47.9	0.7	0.9
Simulation 2	−2617.2	55.8	−6.6	−42.6
Simulation 3	−979.3	34.9	1.7	8.2
Simulation 4	—	—	−8.3	−18.0
Simulation 5	−2,482.6	58.5	−1.8	−4.4

—Not available.
Source: Authors' calculations.

• In the earlier period, inequality fell. This finding is best accounted for by changes in the reward structure and the population structure.

• In the later period, mean income rose substantially, and the poverty rate fell substantially. The changes in the population structure and the reward structure each made important contributions.

• Inequality change in the later period, as well as mean income and poverty changes in the same period, is best explained by changes in the population structure and the reward structure.

Notes

1. The 1973 Postenumeration Survey was not fully comparable with the surveys in later years.

2. This phenomenon is also called *first-order stochastic dominance*. It implies that for any poverty line, high or low, a smaller percentage of individuals are in poverty in the dominating distribution (in this case, 1997) than in the dominated one.

3. The poverty line used in this study is half the 1984 median for per capita household income.

4. Earnings also depend on hours worked in each type of employment, but such information is not present in the Malaysian data.

5. A "residual effect" may be defined implicitly by the adding-up requirement that the total change be expressed as the sum of the reward structure effect $B_{tt'}$, the occupational position effect $O_{tt'}$, the population structure effect $P_{tt'}$, and a residual:

$$D_{t'} - D_t = B_{tt'} + O_{tt'} + P_{tt'} + R_{tt'}.$$

This decomposition will not be pursued further here.

6. Because mean income is kept constant, such a change is of no interest in understanding differences in the location of two years' distributions.

7. The Malaysian data do not permit multiple classifications.

8. The spline, in this case, consists of three connected line segments, which allow for the dependent variable to change at one rate for each additional year of primary schooling, at a different rate for each additional year of secondary schooling, and at a third rate for each additional year of higher education.

9. The Malaysian data set did not include ownership of land or of other productive assets. If it had, we would have included it.

10. The head's occupational position may be thought of as a proxy for the existence of a family business, thus affecting the occupational choice of other members. As with any proxy, there may be some reporting error.

11. Statistical significance of the individual variables implies joint significance of the four variables taken together.

12. Industrial sector dummy variables were not used because of coding changes between 1997 and the other years. The only industrial control that could be trusted was agriculture, whose effect is picked up by the occupation controls.

13. Note that, in this simulation, the educational endowments change income distributions only through the fact that people possess more years of schooling and earn higher incomes in their preexisting occupations. The occupational structure is kept fixed.

14. Because the actual Lorenz curves lie so close together, visual inspection is uninformative, so we have not presented those curves here.

References

Ahuja, Vinod, Benu Bidani, Francisco Ferreira, and Michael Walton. 1997. *Everyone's Miracle? Revisiting Poverty and Inequality in East Asia.* Washington, D.C.: World Bank.

Atkinson, Anthony B. 1970. "On the Measurement of Inequality." *Journal of Economic Theory* 2(3): 244–63.

Milanovic, Branko. 1999. "Inequality and Determinants of Earnings in Malaysia, 1989–97." World Bank, Washington, D.C. Processed.

World Bank. n.d. "Social Crisis in East Asia: Poverty and Malaysia." Available online at http://www.worldbank.org/poverty/eacrisis/countries/malay/pov1.htm.

8

Can Education Explain Changes in Income Inequality in Mexico?

Arianna Legovini, César Bouillón,
and Nora Lustig

> *Social institutions must combat, as much as is possible, this*
> *inequality [in education] which produces dependency.*
>
> —Condorcet

Mexico experienced a sharp increase in inequality in earnings and household income in 1984–94. The ratio of average to low-skilled earnings, for example, rose by 27 percent for wage earners and by 25 percent for self-employed workers. Those at the bottom of the earnings distribution experienced severe losses in earnings, and those at the top experienced substantial gains (see figure 8.1). Those in the middle were mostly unaffected. The Gini coefficient for earnings increased by 8 points, and that for household income increased by 6 points (see table 8.1).

We have used an empirical framework to identify the contributions of microeconomic factors to the observed rise in inequality in earnings and household income. Briefly, the framework consists of estimating a labor-market model at two (or more) points in time and simulating the effect on the distribution of earnings and household income from observed changes in behavior (such as labor-force participation), changes in the returns to particular factors (such as education), and changes in the structure and distribution of those factors (see chapter 9).

Figure 8.1 Observed Change in Individual Earnings by
Percentile in Mexico, 1984–94

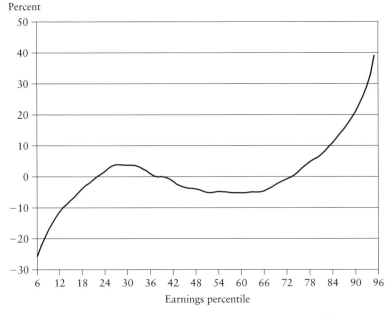

Percent

Source: Authors' calculations based on data from the 1984 and 1994 Encuesta
Nacional de Ingresos y Gastos de los Hogares (National Household Income and
Expenditure Surveys, or ENIGH).

Among the factors that we analyze are changes in demographic
structure (including changes in the level and distribution of education), geographic location, and labor-supply decisions. Our prior is
that education and the returns to it explain a large portion of the
change in income distribution. Drawing on the results of a previous
study, we also believe that divergence in conditions between rural
and urban areas plays an important role (Bouillon, Legovini, and
Lustig 2001). A comparison of the effect of those factors on inequality in individual earnings with their effect on inequality in household income provides useful insights into the role of the family and
its response to labor-market conditions.

Changes in Demographics and Labor-Force Behavior in 1984–94

Significant demographic changes in the 10 years between 1984 and
1994 may have affected the distribution of income. The Mexican
labor force became younger and more educated. Average education

Table 8.1 Inequality in Earnings and Household Income in Mexico, 1984 and 1994

Indicator	1984				1994				Percentage change			
	Gini coefficient	E_0	E_1	E_2	Gini coefficient	E_0	E_1	E_2	Gini coefficient	E_0	E_1	E_2
Earnings inequality	49.4	53.5	45.5	76.4	57.3	71.4	68.8	193.0	16.0	33.5	51.1	152.6
Household income inequality	49.1	42.8	45.6	87.5	54.9	54.0	60.2	130.1	11.7	26.2	32.0	48.7
Static decomposition of between- and within-group inequality in earnings												
All labor categories (by gender, occupation, and location)												
Between group	42.0	16.8	16.9	9.2	50.0	23.7	20.7	7.0	19.2	41.8	22.6	−24.3
Within group	58.0	83.2	83.1	90.8	50.0	76.3	79.3	93.0	−13.9	−8.4	−4.6	2.5
Occupation												
Between group	17.1	2.8	3.2	1.9	15.6	2.6	2.6	0.9	−9.0	−5.5	−19.3	−53.3
Within group	82.9	97.2	96.8	98.1	84.4	97.4	97.4	99.1	1.9	0.2	0.6	1.0
Location (urban and rural)												
Between group	29.7	10.5	11.1	6.1	37.8	17.5	15.6	5.0	27.0	66.9	40.8	−17.6
Within group	70.3	89.5	88.9	93.9	62.2	82.5	84.4	95.0	−11.4	−7.8	−5.1	1.1
Gender (male and female)												
Between group	14.5	2.7	3.0	1.7	14.8	2.6	2.5	0.8	2.1	−5.2	−15.7	−49.2
Within group	85.5	97.3	97.0	98.3	85.2	97.4	97.5	99.2	−0.4	0.1	0.5	0.8

Note: E_0 is the mean log deviation, E_1 is the Theil index, and E_2 is the modified coefficient of variation.
Source: Authors' calculations based on data from the 1984 and 1994 ENIGH.

increased, and the distribution of years of schooling improved. Female labor-force participation rose markedly at both the top and the bottom of the skill distribution. And wage work replaced self-employment.

The proportion of young people in the labor force increased as a result of declining labor-force participation in the 56–65 age group and growing participation among young women (table 8.2). Education among workers rose from an average of 5.6 years of schooling in 1984 to 6.9 years in 1994. The share of workers with secondary or higher education increased by half (from 30 percent of the labor force to 45 percent).

The improvement in the distribution of years of education—with the Gini coefficient falling from 0.42 to 0.37—appears to arise from a better-than-average performance by the middle of the income distribution rather than the bottom. While the middle four deciles of the household per capita income distribution experienced a 31 percent increase in schooling, the bottom three deciles had a 19 percent increase and the top three had a 22 percent increase.

This statement, however, is not necessarily descriptive of what happened to individuals. Because education and income are highly correlated, those who achieved higher levels of education than others in their decile moved upward, and vice versa. Thus, a person who lived in a poor household in 1984 and who became highly educated would be recorded in a higher decile in 1994, whereas a person who was from a richer household and who obtained less education would be found in a lower decile. Thus, people in the lower deciles appear to have gained less than they actually did, but the issue is difficult to investigate without panel data. (Later we present results from a simulation of educational gains across the distribution using a clustering method.)

Education levels lagged in rural areas. Rural workers had an average of only 4.5 years of schooling (less than a primary education) in 1994—and almost 80 percent had a primary education or less. Those results are affected by rural-urban migration, however. Although primary schools are available to most in rural areas, secondary schools are scarce. Students must move away to continue their studies and may never return. In addition, more educated people are attracted to the cities, which promise better-paying jobs.

Fertility rates fell during the period, reducing family size by 9 percent and dependency ratios by 17 percent. Low-income families declined somewhat more in size (by 11 percent), and urban households declined more than rural households. The drop in fertility coincides with women's larger-than-average gains in education and with a solid increase in their labor-force participation.

Table 8.2 Characteristics of the Labor Force in Mexico, 1984 and 1994

Characteristic	Total			Men			Women		
	1984	1994	Percentage change	1984	1994	Percentage change	1984	1994	Percentage change
Age structure (percent)									
18–35 age group	55.1	57.0	3.5	54.8	55.9	2.0	55.8	59.4	6.4
36–55 age group	35.8	35.4	-1.2	35.7	35.8	0.3	36.1	34.5	-4.3
56–65 age group	9.1	7.6	-16.7	9.5	8.3	-12.5	8.1	6.1	-24.9
Education structure (percent)									
National									
Primary school and below	70.3	54.8	-22.0	70.9	56.8	-19.9	68.7	50.7	-26.1
Secondary and preparatory school	22.6	34.4	51.8	21.6	32.3	49.4	25.3	38.8	53.1
More than preparatory school	7.1	10.8	52.5	7.5	10.9	46.0	6.0	10.5	75.2
Urban									
Primary school and below	60.4	39.2	-35.1	60.6	40.6	-33.0	60.0	36.7	-38.9
Secondary and preparatory school	29.1	43.9	50.6	27.9	41.5	48.6	32.0	48.3	51.0
More than preparatory school	10.4	16.9	62.1	11.4	17.9	56.3	8.0	15.0	88.3
Rural									
Primary school and below	87.4	77.7	-11.2	87.4	78.0	-10.7	87.5	76.7	-12.4
Secondary and preparatory school	11.3	20.4	81.1	11.4	20.2	76.3	10.8	21.2	95.8
More than preparatory school	1.3	1.9	49.7	1.1	1.8	58.1	1.7	2.1	27.9
Years of schooling									
Total	5.6	6.9	23.8	5.6	6.8	22.9	5.7	7.1	25.2
Urban	6.7	8.5	27.4	6.7	8.5	26.8	6.6	8.5	29.2
Rural	3.6	4.5	24.6	3.6	4.6	25.4	3.6	4.5	22.5
Deciles 1–3	3.1	3.7	19.2	3.2	3.9	22.7	2.8	3.1	9.6
Deciles 4–7	4.6	6.1	30.9	4.7	6.2	31.4	4.5	5.9	30.9
Deciles 8–10	8.0	9.8	22.0	8.2	9.8	19.7	7.6	9.6	27.5

(Continued on the following page)

Table 8.2 *(Continued)*

Characteristic	Total			Men			Women		
	1984	1994	Percentage change	1984	1994	Percentage change	1984	1994	Percentage change
Participation (percent)									
Working age	61.8	66.0	6.8	93.9	93.9	0.0	33.1	41.0	23.9
18–35 age group	60.7	67.2	10.7	92.1	93.9	2.0	32.8	43.3	32.1
36–55 age group	63.7	66.8	4.9	96.7	95.8	−0.9	34.2	40.6	18.4
56–65 age group	61.6	55.8	−9.5	94.7	86.4	−8.7	30.2	27.9	−7.4
Occupation (percent)									
Wage employment	55.5	62.1	11.9	54.5	63.0	15.7	58.1	60.0	3.4
Mixed activities	9.0	4.7	−47.7	11.4	6.0	−47.9	2.7	2.1	−22.4
Self-employment	35.5	33.2	−6.4	34.1	31.0	−9.0	39.2	37.8	−3.4
Earnings									
Wage earners									
Average hourly real earnings (1994 pesos)	5.9	6.9	15.4	6.0	6.9	15.1	5.7	6.6	16.5
Earnings premium (ratio)									
Average- to low-skilled earnings	1.6	2.0	27.3	1.5	1.9	29.2	2.0	2.4	19.7
High- to low-skilled earnings	3.9	6.1	57.8	3.8	6.7	75.8	4.4	5.5	24.9
Self-employed									
Average hourly real earnings (1994 pesos)	4.7	5.0	6.6	4.5	5.5	20.5	4.9	4.0	−19.3
Earnings premium (ratio)									
Average- to low-skilled earnings	1.4	1.8	25.5	1.3	1.5	17.2	1.5	1.4	−2.7
High- to low-skilled earnings	5.3	7.9	47.7	5.3	7.8	46.4	0.9	6.5	603.3
Family size (number of individuals)									
Total	5.16	4.68	−9.1						
Rural	5.40	5.05	−6.4						
Urban	5.02	4.45	−11.4						

Source: Authors' calculations based on data from the 1984 and 1994 ENIGH.

The increase in women's participation in the labor force was per-haps the most salient change in labor-market behavior during the period. In 1984, only 33 percent of working-age women were in the labor force; in 1994, 41 percent were. The greatest increase (88 per-cent) was among women with very high levels of education—probably in response to the greater market incentives and opportu-nities for highly skilled individuals (figure 8.2). Women with little education also entered the labor force in greater numbers—in this case to supplement spouses' dwindling real incomes and to substi-tute for migrating agricultural workers. The changes in women's participation are even sharper when broken down by cohort: par-ticipation by women ages 18–35 increased from 33 percent to 43 percent between 1984 and 1994, but participation by women ages 56–65 declined. Participation by men ages 56–65 declined even more (by 8 percentage points), whereas participation by men ages 18–35 increased. The higher participation of younger cohorts gen-erates a proportional increase in wage employment, because younger cohorts are less likely to enter self-employment.

Figure 8.2 Change in Women's Labor-Force Participation by Education Level in Mexico, 1984–94
(percent)

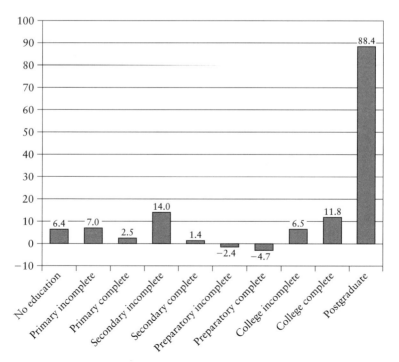

Source: Authors' calculations based on data from the 1984 and 1994 ENIGH.

As we will see, all these changes in demographics and labor-force behavior, combined with the sharp increase in the skill premium (which we take as given in our empirical analysis), help to explain the rising inequality in earnings and household income observed in the period.

Method and Data

From a microeconomic point of view, changes in income distribution can come from changes in decisions regarding labor-force participation, in demographic characteristics, and in the returns to those characteristics. The method we use is designed to measure the relative importance of those different sources of change. It provides a complete description of the effect of these microeconomic determinants on the entire vector of incomes. In other words, the method computes whole new sets of vectors of earnings and household incomes under different assumptions, and differences between these vectors describe the composition of different effects across the entire sample of observations.

We proceed in three steps. First, we estimate a standard labor-market model for individual earners for 1984 and 1994. The model includes labor choice and earnings functions for men and women in urban and rural locations and in the wage employment and self-employment sectors.

Second, we simulate the contribution of the labor-choice effect, the price effect, the population effect, and the effect of unobservable factors to the change in the distribution of individual earnings. *Labor-choice effect* refers here to the effect of changes in the probabilities of participation and occupational choice decisions; *price effect* refers to the effect of changes in the returns to education and experience; *population effect* refers to the effect of changes in the distribution of education, experience, and location; and the *effect of unobservable factors* refers to the effect of changes in the distribution of the errors in the earnings equations.

We perform this simulation by reestimating the vector of incomes, changing one microeconomic factor at a time. For example, say that we have estimated the vector of earnings for 1984 as:

$$(8.1) \qquad \hat{y}_{84} = \hat{a}_{84} + \hat{b}_{84} X_{84}$$

and that we are interested in determining the effect of the changes in the price of X on the distribution of y. We simply replace the estimated parameter for 1984 with that for 1994 to obtain a new vector of y:

$$(8.2) \qquad \hat{y}_{84}^{b94} = \hat{a}_{84} + \hat{b}_{94} X_{84}.$$

The differences between the two vectors describe the changes in income attributable to changes in b across the entire distribution. We do this for each parameter and independent variable in the labor-choice and earnings equations for both 1984 and 1994. The exercise provides us with a full description of the effect of each microeconomic determinant on the distribution of individual earnings in the two years.[1] These descriptions can be visualized using graphs. Alternatively, we can use conventional measures of income inequality reestimated for each simulated vector of income to obtain estimates of the proportional contribution of each factor.

Third, we obtain a description of the impact of microeconomic determinants on the distribution of household income. To do this, we aggregate the already calculated vectors of individual incomes by household and add nonlabor household income. Again, these vectors can be compared graphically, or indicators of income inequality can be calculated and compared.

We use four conventional measures of income inequality to summarize our results: the Gini coefficient and three measures from the generalized entropy class: the mean log deviation (E_0), the Theil index (E_1), and the transformed coefficient of variation (E_2). Because the mean log deviation gives greater weight to observations at the bottom, the Theil index gives equal weight to observations across the distribution, and the transformed coefficient of variation gives greater weight to observations at the top (Cowell 1977), differences among the results for the three measures provide insight into the portion of the distribution responsible for the change, just as observing the entire distribution would.

The analysis relies on data from the Mexican National Household Income and Expenditure surveys (Encuesta Nacional de Ingresos y Gastos de los Hogares, or ENIGH) for 1984 and 1994, conducted by the Instituto Nacional de Estadística, Geografía y Informática. The surveys have national coverage, with a sample size of 4,735 households in 1984 and 12,815 households in 1994. Income data were adjusted to account for regional differences in inflation using the regional consumer price indexes estimated by the Bank of Mexico. This adjustment facilitated the interpretation of changes in interregional differences.

Empirical Specification of the Labor-Market Model

OCCUPATIONAL CHOICE

We assume that individuals can choose one of four options: to not participate in the labor market, to pursue wage work, to pursue self-employment, or to have multiple occupations. We assume that the decision to participate in the labor market and the choice of occupation will differ among heads of household, spouses, and other members of the family, as well as between rural and urban dwellers. We assume that the implicit (latent) reservation earnings depend on potential household income, on household size and composition, on the education level of other household members, and on the characteristics of household assets. The labor-choice decisions of spouses and other members of the family are controlled for the labor status of the head of household because we assume that the activity of the head of household may influence those decisions (for example, a self-employed head of household might offer work to other family members, and an unemployed one might induce his spouse to enter the job market). To estimate the probability of each occupational choice j, we fit multinomial logit equations for each category (heads of household, spouses, and other members of the family in urban and rural areas) and in each period (1984 and 1994). Individual i in period t will select option j whenever the utility of option j exceeds the utility of any other option k, including inactivity.

$$(8.3) \qquad P_{itj} = prob\,(u_{itj} > u_{itk})$$
$$= prob\,(Z_{itj}\,\lambda_{tj} - Z_{itk}\,\lambda_{tk} > 0)\ldots \quad \text{for all } k \neq j$$

where Z is the matrix of independent variables and λ is the vector of coefficients.

EARNINGS EQUATIONS

We assume that earnings are a function of skills as proxied by education and experience, and we control earnings for regional variation. We fit earnings equations separately for 12 labor categories on the basis of gender, urban or rural location, wage employment, self-employment, and mixed-activity employment.[2] Except for separate error terms, this process is equivalent to running a single regression with fully interacted dummy variables for gender, location, and activity. We estimate the following using ordinary least squares:[3]

$$(8.4) \qquad \log(y) = X\beta + \varepsilon = \alpha + Edu\beta_1 + Edu^2\beta_2 + Exp\beta_3$$
$$+ Exp^2\beta_4 + R\gamma + \varepsilon$$

where
$\quad y =$ individual monthly earnings
$\quad Edu =$ years of schooling
$\quad Exp =$ work experience (age $- Edu - 6$)
$\quad R = \{R_1, R_2, R_3, R_5, R_9, R_{so}\}$ regional dummy variables
$\qquad$ (excluded category: $R_4 =$ Center-West [Aguascalientes, Colima, Guanajuato, Jalisco, Michoacán])
$\quad R_1 =$ Northwest (Baja California, Baja California Norte, Sinaloa, Sonora, Nayarit)

R_2 = Northeast (Tamaulipas, Nuevo León)
R_3 = North (Coahuila, Chihuahua, San Luis Potosí,
    Zacatecas, Durango)
R_5 = Center (Hidalgo, Querétaro, Tlaxcala, México,
    Morelos, Puebla)
R_9 = Federal District
R_{so} = Southern region dummy variable; includes South (Tabasco,
    Veracruz); Southeast (Chiapas, Guerrero, Oaxaca); and
    Southwest (Campeche, Quintana Roo, Yucatán).

We convert school achievement (degrees earned) into years of schooling and then estimate the model assuming a quadratic relationship between earnings and education. To ensure that the resulting convexity and convexification of returns to education are not driven by higher education alone, we reestimate our model using school achievement dummy variables. The results are nearly unchanged.

SIMULATION OF THE DISTRIBUTION OF EDUCATION, EXPERIENCE, REGIONAL LOCATION, AND UNOBSERVABLE FACTORS

To simulate changes in years of schooling and experience, we cluster observations by gender and location, estimate the distribution of these factors in each cluster (mean and standard deviation), and replicate the distribution of the cluster in 1984 into the corresponding cluster in 1994, and vice versa. In other words, for each x in cluster j, we apply a simple transformation:

$$(8.5) \qquad x_{j84}^{distr94} = (x_{j84} - \mu_{j84}) \frac{\sigma_{j94}}{\sigma_{j84}} + \mu_{j94}$$

where the μs and σs are the means and standard deviations in each cluster.

To simulate regional distribution, we use the weights from the household surveys and reweigh observations of one survey—say, that for 1984—with the weights of the other—say, 1994—to ensure that the resulting regional distribution of the population across all regions matches that observed in 1994, and vice versa.

The distribution of the residual terms can be modified in several ways—for example, by randomly drawing error terms for each observation given an assumed distribution or by modifying the original estimated error terms by assuming a different variance. Juhn, Murphy, and Pierce (1993) compute residuals based on the actual income percentile of a household in a particular year and the average cumulative distribution over time. If we assume a normal distribution, this procedure, which we use here, is equivalent to scaling the error terms in one year by the standard deviation in the other year.

Decomposition Method

Let $D(y, P)$ be any measure of income distribution, where y is earnings and P is the probability of labor-force participation and occupational-choice decisions (as defined in equations 8.4 and 8.3). Let β be the estimated parameters in the earnings equations; let X be the independent variables of education, experience, and regional location; let ε be the error terms in the earnings equations; and let λ be the estimated parameters in the occupational-choice equations. We can then rewrite $D(y, P)$ as $D(\beta, X, \varepsilon, \lambda)$. This decomposition exercise consists of estimating the effects on the joint distribution of income and labor choice by changing one or more arguments of $D(.)$. The labor-choice effect is estimated by modifying λ_t (the estimated parameters in the occupational-choice equations). The price effect is estimated by changing β_t (the estimated returns to education, experience, and location in the earnings equations); the population effect is estimated by modifying the structure of X_t (such as the distribution of years of schooling, experience, and location); and the effect of unobservable factors is estimated by simulating the distribution of residuals, as described above.

Let y be income and P the probability of an occupation in the initial year 0 (1984), and y' and P' income and occupation in final year 1 (1994). We are interested in explaining the change in income distribution between year 0 and year 1:

(8.6) $\quad \Delta D = D(y', P') - D(y, P) = D(\beta', X', \varepsilon', \lambda') - D(\beta, X, \varepsilon, \lambda)$.

This change in the distribution of income can be decomposed into the effect of changing prices, the effect of changing unobservable factors (after having changed prices), the effect of changing the Xs (after having changed prices and unobservable factors), and the effect of changing labor-choice behavior (after having changed all other factors). This decomposition can be stated as:

(8.7) $\quad \Delta D = [D(\beta', X', \varepsilon', \lambda') - D(\beta, X', \varepsilon', \lambda')] + [D(\beta, X', \varepsilon', \lambda')$
$\qquad - D(\beta, X', \varepsilon, \lambda')] + [D(\beta, X', \varepsilon, \lambda') - D(\beta, X, \varepsilon, \lambda')]$
$\qquad + [D(\beta, X, \varepsilon, \lambda') - D(\beta, X, \varepsilon, \lambda)]$

which, simplifying notation, can be expressed as follows:

(8.8) $\quad \Delta D = D_\beta(X', \varepsilon', \lambda') + D_\varepsilon(\beta, X', \lambda') + D_X(\beta, \varepsilon, \lambda') + D_\lambda(\beta, X, \varepsilon)$

where each D subscript represents the change in the distribution resulting from changing the subscript variable.

This equation represents an exact "sequential" decomposition of price, unobservable factors, population, and labor-choice effects.

This decomposition does not, however, keep final (1994) conditions constant at each step of the simulation. To keep final conditions unchanged, we apply a simple transformation and rearrange terms to obtain:

$$
\begin{aligned}
(8.9) \quad \Delta D = {} & D_\lambda(\beta', X', \varepsilon') && \textit{labor-choice effect} \\
& + D_\beta(X', \varepsilon', \lambda') && \textit{price effect} \\
& + D_\varepsilon(\beta', X', \lambda') && \textit{effect of unobservable} \\
& && \textit{factors} \\[4pt]
& + D_X(\beta, \varepsilon, \lambda') && \textit{population effect} \\
& + [D_\varepsilon(\beta, X') - D_\varepsilon(\beta', X')] \\
& + [D_\lambda(\beta, X, \varepsilon) \\
& \quad - D_\lambda(\beta', X', \varepsilon')] && \textit{remainder.}
\end{aligned}
$$

Or, alternatively, to keep initial (1984) conditions unchanged:

$$
\begin{aligned}
(8.10) \quad -\Delta D = {} & D_\lambda(\beta, X, \varepsilon) + D_\beta(X, \varepsilon, \lambda) + D_\varepsilon(\beta, X, \lambda) \\
& + D_X(\beta', \varepsilon', \lambda) + [D_\varepsilon(\beta', X) - D_\varepsilon(\beta, X)] \\
& + [D_\lambda(\beta', X', \varepsilon') - D_\lambda(\beta, X, \varepsilon)].
\end{aligned}
$$

Equations 8.9 and 8.10 state that the total change in the joint distribution of y and P can be expressed as the sum of the effects of labor-choice changes, price changes, and change in the distribution of unobservable factors—given final (initial) conditions—plus the effect of changes in population—given initial (final) conditions.

The interpretation of the two remainder terms in this formulation is that of an interaction term between different factors being simulated. In other words, the combined effect of modifying two or more factors at the same time—say, prices and population characteristics—is not equal to the sum of the components (that is, the effect of changing prices while keeping education, experience, and location fixed and the effect of changing education, experience, and location while keeping prices fixed).

The results from decompositions 8.9 and 8.10 represent the upper and lower bounds for the estimates if we make the reasonable assumption of monotonicity of the decomposition relative to changes in those factors.[4] Using this assumption, we base the analysis of the results on the average of the upper and lower bounds.

The decomposition described here is a simplification of what is actually applied. Because we simulate the effect of each price and independent variable in turn (holding all else constant), the results will include several different remainders, each being the difference between the effect of simulating two or more prices or factors at the same time and the separate effect of each price or factor. Empirically, the most notable remainder is that of the overall population effect; the reason is that the overall population effect is calculated as the observed change in distribution minus the calculated effects of labor choice, prices, and unobservable factors. In turn, the overall population remainder is calculated as the overall population effect minus the calculated effects of those factors being simulated—education, experience, and regional location. Thus, the overall population remainder incorporates all other effects that we cannot account for from within our framework.

Changes in Labor-Choice and Earnings Functions in 1984–94

For this chapter, we discuss only major changes shown by the estimation results for the 1984–94 period—those most relevant to understanding the changes in distribution. Among them are significant changes in labor-force participation, in returns to skills, and in regional conditions.

Labor-Force Participation

The results of the multinomial labor-choice equations indicate some significant changes in labor-force participation behavior and in choice of activity in 1984–94.[5] One important change relates to experience. For heads of household, the positive elasticity between experience and inactivity increased tremendously in the period. A head of household with more-than-average experience was more likely to be inactive in 1994 than in 1984. Experience clearly proxies for age, and the increased speed with which skills become obsolete makes older workers less attractive in the market. This change was more marked in urban areas, where greater technological change has taken place.

Another important change was in the relationship between women's education and their occupational choices. Generally, an increase in years of schooling reduced the probability of inactivity for all household members, and this effect was stronger in 1994 than in 1984. But for spouses—most of whom were women—the effect was more often than not in the opposite direction. In 1984, urban spouses at all levels of education who experienced a marginal increase in education were more likely to revert to inactivity and away from self-employment—and the effect was stronger at higher levels of education. In 1994, however, women with higher levels of education were more likely to enter self-employment. Those with primary education were more likely to become active, and those with higher levels of education were less likely to be inactive. Apparently, the urban woman of 1994 was more independent than her cohort in 1984—that is, she was more likely to respond to market opportunities for her human capital. This interesting development may reflect cultural changes more than economic ones.

In contrast, a rise in the potential income of the household—which controls for characteristics of other household members—increased the probability of inactivity for spouses (and for other members of the household) more in 1994 than in 1984. This finding is not a general result. Because this elasticity is evaluated at the mean, it reflects the decisions of women with a secondary education whose participation dropped. One interpretation of this drop in participation is that these are women in support positions—for example, secretarial jobs—who may have seen their opportunities reduced as they were replaced by slightly more educated people and those with computer skills.

Some changes across regions were also of interest. In rural areas, a working head of household increased the probability of self-employment for other members of the household in 1994 but not in 1984. We usually think of self-employed heads of household as providing work for the rest of their families. One interpretation of the change is that, as conditions in rural areas deteriorate, job opportunities become more segmented; more of the people who stay must work, and these people resort to the family business, while the other family members migrate to urban areas. Another part of this interpretation is that the uneducated women who join the labor market—usually without formal work experience—do so by working in the family business (which counts as self-employment).

Finally, living in Mexico City significantly reduced the probability of inactivity, with the effect much stronger in 1994 than in 1984. This result reflects major changes in the relative availability of job opportunities, together with self-selection in migration, which ensures that the most entrepreneurial people move to cities, while those with less potential stay behind.

Returns to Skills

Results from the earnings equations show that the most important change between 1984 and 1994 is the convexification of the returns to schooling (table 8.3). As observed in other economies, in Mexico the wage gap related to skills, as measured by the returns to education, widened in the period. The curvature of the functions for returns to education increased (that is, the functions became more convex), and the returns to low and medium levels of education

Table 8.3 Selected Results from Earnings Equations for Mexico

Indicator	Wage earners		Self-employed	
	1984	1994	1984	1994
Urban men				
Years of schooling	0.099*	0.051*	0.138*	0.044**
Years of schooling squared	0.000	0.004*	−0.001	0.004*
Years of experience	0.078*	0.064*	0.073*	0.079*
Years of experience squared	−0.001*	−0.001*	−0.001*	−0.001*
Southern region	−0.040	−0.226*	0.333*	−0.228*
Mexico Distrito Federal	0.162*	0.106*	0.141	0.275*
Constant	5.150*	5.404*	4.525*	5.156*
R^2	0.376	0.468	0.215	0.292
Urban women				
Years of schooling	0.193*	0.113*	0.144*	0.034
Years of schooling squared	−0.004*	0.001*	−0.004	0.006*
Years of experience	0.065*	0.057*	0.047*	0.053*
Years of experience squared	−0.001*	−0.001*	−0.001*	−0.001*
Southern region	0.034	−0.173*	0.140	−0.238*
Mexico Distrito Federal	0.312*	0.196*	0.482*	0.530*
Constant	4.620*	4.922*	4.248*	4.537*
R^2	0.341	0.411	0.108	0.192
Rural men				
Years of schooling	0.135*	0.071*	0.177*	0.159*
Years of schooling squared	−0.001	0.003*	−0.005**	0.001
Years of experience	0.095*	0.069*	0.069*	0.087*
Years of experience squared	−0.001*	−0.001*	−0.001*	−0.001*
Southern region	−0.179**	−0.363*	−0.064	−0.649*
Constant	4.632*	5.044*	4.435*	3.903*
R^2	0.370	0.250	0.215	0.209
Rural women				
Years of schooling	0.232*	0.129*	0.132	0.132*
Years of schooling squared	−0.004	0.002**	0.002	0.003
Years of experience	0.068*	0.060*	0.078*	0.037*
Years of experience squared	−0.001*	−0.001*	−0.001*	0.000*
Southern region	0.128	−0.252*	−0.145	−0.623*
Constant	3.690*	4.564*	3.168*	3.865*
R^2	0.453	0.343	0.079	0.112

*Significance at the 5 percent level. **Significance at the 10 percent level.

Note: Excludes results for some regional dummy variables and mixed employment. Full estimation results available from the authors on request.

Source: Authors' calculations based on data from the 1984 and 1994 ENIGH.

declined, while returns to high levels of education increased.[6] For example, for all male workers, except men who were self-employed in rural areas, the marginal private returns to any year of primary education fell, while those to higher and college education rose. For male workers who were self-employed in rural areas, marginal returns to education fell for all levels of schooling (figure 8.3). These changes were not driven by a dramatic increase in the returns for a few people at the top. When the quadratic specification for education is replaced by one with dummy variables for schooling levels, the change in curvature closely resembles that in the quadratic specification.

The widening gap in the returns to education reflects the timing of demand and supply factors affecting the labor market. In the short run, technological change increases the demand for skills. This effect raises the relative wages of the skilled, because it takes time for more educated cohorts to enter the labor force, even when the public policy response is immediate, which has not been the case in Mexico.

As many authors have argued, trade liberalization may also raise the demand for skills, contrary to the predictions of the two-sector Heckscher-Ohlin model. Hanson and Harrison (1995), for example, found that 23 percent of the increase in relative wages for skilled workers in Mexico during 1986–90 can be attributed to the reduction in tariffs and the elimination of import license requirements. Revenga (1995) suggests that employment and wages for unskilled labor are more sensitive and liable to reductions in protection than employment and wages for skilled labor, because of the concentration of unskilled workers in sectors more affected by liberalization. Tan and Batra (1997) find that investments in technology and export orientation have a large effect on wages for skilled workers and a relatively smaller effect on wages for unskilled workers. Cragg and Epelbaum (1996) present evidence suggesting that the effect of skill-biased technological change is to expand the wage premium for skilled workers. In addition, Robertson (2000) points to empirical evidence suggesting that trade liberalization in Mexico has sharpened the demand for skilled workers and increased wage inequality.

Several forces explain these results. First, Mexico has tended to protect less skill-intensive industries, and as a result trade liberalization increased the relative price of skill-intensive goods. Second, foreign investors tend to outsource tasks that are relatively less skill intensive in the United States but are nonetheless relatively skill intensive in Mexico. Third, domestic firms invest in technology, thereby increasing the demand for complementary skills. Trade liberalization and technology absorption may thus partially explain

Figure 8.3 Returns to Education for Men by Location, Education Level, and Type of Employment in Mexico, 1984 and 1994

A. Urban men in wage employment

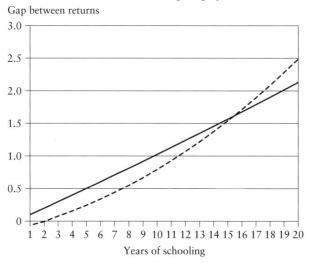

B. Rural men in self-employment

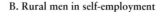

—— 1984   - - - 1994

Source: Authors' calculations based on data from the 1984 and 1994 ENIGH.

the observed increases in income inequality through a change in the rewards for skills as proxied by education. They also may have contributed to the increased divergence of conditions between urban and rural labor markets, because foreign investment remains concentrated in cities on the U.S.-Mexico border (Hanson 1996).

The increased returns to higher education are mirrored by falling returns to experience in wage employment. This finding is consistent with technological innovation, the obsolescence of older cohorts' skills, and the greater likelihood that young cohorts will enter wage work. Younger cohorts, for example, are more likely to have acquired the computer skills required in the modern work environment. With technological innovation, these skills become more important to an employer than work experience. Among the self-employed, however, experience was valued more in 1994 than in 1984, perhaps as a result of a shift in demand toward goods requiring more experience.

Regional Conditions

In 1984, most regional effects were insignificant at 95 percent or greater confidence. In 1994, most were negative and highly significant. This change indicates that conditions diverged across regions and that growth was uneven. Indeed, the central regions of Mexico have been growing at a faster pace than the rest of the country, with Mexico City in particular doing better than other regions. Poor agricultural areas in the south have suffered the greatest relative decline, in part because of falling crop prices. The northern regions have shown uneven growth: The northwest has seen growth spurred by significant foreign investment, but the northeast has lagged behind.

Unobservable Factors

The variance of the residuals of the earnings function for men increased during the period 1984–94. A standard interpretation would be that the dispersion of the unobservable talents of men, such as innate ability and entrepreneurship, increased. This interpretation is an appealing one for Mexico, where market-oriented reforms increased economic competition and reduced protection. The value of entrepreneurship in determining outcomes must have risen, and this effect shows up in the increased variance of the residuals.

For women, however, the variance of the residuals of the earnings function declined. Here the change in the variance may capture the dispersion in the hours worked. The strong participation of younger women, who are more likely than older women to work full time, should reduce the dispersion in hours of work.

Results from Decomposing Changes in Earnings Inequality for Individuals

We now present the results from the decomposition, which estimates the proportional contribution of changes in labor choice, prices, and observed and unobserved labor characteristics to the changes in income distribution. This section provides the results for individual earnings; the results for household income follow in the next section. Comparison of the two sets of results provides added insight into household dynamics and decisionmaking. Each set of results represents the average of the results from two separate simulations—one relating to the contributions of each factor with 1984 as the base year, and the other relating to those with 1994 as the base year.

Earnings inequality rose markedly in 1984–94. The Gini coefficient rose by 8 points, the mean log deviation (E_0) rose by a third, the Theil index (E_1) rose by a half, and the transformed coefficient of variation (E_2) rose by one and a half. Changes in labor choice, in education and the returns to education, and in rural-urban disparities explain more than two-thirds of this increase in earnings inequality (table 8.4). The largest contributions came from changes in the price and population effects for education, which together explain 41 percent of the change in the Gini coefficient (24 percent and 17 percent). Also very important are the growing disparities in returns between rural and urban areas, which accounted for 21 percent of the change in the Gini coefficient (table 8.5). Finally, labor-choice effects, driven by the choices of the increasing number of working women, accounted for 6 percent of the change in the Gini coefficient.

Labor-Choice Effect

The first simulation modifies the structure of parameters in the equations for labor participation and occupational choice, while keeping the structure of earnings unchanged. This question is addressed: What would the distribution of earnings be like if labor participation and occupational choice in 1984 were modified to reflect labor participation and occupational choice in 1994, and vice versa?

Overall, the effect of changes in labor participation and occupational choice is unequalizing, especially at the top of the distribution. This effect represents 6 percent of the change in the Gini

Table 8.4 Decomposition of Changes in Inequality in
Earnings and Household Income in Mexico, 1984–94
(average; percent)

Indicator	Gini coefficient	E_0	E_1	E_2
Earnings				
Labor-choice effect	6.4	5.5	10.7	27.6
Male	−1.0	−4.4	4.4	19.2
Female	7.8	10.4	6.4	8.3
Price effect	38.7	44.7	34.7	31.8
Education	24.0	19.0	23.7	21.5
Experience	−0.9	−1.4	−0.1	2.5
Regions	−4.3	−4.5	−3.4	3.8
Constant	21.7	32.8	17.9	14.0
Remainder	−1.9	−1.3	−3.4	−10.1
Population effect	53.4	42.5	54.1	51.8
Education	16.5	13.8	10.7	6.7
Earnings-induced effect	19.6	18.0	13.2	8.0
Labor-choice-induced effect	−2.3	−3.7	−2.5	−2.2
Remainder	−0.7	−0.4	0.0	0.8
Experience	1.7	1.5	1.7	1.9
Earnings-induced effect	2.2	1.7	2.0	2.4
Labor-choice-induced effect	−0.5	−0.1	−0.4	−0.5
Remainder	0.0	−0.1	0.0	0.0
Regions	6.2	6.2	5.0	1.7
States	5.4	6.7	4.1	0.6
Remainder	28.9	20.9	36.7	41.5
Effect of unobservable factors	−0.6	2.5	−2.7	−9.0
Remainder	2.1	4.8	3.3	−2.2
Household income				
Labor-choice effect	−2.6*	−1.5*	0.6*	5.1*
Male	−0.7	0.0	2.5*	8.4*
Female	−2.0*	−1.6*	−1.9*	−3.5*
Price effect	38.7*	42.5*	33.6*	29.4*
Education	24.5	23.0	24.7	25.3
Experience	1.5	2.0	2.1	6.2
Regions	−4.2	−4.4	−5.7*	−10.4*
Constant	18.8*	23.6*	16.1*	16.5
Remainder	−2.0*	−1.7*	−3.7*	−8.1
Population effect	64.5	58.4	66.2	69.2
Education	15.4*	15.1	11.9	5.4*
Earnings-induced effect	13.1*	14.6*	11.2*	8.2
Labor-choice-induced effect	2.4	1.0	0.1	−5.6*
Remainder	−0.1	−0.4	0.6	2.8

(*Continued on the following page*)

Table 8.4 (*Continued*)

Indicator	Gini coefficient	E_0	E_1	E_2
Experience	3.6	3.1	2.6	1.5*
Earnings-induced effect	3.2	3.1	2.5	1.8*
Labor-choice-induced effect	0.3	−0.1*	0.0	−0.4
Remainder	0.1	0.1	0.1	0.1
Regions	1.9*	1.3*	2.8*	4.7
States	−0.4*	−1.1*	1.8*	5.8
Remainder	43.6	38.8	48.9	57.6
Effect of unobservable factors	−3.4*	−2.5*	−5.0*	−13.7*
Remainder	2.0*	5.7	0.2*	−3.3*

*Effects that are less unequalizing for household income than for individual earnings.

Note: E_0 is the mean log deviation, E_1 is the Theil index, and E_2 is the modified coefficient of variation.

Source: Authors' calculations based on data from the 1984 and 1994 ENIGH.

coefficient and as much as 28 percent of the change in the transformed coefficient of variation. Driving this result is the effect of increased female participation in the labor force: male occupational choices temper the result.

Changes in employment participation decisions of females have a large and unequalizing effect on the distribution of earnings, while changes in employment participation decisions of males have an equalizing effect at the bottom of the distribution and an unequalizing one at the top (figure 8.4). The reason for this difference is that women enter at the two extremes of the skill distribution. Those with little education enter self-employment in agriculture to substitute for poorly educated men moving out of agriculture and into the wage sector. Women's entry into the least remunerated activity increases inequality, whereas men's movement out of agriculture and into better-paid activities reduces it. At the top of the skill distribution, highly educated women increase their participation greatly, entering self-employment (once the domain of women with low education) in services (figure 8.2). Similarly, highly educated men flee wage employment in manufacturing to enter self-employment in services, which explains why the male labor-choice effect is unequalizing at the top of the earnings distribution (see the results for E_2 in table 8.4).

Price and Population Effects

The second step in the decomposition is to modify returns to skills and to location and to modify the independent variables in the

Table 8.5 Rural Effect in the Decomposition of Changes in Inequality in Earnings and Household Income in Mexico, 1984–94

(average; percent)

Indicator	Gini coefficient	E_0	E_1	E_2
Earnings				
Price effect	38.9	44.9	34.8	31.9
Average prices	18.9	10.4	20.9	25.6
Education	21.2	15.0	20.8	18.2
Experience	0.5	0.0	1.2	4.2
Regions	1.0	1.6	1.7	9.1
Constant	−2.4	−5.2	−0.6	0.8
Remainder	−1.3	−0.8	−2.3	−6.7
Rural prices	20.6	35.9	15.1	8.3
Education	1.4	2.6	1.5	2.2
Experience	−0.2	−0.1	0.0	0.0
Regions	−1.3	−1.4	−1.0	−0.7
Constant	21.5	35.2	15.6	8.8
Remainder	−0.9	−0.4	−1.1	−2.0
Household income				
Price effect	38.9*	42.7*	33.7*	29.6*
Average prices	20.3	18.8	20.2*	19.9*
Education	21.2*	18.9	21.3	20.9
Experience	2.1	2.8	3.0	7.6
Regions	−0.1*	0.8*	−1.5*	−4.1*
Constant	−1.9	−2.8	−0.6*	0.1*
Remainder	−1.0	−0.9*	−2.0	−4.5
Rural prices	18.9*	24.6*	14.3*	11.0
Education	2.4	3.0	2.6	2.9
Experience	0.1	0.3	0.0	0.0
Regions	−1.0	−1.4	−0.9	−0.8*
Constant	18.3*	23.6*	14.0*	11.4
Remainder	−1.0*	−0.9*	−1.5*	−2.5*

*Effects that are less unequalizing for household income than for individual earnings.

Note: The overall price effects differ slightly from those in table 8.4 because of the restrictions imposed on the error terms. E_0 is the mean log deviation, E_1 is the Theil index, and E_2 is the modified coefficient of variation.

Source: Authors' calculations based on data from the 1984 and 1994 ENIGH.

Figure 8.4 Effect of Labor Choices on Earnings by Percentile in Mexico, 1984–94

(base year 1984)

Source: Authors' calculations based on data from the 1984 and 1994 ENIGH.

earnings equations to investigate what effect skills and location would have on the distribution of income if participation and occupational-choice decisions were left unchanged. Not surprisingly, the dominant factor is the change in the structure of returns to education. Unexpected, however, are the results for years of education.

THE UNEQUALIZING EFFECT OF EDUCATION

The change in the structure of returns to education engenders a large, unequivocal increase in inequality. But it is not only the change in the returns to education that produces higher income inequality; the improvement in the distribution of education also produces higher income inequality.

Two elements contribute to this surprising result. As we saw in the comparison of educational achievement across the distribution in 1984 and 1994, there was a larger proportional increase in years of schooling in the middle of the distribution than at the bottom or the top (table 8.2). In addition, marginal rates of return are higher for higher levels of education. This means that someone with little education gains less from an additional year of schooling than does someone who is more educated. Only much larger educational gains at the bottom would have resulted in increased income equality.

Why is the bottom of the distribution slow to adjust? One explanation is that poor people face greater constraints in adjusting to increased demand for skills. Those constraints may be on both the demand side (inability to afford the costs of attending school) and the supply side (unavailability of schools in poor areas). Thus, greater efforts are needed to provide access to education and to stimulate demand for education across the distribution. Among cohorts already in the labor force, those with some education may find it easier to acquire additional skills than those with no education at all. The importance of a universal basic education for increased flexibility in responding to changing labor-market conditions cannot be overstated.

Other interpretations also exist regarding the slow adjustment at the bottom: these are cohort effects and mobility effects. Older, less educated cohorts do not invest in additional education and end up swelling the bottom of the distribution. Indeed, the first decile of the income distribution is the only one in which the average age of the labor force increased. Younger individuals from poor households who become more educated move upward in the income distribution. Both effects lower the recorded gains in education at the bottom.

To gain a better understanding of the ex ante changes in education across the distribution, we simulate educational gains while keeping the 1984 ranking of individuals by earnings. We then calculate the effect of educational gains on the distribution of earnings. The results, presented in figure 8.5, are quite interesting. The jagged line in the figure represents proportional gains in education by percentile. Educational gains are about 15 to 20 percent for the bottom half of the distribution, significantly larger than the 10 to 15 percent gains for the top half. The smoother, upward-sloping curve represents the effect of educational gains on earnings. These gains are distributionally neutral up to the 60th percentile. Above that, the very high marginal returns to higher education contribute to increasing inequality. At the very top of the income distribution, relatively small educational gains translate to a 20 percent increase in earnings (compared with only a 10 percent increase for the bottom three quintiles).

Heckman, Lochner, and Taber (1998) offer another interpretation of why the bottom may be slow to adjust in the context of a heterogeneous agent, general equilibrium model. Their interpretation relates to the time people spend actually working and investing

Figure 8.5 Effect of Educational Gains on Earnings by
Percentile in Mexico, 1984–94

(individuals ranked by 1984 earnings; base year 1984)

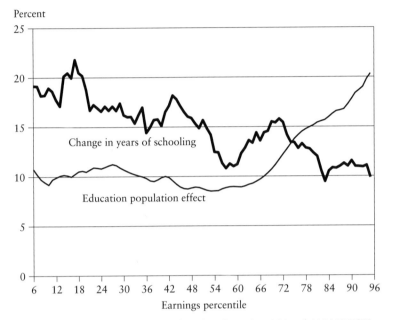

Source: Authors' calculations based on data from the 1984 and 1994 ENIGH.

in learning-by-doing (neither of which is observed empirically). In
their model, the best response for the poorly educated to an expected
fall in the relative returns to unskilled labor is to work now (when
the returns are high) and invest in learning later (when the returns
are low). For the more educated, who would expect their returns to
improve in the future, the optimal choice is to invest in learning
now and work more later. These strategies would increase measured
income inequality in the medium term. They would also lead to a
smaller increase in education levels at the bottom of the income
distribution than would be necessary to avoid an increase in the
earnings gap associated with skills.

The distribution of education also affects occupational choice—a
participation-induced effect. This effect is consistently equalizing
and somewhat tempers the inequality-increasing earnings effect.[7] As
the distribution of education improves, the relatively less educated
get more benefit from it—in terms of expanding opportunities—
than do more educated people. This result makes sense. Overcom-
ing illiteracy, for example, enlarges opportunities more than does
staying in high school or college for one more year. Therefore, the

participation-induced effect is strongest at the bottom of the distribution.

If upward-sloping convex returns to education lead to improvements in the distribution of education and thus contribute to income inequality, the more pronounced convexity in the returns observed in 1994 can only contribute more to inequality. As we noted, returns to lower education fell while returns to higher education increased in every labor category. The convexification of returns is highly unequalizing. The changes in returns to education led to some gains at the bottom of the distribution, to substantial losses in the middle, and to very large gains at the top (figure 8.6). Together, changes in education and in returns to education account for 41 percent of the change in earnings inequality as measured by the Gini coefficient and about a third of the change in other inequality measures.

THE WEAKLY UNEQUALIZING EFFECT OF EXPERIENCE

The price and population effects of experience tend to cancel each other out and, when combined, these two effects account for barely 1 percent of the increase in the Gini coefficient. The price effect is

Figure 8.6 Effect of Changes in Returns to Education on Earnings by Percentile in Mexico, 1984–94

(base year 1984)

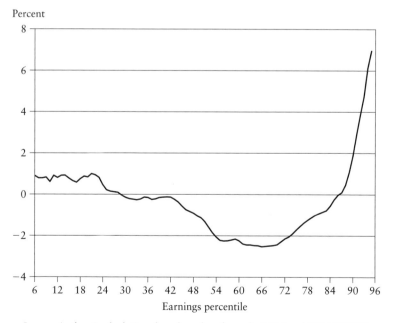

Source: Authors' calculations based on data from the 1984 and 1994 ENIGH.

small and equalizing, because returns on experience fell overall and became more concave. In contrast, the distribution of experience became more unequal during the period (the Gini coefficient for years of experience increased from 0.39 to 0.41), and this result contributed to an increase in earnings inequality.

THE LARGE AND UNEQUALIZING EFFECT OF URBAN-RURAL DISPARITIES

The constant-term effect from the earnings equations is large and unequalizing. This effect captures the changes in the differences between the constant terms of the regressions in the 12 labor categories. Our guess was that the fall in real labor earnings in rural areas in absolute terms and relative to real earnings in urban areas was responsible for this large and unequalizing effect. Applying a static decomposition of inequality within rural and urban areas and between them, we find that the inequality between rural and urban areas rose (table 8.1).

To confirm this change and to calculate its proportional effect on the increase in inequality within our framework, we reestimate the earnings equations, this time combining urban and rural earners (though separating them by gender and occupation), yet leaving all rural coefficients unrestricted. Although this procedure is identical to regressing rural and urban data separately except for the common error term, it allows us to isolate the marginal effect of rural returns from the effect of overall returns in the decomposition.

The results confirm that the deterioration of conditions in rural areas compared with conditions in urban areas explains a large part of the increase in income inequality (table 8.5). In particular, the fixed effect of living in rural areas, as reflected by the rural constant term, has a large, unequalizing impact, only partially counterbalanced by the convergence of urban and rural returns to both education and experience. The urban-rural disparity represents 22 percent of the change in the Gini coefficient. When we plot the simulated change in income by percentile caused by the urban-rural effect, we find that the urban-rural effect heavily penalizes the bottom half of the earnings distribution (figure 8.7). The bottom half of the distribution experiences an earnings loss of 10 to 25 percent, compared with 5 to 10 percent for the top half of the distribution.

THE MILDLY UNEQUALIZING EFFECT OF REGIONAL DISPARITIES

The coefficients of regional dummy variables have an equalizing effect, but this effect is outweighed by the change in the geographic distribution of the population. An appropriate description of these

Figure 8.7 Effect of Urban-Rural Disparities on Earnings by Percentile in Mexico, 1984–94

(base year 1984)

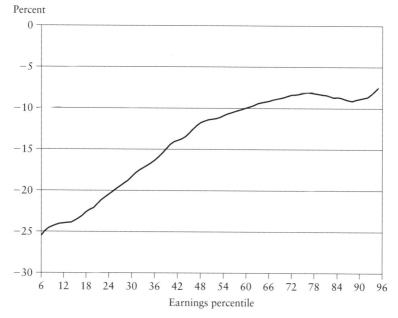

Percent

Source: Authors' calculations based on data from the 1984 and 1994 ENIGH.

results might be called "voting with their feet." As economic conditions change, people move to compensate for those changes. The reverse may hold as well: as people move to take advantage of opportunities, returns equalize across regions.

Evidence suggests that migratory flows were significant during the 1984–94 period. For example, the 1990 census showed that an estimated 30 percent of the people in the northern border regions were immigrants from other regions, and urbanization rates in the northern cities far exceeded those in other major urban centers (Anguiano Téllez 1998).

THE LARGE AND UNEQUALIZING REMAINDER POPULATION EFFECT

The size of the remainder term in the population effect requires an explanation. Once education, experience, and interregional migratory effects are considered, the unexplained portion of the population effect remains very large and unequalizing. Part of this effect comes from sampling errors in the surveys: the 1994 survey significantly oversamples rural areas compared with the 1984 survey, and this error may bias population effects upward.[8] Most of the effect, however, reflects our inability to capture urbanization and inter-regional migratory movements. The importance of selection in explaining migration is widely recognized: entrepreneurial and resourceful people are more likely to migrate. Without panel information or a variable relating migrant status, it is impossible to satisfactorily simulate the effect of migratory movements. There is a strong presumption, however, that the population effects from migration are very important in explaining increased income inequality. As the best and the brightest leave depressed areas for more successful areas, the depressed areas lose, and the successful areas gain even more.

The Effect of Unobservable Factors

The last step in the decomposition is to modify the distribution of residuals to investigate the effect of unobservable factors on the distribution of income if other factors in the earnings equations and in the participation and occupational-choice decisions remain unchanged.

The effect of unobservable factors is small (except at the top of the distribution) and ambiguous. This finding is not surprising, because, as we have seen, the increase in the variance of the residuals of the male earnings equations is counterbalanced by the decline in the variance of the residuals of the female earnings equations. The relatively large equalizing effect of unobservable factors at the top of the distribution is interesting. One possible interpretation is that the female entrants at the top of the distribution work full time, reducing the variance in overall hours of work.

Results from Decomposing Changes in Household Income Inequality

Household income inequality rose less than individual earnings inequality in 1984–94, yet the increase was still substantial. The Gini coefficient rose by 6 points, the mean log deviation (E_0) rose by a quarter, the Theil index (E_1) rose by a third, and the transformed coefficient of variation (E_2) rose by a half.

By grouping individuals back into their own household and adding nonlabor sources of income, we obtain household income vectors and can observe the changes in the distribution of household income. The decomposition of the change in household income inequality in 1984–94 is consistent overall with the decomposition of the change in individual earnings inequality (table 8.4). The differences, however, point to the household as an important mechanism for tempering the rise in earnings inequality. Because the two decompositions are based on the same econometric estimations and merely reflect a different grouping of individuals, any difference between them is by definition statistically significant.

The largest single contribution to the increase in household income inequality remains the increase attributable to price and population effects for education, which together explain about 40 percent of the change in the Gini coefficient (25 percent and 15 percent; see table 8.4). The effect on household income of the growing disparities in returns between rural and urban areas is comparable to the effect on earnings (19 percent of the change in the Gini coefficient; see table 8.5). Much less important and ambiguous are labor-choice effects (-3 percent of the change in the Gini coefficient and 5 percent of the change in E_2). Much greater is the impact of unexplained population effects (44 percent of the change in household income inequality, compared with 29 percent for earnings inequality).

Labor-Choice Effect

The most important result is that household dynamics eliminate the unequalizing effect of decisions about labor participation and occupational choice on individual earnings. Female labor choices that are very unequalizing for individual earnings become equalizing for household income.

Two factors are at play. First, the highly educated women who entered the labor force in large numbers did not come from the richest households (those with very high nonlabor income) but from upper-middle-class households. Their high wages contributed to the increase in earnings inequality, because they were among the highest earners. Their wages, however, also helped close the gap with the households that had the highest nonlabor income, because women from the richest households tended not to participate in the labor market.

Second, at the opposite end of the income distribution, women with little or no education who belonged to the poorest households contributed to earnings inequality by earning wages lower than those of unskilled male workers. But as they entered agricultural activity to substitute for male labor moving to wage employment, they complemented their spouses' income and raised household income closer to that of less poor households—and thus reduced household income inequality.

The changes in the male participation effect were similar to those in the female participation effect for educated men, but not for uneducated men. Participation increased for men with higher education, and those highly educated men contributed to the increasing inequality in earnings—just as highly educated women did—but the effect was hampered at the household level, because these men did not belong to households with high nonlabor income. Men with little education tended to contribute to the equalizing of earnings by moving to the wage sector, but they had no effect on the distribution of household income. The reason is that the wage sector offers better and less unequally distributed earnings than self-employment. The more equal distribution in the wage sector reduces overall earnings inequality.

Price and Population Effects

Several price and population effects are notable.

• *The more unequalizing effect of education.*   The effect of the changes in returns to education is more unequalizing at the household level. This result is intuitive: since the correlation between education levels is positive and very high among family members, the change in relative wages tends to affect all members of a household in the same direction. For example, an educated man is more likely than an uneducated man to have an educated spouse. When the earnings gap associated with skill increases, both educated spouses will benefit, and both uneducated spouses will be harmed. Indeed, it is surprising that the difference in effect between individuals and households is not larger. This finding may reflect the still relatively low participation of women in the labor force.

• *The more unequalizing effect of experience.*   The effect of experience differs more markedly between individual earnings and household incomes than does the effect of education (relative to the size of the effect). This finding reflects the fact that spouses age together. As returns to experience fall, older couples lose compared with younger couples. Their combined loss is greater relative to the household income distribution than their individual losses in the earnings distribution.

• *The less unequalizing effect of urban-rural disparities.*   The effects of the divergence between urban and rural areas are less marked at the household level. The reason is that household income includes nonlabor income, and any change in earnings affects total income by a smaller proportion than it would labor income. In addition, reported nonlabor income falls more in urban than in rural areas, countering the decline in rural labor income.

• *The more unequalizing remainder population effect.* The remainder population effect is more important in explaining changes in household income inequality than it is in explaining changes in earnings inequality. One reason is that this term captures the distributional effects of nonlabor income (not modeled here). Nonlabor income contributes to increasing inequality because its distribution has become more unequal and because the correlation between labor and nonlabor per capita income almost doubled between 1984 and 1994, from 16 percent to 27 percent, according to our calculations.

The Effect of Unobservable Factors

The effect of unobservable factors is more equalizing for household income than for earnings. This finding probably reflects diversification in the activities of working household members, such that the variance of the sum of their residuals is lower than the sum of the variances of those residuals.

Conclusion

Our analysis of the microeconomic determinants of the marked rise in inequality in earnings and household income in Mexico during 1984–94 indicates that changes in the levels of and returns to education are responsible for about two-fifths of the increase in inequality (as measured by the Gini coefficient). Divergence between rural and urban fixed factors accounts for another fifth. These results are consistent across decompositions of the changes in inequality in earnings and household income.

The first result points to the importance of education—in particular, structural shifts that affect the labor-market returns to education—in determining the changes in income distribution. Most earners—all except those with tertiary education—experienced falling marginal returns to their education. The consequences for private incentives to invest in education pose a policy dilemma. To reverse the trend of falling returns to lower levels of education, more has to be invested in education, not less. The market incentives for all but those with the highest levels of education, however, work in the opposite direction.

In what may at first seem a paradox, the gains in average education and the more equal distribution of education across the working population contribute to rising income inequality. The reason is that marginal returns to education increase at higher education levels, so a marginal increase in education brings smaller rewards for the less educated than for the more educated. Part of the effect is due to the behavior of older cohorts. Because these cohorts no longer invest in education (and at the same time are not rewarded for their greater experience), they end up lagging behind and swelling the bottom of the income distribution.

Despite the paradoxical effects of the gains in education and its distribution, too little emphasis has gone to improving education for all, particularly those least able to improve their education on their own. Education helps reduce poverty no matter what its consequences are for distribution. Moreover, educating children at the bottom of the income distribution is necessary to outweigh the convexity of the returns to education.

The observed drop in marginal returns to primary—and, in some cases, secondary—education implies weaker private incentives to invest in education for all parents who would expect to be able to provide their children with only a basic education. Facing constraints on their ability to meet the direct costs and the opportunity costs of schooling, more parents may choose to delay or cut short their children's education. These considerations raise some important policy issues.

First, skill-biased technological innovation and, possibly, trade liberalization may have caught Mexico unprepared. Avoiding negative repercussions for poverty and income distribution requires building the human capital asset base, particularly of the poor and the least educated individuals. This type of change takes both time and substantial investment. The investment needs to be multisectoral—in health, nutrition, and education—to improve children's ability to learn and to achieve.

Second, as the marginal returns to primary and secondary education in the labor market fall, the gap between social and private returns to education is probably expanding. While most parents send their children to school because they value learning beyond what is strictly captured by the present value of future earnings, public policy may need to address the needs of families too poor to provide their children with even minimal schooling, nutrition, and health care.

Although most school-age children in Mexico today are already enrolled in primary school, a small but significant number of children are not, particularly in poor, isolated rural areas. The ultimate challenge, of course, is to ensure that the new generation acquires an education, enabling them to meet the increasing demands for skills—whether through a technical education or a college education. It is also critical to ensure universal basic education, so that children's opportunities to obtain higher education are as equal as possible.

The other important source of inequality is the divergence in conditions between rural and urban areas and the absolute fall in rural real incomes. Although countries that have made substantial efforts to liberalize trade have reaped significant gains (Ingco 1997), these gains do not necessarily benefit all workers. This pattern reveals itself in Mexico. Although trade liberalization has contributed to higher average wages, the increase is not uniform across workers (Revenga 1995). Agricultural workers suffered a severe decline in real income—on the order of 45 percent—as a result of terms of trade reversals in their principal crops, including coffee and cocoa, and the elimination of agricultural price support schemes. This outcome for agricultural workers may reflect, in part, the relative lobbying power of sectors benefiting from large foreign direct investment flows. Self-selection in migration also contributed to the fallout for rural economies: the most entrepreneurial workers may have moved to the city, leaving behind those least able to adjust to changing rural conditions.

These trends point to clear public policy objectives: expanding nonfarm productive opportunities in rural areas and building up the lagging asset base of rural households, particularly the human capital. Such a policy might include resolving coordination failures in the production and export of local manufactures and processed foods, developing incentives and partnerships for private sector investment in rural areas, and providing technical training for rural populations that responds to private sector demands. Failure to address rural poverty issues increases the incentives for migration and urbanization, worsening the already pressing problems of overcrowding and urban violence. Economic integration with the United States might well be part of such a policy, because it might contribute to the industrialization of rural areas—at least in the northern regions.

To help improve poor people's acquisition of human capital, in 1997 the Mexican government pioneered a poverty reduction program—Progresa (Programa de Educación, Salud y Alimentación, or Program for Education, Health, and Nutrition). Targeting poor rural households, the program is aimed at improving nutrition and increasing the demand for education and health care for children. Progresa provides monetary and nutritional transfers to families that commit to sending their children to school and completing periodic health care visits; it also provides monetary transfers to pregnant women for pre- and postnatal care. By September 1999, the program had been implemented in 51,300 localities throughout all 31 states, reaching 2.3 million poor, rural households.

Progresa focuses on two of the problem areas we have identified. It targets the schooling, health, and nutrition of poor children, thereby aiming to accelerate improvements in the distribution of human capital and in the productive capacity of the next generation. It also targets poor rural areas, which lag behind in average human capital and have lost ground compared with the rest of the country. Impact evaluation studies attest to Progresa's important effect on poverty.

Because we are interested in the effect such a program could have on distribution, we use the framework of this chapter to perform a simple simulation exercise. Using the 1994 survey as a base, we simulate household income by artificially awarding an increase in income equivalent to the Progresa transfer to the poorest 40 percent of rural households (mimicking Progresa coverage levels); this increase is equal to an average of 18.6 percent of household income in the bottom two quintiles, or 124.4 pesos (1994 pesos). The exercise assumes perfect targeting, 100 percent compliance by beneficiaries, and no change in the amount of education or in any other variable or price. Under those assumptions, we find that the Gini coefficient for household income would have fallen by less than half a point. The largest effect would have been in the mean log deviation (E_0), which would have fallen from 0.54 to 0.52. In other words, if Progresa were only a transfer program, however perfectly targeted, it would have had little effect on the distribution of income. Once the human capital gains of the poor start to affect their earnings—as children come of age and enter the labor force—Progresa may have a stronger effect on distribution.

Notes

The authors would like to thank François Bourguignon for his invaluable advice and support and Luis Tejerina and José Montes for their research assistance.

1. The simulations are path dependent. The estimated effects in each year represent an upper and a lower bound for each factor's effect.

2. The 12 categories are wage-earning urban men and women, mixed-employment urban men and women, self-employed urban men and women, wage-earning rural men and women, mixed-employment rural men and women, and self-employed rural men and women.

3. We tried estimating the earnings equations using a Heckman procedure to control for self-selection. Because we were unable to find good instruments for explaining self-selection in the different activities, we decided to drop the procedure.

4. We have tested monotonicity by calculating the population effect using average 1984–94 returns.

5. Full estimation results can be obtained from the authors.

6. Indeed, the quadratic term is highly significant in 1994 in almost all regressions but barely significant in 1984.

7. The participation-induced effect of education is calculated by substituting the distribution of education into the equations for labor participation and occupational choice. The earnings effect is calculated by substituting the distribution of education into the earnings equations.

8. Census data show that the proportion of the population living in urban areas grew from 66 percent to 74 percent between 1980 and 1999. Household survey data, however, report that this proportion fell from 63 percent to 58 percent between 1984 and 1994 (and that the urban labor force fell from 64 percent to 60 percent in the same period).

References

Anguiano Téllez, María Eugenia. 1998. "Migración a la Frontera Norte de México y Su Relación con el Mercado de Trabajo Regional." Working paper. El Colegio de la Frontera Norte, Population Studies Department, Tijuana, Mexico.

Bouillón, César, Arianna Legovini, and Nora Lustig. 2003. "Rising Inequality in Mexico: Household Characteristics and Regional Effect." *Journal of Development Studies* 39(4): 112–33.

Cowell, Frank. 1977. *Measuring Inequality*. Handbooks in Economic Series. London: London School of Economics and Political Science.

Cragg, Michael Ian, and Mario Epelbaum. 1996. "Why Has Wage Dispersion Grown in Mexico? Is It the Incidence of Reforms or the Growing Demand for Skills?" *Journal of Development Economics* 51: 99–116.

Hanson, Gordon H. 1996. "U.S.-Mexico Integration and Regional Economies: Evidence from Border-City Pairs." NBER Working Paper 5425. National Bureau of Economic Research, Cambridge, Mass.

Hanson, Gordon H., and Ann Harrison. 1995. "Trade, Technology, and Wage Inequality in Mexico." NBER Working Paper 5110. National Bureau of Economic Research, Cambridge, Mass.

Heckman, James J., Lance Lochner, and Christopher Taber. 1998. "Explaining Rising Wage Inequality: Explorations with a Dynamic General Equilibrium Model of Labor Earnings with Heterogeneous Agents." NBER Working Paper 6384. National Bureau of Economic Research, Cambridge, Mass.

Ingco, Merlinda D. 1997. "Has Agricultural Trade Liberalization Improved Welfare in the Least-Developed Countries? Yes." Policy Research Working Paper 1748. World Bank, Washington, D.C.

Juhn, Chinhui, Kevin Murphy, and Brooks Pierce. 1993. "Wage Inequality and the Rise in Returns to Skill." *Journal of Political Economy* 3(3): 410–48.

Revenga, Ana. 1995. "Employment and Wage Effects of Trade Liberalization: The Case of Mexican Manufacturing." Policy Research Working Paper 1524. World Bank, Latin America and the Caribbean Region, Country Department 2, Washington, D.C.

Robertson, Raymond. 2000. "Trade Liberalization and Wage Inequality: Lessons from the Mexican Experience." Macalester College, St. Paul, Minn. Processed.

Tan, Hong, and Geeta Batra. 1997. "Technology and Firm Size-Wage Differentials in Colombia, Mexico, and Taiwan (China)." *World Bank Economic Review* 11(1): 59–83.

9

Distribution, Development, and Education in Taiwan, China, 1979–94

François Bourguignon, Martin Fournier, and Marc Gurgand

Investing massively in the education of the poor is one of the few instruments through which it seems possible to both accelerate growth and improve the distribution of income. Such a strategy has been repeatedly recommended in the development literature over the past 30 years, from the well-known book *Redistribution with Growth* (Chenery and others 1974) to the influential 1990 and 2000 *World Development Reports* (World Bank 1990, 2000) on poverty. But although an important literature has developed on the effects of the expansion of education on growth, relatively little is known of its effects on the distribution of income.[1]

The present volume provides an empirical framework for studying some aspects of the relationship between educational expansion and income distribution in the course of development. This framework essentially tries to isolate observed changes in the distribution of individual income and earnings that may be attributed respectively to changes in the sociodemographic structure of the population, especially changes in education; to changes in labor-force participation and occupational-choice behavior; and, finally, to changes in the return structure of individual earnings. This decomposition is done at the microeconomic level on the basis of the data typically available in household surveys.

Taiwan, China, may be considered an almost ideal case study. It is probably one of the earliest and most dramatic development success stories in which education is often said to have played a leading role and to have been a powerful engine of growth. Indeed, educational expansion in Taiwan, China, has been extremely rapid. During the quarter-century starting in 1970, the average formal schooling of the labor force increased by more than 50 percent, from 6 years—the level observed today in many middle-income countries—to 9.5 years, a level comparable with what is observed in industrial countries.[2] At the same time, Taiwan, China, is somewhat remarkable in terms of the distribution of income, because of its low level of inequality and of its limited variability over time. After a large drop in the 1950s and 1960s, essentially initiated by an extremely successful land reform and reinforced by a vigorous industrialization process, the Gini coefficient for individual income stabilized at a level slightly above or below 0.30.[3] That level is still observed today. How income distribution could remain more or less the same despite the drastic growth-related changes that occurred simultaneously in the structure of the economy and in the sociodemographic characteristics of the population, including schooling, is the issue we analyze in this chapter. We do so by showing that the observed evolution is the result of various mutually compensating phenomena, which we seek to identify.

Possibly because the country's experience during the 1950s and 1960s has often been cited as one of the clearest cases of development with employment expansion and income equalization, there is a rather sizable literature on income distribution in Taiwan, China. As pointed out by Chu (1997), however, a detailed study of the evolution of the distribution of income in Taiwan, China, is still much needed, for two reasons. First, the existing literature is at too aggregate a level to generate an understanding of the mechanisms through which income distribution is affected by structural changes in the economy or in the sociodemographic structure of the population. Second, the literature also tends to focus on a single aspect of the problem—for example, trade, competition, or education—while ignoring other aspects and the way they interact to produce the observed change in the distribution of income.

Several authors have recently tried to overcome those difficulties, mostly through some kind of decomposition of income inequality, either by income source or by income groups, at various points in time. Chu (1997) distinguishes two periods in the recent history of Taiwan, China. By a decomposition analysis based on standard wage regression, he shows that approximately half the fall in wage inequality between 1966 and 1977 is due to changes in both the educational structure of the population and the rate of return to schooling. Between 1981 and 1992, he finds that the distribution of household wage income remained relatively stable but that the inequality of household incomes rose because of changes in participation behavior and in family composition. Using another decomposition methodology based on Shorrocks's (1982) decomposition of inequality by income sources, Fields and O'Hara (1996) found that the expansion of education in Taiwan, China, between 1980 and 1994 contributed to a reduction of the inequality in the distribution of human capital among individual earners. However, the impact of this evolution on the distribution of earnings was mitigated by an increase in the rate of return to education.[4]

All those results agree with the conjecture that below the surface of an apparently unchanging distribution of income, powerful phenomena may have been at work in Taiwan, China—phenomena that, taken in isolation, might have produced significant changes in the distribution of income but tended to offset each other. The reason may not be circumstantial, though. The expansion of education may not be independent from the change in the rates of return to schooling and the structure of wages; it may also be the cause of the observed changes in participation behavior and occupational choices. It is precisely the objective of this study to understand and measure those various effects and the way they interacted.

The chapter is organized as follows. The first section briefly presents the basic quantitative facts about the evolution of the economy of Taiwan, China, over the past two decades, with some emphasis on education and income distribution. The methodological framework is briefly discussed in the second section. The results obtained from applying this methodology to household surveys in Taiwan, China, over the period 1979–94 are then presented.[5] The third section summarizes the observed evolution of the structure of earnings and of occupational-choice behavior, as well as the role played by education in that evolution.[6] The fourth section presents the results of a decomposition of the evolution of the household income distribution and identifies the distributional effects of the observed changes in the educational structure of the population. The last section summarizes the results and concludes.

Basic Facts about Economic Development, Educational Expansion, and Income Distribution in Taiwan, China, since 1979

Several features with potentially strong implications for the distribution of income are readily apparent in the evolution of the sociodemographic structure of the population of Taiwan, China,

Table 9.1 Evolution of the Structure of the Population at
Working Age, 1979–94

Characteristic	1979	1983	1986	1989	1992	1994
Population (million)	11.0	12.1	12.8	13.4	14.0	14.4
Age structure (percent)						
15 to 29	44.9	42.5	40.4	37.1	34.9	34.7
30 to 49	38.2	39.0	40.1	43.0	44.9	45.3
50 to 65	16.9	18.5	19.5	19.9	20.2	20
Educational structure (percent)						
Illiterate	12.9	10.9	9.7	8.4	7.2	6.2
Primary school educated	37.6	33.6	31.4	29.4	26.1	24.3
Secondary school educated	40.1	44.2	46.9	49.4	51.1	52.5
University educated	9.4	11.2	11.9	12.9	15.5	17
Average number of years of *schooling by age groups*						
Age 15–29	9.6	10.2	10.6	11.0	11.3	11.5
Age 30–49	6.9	7.6	8.1	8.8	9.6	9.9
Age 50–65	5.1	5.4	5.4	5.4	5.6	6
Individuals in agricultural *households (percent)*	30.4	27.3	23.3	21.2	19.4	16.2
Average participation rate (percent)						
All individuals	63.9	62.8	63.0	64.0	64.0	63.3
Women	46.1	45.4	47.5	48.8	49.5	50.2
Men	81.5	80.3	78.4	78.9	78.4	76.3
Agricultural	57.1	58.2	59.2	59.9	60.3	60.7
Nonagricultural	79.6	75.0	75.7	79.3	79.3	76.5
Average total size of *households (number of persons)*						
Agricultural	5.7	5.4	5.1	4.6	4.5	4.4
Nonagricultural	4.6	4.5	4.4	4.2	4.0	3.9

Source: Household surveys, Directorate-General of Budget, Accounting, and
Statistics (DGBAS). Population statistics are from *Statistical Yearbook,* DGBAS.

over the past 15 years or so (see table 9.1). The population is becoming better educated, older, and more urbanized. At the same time,
women's labor-force participation is increasing and household composition is changing.

Most of this evolution is taking place at a striking pace. Some
45 percent of the working-age population was younger than 30 in
1979. By 1994, this figure was 35 percent. Almost 20 percent of
working-age individuals had then gone beyond secondary school, a
figure that had nearly doubled in the previous 15 years. Conversely,
the share of the population with no education or no more than primary education fell from 50 percent to 30 percent. A still more

impressive figure is the average number of years of schooling of the middle age group—those ages 30 to 49—which went up by almost 50 percent between 1979 and 1994, from 6.9 to practically 10 years.

Equally impressive is the fast evolution of the rural-urban structure of the population. During the period under analysis, the number of working-age individuals living in rural areas or in households dedicated to some agricultural activity approximately halved. This process corresponded partly with a drop in the number of agricultural households and partly with a change in the composition of rural households, the size of which diminished quite substantially: from 5.7 to 4.4 persons. This relative loss in the importance of agriculture is among the driving forces behind the evolution of other dimensions of the sociodemographic structure of the population. It partly explains the drop in the average household size, although it may be seen in table 9.1 that family size decreased significantly and continuously in both the rural and the urban sides. It should also have had a positive effect on the overall participation rate because participation in the labor force is traditionally lower in agricultural households. Although not shown in table 9.1, it turns out, however, that the participation rate of married women increased in both agricultural and nonagricultural households.

The evolution of the structure of gross domestic product (GDP) paralleled that of the population. The extremely high growth of GDP recorded over the period under analysis—7.8 percent per year on average—was accompanied by a dramatic change in its structure, which itself corresponds to the superposition of two evolutions. First, the agricultural sector kept losing relative importance. Its share of GDP went from approximately 10 percent in 1979 to less than 3 percent in 1994. Until 1984, the corresponding share of GDP went to the manufacturing sector, a continuation of the process observed since the takeoff of economic growth in the 1960s. In the late 1980s, however, the industrialization process itself came to an end and the "tertiarization" of the economy began. Between 1988 and 1995, the manufacturing sector as a share of GDP lost ground to services to the business sector and, to a lesser extent, commerce and personal services.

Structural changes were not limited to aggregate one-digit sectors, though. Within the manufacturing sector, the deceleration of growth is associated with substantial changes in the relative importance of the various activities. Starting in the mid-1980s, traditional manufacturing sectors such as food, textile, wood, and paper products lost in relative importance to the chemical industry, metal industries, and the electrical and electronic machinery sector. As with the

Figure 9.1 Evolution of Income Inequality, 1979–94

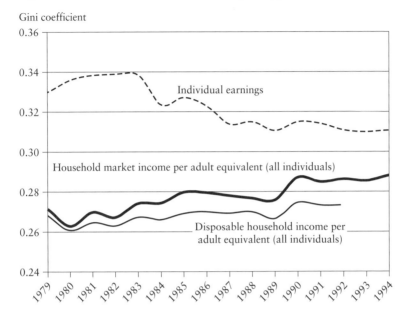

evolution of the population, the period under study thus is one of intense structural changes in the economy and, therefore, on the demand side of the labor market, clearly a rather constant feature of Taiwan, China, over the past 40 years or so.

Given the sizable changes that took place in the social and economic structure of Taiwan, China, in the past decade and the speed at which they occurred, one would expect the distribution of income to have also undergone substantial alterations. Whether or not such alterations took place depends on the definitions of *income* and *income recipients* that one adopts. Three different evolutions are observed in figure 9.1, which summarizes the evolution of income and earnings inequality during the 1980s and the first half of the 1990s. First, the inequality in the distribution of equalized household disposable income—that is, the distribution of individual incomes with every individual being given the disposable income per adult equivalent of the household he or she belongs to—is approximately constant over time.[7] Second, the Gini coefficient of the distribution of equalized household market income—that is, income before taxes and (public or private) transfers—shows a slight ascending trend. This trend accelerates in the early 1990s. Finally, the inequality of individual earnings—nonwage workers excluded— has been decreasing quite substantially since 1984.

Several studies have noted a recent increase in inequality. It seems to have become a stylized fact about the distribution of income in Taiwan, China, that the household income inequality made a U-turn around the beginning of the 1980s (see in particular Hung 1996 and also Chu 1997), whereas individual earnings inequality remained constant and even declined. The U-turn appears more clearly if the distribution is defined in terms of income per household, as in official statistics in Taiwan, China, rather than income per capita or adult equivalent.

This contradictory evolution of the individual and household income distribution is interesting. It suggests that several forces may indeed have contributed to changing the distribution of income in Taiwan, China, over the period under analysis. As different definitions of the distribution may give more or less weight to these forces, it is not surprising that they also may lead to diverging views about whether inequality increased, decreased, or stayed the same. The main objective of the present study is to uncover these forces.

Explaining the Evolution of the Distribution of Household Income: The Microsimulation Decomposition Methodology

Generally speaking, changes in the distribution of individual earnings and equivalized household incomes over time may come from three sources:

1. *The price effect.* People with given characteristics, or endowments, in a given occupation get a different income because remuneration rates or prices in the labor and possibly the output markets have changed.

2. *The participation or occupation effect.* People with given characteristics do not make the same occupational choices, so that the population of earners is modified within and across households.

3. *The population or endowment effect.* The sociodemographic characteristics of the population of households and individuals—for example, educational levels—change over time.

Decomposition Principle

The income y_{it} of household i observed at time t is assumed to depend on four sets of arguments: the observable sociodemographic characteristics of its members (x), its unobservable characteristics (ε), the set of prices and labor-remuneration rates it faces (β), and a set of parameters defining the participation and occupational choice behavior of its members (λ):

(9.1) $$y_{it} = Y(x_{it}, \varepsilon_{it}; \beta_t; \lambda_t)$$

The overall distribution of household income at time t, D_t, is obtained by combining total household incomes y_{it} and some demographic characteristics included in x_{it}, such as its size or composition. It may thus be expressed as a (vector) function of the distribution of observable and unobservable household characteristics at date t, the price vector, β_t, and the vector of behavioral parameters, λ_t. Let $H(\ )$ be that function:

(9.2) $$D_t = H(\{x_{it}, \varepsilon_{it}\}, \beta_t, \lambda_t)$$

where $\{\ \}$ refers to the distribution of the corresponding variable in the population.

With such a definition of the overall distribution, the various effects defined above to explain the evolution of the distribution between two dates t and t' can be simply computed as follows:

(9.3)   Price effect: $B_{tt'} = H(\{x_{it}, \varepsilon_{it}\}, \beta_{t'}, \lambda_t)$
$$-H(\{x_{it}, \varepsilon_{it}\}, \beta_t, \lambda_t)$$

(9.4)   Participation effect: $L_{tt'} = H(\{x_{it}, \varepsilon_{it}\}, \beta_t, \lambda_{t'})$
$$-H(\{x_{it}, \varepsilon_{it}\}, \beta_t, \lambda_t)$$

(9.5)   Population effect: $P_{tt'} = H(\{x_{it'}, \varepsilon_{it'}\}, \beta_t, \lambda_t)$
$$-H(\{x_{it}, \varepsilon_{it}\}, \beta_t, \lambda_t).$$

In other words, the population effect, P, is obtained by comparing to the actual distribution at date t the hypothetical distribution obtained by simulating on the population observed at date t' the remuneration structure and the behavioral parameters of period t. Likewise, the effect of the change in prices is obtained by comparing to the initial distribution the hypothetical distribution obtained by simulating on the population observed at date t the remuneration structure observed at date t'.

This methodology is very simple and may be seen as an extension of the well-known Oaxaca-Blinder methodology to decompose the effects of discrimination among two groups of individuals into differences in mean incomes caused by different mean characteristics of individuals in the two groups—that is, our population effect—and differences in the way these characteristics are remunerated within each group—that is, our price effect. The main differences are, first, that the decomposition is made on the full distribution rather than on means and, second, that the income-generating model—that is, the function $Y(\ )$ in (9.1) may be more complicated than the linear regression model originally used by Blinder (1973) and Oaxaca (1973).[8]

Even though the preceding definition of price, participation, and population effects may seem elementary, it must be stressed that the corresponding decomposition may be strongly path dependent. In particular, the price effect and the participation effect are likely to depend on the population that is used to evaluate them. In other words, it is generally the case that:

$$B_{tt'} \neq B_{t't}, \; L_{tt'} \neq L_{t't}, \; P_{tt'} \neq P_{t't}.$$

For the same reason, the decomposition of the change in inequality as the sum of the three preceding effects is not perfect:

$$D_{t'} - D_t \neq B_{tt'} + L_{tt'} + P_{tt'}.$$

For this decomposition to be nearly perfect, the structure of the population at dates t and t' as well as the price structure and the behavioral parameters λ should be close to each other, which is unlikely to be the case over the medium or long run in an economy subject to strong structural changes. In the application that follows, this ambiguity will be taken into account as we simultaneously consider alternative possible definitions of the various effects.

We would like also to be able to decompose the population effect itself into what may be due to unobservable and observable factors. This task should be easy once a model allowing for the identification of the unobservable terms ε_{it} is available. Assuming that unobservable factors are orthogonal to observable factors, it is possible to simulate a change in their distribution through rank-preserving transformations.[9] When this distribution is assumed to be normal with zero mean, this transformation is equivalent to

$$\varepsilon_{it} \rightarrow \varepsilon_{it}\sigma_{t'}/\sigma_t$$

where σ_t is the standard deviation of the distribution at time t. It is also possible to identify what is due to a specific component of vector x in the population effect—for instance, individual education—by changing the individual values of that variable at one date so as to make its distribution—conditional on other variables—identical to that observed at another date. This procedure can also be implemented through a rank-preserving transformation.

Modeling Household Incomes

The main difficulty of modeling household incomes in most developing countries arises from the fact that income may be obtained from different activities: wage income for all members employed outside the household and farm or self-employment income obtained jointly by all those members working, possibly part time, in the household. To make the presentation simpler, however, we assume in a first stage that all persons in a household can only earn income as wage workers.

Under the preceding assumption, let X_{mi} be the characteristics of person i in household m that determine his or her wage rate in the labor market and u_{mi} be the associated unobserved determinants. Let also Z_{mi} be the characteristics of person i and those of the household—that is, of the other members of the household—that may affect the labor supply of that person. The basic form of the income-generating model for a household observed at period t is then given by:

$$\text{Log } w^t_{mi} = X^t_{mi} \cdot \beta^t + u^t_{mi}$$

(9.6)
$$L^t_{mi} = Sup\left[0, \lambda^t_0 \cdot X^t_{mi} + Z^t_{mi} \cdot \lambda^t + v^t_{mi}\right]$$

$$y^t_m = \sum_{i=1}^{n_m} L^t_{mi} \cdot w^t_{mi} + y^t_{0m}.$$

The first equation is a standard wage equation, where the coefficients and the distribution of the residual term (which is meant to represent unobservable determinants of earnings and possibly transitory components) depend on the period of observation. The second equation is a conventional labor-supply function. Note, however, that this equation is a reduced form because the labor supply does not depend explicitly on the wage rate an individual is facing but on the exogenous determinants, X, of that rate. Here again the residual term, v^t_{mi}, stands for unobserved components or, possibly, transitory effects. Finally, the last equation sums actual earnings over all household members and adds to it some exogenous income, y_0, to obtain total household income, y_m.

All the coefficients of this model, β and λ, as well as the standard deviations of u and v, may be estimated by standard econometric techniques on data available at time t. As is well known, however, some precaution must be taken because of the simultaneity between the wage and the labor-supply equation and the fact that wages are observed only for those persons who actually work.

We use this basic model to simulate the following situation: what would have been the income of household m had it adopted at period t the labor-supply behavior of period t', or had earners been paid according to the wage equation observed at period t'? To see what would have happened, we can modify the set of coefficients (β^t, λ^t) for the values observed in period t', while keeping all the observed characteristics, X^t_m and Z^t_m, constant. Concerning the residual terms or the unobserved variables behind them, we also assume that adopting the behavior of period t' would have modified their absolute but not their relative value according to the rank-preserving transformation discussed above.

The only real difficulty in the preceding microsimulation method occurs for persons who were inactive in period t. For them, no value of the residual term, v_{mi}^t, nor of term u_{mi}^t is observed. The solution consists of drawing the values of these two terms randomly in a way consistent with the original model. Thus, the pair (u_{mi}^t, v_{mi}^t) must be drawn in the distribution estimated on the basis of active persons, which for simplicity may be assumed to be a normal bivariate, in such a way that the *Sup* condition in the second equation is satisfied with $L = 0$. Once those two terms are available, it is a simple matter to see whether the change in the wage equation—that is, from β^t to $\beta^{t'}$—modifies the labor status of an inactive person, and if it does, how the income of the household is itself altered. The opposite case of an active person becoming inactive is easier to handle, because it is not necessary to reconstitute the unobserved variables' terms. Doing the same type of simulation with labor-supply behavior or changing one individual characteristic following the methodology indicated above raises no specific problem.

As mentioned above, the actual household income-generation model is slightly more complicated than the preceding model because household members may have to choose between various types of activities. Adding the possibility that each household member devotes part of his or her time to the family farm or some other family independent business such as retail trade leads to the following model specification:

$$\text{Log } w_{mi}^t = X_{mi}^t \cdot \beta^t + u_{mi}^t$$
$$(9.7) \qquad L_{mi}^t = Sup\left[0, \lambda_0^t \cdot X_{mi}^t + Z_{mi}^t \cdot \lambda^t + v_{mi}^t\right]$$
$$L_{mi}^{At} = Sup\left[0, \lambda_0^{At} \cdot X_{mi}^t + Z_{mi}^t \cdot \lambda^{At} + v_{mi}^{At}\right]$$

$$y_m^t = \sum_{i=1}^{n_m} L_{mi}^t \cdot w_{mi}^t + \Pi\left[\beta_A^t, Z_m^{Tt}, \sum_{i=1}^{n_m} L_{mi}^{At}, \overline{X}_m^t\left(L_m^{At} > 0\right), s_m^t\right] + y_{0m}^t$$

where L_{mi}^{At} stands for the labor supplied by member i in the family farm or business and depends on the same set of variables as wage labor supply, L_{mi}^t, and where $\Pi(\ )$ is the associated profit function. As written, this function depends on those household characteristics, Z_m^t, that describe cultivable land or nonfarm business capital available, the total family labor input, the mean personal characteristics of those members who work in the family business, $\overline{X}_m^t$ $(L_m^{At} > 0)$, and unobservable variables, s_m^t. It also depends on a set of coefficients β_A^t that may be interpreted as the price or remuneration rate of the preceding factors. Except for that profit function, the other difference with the previous model is that there are now two labor-supply functions and the set of labor-supply parameters, λ, has been expanded. There is now a set of coefficients describing wage labor supply and another set, λ^A, describing the supply of labor to the family farm or nonfarm business.

The structure of the model is now complete. The full model (equation 9.7) plays the role of the income-generating function $y_{it} = Y(x_{it}, \varepsilon_{it}; \beta_t; \lambda_t)$ used above in the description of the decomposition principles, with the following set of equivalence between notations: Observable characteristics x_{it} now correspond to the set of general characteristics of a household and its members observed at period t—respectively, Z_m^t and X_{mi}^t. Unobservable characteristics, ε_{it}, are summarized by the set of residual terms $(u_{mi}^t, v_{mi}^t, v_{mi}^{At}, s_m^t)$ that enter the individual earnings functions, the individual labor-supply equations, and the household profit function if the household is engaged in farm or independent business activities. The price system includes the coefficients of the earnings equations, β^t, and of the profit functions, β_t^A. Finally, the set of behavioral parameters λ_t is the whole set of coefficients that enter the labor-supply functions and the profit functions—that is, $(\lambda^t, \mu^t, \lambda^{At}, \mu^{At})$.

It is important to stress that the model in equation 9.7 is in reduced form, rather than in structural form, in the sense that the labor-supply functions do not depend explicitly on the remuneration of labor in each possible activity. So price effects affect individual and household incomes only directly through the earning and profit equations and not indirectly through changes in occupational choice.[10]

Econometric Specifications

For several reasons, estimating the complete household income model (equation 9.7) in its general form above is practically impossible or at least would be a formidable undertaking. First, all the equations of the model must clearly be estimated simultaneously with nonlinear estimation techniques because of the non-negativity constraint on labor supply and the very likely correlation between the residual term in the various equations. Although intricate, this task might be manageable—under some simplifying assumptions—if there were a single individual in each household. But the obvious correlation across the earnings equations and labor-supply equations of the working-age members in a given household, whose number varies across households, makes this task hopelessly complicated. An additional risk would be that the results of such a complex model would be less than robust and would show artificially high time variability, thus jeopardizing the decomposition principle of interest.

The microeconomic estimation work undertaken for Taiwan, China, relies on a simplified, but more robust, specification based on the following principles.

• Individual earnings functions and household profit functions—if applicable—are estimated separately and consistently through the instrumentation of endogenous right-hand-side variables and the correction of selection bias. Residual terms of these functions are assumed to be independent within any household.

• For lack of information on hours of work in the data, labor-supply behavior is estimated in a discrete way. Household members are assumed to have the choice between the following activities: (a) inactivity, (b) wage work, (c) work on a family farm, (d) work in a family nonfarm business, and (e) combinations of (b) and (c). This choice is specified as a multinomial logit model, which may be considered as an approximation of the more structural model (equation 9.7).

• The simultaneity of household members' labor-supply decisions is taken into account by considering sequentially the behavior of household heads and that of the other members, as conventionally done in most of the labor-supply literature. Thus, the labor-supply decision of the household head is estimated first with the preceding multinomial logit model, using both the general exogenous characteristics of the household and those of all household members as explanatory variables. Second, the labor-supply and occupational choices of other members are estimated conditionally on the decision made by the household head and possibly on his or her income, in case he or she is engaged in wage work. In addition, different models were estimated depending on the position of a person in a family. Indeed, it seems natural that, other things being equal, the spouse of the household head would not behave in the same way with respect to labor supply as would the daughter of the household head. The categories for which distinct labor-supply models have been estimated are spouses, sons, daughters, and other household members.

• It would have been possible to use the results of the multinomial logit labor-supply models to control for selection in the estimation of earnings equations and profit functions.[11] The usual Heckman two-step procedure with an intermediate probit estimation of the probability that an individual is a wage worker (whether or not the individual also works on a family farm) led to equivalent results.

• The lack of robustness of the estimates of some coefficients in the various behavioral equations of the model and the corresponding variability over time would clearly introduce some noise in the decomposition technique described above. Say, for instance, that for a regional dummy variable—for example, working in the Taipei area—the coefficient in the earnings equation is very imprecisely estimated. The estimate of this coefficient will thus tend to vary widely but not significantly from one year to the next. As a consequence, the decomposition method will falsely impute to changes in the geographical structure of earnings part of the observed changes in the distribution of household incomes. To avoid this confusion, we have submitted all the original estimates obtained in the various cross-sections to the following time-smoothing treatment. For each series of estimates c^t of a coefficient of the model, a simple regression was run on a time polynomial of order 2:

$$(9.8) \qquad\qquad c^t = a_c + b_c \cdot t + d_c \cdot t^2.$$

Only the terms significantly different from zero in this regression were kept, and the original estimates c^t were then replaced by the value predicted by equation 9.8. All the behavioral equations were then rerun to adjust the intercept accordingly.

Changes in Earnings and Labor-Supply Functions over the 1976–94 Period

Discussing in detail the results of the estimations of the preceding models would have taken too much space. We only sketch here those conclusions drawn from this estimation work that are important for understanding the decomposition of the change in the distribution of income shown in the next section.[12]

Three changes are of major importance for the understanding of the evolution of income distribution in Taiwan, China, since 1979: (a) an increase in the rate of return to schooling in earning equations, (b) a drop in the variance of the residual term of the earnings equations, and (c) a reduced dependency of spouses' labor supply and occupational choice on household heads' income and occupation. We analyze briefly each issue in turn.

Tables 9.2 and 9.3 report the estimates of the standard Mincerian earnings for various years during the period under analysis. Education is specified alternatively as the number of years of schooling or as a set of dummy variables corresponding to the various schooling degrees, so as to take into account the possible linearity of the (log) earning-education relationship.[13] Experience is defined in the usual

Table 9.2 Wage Functions for Men, Corrected for Selection Bias, Selected Years

Function	1979	1983	1987	1991	1994
Primary education	0.1655	0.2092	0.1577	0.2063	0.1541
	0.0157	*0.0160*	*0.0169*	*0.0193*	*0.0227*
Lower secondary	0.2423	0.3426	0.3309	0.3665	0.3019
education	*0.0186*	*0.0186*	*0.0190*	*0.0210*	*0.0242*
Higher secondary	0.2625	0.2547	0.3104	0.3492	0.3130
education (dropout)	*0.0403*	*0.0355*	*0.0309*	*0.0313*	*0.0343*
Higher secondary	0.3428	0.4681	0.4572	0.5154	0.4407
education	*0.0196*	*0.0196*	*0.0197*	*0.0216*	*0.0247*
(graduated)					
Higher secondary	0.4224	0.6113	0.6201	0.6943	0.6205
education	*0.0244*	*0.0232*	*0.0225*	*0.0242*	*0.0269*
(vocational)					
Higher education	0.4330	0.6790	0.7413	0.8481	0.7956
	0.0254	*0.0245*	*0.0245*	*0.0256*	*0.0283*
Years of schooling[a]	0.0325	0.0502	0.0562	0.0620	0.0582
	0.0015	*0.0016*	*0.0016*	*0.0017*	*0.0018*
Experience	0.0694	0.0704	0.0697	0.0590	0.0641
	0.0021	*0.0019*	*0.0017*	*0.0016*	*0.0016*
Experience squared	−0.0014	−0.0013	−0.0013	−0.0010	−0.0012
	0.0000	*0.0000*	*0.0000*	*0.0000*	*0.0000*
Part-time dummy	−0.1142	−0.1052	−0.0862	−0.0592	−0.0627
variable	*0.0029*	*0.0027*	*0.0027*	*0.0028*	*0.0029*
(instrumented)					
Mills ratio	0.1961	0.3173	0.3063	0.1450	0.2082
	0.0313	*0.0331*	*0.0330*	*0.0342*	*0.0358*
Constant	10.6556	10.5336	10.7701	11.2773	11.3544
	0.0377	*0.0372*	*0.0380*	*0.0407*	*0.0459*
Residual variance	0.2017	0.2071	0.1807	0.1770	0.1856
Number of	12,711	14,217	13,428	13,034	12,724
observations					
Adjusted R^2	0.51	0.52	0.49	0.48	0.45

Note: In this table, the dependent variable is log earnings. Other explanatory variables include dummies for area of residence and position in the household. White robust standard errors are in italics.

a. Coefficient obtained by replacing all educational dummy variables by years of schooling.

Source: Authors' calculations from DGBAS household surveys.

Table 9.3 Wage Functions for Women, Corrected for
Selection Bias, Selected Years

Function	1979	1983	1987	1991	1994
Primary education	0.1908	0.1937	0.1370	0.1115	0.1438
	0.0213	*0.0204*	*0.0191*	*0.0206*	*0.0226*
Lower secondary	0.3072	0.3477	0.3243	0.2873	0.3299
education	*0.0265*	*0.0249*	*0.0229*	*0.0243*	*0.0256*
Higher secondary	0.2776	0.3810	0.3911	0.3452	0.4407
education (dropout)	*0.0463*	*0.0413*	*0.0350*	*0.0390*	*0.0391*
Higher secondary	0.4962	0.5566	0.5080	0.5538	0.5924
education	*0.0286*	*0.0268*	*0.0247*	*0.0258*	*0.0269*
(graduated)					
Higher secondary	0.7522	0.8381	0.7911	0.8762	0.8774
education	*0.0359*	*0.0331*	*0.0301*	*0.0304*	*0.0312*
(vocational)					
Higher education	0.8745	0.9987	0.9336	1.0809	1.1212
	0.0441	*0.0398*	*0.0361*	*0.0356*	*0.0358*
Years of schooling[a]	0.0571	0.0679	0.0663	0.0794	0.0822
	0.0024	*0.0025*	*0.0023*	*0.0025*	*0.0024*
Experience	0.0406	0.0453	0.0418	0.0463	0.0435
	0.0030	*0.0028*	*0.0026*	*0.0025*	*0.0023*
Experience squared	−0.0009	−0.0009	−0.0008	−0.0009	−0.0008
	0.0001	*0.0001*	*0.0001*	*0.0001*	*0.0001*
Part-time dummy	−0.0626	−0.0600	−0.0435	−0.0379	−0.0273
variable	*0.0033*	*0.0032*	*0.0029*	*0.0029*	*0.0028*
(instrumented)					
Mills ratio	0.0604	0.0154	0.0212	0.0901	−0.0004
	0.0380	*0.0357*	*0.0330*	*0.0346*	*0.0332*
Constant	10.6194	10.6551	10.9973	11.2097	11.3246
	0.0421	*0.0410*	*0.0402*	*0.0437*	*0.0465*
Residual variance	0.1913	0.2052	0.1658	0.1747	0.1609
Number of	5,780	7,403	7,448	7,729	8,108
observations					
Adjusted R^2	0.46	0.44	0.38	0.43	0.43

Note: In this table, the dependent variable is log earnings. Other explanatory
variables include dummies for area of residence and position in the household. White
robust standard errors are in italics.

a. Coefficient obtained by replacing all educational dummy variables by years of
schooling.

Source: Authors' calculations from DGBAS household surveys.

way as age minus years of schooling minus 6. Other variables include a dummy variable for those wage earners who report also working as family farm workers and the Mills ratio, which controls for selection into wage-earner jobs. In the absence of data on hours of work, wage earners also working on family farms are the only wage workers who may be guessed to be employed part time. The first variable is instrumented by all variables that appear in the occupational-choice model—that is, all individual and household characteristics. The Mills ratio is computed on the basis of a probit model in which wage work is the dependent dummy variable and explanatory variables are again all the variables that appear in the occupational-choice model.

The striking result in tables 9.2 and 9.3 is the increasing trend in the coefficient that measures the return to education for both men and women, although a slight reversing of that trend seems to have taken place for men at the end of the period. Roughly speaking, over the 14-year period analyzed here, the rate of return for an additional year of schooling increased from a little more than 3 percent to 6 percent for men, and from 6 percent to almost 8 percent for women. Judging from the coefficients obtained by specifying schooling as a set of dummy variables for the various degrees, the structure of earnings by educational levels was substantially modified during the period under analysis. The earning differential between workers with higher secondary or university education and workers with primary or lower secondary increased quite substantially and, as a matter of fact, more than proportionally to the numbers of years of schooling. From the coefficients in tables 9.2 and 9.3, we can conclude that the marginal return by year of schooling increased significantly at the higher secondary level and for higher education, whereas it remained constant for lower secondary and even dropped for primary education. It is also interesting that this evolution is more pronounced for women than for men.

Previous studies of the evolution of the wage structure in Taiwan, China, are not in contradiction with the preceding results, although they point to a somewhat milder unequalizing trend. Using the Labor-Force Survey of the Taiwan, China, Area for 1978–91, Gindling, Goldfarb, and Chang (1995) found a slowly increasing trend in the earnings differential between higher and primary education until approximately 1988 for men, with a small drop afterward, and a continuously increasing trend until 1991 for women. Using the same data source, Fields and O'Hara (1996) also found that the coefficient of the number of years of schooling in the typical log wage regression increased significantly, from .050 to .057 between 1980 and 1993 in a sample including both men and women.[14]

The evidence obtained from the household surveys on the increase of the return to education is thus more pronounced than with the labor-force surveys. A possible explanation of this difference is the fact that the number of hours of work is not observed in the household survey, whereas it is explicitly taken into account in the studies just mentioned. Those studies also make use of other variables not available in the household survey, such as tenure in the current main job, job mobility over the previous five years, and whether the person has a second job. A possible explanation of the stronger increase in the coefficient of education found in the present study would be that the correlation between all these variables and education may have changed in some systematic way over time. Our specification would thus appear as some kind of reduced form of more complete earning models.

From a macroeconomic point of view, the increase in the return to education in Taiwan, China, may seem somewhat surprising. In a competitive framework, it suggests that the demand for educated workers over the period under analysis increased faster than the supply, which we have seen grew at an accelerated rate over the period. The growth of demand has to do obviously with the overall growth rate of the economy but doubtlessly also with the change in the structure of the economy, which we have seen has been quite dramatic.

The second striking feature in tables 9.2 and 9.3 is the fall in the variance of the residual term of the earnings equation. Since the analysis of Juhn, Murphy, and Pierce (1993) for the United States, it has become customary to interpret this term as representing the dispersion of the remuneration of unobserved productive talents. In the case of Taiwan, China, the evidence would thus suggest that unobserved talents were remunerated in a more homogeneous way in the 1990s than in the late 1970s. It is not clear, however, that this interpretation would be right. It must be kept in mind that we control for hours of work very poorly in the earning equations. We essentially do so through a dummy variable indicating that a wage earner has another self-employment activity and implicitly through the selection bias correction factor, which in some sense may be interpreted as linked to labor supply.[15] Under those conditions, it is quite possible that the drop in the variance of the residual term of the earnings equations corresponds to more homogeneity in the working hours of wage earners. To check whether this hypothesis is actually the case would require reestimating earnings equations with another database that included hours of work. For our decomposition purpose, there thus remains an ambiguity about the actual interpretation to be given to the drop in the variance of this residual term.

Income regressions were also estimated for farm and nonfarm profit functions. None of those functions show very significant changes over time. In particular, the rate of return to schooling shows no significant evolution. As self-employed workers tend to concentrate toward the bottom of the educational scale, this result is consistent with what was obtained for wage earners. For lack of space, these regressions are not reported.

The last major change in the estimated household income model is concerned with the occupational choices of married women. As mentioned above, these choices are modeled through a multinomial logit model. Explanatory variables include the characteristics of the household head (gender, age, and education); the sociodemographic composition of the rest of the household with respect to the same variables; the area of residence; land ownership; and financial wealth, which is approximated by capital income. Different models were estimated for household heads, spouses, and other members in the household. Describing the details of all these models would be cumbersome. We insist here on a single change, which is the increasing autonomy of married women in their occupational choices. Figure 9.2 shows the evolution of the estimated mean elasticity of the probability that married women will take up various occupations with respect to their husband's earnings—in cases where he indeed is a wage worker. It can be seen that the woman's choice is less and less dependent on the husband's income, this situation being the case in particular for wage work and self-employment, and to a lesser extent for participation. If we were to restrict the population to those households whose head is a wage earner—that is, approximately 75 percent of the population—it would, thus, be the case that the correlation between husbands' and wives' incomes tended to increase over time, fewer wives being inactive or having low-paid self-employment jobs in households in which the heads have a relatively high wage.

This evolution may be explained, on the one hand, by the general increase observed in women's labor-force participation seen above and, on the other hand, by the increase in wage employment opportunities permitted by the growth of the economy. In both cases, women who were initially less likely to be active or to be employed as wage workers are those who took over these new jobs. Other things being equal, they were predominantly in households with relatively well-off household heads.

Other features are notable in the evolution of the coefficients of the occupational-choice models over the period under analysis, all of which are likely to have had some influence on the evolution of the distribution of income. These features are quantitatively less

Figure 9.2 Elasticity of Spouses' Occupational Choice with Respect to Head of Household's Earnings

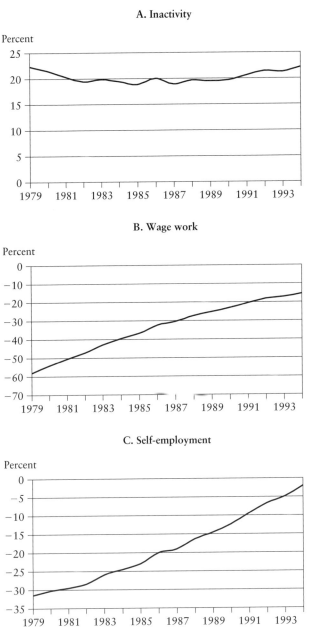

A. Inactivity

B. Wage work

C. Self-employment

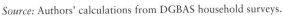

Source: Authors' calculations from DGBAS household surveys.

important, however, and we prefer to leave them aside for the clarity of the argument.[16]

Decomposition of the Change in the Distribution of Income over 1979–94

We are now in a position to apply the decomposition methodology presented above and to estimate the separate effects on the distribution of income of the changes in the structure of wages and prices, in labor-supply behavior and occupational preferences, and finally in the structure of the population. To make the analysis clearer, we consider only the initial and terminal years of the period. However, because we have seen that the decomposition methodology was sensitive to the sample chosen as a reference, we use several combinations of the two initial years (1979 and 1980) and the two terminal years (1993 and 1994). We apply the decomposition methodology presented above between two years, using alternately the initial and the terminal years as a reference sample. Overall, this procedure leads to eight possible ways of defining the price, participation, population, and education effects.[17] Using these combinations enables us to identify some rough "intervals of confidence" for the various effects or, alternatively, to measure the extent to which the combinations are sensitive to the population that is chosen as a reference. In tables 9.4 and 9.5, we report the average change in the Gini coefficient computed for these eight alternative combinations as well as the two extreme values.[18]

The Evolution of the Distribution of Individual Earnings

The results of our decomposition methodology applied to individual earnings are summarized in table 9.4 for Gini coefficients and in figures 9.3 through 9.5 for the full distribution.

THE PRICE EFFECT AND THE UNEQUALIZING EFFECT OF THE INCREASE IN EDUCATIONAL RETURNS

The first step in the decomposition consists of modifying the structure of earnings while keeping the population of wage earners constant. By doing so, we ignore the possible effects of a change in the level and structure of earnings on participation and occupational decisions.

The dominant effect in the evolution of the structure of earnings is, of course, the observed increase in the return to education. Not surprisingly, this produces an unambiguous increase in the inequality of the distribution. Depending on the population that is used to

Table 9.4 Decomposition of the Evolution of the Inequality of Individual Earnings, 1979–80 and 1993–94

(absolute change in Gini coefficient)

Indicator	Mean change	Minimum change	Maximum change
Observed variation	−0.024	−0.027	−0.021
Price and participation effect	0.015	0.006	0.025
Price effect (occupation held constant)	0.025	0.016	0.034
Overall participation effect	−0.010	−0.013	−0.009
Change in earning equation's residual variance	−0.029	−0.038	−0.022
Overall population effect	−0.009	−0.019	0.003
Education effect	−0.011	−0.013	−0.010
Education with fixed school enrollment	−0.008	−0.012	−0.004
Education with fixed school enrollment and fixed occupation	−0.008	−0.012	−0.005
School enrollment effect	−0.002	−0.005	0.002
Education of women	−0.014	−0.020	−0.010
Education of women with fixed school enrollment	−0.012	−0.019	−0.007
Education of men	0.003	0.000	0.005
Education of men with fixed school enrollment	0.003	0.002	0.005

Note: Minimum and maximum values among all combinations of initial and terminal years and initial or terminal population samples for decomposition methodology. Mean change computed on all combinations.

Source: Authors' calculations from DGBAS household surveys.

evaluate this effect, the change in the Gini coefficient ranges from 0.016 to 0.034, with an arithmetic mean equal to 0.025. There is nothing really surprising in the amplitude of this range. It is indeed to be expected that the effect of a change in the return to education on the distribution of earnings depends on the distribution of schooling in the population, which we have seen has drastically changed over the 15-year period studied in Taiwan, China. The effect of a rising earning differential between highly and poorly educated workers depends on the weight of each group in the population, and these weights are substantially different in 1979 and in 1994.

Figure 9.3 gives another representation of the unequalizing effect of the increase in the return to education. It shows the simulated

Table 9.5 Decomposition of the Evolution of the Inequality of Equivalized Household Incomes, 1979–80 and 1993–94

(absolute change in Gini coefficient)

Indicator	Mean change	Minimum change	Maximum change
Observed variation	0.019	0.013	0.025
Price and participation effect	0.037	0.013	0.062
Price effect (occupation held constant)	0.024	0.010	0.037
Overall participation effect	0.013	0.003	0.025
Change in earning equation's residual variance	−0.020	−0.028	−0.014
Overall population effect	0.002	−0.026	0.032
Education effect	−0.002	−0.010	0.006
Education with fixed school enrollment	−0.003	−0.008	0.000
Education with fixed school enrollment and fixed occupation	−0.004	−0.006	−0.003
School enrollment effect	0.003	−0.002	0.009
Education of women	0.004	0.001	0.008
Education of women with fixed school enrollment	0.003	0.001	0.005
Education of men	−0.005	−0.009	0.001
Education of men with fixed school enrollment	−0.005	−0.008	−0.003
Number of children	−0.008	−0.015	−0.001
With fixed participation	−0.007	−0.011	−0.004

Note: Minimum and maximum values among all combinations of initial and terminal years and initial or terminal population samples for decomposition methodology. Mean change computed on all combinations.

Source: Authors' calculations from DGBAS household surveys.

change that would have occurred in the earnings of individual wage workers observed in 1979 had they been paid in accordance with the earning function observed in 1994. On average, earnings would have increased by approximately 70 percent, but because of the rise in the rate of return to education, the gain in earnings is an increasing function of the rank in the distribution. Earners in the bottom quartile would have gained slightly more than 60 percent over the whole period, whereas those in the top quartile would have gained approximately 75 percent.

Interestingly, it turns out that most of the preceding evolution is due to the change in the structure of earnings by educational level.

Figure 9.3 1979–1994 Variation in Individual Earnings
Caused by the Price Effect, by Centiles of the 1979 Earnings
Distribution

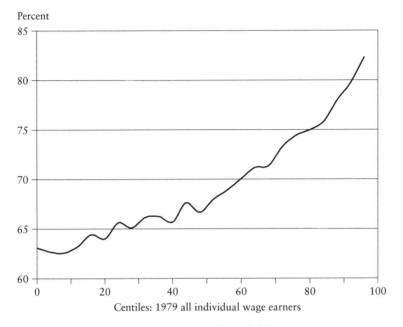

Percent

Centiles: 1979 all individual wage earners

Source: Authors' calculations from DGBAS household surveys.

Changes in the returns to experience or in geographical earning differentials were too small to have any sizable effect on the distribution.

THE EQUALIZING EFFECT OF CHANGES IN PARTICIPATION AND OCCUPATIONAL CHOICE

The effects of changes in participation and occupational choice
behavior are a bit more subtle to analyze than the pure price effects
because they correspond to a modification of the population of individual earners. Figure 9.4 represents these modifications by showing
the simulated entries in and exits from the 1979 wage labor force
that would have occurred had people adopted the participation and
occupational-choice behavior observed in 1994. Considering all
wage earners at the same time, we first see in panel A of figure 9.4
that there has been an equalizing effect, with net exits from the
wage labor force at the two extremes of the distribution and no net
change at the middle. Interestingly, this overall evolution results
from various phenomena and, in particular, from opposite tendencies among men and women.

   The participation of men in the wage labor force fell over the
period under analysis, mostly as a result of people retiring sooner.

Figure 9.4 Simulated Entries into and Exits from
the Wage Labor Force

A. All individuals

Percentage of total population

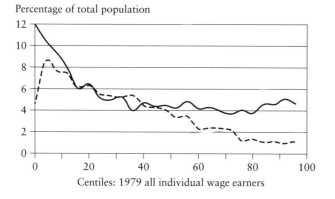

Centiles: 1979 all individual wage earners

B. Men/men's wages

Percentage of total population

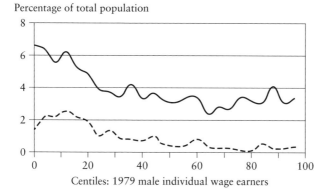

Centiles: 1979 male individual wage earners

C. Men/individual wages

Percentage of total population

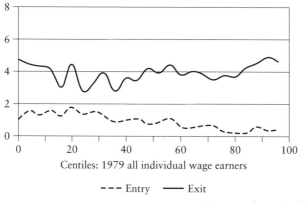

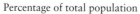

Centiles: 1979 all individual wage earners

--- Entry —— Exit

(Continued on the following page)

Figure 9.4 (Continued)

D. Women/women's wages

Percentage of total population

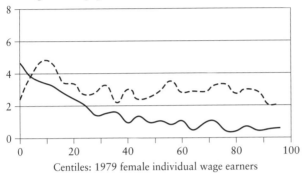

Centiles: 1979 female individual wage earners

E. Women/individual wages

Percentage of total population

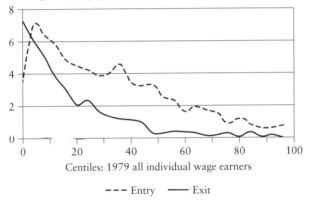

Centiles: 1979 all individual wage earners

- - - Entry   ——— Exit

Source: Authors' calculations from DGBAS household surveys.

This net drop is approximately constant along the male wage scale but is a little more pronounced in the first two deciles (see panel B of figure 9.4). However, because there are more men than women at the top of the distribution of wage earners, this drop in participation is responsible for a higher net exit rate at the top of the distribution, as may be seen in panel C of figure 9.4.

For women, there were more entries than exits because of the participation effect mentioned earlier. This phenomenon tended to be stronger at the top of the female wage scale and was actually in the opposite direction in the bottom percentiles (see panel D of figure 9.4). But because most women are located in the bottom part of the overall distribution of wages, this phenomenon contributed to a net entry of wage workers at the middle of the overall wage scale and was, therefore, equalizing (see panel E of figure 9.4). Overall, the change in participation behavior, which essentially consisted of a drop in the wage labor-force participation of men and an increase in that of women, thus had an unambiguous equalizing effect on the overall distribution of individual earnings.

THE EQUALIZING EFFECT OF THE DROP IN RESIDUAL EARNING VARIANCE

The drop in residual earning variance corresponds to a rather tautological step in the decomposition methodology. We have seen that earnings heterogeneity, as described by the residual terms of earning equations, fell substantially over time. This fall reflects either a true decline in the heterogeneity of the productivity of workers with identical observed characteristics or less disparity in working hours. The only lesson to be drawn from the decomposition appearing in table 9.4 is that this effect is responsible for a drop of 2.2 to 3.8 points in the Gini coefficient of individual earnings, a rather sizable effect.

POPULATION AND EDUCATION EFFECTS

Taking the preceding effects out of the actual change in the Gini coefficient of the distribution of individual earnings yields the population effect as a residual. It amounts to a drop of approximately 1 point in the Gini coefficient. But it must be noted that, more than for the effects already discussed, this effect depends very much on the path followed in decomposing the change in inequality.[19] Thus, there is some ambiguity in the conclusion that the change in the sociodemographic structure of the population helped equalize the distribution.

More interesting and much less ambiguous is the effect of the change in the educational structure of the population. On average, this change represents a little more than a 1 point drop in the Gini coefficient of individual earnings, with a rather narrow range of variation.

An illustration of the way the change in the educational structure of the population modifies the distribution of individual earnings is shown in figure 9.5, which was built along the same lines as figure 9.3. Here again, the starting point is the 1979 population. We apply to that population the distribution of education observed by gender and age groups in 1994. As mentioned above, we do so through a rank-preserving transformation. The most educated person in a gender and age group in 1979 is given the educational level of the most educated person in the same group in 1994; the same thing is then done for the next most educated person, and so on. Panel A of figure 9.5 shows the change in earnings that would have resulted from this modified level of schooling for the 1979 population of wage earners.

Figure 9.5 Simulation of the 1994 Education
Structure on the 1979 Population

**A. Relative wage variation by centiles of the 1979
wage distribution (constant composition)**

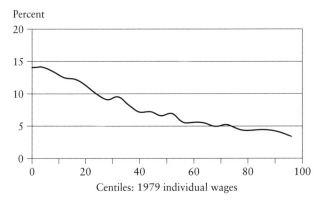

Centiles: 1979 individual wages

B. Entries in and exits from the wage labor force

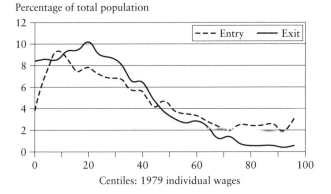

Centiles: 1979 individual wages

C. Mean wage variation by centile (variable composition)

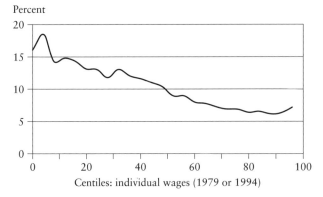

Centiles: individual wages (1979 or 1994)

Source: Authors' calculations from DGBAS household surveys.

Of course, this simulated change in the level of schooling also modifies the participation and occupational choice behavior of people; hence, panel A actually refers only to those wage workers in 1979 who would have remained wage workers despite the change in their educational level. It does not include those who, being initially inactive or in a nonwage activity, would have entered wage work because of more schooling.

Panel A illustrates that the change in the average level of schooling of a population is not distribution neutral. Because there is a limit to the number of years of schooling, workers who initially were at the top of the wage scale—and therefore better educated—gained proportionally fewer years of schooling than people at the bottom who initially had a low level of schooling. It follows that the expansion of schooling had a significant equalizing effect on the distribution of individual earnings. Roughly speaking, this evolution may have caused a 10 percent increase of earnings in the bottom half of the distribution and only a 5 percent increase in the top half.

The change in the structure of schooling in the population also brought about changes in participation behavior. One of these changes is purely mechanical. With the expansion of education, young people stay longer in school and out of the labor force. This effect produces some "exits" from the wage labor force, which are concentrated at the bottom of the distribution because the young workers in question receive relatively low wages. The second change is of a more economic nature. With higher schooling and higher market wages, more individuals enter the wage labor force. This phenomenon is more or less uniform across the wage scale for men and concentrates a little more at the bottom of the distribution for women. On balance, it may be seen in panel B of figure 9.5 that the expansion of education produces net exits from the wage labor force at the bottom of the distribution and net entries at the top. In terms of inequality, this pattern produces ambiguous effects: poor people become relatively poorer but less numerous. The second effect tends to dominate with the Gini coefficient, which explains why the drop in inequality owing to the education effect tends to be lower in table 9.4 when occupation and school enrollment are kept fixed.

That the sum of these two effects on the distribution of income is unambiguously equalizing is shown by panel C of figure 9.5. The difference between panel A and panel C is that in panel C exits from and entries into the wage labor force have been taken into account at the same time as individual earnings were modified because of the change in schooling. This combination leads to a redefinition of the percentiles of the original 1979 distribution, because the population is not the same and some income reranking may have taken place.

Thus, we are now comparing percentiles of individual wage earners with different compositions. The relative income gain is still a decreasing function of the wage level, so that the Lorenz curve of the simulated distribution of wages in 1994 dominates that of 1979. For the bottom centiles, the effect is quite substantial, amounting to approximately 17 percent. This finding is not out of proportion with the 60 percent pure price effect appearing in figure 9.3, an effect that may be interpreted as a pure productivity effect.

Changes in the Gini coefficient appearing in table 9.4 are consistent with this analysis of the effect of the expansion of education upon income distribution. An additional and seemingly puzzling effect appears there. It is a strong asymmetry between the effects of the expansion of the education of men and women on the overall distribution of earnings. There is no paradox here, simply the consequence of an earnings differential in favor of men. In view of that differential, increasing the education of men but not that of women would have the equalizing effect seen above; it would also contribute to an increase in the inequality between men and women. The second effect dominates the first. The opposite occurs for women. The equalizing effect of the expansion of education is reinforced by the reduction in the male-female differential.

Overall, it thus appears that the reduction in the inequality of individual earnings in Taiwan, China, over the period 1979–94 results from several strong influences that have not all played in the same direction. On the unequalizing side, there is the increase in the returns to education, which reinforced earnings disparities. On the equalizing side, three phenomena of unequal importance have overcompensated that increase. By order of importance, they are (a) the fall in the variance of the unobserved determinants of earnings, (b) the change in schooling and the distribution of schooling within the population of wage earners, and (c) the change in participation and occupational-choice behavior, which brought more women into the wage labor force and took out some men. The latter evolution was equalizing because of the initial earnings gap in favor of men.

Decomposition of the Evolution of the Distribution of Household Income

Interestingly, the decomposition of the evolution of the distribution of equivalized primary incomes along the same lines does not lead to the same conclusions. As a matter of fact, the overall balance of all the preceding effects must even be the opposite of what was found for individual earners, because we know that the distribution of equivalized household income became substantially more unequal over the period. In the following subsections, we review the same issues as for individual earnings and try to identify where the difference may lie.

PRICE EFFECTS

The increase in the rate of return to schooling should have the same unequalizing effect on household incomes as on individual earnings, but its magnitude may be expected to be smaller. Even though there is some correlation between the level of schooling of the various members in a household, it is not perfect, which is an equalizing factor. In addition, it turns out that the returns to education remained approximately stable in farm and nonfarm profit functions. This stability should dampen somewhat the effect of increased individual wage inequality on household incomes. Of course, this effect may be compensated by changes in the coefficients of profit functions, which would contribute to more inequality among households receiving this type of income. Although it was seen that the latter effects were not substantial, they indeed seem to compensate for the dampening effect on wage inequality of switching from household to individual incomes. The increase in the Gini coefficient attributable to the price effect is approximately the same for households as for individual earners—namely, 2.4 points. The lower bound of the confidence interval proves to be smaller, though. Likewise, the curve in figure 9.6 showing the 1979–94 price effect on the distribution of household income is flatter than the curve in figure 9.3.

PARTICIPATION EFFECTS

In the case of participation effects, the difference with individual earnings is still more pronounced. Changes in participation and occupational-choice behavior that were unambiguously equalizing in the case of individual earnings are not so any more. As may be seen in table 9.5, they are even unequalizing.

Two phenomena explain this difference. The first one has been alluded to in the preceding section and has been analyzed in some detail in Fournier (1997). It is the drop in the (negative) income effect of husbands' incomes on married women's labor-force participation. Because of this evolution, we expect that applying the participation and occupational-choice behavior of 1994 to the 1979 sample of households will lead to relatively more women—in net terms—entering the labor force at the top of the distribution of household incomes, where household heads' earnings are relatively high. This outcome is exactly what appears in panel A of figure 9.7, which shows the variation of income due to simulated entries and exits from the labor force by percentiles of 1979 households ranked by equalized income.[20]

Figure 9.6 1979–94 Variation in Household Income Caused by the Price Effect, by Centiles of the 1979 Distribution of Equivalized Household Income Per Capita (EHIP)

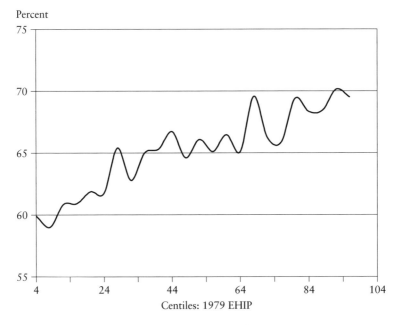

Centiles: 1979 EHIP

Source: Authors' calculations from DGBAS household surveys.

But there is another explanation. It was seen in panel D of figure 9.4 that women who entered the wage labor force between 1979 and 1994 were, on average, better educated than women who were already active. This fact had an equalizing effect on the distribution of individual earnings, because these women were in the middle of the overall distribution of wages. The situation is different for household incomes, however. Better-educated women tend to be in relatively richer households, and their entry into the wage labor market contributes to a larger increase of household income in the upper part of the scale.

Nothing of this type is observed for men. It was seen above that they tended to exit the labor force in a more or less neutral way with respect to the distribution of male individual earnings. Panel B of figure 9.7 suggests that there is approximately the same neutrality with respect to household income. This finding is not unexpected. Indeed, household incomes generally are well correlated with the income of household heads, who are generally taken to be males. Overall, it is, therefore, mostly the change in women's labor-force participation

Figure 9.7 Entries into and Exits from the Labor Force: Overall Participation Effect

A. Women

Percentage of total population

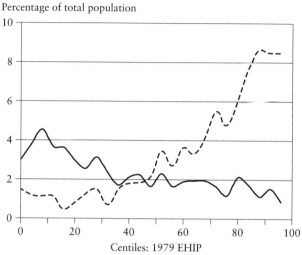

Centiles: 1979 EHIP

B. Men

Percentage of total population

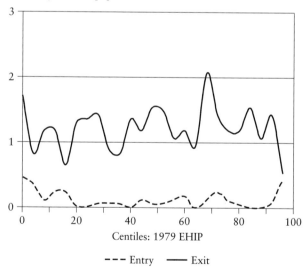

Centiles: 1979 EHIP

--- Entry ——— Exit

Source: Authors' calculations from DGBAS household surveys.

that explains the unequalizing effect of the changes in participation behavior and occupational choice on household incomes.

THE EFFECT OF EARNINGS' RESIDUAL VARIANCE

As for the effects of the returns to education, the fact that there are various wage earners in a household should reduce the distributional effect of this drop in the variance of the unobserved determinants of individual earnings. This result is indeed seen in table 9.5. The drop in the Gini coefficient of equivalized household incomes is only 0.020, whereas it was 0.029 for individual earnings.[21]

POPULATION AND EDUCATION EFFECTS

Another important difference with the decomposition of changes in individual earnings is that the effect of changes in the sociodemographic structure of the population on the distribution of household incomes is close to zero when the Gini coefficient is used to measure income inequality. Alternatively, one may say that the interval of confidence appearing in table 9.5 suggests a much more ambiguous effect, whereas that same effect was (almost) unambiguously equalizing in the case of individual earnings. What is more puzzling is that this ambiguity still holds when one focuses on the effect of the change in the educational structure. Indeed, the change was unambiguously and strongly equalizing in the case of individual earnings. On the one hand, the change in the educational structure of the population may be expected to have a lesser equalizing effect for household income than for individual earnings because of the diversification of educational changes within the household. On the other hand, there are additional unequalizing effects that were not present for individual earnings.

As in the argument about the price effect or the residual variance earlier, the lesser equalizing effect of the expansion of education observed with household incomes corresponds to the diversity of initial individual levels of schooling within a household. If schooling levels were perfectly correlated across the various members of a household, the income-equalizing effect of the expansion of schooling would be the same as for individuals. At the other extreme, if schooling levels were totally uncorrelated, the expansion of schooling would have the same income effect on all household members, so that the distribution would hardly change. Reality lies somewhere between these two extremes. When the effect of the expansion of education is evaluated with fixed occupations—in other words, when only the income effect of an increase in education is taken into account—the distribution of household income unambiguously improves. But the change in the Gini coefficient is smaller than for individual earners. In table 9.5, this change is −0.4 points, with a confidence interval ranging from −0.3 to −0.6. This change was −0.8 points in table 9.4. It is likely, however, that we slightly overestimate the equalizing effect of the expansion of education on household incomes because changes in individual levels of schooling were simulated independently among the members of the same household, whereas some partial correlation should have been taken into account.

Unlike with individual earnings, it may be seen in panel A of figure 9.8 that participation effects induced by the change in the distribution of schooling have little influence on the distribution of equivalized household incomes. The proportion of net exits from the labor force, which results on the one hand from more people going to school longer and on the other hand from more people participating because of their increased earning potential, turns out to be approximately the same across the various income groups. Gross flows in and out of the labor force are strongly income dependent, however, with larger flows being observed at the highest income levels. The explanation is rather simple. First, the drop in participation due to longer schooling years and more school enrollment may be observed only for individuals who are going to school long enough for the choice between schooling and activity to be truly relevant. For instance, workers in relatively rich households who are 18 years old are more likely than those in relatively poor households to switch from activity to school because of the general expansion of education. This fact is explained by a larger proportion of children in richer households already going to school until age 17. Second, the increase in the level of education among older people led some of them to enter into the labor force. This phenomenon is stronger among women who reach higher levels of education and, therefore, belong to relatively well-off households.

The overall effect of the expansion of education is represented in panels B and C of figure 9.8. In panel B, individuals are ranked according to the 1979 level of equivalized income in their household. This panel shows the average change in income owing to both higher earnings and profits of active household members and changes in participation behavior. It may be seen that the drop in income due to less participation is overcompensated by the higher income of active people at low initial income levels but not at the other extreme of the distribution. On the basis of panel B, it would seem that the expansion of education is unambiguously equalizing even when one takes into account its consequences for labor-force participation. However, the argument behind panel B ignores the fact that those changes in participation are bound to generate

Figure 9.8 Effects of Imposing the 1994 Education Structure on the 1979 Population

A. Entries in and exits from the labor force

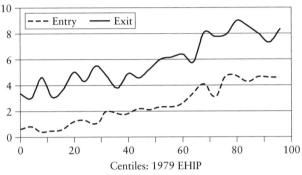

Percentage of total population

Centiles: 1979 EHIP

B. Relative income variation by centile of the 1979 distribution of equivalized household income

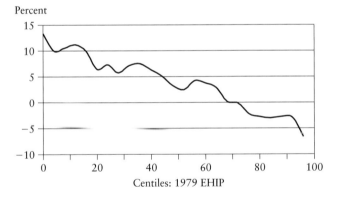

Percent

Centiles: 1979 EHIP

C. Mean EHIP variation by centile (variable composition)

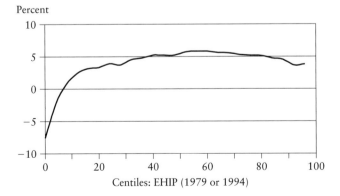

Percent

Centiles: EHIP (1979 or 1994)

Source: Authors' calculations from DGBAS household surveys.

some substantial reranking of households. In fact, exits from the labor force caused by longer schooling are responsible in some households for a substantial drop in income, which may modify the ranking of households. Symmetrically, more participation may explain why a household shifts to a higher percentile. So the bottom percentiles of the new distribution include many households whose income has fallen because of the negative effect of longer schooling on participation in the labor force.[22] At the top of the distribution, one should find some households in which an additional member switched from inactivity to work or from self-employment to wage work because of the change in his or her level of schooling.

It may be seen in panel C of figure 9.8 that this reranking is causing an ambiguous change in the distribution of income. On average, those households in the first percentiles of the 1979 distribution are gaining with the expansion of education (panel B of figure 9.8), but some of them are losing a lot because a member became inactive. Because of this loss, those households shift toward the bottom of the distribution and the bottom percentiles of the distribution appear poorer than they actually were in 1979. As a result, the effect of the expansion of schooling on the distribution of household income is essentially ambiguous, a conclusion that is in direct opposition to that obtained for individual wage earners. Isolating this school enrollment effect, as was done in table 9.5, confirms that it contributes to an increase in the level of inequality.

This conclusion may seem surprising, and one may wonder whether it is not built in the methodology being used. Clearly, it may have to do with the absence of an explicit model of household demand for schooling in our decomposition methodology and, therefore, to the fact that changes in schooling and their implications for participation are allocated randomly and uniformly in the population. In practice, there certainly has been some selection in the process of schooling expansion, with schooling expanding less among poorer households. However, it must be stressed that the magnitude of the expansion of schooling over the period under analysis has been so great that it is difficult to imagine that such temporarily unequalizing forces have not been present. One must also note that the negative income effect associated with longer schooling took place during a period in which the income of the active household members increased quite rapidly, by approximately by 60 percent. Thus, it is unlikely that the overall income of those households in which a member became inactive has fallen. It simply has increased at a slower rate than that of other households. Of course, such a relative and absolute income loss (and therefore this expansion of schooling in the bottom part of the distribution) would probably have been impossible without the general increase in labor productivity observed throughout the period. In other words, more inequality may have appeared through this channel because of the fast increase in the mean income of the population.

The differential effect of the expansion in education for men and women is reported in table 9.5. Here again, the difference from the results obtained for individual earnings is striking. The expansion of women's education is now unequalizing, whereas that of men's education is equalizing. The explanation of that difference is simple. It lies in the filtering caused by labor-force participation. The expansion of men's education is equalizing because men's labor-force participation is more or less uniform across the household income scale and, as seen for individual earners, men's educational gains are relatively more important at the bottom of the distribution. For women, the situation is different. Their participation is more frequent in the upper part of the distribution of household income, so that the expansion of their education and the consequent rise in their earnings have an unequalizing effect. This effect offsets that of a more equal distribution of schooling among the whole female population.

FAMILY SIZE AND OTHER POPULATION EFFECTS

More factors are likely to influence the distribution of household income than that of individual earnings. This is true in particular of the evolution of the demographic composition of families. To isolate the influence of that factor on the change in the distribution of household income is a difficult task because that evolution is clearly linked to economic and social phenomena behind the price and occupational-choice effects analyzed earlier.

Things may be a little simpler if attention is restricted to children under working age, who were considered as exogenous in the household income model. The last rows of table 9.5 and figure 9.9 report the results obtained with a very simple simulation consisting of a rank-preserving transformation of the distribution of the number of children in groups of households defined by age, area of residence, and education of household heads. The transformation is of the same type as for education. The household in a given group with the largest number of children in 1979 is given the number of children of the household with the largest number of children in the same group in 1994. The same is then done for the household with the next largest number of children in that group and so on in each group of households. This simulation unambiguously contributes to equalizing the distribution of equivalized household income. The Gini coefficient falls on average by 0.8 percentage points, and it may be seen in figure 9.9 that the average gain in net equivalized income

Figure 9.9 Effects of Imposing the 1994 Children Structure on the 1979 Population: Relative Variation by Centile of the 1979 Distribution of Equivalized Household Income

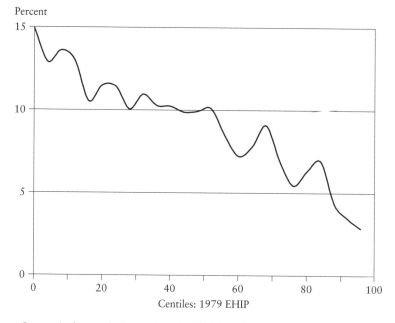

Percent

Centiles: 1979 EHIP

Source: Authors' calculations from DGBAS household surveys.

decreases as one moves up in the 1979 distribution scale. As for education, this overall effect includes the consequences of a change in participation behavior. Because there are fewer children to take care of, older household members modify their occupational choice, which in turn modifies the income of the household. It may be seen in table 9.5 that this effect is extremely small, though.

Other changes in the structure of the population may have had an important influence on the distribution of equivalized household incomes. They may be measured by the residual of the effects of education (−.002) and that of the number of children (−.008) with respect to the overall population effect (.002), which amounts to an increase of 1.2 percentage points in the Gini coefficient. However, these changes are more difficult to identify directly. Because they were practically negligible for individual earners and because the main difference in household composition has already been taken into account, it is tempting to relate them with the matching of individuals within households—for instance, the correlation between the earning potential of household members. The consequences of a change in this matching is analyzed in Fournier (1999).[23]

Conclusion

Using a decomposition analysis of inequality in Taiwan, China, over the 1979–94 period, this chapter proposed some explanations of the observed evolution of the distribution of income among individual earners and households. It also revealed the influence of some of the dramatic transformations that took place in the structure of the population and the economy during that period.

Four phenomena were shown to be important in the evolution of the distribution of individual earnings:

1. An increase in the returns to schooling, which took place despite a dramatic growth in the supply of educated workers and contributed to an increase in inequality. This effect was more than offset by the three other phenomena.

2. A drop in the variance of the effect of unobserved determinants of individual earnings.

3. A change in participation behavior, which contributed to increasing the relative weight of the middle earners.

4. The expansion of education, which equalized the distribution of schooling and, therefore, of earnings.

Together these four tendencies produced a significant drop in the inequality of individual earnings. Note, however, that there is some ambiguity about the interpretation of the second phenomenon. If we ignore that component, then it may be said that the expansion of schooling and the change in occupational behavior more or less offset the unequalizing effect of the increase in the rate of return to education.

The same phenomena affected the evolution of the distribution of equivalized household incomes, but their effects were somewhat different, whether they were taken separately or jointly. Also, other forces were present, so the overall outcome was rather different. Inequality unambiguously increased between 1979 and 1994. This increase was shown to result from the combination of the increase in the rate of returns to education and of the changes in participation and occupational-choice behavior, which turned out to be unequalizing at the household level instead of equalizing, as for individual earners. This apparent contradiction is explained by the fact that the net entrants into the labor force, mostly women, belonged to the upper part of the distribution of household income and the middle part of the distribution of individual earners. Taken together, the effect of the increase in the rate of return to education and of the change in occupational choices may have been responsible for an increase of 3.7 points in the Gini coefficient of the distribution of household income.

This increase in inequality was partly offset by the drop in the variance of the unobserved determinants of earnings. Unlike the case with individual earnings, however, no offsetting force came from the change in the educational structure of the population. A more equal distribution of schooling around a higher mean could have contributed to more equal household incomes, although to a lesser extent than for individual earners because of individual diversity within households. But this tendency was offset by the unequalizing effects of induced changes in participation and, in particular, the withdrawal from the labor force originating from longer schooling and higher school enrollment.

Other potentially important influences on the distribution of household incomes include changes in the distribution of household size. These changes were shown to have contributed to more equality in the distribution of household incomes but were probably offset by other changes in the sociodemographic structure of the population of households.

If one were to summarize all that evolution and relate it to the economic trends in Taiwan, China, during the period, the story suggested by the decomposition undertaken in this chapter could be as follows. Continued accelerated economic growth caused an increase in the demand for educated labor that went beyond the rapidly increasing supply resulting from the general expansion of education and of participation rates. As a consequence, the rate of returns to education went up, earnings differentials widened, and inequality increased among both individual earners and households. In the case of individual earners, this movement was offset by the equalizing influence of a more equal distribution of schooling and the fact that net entrants to the labor force were predominantly women at the middle of the earning scale. For households, however, those women contributed to an increase in inequality because they came from households in the upper half of the distribution. At the same time, longer schooling and its negative effect on labor-force participation considerably dampened the equalizing potential of the expansion of education.

Notes

1. On both subjects, the analysis is essentially aggregate and cross-sectional. For an account of the relationship between growth and education, see Pritchett (1996). On the relationship between education and income distribution, see Bourguignon (1995).

2. The 1970 figure is from Jiang (1992). The 1995 figure is ours and is computed from the household survey.

3. This is the process eloquently described and analyzed by Fei, Ranis, and Kuo (1979, 1981) and Ranis (1974).

4. Based on a methodology of the Oaxaca-Blinder type, the results obtained by Jiang (1992) for the early 1980s seem to go in the opposite direction. This finding suggests that the evolution brought to light by Fields and O'Hara might have taken place in the late 1980s and early 1990s.

5. It would certainly have been quite interesting to conduct this analysis on a longer period extending back to the 1960s or the 1950s. Unfortunately, the available data were not comparable. As a matter of fact, even the surveys taken in 1976–78 proved not to be fully comparable, in particular in terms of sample size, to earlier ones. It would also have been interesting to extend the period of analysis to more recent years: 1994 was the last survey available when this project started.

6. A more detailed analysis of changes in occupational-choice behavior and their consequences for labor supply and the labor market is made in Bourguignon, Fournier, and Gurgand (1999b).

7. The equivalence scale used here is such that the number of adult equivalents in a household is equal to the square root of the number of household members.

8. A decomposition similar to the present one with a linear income-generating function has been proposed by Juhn, Murphy, and Pierce (1993).

9. Formally a rank-preserving transformation of the distribution of ε_{it} into the distribution observed at time t' is obtained as follows: $e_{it''} = F^{-1}_{t'}[F_t(\varepsilon_{it})]$, where $F(\ )$ is the cumulative function of the distribution.

10. A structural model is used in Bourguignon, Fournier, and Gurgand (1999b).

11. An equivalent to the well-known Heckman two-stage procedure for the correction of the selection bias in the case of a dichotomous choice represented by a probit exists with polytomous choices and the multinomial logit model. See Lee (1983).

12. More detail on the estimation work and its results is given in Bourguignon, Fournier, and Gurgand (1999a).

13. All simulations in the next section rely on the most complete specification with dummy degree variables.

14. Jiang (1992) found a "wage compression effect" across educational levels between 1978 and 1986, although he also uses the labor-force surveys. However, his conclusion is likely because he simultaneously controlled for the sector of activity of wage earners and their occupation, both variables being highly correlated with formal education.

15. In other words, the latent variable in a probit participation model may be interpreted as proportional to the desired number of hours of work.

16. A detailed discussion of these models as well as of the household profit functions may be found in Bourguignon, Fournier, and Gurgand (1999b).

17. That is, four different combinations of initial and terminal years and, for each combination, two decompositions, depending on whether the initial or terminal population sample is used as a reference.

18. Shorrocks (1999) shows that focusing on the average may be justified by an argument relying on Shapley values.

19. It could also depend on the choice of the initial and terminal years, but closer scrutiny shows that path dependence is the main source of ambiguity.

20. Note that this figure is the equivalent of panels C and E of figure 9.4 for individual earners, except for two differences. First, entry and exit are defined with respect to the whole labor force—that is, participation—rather than the wage labor force. Second, individuals entering or leaving the labor force are ranked according to the equivalized income of the household they belong to rather than their own actual or potential wage.

21. No attempt has been made to simulate the effect of observed changes in the variance of the residuals of farm and nonfarm profit functions because this change happens to be very small.

22. Of course, this fall did not actually happen because of the increase in the income of those household members who remained active. It must also be stressed that this fall in income is the counterpart of an increase in the future income of children. The unequalizing effect put into evidence here may thus be purely transitory.

23. Following the methodology in Burtless (1999).

References

Blinder, Alan S. 1973. "Wage Discrimination: Reduced Form and Structural Estimates." *Journal of Human Resources* 8(Fall): 436–55.

Bourguignon, François. 1995. "Growth, Distribution, and Human Resources: A Cross-Country Analysis." In Gustav Ranis, ed., *En Route to Modern Growth*. Washington, D.C.: Inter-American Development Bank.

Bourguignon, François, Martin Fournier, and Marc Gurgand. 1999a. "Fast Development with a Stable Income Distribution: Taiwan, 1979–1994." Working Paper 9921. CREST, Paris.

———. 1999b. "Female Labor Supply in the Course of Taiwan's Development, 1979–1994." Working Paper 9920. CREST, Paris.

Burtless, Gary. 1999. "Effects of Growing Wage Disparities and Changing Family Composition on the U.S. Income Distribution." *European Economic Review* 43(4–6): 853–65.

Chenery, Hollis, Montek S. Ahluwalia, C. L. G. Bell, John H. Duloy, and Richard Jolly, eds. 1974. *Redistribution with Growth*. New York: Oxford University Press.

Chu, Yun-Peng. 1997. "Employment Expansion and Equitable Growth: Taiwan's Postwar Experience." Sun Yat-Sen Institute for Social Science and Philosophy, Academia Sinica, Taipei, Taiwan, China. Processed.

Fei, John, Gustav Ranis, and Shirley Kuo. 1979. *Growth with Equity: The Taiwan Case.* New York: Oxford University Press.

———. 1981. *The Taiwan Success Story.* Boulder, Colo.: Westview Press.

Fields, Gary, and Jennifer O'Hara. 1996. "Changing Income Inequality in Taiwan: A Decomposition Analysis." Processed.

Fournier, Martin. 1997. "Inequality and Economic Development: A Microsimulation Study of the Taiwan Experience (1976–1992)." Processed.

———. 1999. "Inequality Decomposition by Factor Component: A New Approach Illustrated on the Taiwanese Case." Etudes et documents du CERDI, 99-20. Centre d'Études et de Recherches sur le Développement International, Clermont-Ferrand, France.

Gindling, Thomas, Marsha Goldfarb, and Chun-Chig Chang. 1995. "Changing Returns to Education in Taiwan: 1978-91." *World Development* 23(2): 343–56.

Hung, Rudy. 1996. "The Great U-Turn in Taiwan: Economic Restructuring and a Surge in Inequality." *Journal of Contemporary Asia* 26(2): 151–63.

Jiang, Feng-Fuh. 1992. "The Role of Educational Expansion in Taiwan's Economic Development." *Industry of Free China* 76(4): 37–68.

Juhn, Chinhui, Kevin Murphy, and Brooks Pierce. 1993. "Wage Inequality and the Rise in Returns to Skill." *Journal of Political Economy* 101(3): 410–42.

Lee, Lung-Fei. 1983. "Generalized Econometric Models with Selectivity." *Econometrica* 51(2): 507–12.

Oaxaca, Ronald. 1973. "Male-Female Wage Differentials in Urban Labor Markets." *International Economic Review* 14(3): 693–709.

Pritchett, Lant. 1996. "Where Has All Education Gone?" World Bank, Washington, D.C. Processed.

Ranis, Gustav. 1974. "Taiwan." In Chenery, Hollis, Montek S. Ahluwalia, C. L. G. Bell, John H. Duloy, and Richard Jolly, eds., *Redistribution with Growth.* New York: Oxford University Press.

Shorrocks, Anthony. 1982. "Inequality Decomposition by Factor Components." *Econometrica* 50(1): 193–211.

———. 1999. "Decomposition Procedures for Distributional Analysis: A Unified Framework Based on the Shapley Value." University of Essex, Essex, U.K. Processed.

World Bank. 1990. *World Development Report.* New York: Oxford University Press.

———. 2000. *World Development Report.* New York: Oxford University Press.

10

A Synthesis of the Results

François Bourguignon,
Francisco H. G. Ferreira, and Nora Lustig

Chapters 3 to 9 describe applications of essentially the same methodology to seven very different economies, thus providing a unique opportunity for comparison. In this chapter, we first summarize the results for each case study and then discuss how these results compare with one another. At the end of the chapter, we also discuss the apparently paradoxical result that a more equal distribution of the stock of education can result in higher income inequality. As we shall see, this result follows from increasing returns to years of schooling, a feature that characterizes all the case studies included in this book.

The Empirical Results by Case Study

This section reviews the main results on the nature of the dynamics of income distribution for each of the countries included in this book: Argentina (Greater Buenos Aires), 1986–98; Brazil (urban areas), 1976–96; Colombia, 1978–95; Indonesia, 1980–96; Malaysia, 1984–97; Mexico, 1984–94; and Taiwan (China), 1979–94. It should be clear from the outset that the analysis for Argentina and Brazil refers to the Greater Buenos Aires and urban areas, respectively. The Greater Buenos Aires area accounted for some 35 percent of the Argentine population in 1986 and 34 percent in 1998. Brazil's urban areas contained 68 percent of the country's people in 1976 and 77 percent in 1996.

Each of the seven economies experienced important structural changes in their sociodemographic and economic profiles over the period under consideration (see table 10.1). At the same time, the evolution of inequality was diverse, rising more in some economies than in others and remaining basically unchanged in Brazil. The individual analysis of each economy sheds light on the relative importance of changes in endowments (such as the distribution of the stock of education), changes in labor-market decisions (such as the rate and determinants of female participation in the labor force), changes in prices or returns (such as the returns to education or experience), and changes in unobservable factors. It also reveals the extent to which strong—and sometimes surprising—countervailing trends are at work. Beneath a deceivingly small change in inequality (or even no change at all), interesting distributional dynamics are often taking place. The summaries for the seven case studies are presented in alphabetical order.

Argentina

Income inequality in Argentina has fluctuated around an increasing trend which began in the mid-1970s. Gasparini, Marchionni, and Sosa Escudero (in chapter 3) focus the analysis on three years of relative macroeconomic stability—1986, 1992, and 1998—using microeconomic data from the Encuesta Permanente de Hogares (Permanent Household Survey, or EPH) of the Greater Buenos Aires area. Although inequality did not change significantly between 1986 and 1992, it increased dramatically in the next six years. The Gini coefficient for the distribution of equivalent household labor income increased less than 1 point between 1986 and 1992; it jumped 8.5 points between 1992 and 1998. It is not easy to find countries that have such a dramatic change in inequality, especially in times of macroeconomic and political stability, economic growth, and absence of natural disasters.

Many factors may have caused these inequality changes. Gasparini, Marchionni, and Sosa Escudero study seven such factors: (a) returns to education, (b) the gender wage gap, (c) returns to experience, (d) the dispersion in the endowment of unobservable factors and their returns, (e) hours of work, (f) employment, and (g) education of the adult population. For each factor, they first provide evidence from unconditional means, then show the results from multivariate regression models. Finally they apply a variant of the generalized Oaxaca-Blinder decomposition methodology described in chapter 2 in order to assess the relevance of the distributional effect of changes in each of the seven factors in a consistent framework.

Table 10.1 A Summary of the Decomposition Results
(absolute change in Gini coefficient, percentage points)

Indicator	Argentina (urban)[a] 1986–98	Brazil (urban) 1976–96	Colombia (urban)[b] 1988–95	Indonesia 1980–96	Malaysia[b] 1989–97	Mexico 1984–94	Taiwan, China 1979–94
Observed change	9.2	−0.4	4.2	1.6	3.8	5.8	1.9
Overall price effect	2.1	0.3	0.5	−0.9	1.9	1.9	2.4
Education	1.8	−0.2	−0.1	0.1	3.5	1.1	(2.1)[c]
Overall occupation effect	2.9	1.5	−0.4	4.7	−0.6	−0.5	1.3
Distribution of residuals in earning and self-employment income functions	2.1	—	1.1	2.0	—	0.1	−2
Overall population effect	2.1	−2.6	2.9	−4.3	3.5	4.6	0.2
Education effect	0.9	−0.3	0.8	1.3	0.2	1.0	−0.2
Number of children	—	−2.0	−0.4	—	—		−0.8

— Not available.

a. Figures for Argentina refer to the distribution of equivalized, rather than per capita, household income.

b. Because the Colombia and Malaysia chapters do not report decompositions for the entire periods described in table 1.1, results in this table are only for the second subperiod analyzed in each of those two chapters. The dates reflect this modification from table 1.1.

c. This figure is indirectly inferred from various pieces of information in the Taiwan, China, study, as it is not directly available there.

Source: Chapters 3–9.

The wage premium for skilled workers decreased slightly between 1986 and 1992 and increased substantially thereafter. The conditional wage-education profiles became somewhat flatter between 1986 and 1992 and became substantially steeper and more convex in the following six years. The results from the decomposition confirm that changes in the returns to education had a small equalizing effect between 1986 and 1992, and a strong unequalizing effect over the 1990s.

The gender wage gap narrowed over the period under analysis, a fact that had an unambiguous inequality-decreasing effect on the earnings distribution, given that women earn less than men. In contrast, the effect on the equivalent household labor income distribution was negligible. The authors suggest that this fact is due to two factors that act in different directions: (a) the concentration of female workers in the upper part of the household income distribution, which makes the shrinking gender wage gap increase inequality on the household income distribution and (b) the fact that the share of women's earnings in total household income is larger in low-income households, which makes the relative increase in women's wages inequality decreasing. The results of the decompositions suggest that the two factors canceled out.

The age coefficients in the wage equations of 1986 and 1998 are not substantially different. This fact is translated into a small value for the effect of returns to experience over the period. Changes were greater within each of the two periods. For instance, the relative increase in earnings for people older than 50 between 1992 and 1998 implied an equalizing effect on the earnings distribution but an unequalizing effect on the household income distribution, since people older than 50 have lower wages but higher household incomes per capita, compared with the other age groups.

The standard deviation of the error term for the log hourly earnings equation increased sharply over the period. For instance, for household heads the standard deviation was 0.56 in 1986, 0.57 in 1992, and 0.64 in 1998. The results of the decompositions confirm that changes in unobservable factors were mildly unequalizing between 1986 and 1992 and were substantially unequalizing in the next six years. As in the case of the United States, documented by Juhn, Murphy, and Pierce (1993), the increase in the dispersion of unobservable factors was one of the main forces affecting earnings and household inequality in Argentina.

The 1990s saw a dramatic fall in hours of work by low-education workers. Predicted weekly hours of work from a Tobit-censored data model clearly decreased between 1986 and 1998 for the least educated workers, while changes for the rest of the distribution were marginal. From the results of the decompositions, it seems that this fact has had a very significant inequality-increasing impact on the earnings and household income distributions.

Unemployment skyrocketed in the mid-1990s and has remained high since then. The share of the unemployed in the adult population rose from 2.3 percent in 1986 to 3.5 percent in 1992 and 6.5 percent in 1998. It is a widespread belief that the increase in unemployment is the main cause of the strong increase in household inequality (see, for example, González-Rosada and Menendez 2002). However, chapter 3 shows that the increase in unemployment was mainly associated with a fall in the group that was not part of the labor force: women and youths entering the labor force in large numbers and largely failing to find a job. Despite the jump in the unemployment rate, the proportion of people in economically active age groups with zero incomes remained roughly unchanged between 1986 and 1998. For distributional measures, it is irrelevant whether the individual has zero income because he or she is unemployed or not looking for a job. Accordingly, changes in the parameters governing participation in the labor market did not play a significant role in inequality changes.

Substantial changes in the educational composition of the population have been taking place in the past decades in Argentina. Between 1986 and 1998, there was a strong reduction in the proportion of youths and adults with primary education only, while the share of those with a college education increased significantly, particularly between 1992 and 1998. To understand the effects of these changes, the authors think of total inequality as a function of inequality between educational groups and a weighted average of inequality within educational groups (as in a standard Theil decomposition—see chapter 2). An increase in the share of a given educational group in the population can increase inequality (a) if the mean income of that group is far from the overall mean (or median), so that between-group inequality grows, and (b) if within-group inequality for that group is high, so that the weighted average of within-group inequalities goes up. In Argentina the educational structure changed in the 1990s in favor of a group with an earnings distribution that has a relatively high mean and dispersion—the college-educated group—which feeds the presumption of an unequalizing education effect. Indeed, the generalized Oaxaca-Blinder decomposition confirms that the change in the educational structure of the population had an inequality-increasing effect on the earnings distribution and on the distribution of equivalent household income in the 1990s, although the effects were small.

Between 1986 and 1992 all seven factors studied in the paper were rather small, had different signs, and hence had a small overall effect on inequality. In contrast, between 1992 and 1998 nearly all factors were inequality-increasing, and some of them were large. The three most relevant factors were the increase in the returns to education, the change in the distribution of hours of work, and the increase in the dispersion of unobservable factors. Of the 8.5 point increase in the Gini coefficient for the distribution of equivalent household labor income, 2.8 points can be accounted for by changes in the returns to education in terms of hourly wages, 2.5 points by changes in hours of work, and 2.0 points by the increase in the dispersion of unobservable factors.

In summary, the results for Argentina suggest that the small change in inequality between 1986 and 1992 is the result of mild forces that offset one another. In contrast, between 1992 and 1998, nearly all effects acted in the same direction. Changes in the returns to education and experience, changes in the endowments of unobservable factors and their remunerations, changes in hours of work and employment status, and the transformation of the educational structure of the population all had some role in increasing inequality in Argentina to unprecedented levels. The narrowing of the wage gap between men and women, which was a potential force for reducing inequality, did not induce a significant decrease in household income inequality. The increase in the returns to education and to unobservable factors and the relative decline in hours of work for unskilled workers are particularly important in characterizing the growth in inequality. Perhaps surprisingly, although Argentina witnessed dramatic changes in the gender wage gap, the unemployment rate, and the educational structure, those factors appear to have had only a mild effect on household income distribution.

Brazil

In the two decades between 1976 and 1996, Brazil's development was characterized by a seemingly paradoxical coexistence of substantial structural change on the one hand and almost no measurable progress in income levels or distribution on the other hand. Brazil continued to urbanize rapidly over this period, with the share of the population in urban areas rising from 68 to 77 percent. Economic activity continued to shift away from agriculture, predominantly toward services. Educational attainments remained low by international standards, but the mean years of schooling rose from 3.2 to 5.3. Fertility rates—and thus family sizes—fell: on average, from 4.6 people in 1976 to 3.6 people in 1996.

All this change took place with only very limited impact on the aggregate level of economic activity. The average annual growth rate in mean household per capita income—captured in the Pesquisa Nacional por Amostra de Domicilios (National Household Survey, or PNAD)—over the same 20 years was a tiny 0.2 percent. Inequality also appeared to remain essentially constant, with the Gini coefficient measuring 0.595 in 1976 and 0.591 two decades later. Unsurprisingly—given no growth and no change in income inequality—poverty incidence (with respect to a constant line of R$60 per capita per month at 1996 prices) remained stable at 22 percent.

Chapter 4 by Ferreira and Paes de Barros investigates how this stagnation in income levels and distribution was possible, in light of such substantial demographic, sectoral, and educational changes. The first finding is that extreme poverty—or indigence—actually rose during the period. Although poverty incidence was stable with respect to a R$60 line, it rose from 7 percent to 9 percent for a line of R$30. Measures of the severity of poverty, such as [P(2)], rose by even more. It turns out, in fact, that the incomes accruing to each percentile of the distribution were almost identical between 1976 and 1996 for percentiles 15 and above but were lower in 1996 for percentiles below 15.[1]

The authors thus seek to explain two puzzles: (a) why indigence rose in Brazil over those 20 years, when both the mean and inequality seemed so stable, and (b) how the distribution could be so stable above percentile 15, given such massive educational, demographic, and sectoral changes. Although Brazil's PNAD does contain data for rural areas (unlike the EPH in Argentina, for instance), the chapter focuses on urban areas only, given concerns about unusual measurement error from the survey instrument as applied to rural areas (see Ferreira, Lanjouw, and Neri 2003).

Applying the microsimulation methodology common to all studies in this volume, Ferreira and Paes de Barros find that the main factors behind income losses at the very bottom of the income distribution—and thus the rise in extreme poverty—were changes in the occupational structure of the population and declines in the average returns to both schooling and experience. The main changes in occupational structure that accounted for this rise in indigence were increases in unemployment (from 1.8 to 7.0 percent) and informality. The proportion of households with no gainfully employed member rose, as did the share of individuals reporting zero incomes (from 0.6 percent in 1976 to 3.1 percent in 1996). The overall occupational-choice simulation moves the incidence of extreme poverty from 0.068 in 1976 to 0.094, very near the observed value of 0.092 in 1996.

The deterioration in the Brazilian labor markets was not restricted to greater unemployment and informality: absolute returns to education and experience also fell. The overall simulated price effects were neutral with respect to inequality but were poverty-increasing for both wage earners and self-employed workers. The change in the returns to education, on its own, was actually mildly equalizing, because the fall in the average returns to education more than offset an increase in the marginal returns for the higher grades. A reduction in the conditional gender wage gap was also equalizing. However, changes in returns to experience were inequality increasing, and the overall effect was neutral. Poverty, however, rose substantially in the price effect simulations. This rise was driven by declines in the average returns to both schooling and experience, even at lower levels. The overall impact of these changes was to raise the incidence of indigence by almost 3 percentage points and the incidence of poverty by 6 percentage points.

The two effects that helped offset the deterioration in both the occupational structure and the returns profile of the Brazilian labor markets over the period in question were the educational effects and the demographic effects. More years of schooling and reductions in family size contributed to higher levels of income per capita, helping to offset the negative effects of falling returns and of a worsening job market structure. The rightward shift in the distribution of years of schooling was, in itself, broadly neutral with respect to inequality, but it tended to reduce poverty (by some 6 percentage points). When combined with the demographic effect, the education factor became both more powerful—contributing to an 11 percentage point decline in poverty—and more progressive—contributing a 2.4 point reduction in the Gini coefficient.

For the top 85 percent of the household income distribution, this combination of poverty-increasing price and occupational effects with poverty-reducing education and demographic effects effectively canceled out. The net effect was almost zero change in incomes above the 15th percentile, with no changes, for instance, in poverty incidence with respect to the main poverty line.

For the poorest 15 percent of the population, however, the magnitude of the negative occupational effect—with greater unemployment and the rise in the number of very low-paying informal sector jobs—was too great. Rising education and falling fertility were not enough to offset those poor labor-market outcomes. As a result, incomes in the bottom 12 to 15 percent of the distribution of urban incomes in Brazil were lower in 1996 than in 1976. Although reductions in dispersion elsewhere meant that this result hardly affected overall inequality measures, it did show up in measures of extreme poverty. As a result, all three classic P_α measures for indigence rose between 1976 and 1996.

Colombia

There are two stages in the evolution of income inequality in Colombia between 1978 and 1995. For both per capita income and individual earnings, inequality first followed the slowly descending trend observed since the mid-1960s and then fell slightly during the first 10 years of the period under analysis. It then made a U-turn and surged between 1988 and 1995 to its highest level over the previous three decades. This pattern arose from the interaction of two forces. On the one hand, long-run changes in the sociodemographic structure of the Colombian population and in behavior related to participation in the labor force tended to increase inequality throughout the period. On the other hand, macroeconomic fluctuations that tended to offset this tendency during the first 10 years shifted to reinforcing it in the second period. Those two forces are discussed in more detail below. Because the urban sector is responsible for the observed fluctuation in income inequality, the analysis focuses mostly on that dominant part of the Colombian economy.

Three structural factors affect the long-run evolution of the income distribution in Colombia: (a) the increase in educational achievements of the labor force, (b) the rising labor-force participation of women, and (c) declines in fertility and, consequently, in family size. It turns out that the first factor contributes to increasing income inequality, the second contributes to an increase in the inequality of individual earnings but has an ambiguous effect on household income, and the third reduces inequality. In both periods, the overall balance of those effects is positive.

To the extent that large families are among the poorest, it is only natural that the drop in family size reduces the inequality of per capita income. The effect of increased female labor-force participation is more subtle. Participation actually rose among low-educated and middle-educated women, thus increasing the weight of middle- and low-paid individuals among earners and increasing the inequality of earnings. When we consider the distribution of income per capita, however, some ambiguity arises. Married women who entered the labor market around the middle of the earning distribution tended to be more educated than the average woman and lived with educated husbands. This fact tended to make upper-middle-income households richer and contributed to increasing inequality. However, those entering the labor market at the bottom of the earnings distribution were likely to be married to poorer husbands, and their increased participation reduced inequality. It turns out that the first effect dominated in Colombia between 1978 and 1988 and the second effect dominated in the 1990s.

The increase in the educational endowments of the labor force was of even greater importance, leading to an increase in inequality in both the earnings and the income per capita distributions. As discussed in chapter 1, this apparently paradoxical fact is explained by strongly increasing marginal returns to the number of years of schooling. In 1978, the relative earnings difference between workers with six and five years of schooling was 10 percent. It was 15 percent between people with 11 and 10 years of schooling, and this gap increased over time. Under those conditions, if all labor-force participants increased their level of schooling by one year, the earnings of the more educated would rise by proportionately more than those of the least educated, and inequality would thus rise. Something of that type occurred in Colombia, although the number of years of schooling increased more for the least educated than for the most educated. Changes in the educational characteristics of the population were therefore responsible for an increase of more than 3 percentage points in the Gini coefficient between 1978 and 1995.

Other forces that affected the income distribution between 1978 and 1995 are related to macroeconomic phenomena. The most important one is the evolution of returns to schooling or, more generally, the skill differential in earnings during the period. The skill differential fell substantially during the 1980s and then stabilized and even slightly reversed in the early 1990s. That evolution is related to a deceleration in the demand for unskilled labor income in the first half of the 1990s. In effect, employment growth fell quite significantly after 1990—despite slightly faster economic growth. Several explanations have been given for this sluggishness of employment: an appreciation of the exchange rate, labor legislation reforms that increased the relative cost of labor, trade liberalization, and a reorientation of productive activities toward more capital-intensive activities. In any case, the effect on total inequality has been substantial. Whereas the drop in the skill differential could counterbalance the unequalizing effect of the change in the educational structure of the population between 1978 and 1988, it actually reinforced it in the subsequent period.

Two other sources of fluctuation in the distribution of income have to be emphasized. The first one is that earnings differentials between men and women and between wage earners and self-employed workers fell substantially between 1978 and 1988. As a consequence, inequality both in earnings and in per capita income went down. But those earning differentials across labor-market segments went up again in the following period, leading to a rise in inequality. The second source is related to inequality in the residuals of the earnings regressions, which corresponds to the effect of unobserved earning determinants—such as talent or ability—but also possibly to an increase in the variance of transitory earnings. This residual inequality fell during the first period and rose during the second. The authors conjecture that the slackening of the labor market after 1990 may have increased the differential between the most and the least able workers and may increase the variability of earnings over time.

In summary, the dynamics of the income distribution in Colombia over the 1978–95 period were characterized by the conjunction of permanent forces linked to changes in the sociodemographic structure of the Colombian population and fluctuating forces mostly related to the state of the labor market. Overall, permanent forces tended to increase inequality over time, albeit slightly. They were more than offset, in the first period, by a strong labor market. But in the second period, they were actually reinforced by a slowing down of employment growth, which was particularly strong for unskilled workers—thus leading to inequality-increasing price effects.

Indonesia

Between 1980 and 1996, Indonesia's gross domestic product (GDP) per capita grew at an average of 5.7 percent per year. The share of the population living in urban areas rose from 23 percent to 35 percent, and average years of schooling for the population increased from 3.8 to 6 years. The remarkable economic expansion was also characterized by significant changes in the structure of employment and in the relative importance of economic sectors. During the same period, the share of traditional agriculture in GDP fell from 24 to 17 percent, while manufacturing and services rose from 47 to 66 percent. At the same time, the share of inactive people in the working-age population dropped from 30 to 25 percent, and the share of wage income in total income fell from 57 to 50 percent, while nonfarm income from self-employment or small enterprises rose from one-fifth to little less than one-third.

How have those trends affected income distribution in Indonesia? On the surface, not much. For example, the Gini coefficient for household per capita income (using equivalized income) rose by only 1.6 points between 1980 and 1996 (table 10.1), and further analysis indicates that there was a redistribution from the middle to primarily the top of the distribution (and some slight redistribution to the bottom). However, as in the cases of Brazil (and Taiwan, China), this relative stability in the distribution of income is the result of various forces that, taken individually, could have caused significant changes in the direction of either greater or lower inequality but that, when combined, largely offset one another. Using the Susenas survey for

1980 and the Susenas survey complemented by the Savings and Incomes Survey for 1996, Alatas and Bourguignon apply the generalized Oaxaca-Blinder methodology to assess the contribution of these various forces to the evolution of inequality in Indonesia. In particular, they study the contributions of changes in returns (the *price effect*), in labor supply and occupational choice (the *occupational-choice effect*), and in the sociodemographic structure of the population (the *population* or *endowment effect*).

During the period considered, the distribution of earnings (wage income) became more unequal. The net effect of the changes in the rates of return to education and experience was unequalizing, although individual components were moving in opposite directions. For example, the observed drop in the rate of return to education in urban sectors was equalizing, while the rise in the returns in rural areas had the opposite impact. When all wage earners are taken together (including part-time wage earners), the unequalizing impact dominates because the poorest wage earners become even poorer (at constant means). The results also indicate that measures of labor-market segmentation, such as the male-female and urban-rural wage differentials, also contributed to more inequality because those gaps rose during the period under consideration. The third unequalizing factor was the increase in the variance of the residuals of the earning equations. This factor implies an increase in the heterogeneity of unobserved earnings determinants (or in their rates of return), including the number of hours worked—particularly for part-time wage earners. By itself, this last factor would have resulted in a rise of 4 percentage points in the Gini coefficient, underscoring its significance. One equalizing factor was the reduction in the relative disadvantage of wage earners living in Java (the largest island) compared with the rest of the country. All those results were qualitatively robust to the path chosen—the 1980 (1996) earning functions on the 1996 (1980) sample—in performing the decomposition.

The picture for household incomes looks quite different, primarily because household incomes also include incomes from self-employment and profits from farming and nonfarming activities. First, the unequalizing effect of the increase in the returns to schooling is much more moderate because the lower return in the nonfarm profit functions almost fully compensates the higher inequality induced by the increase in returns to schooling among rural wage earners. The higher returns to experience are equalizing (the opposite of what was found for individual earnings), indicating that the number of older self-employed workers was proportionately higher in the bottom part of the distribution. The fall in the income differential between wage earners living on Java and those living elsewhere is equalizing, but less so than in the case of individual earnings, perhaps because the differential changed by a small amount in the case of pure farm incomes. Labor-market segmentation has a lesser unequalizing effect because of income pooling within households. It is also partly offset by a rise in farm self-employment income relative to other income sources and, within farm income, by a proportionally larger increase among small producers.

Altogether, the pure price effect was equalizing and larger in absolute value in the case of household income, and unequalizing and smaller in absolute value in the case of individual earnings or wage income. According to the simulation, it would account for a drop of 1 point in the Gini coefficient. The main factors behind this decrease are the drop in the rate of return on land size (returns to small landholdings rose relatively more during the period), the change in the experience and age structure of wage and self-employment incomes, and the fall in the income differentials between those living in Java and those living elsewhere. But those equalizing trends were more than offset by the increase in the variance of the residuals, which contributed a 2 point increase in the Gini coefficient.

The occupational-choice effect is dominated by a very strong move from wage work to nonfarm self-employment, this evolution being more pronounced in the rural sector. This change in population composition from a group with relatively low inequality to a group with a high level of inequality, in both the urban and the rural sectors, contributed to a sharp increase in household income inequality more than 4 points of the Gini coefficient. However, it is likely that this change in estimated occupational preferences away from wage work is the direct reflection of the strong rural-urban migration process that took place during the period under analysis. If migrants were mostly wage workers—or potential wage workers—with no land and no other assets tying them to the rural sector, it is natural to find that preferences for wage work in the rural sector weakened. An identification problem arises here, one that assigns to occupational preferences a role that may have corresponded to the selectivity of the migration process. This problem essentially arises because of the lack of observation of migrant status in the database.

The endowment or population effect in this exercise is calculated as the difference between the observed change in inequality and that explained by the price effect, the occupational-choice effect, and the changes in the residuals (variance in unobserved variables in the earnings and profit functions). The population effect was strongly equalizing, with a potential reduction in the Gini coefficient of

between 4 and 5 points (the decline is even higher for other measures of inequality). However, because the occupational-choice
effect may suffer from identification problems and because the
population effect is calculated as a difference, this result must be
considered with caution.[2]

The effect of the rural-urban migration is simulated under the
strong assumption that representative rural dwellers migrated to the
cities and instantaneously became representative urban dwellers.
Under this assumption, the simulation results suggest that the impact
of the large rural-urban migration was unequalizing. However, it is
not clear whether this result would still hold if the unobserved selectivity of migration could be accounted for. As seen above, this population movement most likely caused a drop in wage work and an
increase in nonfarm self-employment, which contributed to a further increase in inequality. However, selectivity of migration within
each of these groups might have wiped out those effects, as for
instance if migrants predominantly came from the lower part of the
distribution of income of rural wage workers.

Using a rank-preserving replication of the distribution of schooling, the authors simulate the effect of the changes in the structure of
education between 1980 and 1996. The results indicate that the
progress observed in schooling had an unequalizing effect in the distribution of household income, the same result that was found in
Colombia (and indeed in Mexico, as we shall see below). How can
a rise in the mean and a fall in the variance of years of schooling be
reconciled with such a result? As in the Colombian case, the key is
that returns to schooling are not constant: returns are convex with
respect to years of schooling and are higher for urban wage earners
than for rural wage earners or self-employed workers and higher for
nonfarm activities than for farm activities. Convexity implies that, if
everyone goes to school for an additional year in the population as
a whole, the distribution of income among income earners would
become more unequal. According to the authors, the changes in the
structure of schooling could have contributed to an increase in
inequality of slightly less than 1 point in the Gini coefficient.[3]
Changes in educational structure also affect the distribution of
income through their effect on occupational choice. The simulation
results show that this effect was also unequalizing. Two factors may
explain this result. First, changes away from self-employment to
higher-paid wage employment may have occurred more frequently
in the upper half of the distribution. Second, more years in school
could have meant fewer members in the labor force (teenagers in
particular) for poorer families. As in the case of Taiwan, China, the
overall expansion in living standards allowed poorer families to
keep their children in school longer.

Malaysia

The Malaysian income distribution has also exhibited major changes from 1984 to 1997. The 1997 distribution is characterized both by slightly more inequality and by a substantially higher mean than the one observed in 1984. Within this overall period, however, both the growth and the distribution experience were uneven. If the overall period is divided into a first period from 1984 to 1989 and a second one from 1989 to 1997, then economic growth was much slower during the first period. Also, income inequality followed two distinct phases: income inequality fell in the first period, whereas it rose in the second. However, because the changes in inequality in both periods were modest relative to the magnitude of economic growth, poverty in Malaysia fell continuously—albeit at a slower rate during the slow growth years of the 1980s.

The mean of the 1989 distribution of household income per capita is a mere 3.2 percent higher than the mean in 1984, illustrating the slow growth in this period. During this period, inequality, as measured by the Gini index, fell from 0.49 to 0.46. As a result of economic growth and falling inequality, the percentage of the population living below the poverty line fell 4.2 percentage points, from 37.9 to 33.7 percent. The 1989–97 period shows the opposite behavior, with real incomes rising much faster (88.4 percent) and inequality, as measured by the Gini index, increasing from 0.46 to 0.50. Because of the rapid economic growth, poverty fell 19.3 percentage points to an all-time low of 14.4 percent.

These are the basic distributional changes to be explained. In chapter 7, Fields and Soares ask the following questions:

• Which factors contributed how much to the increase in household income levels and the fall in absolute poverty in the 1984–89 and 1989–97 periods?
• Which factors contributed how much to the falling income inequality from 1984 to 1989 and the rising income inequality from 1989 to 1997?

As in the other case studies, the factors examined are changes in the demographic characteristics of households, including their human capital, individuals' decisions about participation in the labor force and about opportunities to work in various occupations, and the structure of returns to various characteristics of wage employment and self-employment. Distributional changes will therefore be decomposed into the changes in returns to human capital (referred to as the *price effect*), changes in labor participation and occupational opportunities (referred to as the *occupational-choice effect*), and changes in the sociodemographic structure of the population (referred to as the *population effect*). Within this last effect, special emphasis is placed on the results of Malaysia's impressive educational efforts.

During the first subperiod (1984–89), stability is the main outcome to be explained, since there was little change in average incomes and only a slightly greater change in inequality. The income results are that changing population structure overexplains increases in incomes, accounting for 145 to 251 percent of the change, depending on whether the 1984 or 1989 year is used as the baseline. Increases in education explain statistically almost 90 percent of the change. Price effects also contribute slightly to higher incomes, and changes in occupation compensate the demographic overshooting. Poverty reduction during this first period is almost totally explained by population structure (largely meaning increases in education), with none of the other factors playing a significant role.

Although population effects dominated in explaining increases in average incomes, they share with price effects the ability to account for the entire change in inequality, with each of these effects contributing about 50 percent. Occupational-choice changes were not important (explaining −1.4 percent to −6 percent of changes). An interesting result is that the reductions in inequality of labor income (not in household per capita income) for wage-earning men, wage-earning women, self-employed men, and self-employed women were all considerably larger than the total reduction in inequality. This result is due to the increasing correlation between the incomes of different income earners in the household.

The 1989–97 period was much less stable. Population structure and price effects explain almost 100 percent of the very large change observed in the location of the distribution. Occupation effects are unimportant in explaining change in mean incomes, although they are of some importance in explaining poverty (up to 12 percent of the observed change can be explained by occupational choice). Inequality change is harder to account for and once again involves partially offsetting forces. Population and price effects overexplain the increase in inequality, but part of those effects is compensated by occupational choice, which led to greater equality of incomes—although the magnitude varied from −16 percent to −192 percent of the actual change, depending on the period used as the baseline and on the inequality measure used.[4]

An interesting fact is that education-related effects, whether price or population, are relatively unimportant in explaining any of the observed changes. Some other effects contribute considerably more. The first is the change in the constant, which rises 0.5 logarithmic units for wage-earning men and self-employed women. Another is the sharp decline in the population employed in agricultural occupations, for which there is a large negative premium. The first of these results points to the importance of the accumulation of physical capital, as well as to the importance of institutional and technological progress, in raising worker productivity—to some extent, regardless of worker characteristics. Rises in the constant term in earnings regressions are the closest analogue in labor economics to tangible evidence of distribution-neutral growth—a "rising tide that lifts all boats." Distribution-neutral growth is not seen as often as one would like, but it can certainly do wonderful things when it happens. The second phenomenon reminds us that sectoral change remains an important component of economic development in many settings.

In conclusion, the analysis of the microeconomics of changing income distribution in Malaysia reveals that, in the earlier period (1984–89), the modest increase in mean income and the modest reduction in the poverty headcount ratio are accounted for by population structure effects (largely related to the expansion of schooling). In this earlier period, inequality fell. That decline is best accounted for by price and population structure effects. In the latter period, mean income rose substantially, and the poverty rate fell substantially. Both price and population structure effects make important contributions. All three effects—price, population structure, and occupational-choice effects—make important contributions to explaining inequality change in the latter period. Occupational choice—which would have led to reductions in inequality—is more than offset by population and price effects.

Mexico

The distributions of earnings and per capita household income in Mexico became substantially more unequal between 1984 and 1994. The Gini coefficient, for example, rose by 8 and 6 points, respectively, over these years. During that decade, the country went through the aftermath of the debt crisis of 1982 and far-reaching reforms such as the liberalization of trade and investment regimes. The economy was practically stagnant, with GDP per capita growing at the rate of 0.6 percent between 1984 and 1994. The period was also characterized by a significant increase in the skill premium for wage earners and self-employed workers: the ratio of average-to-low skill earnings, for example, rose by 27 and 26 percent, respectively. There were also important changes in the structure of employment and in labor-supply factors. In particular, the share of wage employment rose from 55.5 percent in 1984 to 62 percent in

1994 (self-employment fell). The participation of females in the labor force went up by 8 percentage points, reaching 41.0 percent in 1994. And the population became better educated. In 1984, 48 percent of the population had no education or had not completed primary school. That figure was down to 38 percent in 1994. Average years of schooling increased from 5.6 to 6.9 years. Because more people became more educated at the bottom, the distribution of the stock of education became more equal: the Gini coefficient (for the distribution of years of education) fell from 0.42 to 0.37 during the period under consideration. Another important trend that was observed between 1984 and 1994 was the deterioration of the relative income of workers located in rural areas. Although real labor earnings increased by at least 20 percent for all types of workers living in urban areas, they fell by about 7 percent for rural male wage workers and by about 13 and 20 percent, respectively, for rural male and female self-employed workers.

Using the Encuesta Nacional de Ingresos y Gastos de los Hogares (Household Income and Expenditure Surveys, or ENIGH), Legovini, Bouillon, and Lustig apply the generalized Oaxaca-Blinder methodology in chapter 8 to identify the price, occupational-choice, and population effects behind the observed increase in earnings and household income inequality in Mexico. The estimation of the earnings functions and the occupational-choice model suggest the following trends. The returns to education have become more convex over the period. The returns to high levels of education (postsecondary and university) increased substantially, whereas the returns to low and medium levels fell. Other studies have suggested that this trend is primarily the result of skill-biased technical change and, to a lesser extent, the transitional effects of trade liberalization. The returns to experience fell for wage and mixed-employment workers, while they rose for the self-employed.

The labor-force participation of women increased substantially in Mexico between 1984 and 1994. This increase in participation was concentrated at both ends of the skill distribution: among poorly educated women (with no education, an incomplete primary education, and an incomplete secondary) and highly educated women (with college education). In the case of men, there was a small increase in participation (concentrated in men with college education). The dynamics of labor-force participation in Mexico seem to suggest that, while highly educated women living in richer households benefited from the modernization and increasing opportunities in the economy, women with low levels of education had to enter the labor force to compensate for declines in other incomes in their households. The occupational-choice estimation indicates that in Mexico two strong forces drive labor-force participation decisions. First, the potential income of other members of the household increases the probability of inactivity for any one given member—that is, the elasticity of labor supply with respect to unearned income is negative (as expected) and large; this effect became stronger in 1994 for spouses and members of the household other than the head. Second, education levels increase the incentives to participate in the labor market; this effect became stronger for spouses in urban areas in 1994. Although the latter effect seems to dominate for highly educated women, the former did induce some of the least educated women to enter the labor market to compensate for the falling incomes of their partners.

For the distribution of individual earnings, the decomposition finds that the price effect, the occupational-choice effect, and the endowment effect were all unequalizing. The change in returns accounted for 3.05 points in the rise of the Gini coefficient of earnings. Most of this increase is accounted for by the increase in the returns to education (which would have resulted in an increase in the Gini coefficient of 1.9 points) and the change in the mean income of different categories of workers (which—for male and female workers, urban and rural workers, and wage-earning and self-employed workers—would have resulted in an average increase in the Gini coefficient of 1.7 points). The effect of the change in the mean income of different types of workers is produced mainly by changes of incomes between rural and urban areas. A static decomposition of between- and within-group inequality by gender, occupation, and location using the Theil index reveals that, while between-group inequality fell about 19 and 16 percent between 1984 and 1994 when workers were grouped by occupation and gender, respectively, it increased by 41 percent when workers were grouped by urban and rural location.

The effect of occupational choice—and especially of female labor-force participation—on the distribution of individual earnings was also unequalizing. Labor-supply changes would have caused an increase of 0.51 points in the Gini coefficient. While the change in male labor supply would have caused a decrease in the Gini coefficient of 0.08 points, the change in female labor supply would have caused an increase in the Gini coefficient of 0.62 points. What explains this result? Because low-educated women earned the lowest incomes among workers, the increase in their participation in the labor force more than compensated for the effect of higher participation of better-educated women and caused a deterioration in the distribution of earnings among all workers.

The effect of changes in endowments has been highly unequalizing for individual earnings in Mexico, accounting for an increase in the Gini coefficient of 4.2 points. Of this total, 1.3 points can be attributed to the effect of a more equal distribution of the stock of education. Two elements contribute to this surprising result. In the comparison of education achievement across the distribution in 1984 and 1994, one can observe a larger proportional increase in years of schooling in the middle of the distribution rather than at the bottom or top. The middle four deciles of the distribution of per capita household income experience a 31 percent increase in schooling as compared with 19 and 22 percent for the bottom three and top three deciles, respectively. Furthermore, the relevant portion of the convex returns to education function is the upward-sloping portion, which weighs gains at the bottom of the distribution less than gains at the top of the distribution. The relationship between inequality of education and income inequality has the shape of an inverted U: as education inequality falls, income inequality rises initially and then starts to fall. Only much larger gains among the least educated would have resulted in increased income equality.

Finally, the effect of unobservable factors was negligible, contributing to a decrease in the Gini coefficient of only 0.05 points. This ambiguous effect is explained by the fact that the increase in the variance of the residuals in the regression equations for male earnings was counterbalanced by a decline in the variance of the residuals of the equations for female earnings, which *may* have been driven by greater homogeneity in female hours of work.

The distribution of per capita household income has followed similar dynamics as that of individual earnings, becoming more unequal between 1984 and 1994. As with the distribution of individual earnings, the returns effect and the endowment effect were unequalizing. The increase in the Gini coefficient attributable to the returns effect was equal to 1.9 points, and the increase attributable to the endowment effects was 4.6 points. As in the case of individual earnings, the returns effect is mainly accounted for by changes in the returns to education and changes in the mean income of different types of workers (urban and rural workers especially). Although the impact of the widening gap in returns to education gets somewhat dampened at the household level because correlation between the level of schooling of household members is not perfect, it would have caused an increase in the Gini coefficient of 1.1 points. The change in mean income among different types of workers (wage-earning and self-employed, male and female, and especially urban and rural) would have caused an increase in the Gini coefficient of less than 1 point. The effect of the changes in the stock and distribution of education at the household level is smaller than at the individual earnings level, accounting for an increase of 1 point. This dampening of the effect is also explained by the fact that the correlation between the level of schooling of household members is not perfect.

One of the main differences between the changes in the distribution of individual earnings and those in the distribution of per capita household income is that, at the household level, the effect of changes in occupational choice and labor-force participation is slightly equalizing. It represents a decrease in the Gini coefficient of 0.5 point. This difference can be explained by the change in the effect of female labor supply. At the household level, the change in female labor supply would have contributed to a reduction in inequality, because women with low levels of education who increased their participation to compensate for the lower earnings of their partners were thereby contributing to increases in the incomes of poor households.

Finally, the effect of unobservable factors at the household level is similar in direction to the one at the individual earnings level, but stronger, accounting for a decrease in the Gini coefficient of 0.1 points.

Taiwan, China

Income distribution in Taiwan, China, has remained relatively stable since the 1970s, with the Gini coefficient hovering just below 0.3 (see table 1.1). However, far from being the result of an absence of change, this stable trend is the outcome of significant mutually offsetting forces. Between 1979 and 1994, the population of Taiwan, China, became significantly older, better educated, and more urbanized. Whereas 45 percent of the population was younger than age 30 in 1979, less than a third were in 1994. During the same period, the average number of years of schooling rose by an impressive 50 percent, from 6.0 to 9.5; the average household size declined steadily in both rural and urban areas; and the number of working-age individuals living in rural areas or working in agriculture was almost halved. Another notable trend is not only that female labor-force participation rose, but also that male participation fell. The high GDP growth in Taiwan, China, of 7.8 percent per year in this period was accompanied by significant structural changes, with agriculture diminishing in importance, manufacturing losing ground, and the service sector surging, particularly services directed at business, such as financial services, transportation, and telecommunications.

How can one reconcile these rather large structural changes in the economy and sociodemographic behavior with a relatively stable income distribution? The first point to note is that, whereas the distribution of household disposable income per capita (measured in adult equivalent units) remained practically unchanged, the Gini coefficient before taxes and (public and private) transfers shows a slight upward trend. In contrast, individual earnings inequality has been falling since 1984. Those opposing trends already indicate that both equalizing and unequalizing forces have been at play.

Using the Taiwan Household Surveys for 1979 and 1994, Bourguignon, Fournier, and Gurgand (in chapter 9) apply the generalized Oaxaca-Blinder approach to identify the underlying forces that explain observed trends in inequality. The estimation of the model highlights three important trends. First, the estimated earnings equations indicate that there has been an increase in the rate of return to schooling. The rate of return for an additional year of schooling increased from a little more than 3 percent to 6 percent for men and from 6 percent to almost 8 percent for women. The differential in earnings between workers with higher secondary or university education and workers with primary or lower secondary education rose substantially and proportionately more than the number of years of schooling. The marginal return increased significantly for those at the upper end of the education scale, remained approximately constant for those with lower secondary education, and dropped for those with primary education or less. Such results indicate a skill-biased trend in the demand for labor.[5]

The second observed trend is a drop in the variance of the residual term of the earnings equation. A straightforward interpretation of this result would be that unobserved talents became remunerated in a more homogenous way. The authors argue, however, that a plausible alternative or complementary explanation is that, given the rudimentary way in which hours of work are controlled for in the regressions, the drop in the variance may partly correspond to a greater homogeneity in the number of working hours of wage earners.

The third observed trend is a relative separation of the labor supply and occupational choice of the spouse (wife) from the income and occupation of the head of household (husband). In the past, women who were married to higher-paid men were often either inactive or self-employed, possibly in some informal association with their husband. More recently, the correlation between the husband's and wife's incomes has increased, particularly among wage earners (who constitute 75 percent of the work force). In other words, the women who took advantage of the creation of large numbers of new jobs that resulted from the spectacular growth of the economy lived predominantly in households with higher-paid men.

How did these observed trends and the changes in the distribution of the stock of education affect the trends in inequality? Let's start with the distribution of individual earnings which, as indicated above, became less unequal during the period under study. The generalized Oaxaca-Blinder decomposition suggests that the price effect has been unequalizing. In contrast, the drop in the variance of the residuals in the earnings equation, the occupational-choice effect, and the endowment effect (which is largely driven by the increase in the stock of education and equalization in its distribution) have all been equalizing. All of these effects, combined, have been larger than the returns effect. The decomposition estimates that the rise in returns to education would have resulted in an average increase in the Gini coefficient of 2.5 points. If wage workers in 1979 had been paid according to the returns observed in 1994, the bottom quartile would have gained slightly more than 60 percent, whereas the top quartile would have gained around 75 percent. Returns to schooling are the driving force, because changes in returns to experience or geographic location are too small to have any significant effect on the distribution of income.

The drop in the variance of the residual accounts for a fall of between 2.2 to 3.8 points in the Gini coefficient for earnings, a rather sizable effect. The impact of the occupational choice effect is shown in changes in the behavior of both men and women. Taking all wage earners together, there has been an equalizing force, with net exits from wage employment occurring at both extremes of the distribution. The net drop in participation of male wage earners was the result of men retiring earlier. For women there were more entries than exits, particularly at the top of the female wage scale. However, because the top of the wage scale for women corresponds to the middle of all wage earners taken together (males and females), this shift was equalizing. It would account for a 1 point drop in the Gini coefficient. Finally, the endowment effect also accounted for approximately a 1 point fall in the Gini coefficient.

Unlike the distribution of individual earnings, the distribution of household per capita income before (net) taxes has become more unequal. Like the distribution of individual earnings, the returns effect was unequalizing and approximately of the same order of magnitude: the increase in the Gini coefficient attributable to the returns effect was equal to 2.4 points. Although the effect of the widening gap in returns to education is somewhat dampened at the household level because the correlation between the level of schooling of household members is not perfect, the changes in the coefficients of profit functions contributed to more inequality among households that received this type of income.

Changes in labor-force participation and occupational choice at the household level were also unequalizing (in contrast to their role in the earnings distribution) owing to two phenomena. First, the drop in the cross-wage elasticity in female labor supply, captured as the negative correlation between the income of the husband and the participation of the wife, meant that more women living in richer households were entering the labor force. Second, women who entered the wage labor force were on average more educated than those already active in the labor force. Although this difference had an equalizing effect at the level of individual earnings because of the relative position of those women in the (joint) wage scale, this change in the qualification of new female entrants was unequalizing at the household level. Women with better education tended to live in richer households, and their entry into the labor force increased the income of the households in the upper end of the scale.

Analyzing the endowment effect at the household level gives an interesting result. If households had experienced the observed increase in education without simultaneously enjoying the large rise in incomes resulting from economic growth, poorer households might have faced a sharp decline in their incomes because teenagers who were in the labor market would now be attending school instead of contributing to household income. This fact has two implications: the distributive effect of changes in the stock of education is ambiguous at the household level, but on the other hand the expansion of education among poorer households would have been less likely to occur without the remarkable improvement in average living standards.

Although the distribution of income before taxes became slightly more unequal, the after-tax distribution became less so, implying that the tax and transfer policy implemented by the government offset the unequalizing trends generated by the other factors at play.

The Empirical Results in a Comparative Perspective

In this section, we discuss the wealth of results and analysis presented in this volume in a comparative manner, across the seven economies reviewed above. For the sake of brevity, we restrict our attention to the main general lessons learned from the decomposition of changes in the income distribution into price, occupational-choice, and population effects. In doing so, we will often refer to table 10.1, which reports the decomposition of the change in the Gini coefficient between the initial and terminal years of the periods under analysis. The reader may also want to refer to table 10.2, which provides a schematic summary of the analysis from the case study chapters.[6] Bold entries in table 10.1 refer to the general effects

Table 10.2 Interpreting the Decompositions: A Schematic Summary

Economy	Periods	Main changes	Price effect	Occupation effect	Endowment effect	Basic story
Argentina	1986–92, 1992–98	Inequality was stable in the first period, then rose markedly in second.	β(education) was equalizing in the first period (as the profile grows less convex) and inequality increasing in the second period. The result was heavily influenced by the behavior of returns to college education. Also, it was more marked for other family members than for heads of household. β(experience) was important for earnings distribution but less so for household per capita income. β(gender) (that is, gender wage gap) was equalizing in both periods in the earnings distribution but had no effect on equivalized household income	Estimation is by a Tobit analysis because there are data for hours worked. The decline in hours worked was inequality increasing and impoverishing in the second period, where declines were concentrated in the bottom fifth of the distribution. Unemployment had a limited impact, because a decline in inactivity of a similar magnitude, so the number of zero incomes was stable. This finding was true in both periods. Basically, the entire occupational-choice effect operated through the intensive margin.	A substantial increase in educational endowments did not seem to have much effect on inequality in either period. Unobserved endowments had an important inequality-increasing effect in both periods.	In the first period, inequality first rose and then fell. Stability seems to be due to inequality-increasing returns to experience (and unobserved endowments) offsetting the equalizing effect of β (education). In the second period, inequality rose unambiguously and markedly: price, occupation (reduction in hours worked by the poor), and unobserved endowment effects all drove this rise.

(Continued on the following page)

Table 10.2 (*Continued*)

Economy	Periods	Main changes	Price effect	Occupation effect	Endowment effect	Basic story
			distribution, presumably because of matching.			
Brazil	1976–96	Growth was positive but very low. GDP series was highly volatile. Inequality first fell and then rose again, but it was stable between the endpoints. Headline poverty was also constant. Indigence rose markedly.	Price effects were neutral with respect to inequality over the period but strongly poverty increasing. Returns to education fell and became more convex. The overall effect was mildly inequality reducing and strongly poverty increasing. Returns to experience also fell, a result that was poverty and inequality increasing. "Returns" to being female rose, a result that was poverty and inequality reducing.	Overall, effects were strongly poverty and inequality increasing. The effect operated through a sharp decline in the constant term of the multinomial logit, mainly for household heads, implying tighter constraints on the process of occupational choice and reflecting both higher open unemployment and informal employment. Unlike in most economies studied, but as in Argentina, this effect was driven by household heads, rather than by spouses.	Overall, the effect was poverty and inequality reducing. The increase in levels of schooling was, on its own, broadly inequality neutral but poverty reducing. The decline in fertility and dependency ratios was inequality and poverty reducing. When combined with this demographic effect, the educational effect became more progressive.	Poverty-increasing participation and price effects and poverty-reducing endowment effects mutually offset one another from the 15th percentile upward. Hence, headline poverty and inequality hardly moved over these turbulent 20 years. The strongly immiserizing participation effect predominated below the 15th percentile, however, increasing extreme urban poverty.

Economy	Periods	Main changes	Price effect	Occupation effect	Endowment effect	Basic story
Colombia	1978–88, 1988–95	In the first period, inequality was broadly stable in urban areas. It rose slightly in rural areas but was stable nationally. Positive growth meant that money-metric welfare rose unambiguously. In the second period, inequality fell in rural areas but rose in urban areas and between the two. It also rose for the country as a whole. Social welfare increases were no longer unambiguous in rural areas.	In the first period, all price effects were equalizing in urban areas. In particular, declines in marginal returns to education contributed to declines in inequality. In the second period, price effects were generally neutral, except for those associated with unobserved characteristics, which turned inequality increasing.	During 1978–88, occupational-choice effects were inequality increasing in urban areas, both for individual earnings and for household per capita income. This result was largely due to net exits of men from the middle of the distribution and net entries of men on both tails. In the second period, this effect was inequality increasing for individual earnings but equalizing for household per capita income. This result was caused by a substantial net entry of females from poor households into the bottom of the earnings distribution, which increased	In urban areas, endowment effects were inequality increasing in both periods. More (and more equally distributed) years of schooling led, nevertheless, to greater income dispersion, because of the convexity of the structure of returns: a classic example of the MIID effect. In rural areas, where marginal returns tended to be lower, the educational endowment effect was equalizing. Greater inequality in the distribution of nonlabor incomes also contributed to higher inequality in both periods.	The Colombian story is complex: inequality trends differ substantially between rural and urban areas. Nationally, however, the basic story is as follows. In the first period, inequality was stable. This finding reflected a canceling out between equalizing price effects and inequality-increasing endowment and occupational-choice effects. In the second period, inequality rose. This finding reflected (a) less progressive price effects, (b) continued inequality-increasing endowment effects, and (c) greater inequality between rural and urban areas.

(Continued on the following page)

Table 10.2 (Continued)

Economy	Periods	Main changes	Price effect	Occupation effect	Endowment effect	Basic story
				dispersion there but raised the incomes of poor households.	Operating against these two effects was an equalizing effect from a persistent reduction in the dependency ratio in both periods and in both rural and urban areas.	
Indonesia	1980–96	Economic growth was very rapid (4.5 percent per capita per year). Poverty declined massively. Earnings inequality increased. Household per capita income inequality was moderately higher.	Overall, price effects were inequality increasing both in the distribution of earnings and in the distribution of household per capita income. This outcome reflected inequality-increasing tendencies in returns to unobserved worker characteristics (captured through the variance of residuals), an inequality-increasing tendency in the return to living in urban (as opposed to rural) areas, and mild	Occupational-choice effects were unimportant for the distribution of individual earnings, but they were substantially inequality increasing for the distribution of household per capita income. This result was largely due to an occupational shift away from wage work and toward self-employment, where the distribution of household per capita	Endowment effects were, overall, equalizing. They tended to offset the inequality-increasing occupational-choice effects, leading to a household per capita income distribution only moderately more unequal. This result occurred even though the educational endowment effect on its own was inequality increasing, through the MIDD effect.	Rapid growth, industrialization, and urbanization changed the face of Indonesia over the period. Poverty fell dramatically, though this fall was largely due to growth. Inequality in household per capita income increased, although moderately and ambiguously, because of a combination of effects, some of which were countervailing. Among those that contributed

Economy	Periods	Main changes	Price effect	Occupation effect	Endowment effect	Basic story
			inequality-increasing returns to education (although these returns were equalizing for male urban wage earners). Partly but not entirely offsetting these effects were some equalizing price effects: changes in the returns to experience were equalizing, as was a decline (and reversal) in the return to living outside Java and to being male. So were declines in the relative returns to land and size.	income among wage workers had a lower dispersion (and an average close to the overall average), and the distribution among the self-employed had an average higher than the population mean and a greater dispersion. This movement toward self-employment was driven by (a) rural-urban migration, which appealed more to landless, rural wage workers than to landed, self-employed family farmers, and (b) increases in profitable self-employment opportunities in the cities, which drew more workers than wage work.	The driving force behind this equalizing tendency of the endowment effect appears to have been the selectivity implicit in the rural-to-urban migration process: those who migrated first appear to have been landless (and likely poor) rural people, who then shared in the greater prosperity of urban areas.	to more inequality were higher returns to education, to unobserved characteristics, and to living in urban areas. An occupational shift away from wage work and toward higher-paying but more unequal self-employment also contributed. Finally, increases in educational endowments were also inequality increasing, given the convexity of the returns (the MIDD effect).

(Continued on the following page)

Table 10.2 (Continued)

Economy	Periods	Main changes	Price effect	Occupation effect	Endowment effect	Basic story
Malaysia	1984–89, 1989–97	Growth was positive but low in the first period and high in the second period. Inequality fell in first period, and rose in second period. Poverty fell throughout.	All βs are equalizing in the first period and inequality increasing in the second. In both periods, returns to education were moving in an inequality-increasing way. In the first period, other βs more than offset this move. In the second period, the returns to education effect predominated.	Effects were negligible in both periods.	Endowment effects were most important in both periods: equalizing in the first period and inequality increasing in the second period. The effects comprise both increases in education and the employment shift away from agriculture.	Endowment and price effects always went the same way. In the first period, endowment effects were equalizing on balance, with more education and little shift from agriculture. In the second period, the mix moved the other way.
Mexico	1984–94	Inequality increased markedly in both the earnings and household per capita income distributions, although more so for the former.	Price effects were overall strongly inequality increasing, for both the earnings and the income distributions. This finding was due predominantly to two effects: a convexification of the returns to education and a growing negative	As elsewhere, the action driving occupational-choice effects was the increase in the participation of women in the labor force. This increase was particularly pronounced at the bottom and at the top of the educational distribution. This entry	Endowment effects were inequality increasing and were driven by an increase in the level (and reduction in the inequality) of years of schooling. This result was inequality increasing in terms of both earnings and household per capita income because of the	Returns to education convexified, with actual declines in returns to low and medium skills. Returns to experience fell. Participation of women in the labor force increased, particularly at the top and bottom of the earnings

Economy	Periods	Main changes	Price effect	Occupation effect	Endowment effect	Basic story
			return to living in rural areas. Returns to experience fell for older workers. This effect turned out to be mildly equalizing for earnings and mildly inequality increasing for househo.d per capita income.	pattern was opposite to that observed in Taiwan, China, and so was its effect: inequality increasing for earnings but equalizing for household per capita income. Increases in educational endowments led to greater participation by poor women and to a shift from self-employment toward wage work for poor men, both of which were equalizing.	convexity of returns (the MIDD effect). Migration from rural to urban areas, as well as from poorer to richer regions, also contributed to an increase in inequality.	distribution. Older workers became more inactive, and the labor force became younger. Fertility fell for all, but more so for the poor. Educational endowments grew for all and became more equal, driven by the middle of the distribution. Urban-rural differentials increased markedly.
Taiwan, China	1979–94	Economic growth was very rapid. Earnings inequality declined. Inequality in equivalized household income increased.	Overall, price effects were inequality increasing for both the earnings and the equivalized household income distributions. This result was driven	Overall, occupational-choice effects were equalizing for earnings but inequality increasing for equivalized household income.	Overall, endowment effects were equalizing for earnings, owing to a fall in educational inequality, which was not offset by the MIDD effect.	Rapid growth caused an increase in the demand for educated labor that exceeded the increasing supply. As a consequence, the rates of return to education

(Continued on the following page)

Table 10.2 (Concluded)

Economy	Periods	Main changes	Price effect	Occupation effect	Endowment effect	Basic story
			by higher average and marginal returns to schooling, which contributed to higher inequality in both distributions. The variance of residuals for wages fell, which tended to (incompletely) offset the educational effect. This finding may reflect a decline in the variance of hours worked and might thus be better interpreted as an equalizing occupational-choice effect.	Changes in the participation behavior of men were broadly distribution neutral. The main effects were thus driven by increased labor force participation by women—in particular, by the entry of more educated women, who entered in the middle of the earnings distributions (thus reducing earnings inequality). However, because these women generally belonged to richer households, their earnings contributed to higher equivalized household income inequality.	For the equivalized household income distribution, however, endowment effects were ambiguous. This ambiguity arose because the educational endowment effect was weaker in this distribution, owing to the imperfect correlation of educational levels across household members, and because the educational effect on participation tended to be inequality increasing. The demographic effect was equalizing.	rose, increasing differentials among both earners and households. In the case of earners, this movement was offset by the influence of a more equal distribution of schooling and by the fact that net entrants to the labor force were predominantly women at the middle of the earnings scale. For households, however, the entry of these women contributed to higher inequality, since they came mainly from households in the upper half of the distribution.

Note: "MIDD effect" was named after the Microeconomics of Income Distribution Dynamics project.

identified above: price, occupational choice, and population. The effect of changes in the distribution of earnings residuals is entered separately—and also in bold—because it cannot be decomposed into the part that reflects changes in the distribution of unobserved characteristics (a population effect) and the part that refers to changes in the structure of their remuneration rates (a price effect). The bold entries should add vertically to the observed change in row 1, up to an approximation error. Other entries in that table correspond to some further decomposition of the preceding effects.

The main general lesson from table 10.1—and indeed from a careful reading of the case studies—is that actual changes in inequality are the composite effect of many different forces, some of which are generally acting in opposite directions. Thus, in all but one country (Argentina), there are both positive and negative entries in bold in table 10.1, indicating the existence of countervailing forces acting on the distribution of income. Indeed, one often observes that the absolute value of some effect is larger than the absolute value of the change actually observed (shown in the top row). For example: without counteracting forces, the change in the Gini coefficient in Taiwan, China, could have been 2.4—instead of 1.9—points because of the overall price effect alone. In Brazil and in Indonesia, the occupational-choice effects alone were greater than the overall change in inequality, indicating the existence of offsetting effects from the price and population effects. In the Brazilian case, these offsetting effects were large enough to change the sign of the net outcome.

While bearing in mind the overarching lesson that individual country experiences are unique exactly because they combine various forces in different ways, some patterns can be discerned across the economies. The first of these patterns is that inequality was on the rise in our (obviously unrepresentative) sample of economies over the past two or three decades of the 20th century. Only one case, (urban) Brazil, showed a (very small) decline in inequality over the period under study. Even so, as the chapter on Brazil makes quite clear, this finding reflects in part the fact that the initial year (1976) is a peak in the inequality time series for that country. Had the analysis started in 1981, results presented in the chapter show that inequality would have risen there too. For the other economies, rises in the Gini coefficient were generally moderate in Asia and high in Latin America. But rises they were, everywhere.

A second pattern is that price effects generally contributed to—rather than mitigated—these increases in inequality. Except for Indonesia, their sign was positive everywhere. In Mexico and Taiwan, China, changing the structure of returns in the earnings and self-employment equations and maintaining everything else constant would have led to an increase in the Gini coefficient of equivalized household incomes equal to 1.9 points in Mexico and 2.4 points in Taiwan, China. Almost always, the price effects reflected higher marginal returns to human capital variables, principally education and potential labor-market experience. In particular, a pattern that was observed in a number of economies was the "convexification" of returns to schooling, a phenomenon that occurs when marginal returns fall at low levels of education but rise at higher levels. The education price effect was negative in only two countries, Brazil and Colombia, and even there only mildly so. In Brazil, in particular, this reflected a stagnant labor market, in which the weakly equalizing role of the returns to education arose as a result of falling *average* rather than marginal returns.

The prevalence of this inequality-increasing effect of changes in returns to education is evocative of similar results in a number of industrial countries. For similar findings for the United States, see Katz and Murphy (1992) and Juhn, Murphy, and Pierce (1993). It lies beyond the scope of our approach to determine the ultimate source of these widespread increases in the marginal returns to education. We note only that, because it was contemporaneous with generally large increases in the supply of more educated workers (see the data on years of schooling in table 10.1), these increases must reflect large shifts in labor demand toward higher skills. There is an ongoing debate on the allocation of responsibility for this phenomenon between skill-biased technological progress and greater trade liberalization. See Bound and Johnson (1992) and Katz and Murphy (1992) for the United States. For developing countries, see Sánchez-Páramo and Schady (2003), Tan and Batra (1997), and Wood (1997). Our methodology does not allow us to model labor demand, and we therefore take no position on this issue.

The contribution of gender price effects—that is, the gap between males and females estimated through the coefficient on an intercept dummy variable—was generally equalizing and, thus, tended to go against the convexification of returns to education. In fact, greater gender equality in labor-market remuneration was the only feature of the evolution of labor markets in these economies that was equalizing across all cases.

In some cases, notably Mexico, an additional and important inequality-increasing price effect was the effect of higher remuneration associated with living in certain areas of the country. In Mexico, this effect contributed to higher inequality both between urban and rural areas and between the North-Center and the South of the country. In Indonesia, the price effect was inequality-increasing between rural and urban areas but actually reversed the regional disparity between the previously poorer island of Java and the out-lying islands.[7]

A third feature of table 10.1 is the potentially important role of unobservable factors. The change in the variance of the residuals of the regressions on earnings and self-employment income is respon-sible for a 2 percentage point fall in inequality in Taiwan, China, and a 2 point increase in Argentina and in Indonesia. In Colombia, it contributed with a 1.1 point rise. In comparison, this effect is neg-ligible in Brazil and Mexico. As mentioned above, there is an inher-ent ambiguity attached to the interpretation to be given to this term. It may correspond to a change in the distribution of unobserved income determinants in the population, but it might also be driven by a change in remuneration.[8] But this term may also be given other interpretations. For instance, given that earnings equations reported in this volume often refer to total earnings without necessarily con-trolling for hours worked, a change in the variance of the residual term may correspond to a change in the heterogeneity of working time among wage earners. Unobserved income determinants may also include transitory income or measurement errors.

There are fewer discernible patterns with regard to the occupational-choice and population effects. Occupational-structure effects were small and equalizing in Colombia, Malaysia, and Mexico. They were larger and inequality increasing in Argentina, Brazil, Indonesia, and Taiwan, China. Yet, and perhaps more so than for price effects, similar magnitudes often obscure very differ-ent economic phenomena. In Argentina and Brazil, the positive (inequality-increasing) effects are due to stagnant or deteriorating labor-market conditions. In both countries, the incidence of unem-ployment rose over the period of study, but in neither was it the only factor behind the positive occupational effect. In Argentina, Gasparini, Marchionni, and Sosa Escudero show that the rise in unemployment offset an identical decline in inactivity. They suggest that the true conduit of the occupational structure effect was actually the reduction in hours worked by poorer workers. In Brazil (where data on hours were not available for the early years in the analysis), a rise in informality seemed to be as important as unemployment.

In the two Asian economies, the stories behind the inequality-increasing effect of changes in the structure of occupations were quite different. In Indonesia, the effect was driven by a large-scale move-ment away from wage employment and into self-employment. But unlike the Brazilian case, where a similar movement took place in the context of a stagnant economy and a labor market with little net job creation, in Indonesia the movement took place against the backdrop of very high growth rates and had a strong migratory component, with wage workers in agriculture leaving for the greater opportunities of urban self-employment. In Taiwan, China, yet another story was told. In the other economies, the action was mainly in the changes in the occupational structure of household heads. Bourguignon, Fournier, and Gurgand argue that in Taiwan, China, the effect reflected primarily the entry of educated women into the labor market. Since they came predominantly from richer households, their entry contributed to greater inequality in the distribution of household incomes.

This methodology is rather less powerful in generating readily interpretable population effects, to a large extent, because such effects are often calculated as residuals. As we indicated in chapter 2, another component to that residual makes it impossible to identify the estimated population effect in table 10.1 exactly with the counterfactual effect of changing the joint distribution of observed characteristics and keeping everything else constant. This component is the approximation error arising from (a) the choice of a specific functional form for modeling the various conditional distributions and (b) the estimation of its parameters. It is difficult, therefore, to read too much into the sign and magnitude of the seven entries in the corresponding line in table 10.1.

We can say much more about the specific population effects associated with the demographic and educational transformations of the population, which are summarized in the last two rows of table 10.1. Consider first the component for number of children in the overall population effect. This effect was estimated for three economies (Brazil, Colombia, and Taiwan, China) in a very simple way. A regression was run of the number of children in a household on the age and education of the head and the spouse, if present. In some cases, regional controls were also included. Then the coefficients of year t'—and the distribution of the residual term—were applied to the population structure of year t, thus simulating a counterfactual conditional distribution of the number of children in observed households. This modification directly altered the level of household income per capita and the weight of households in the distribution. It may also have affected the occupational choices of some household members; this indirect effect can be estimated separately, as in the Brazilian study.

The numbers reported in table 10.1 reflect the combined (direct and indirect) effects of changing the demographic structure in the manner just described. In all cases, it was found that the drop in fertility had an equalizing effect on the distribution—for two distinct and mutually reinforcing reasons. First, the proportional decline in fertility rates was higher for families with the highest initial fertility rates, which were strongly concentrated among the poorest families. Second, the effect of a one-child reduction in family size was larger on average for poorer families, largely owing to its knock-on effect on female participation rates. In Brazil, the effect of reducing the number of children in the family on the probability of changing the occupational status of adult women in the household away from inactivity and unemployment was pronounced. As a result of this fact—and of the direct reduction in the denominator of household income per capita—this effect had a very marked equalizing impact—equivalent to two Gini points—in Brazil. It was less pronounced in both Colombia and Taiwan, China, but went in the same direction.

The impact of changes in the educational composition of the populations in these seven economies is not as uniform. The education population or educational endowment effect is generally positive (for five of the countries) but is negative (that is, equalizing) for both Brazil and Taiwan, China. At first, this finding may seem somewhat surprising, given that in all the case studies we observed a strong rise in mean years of schooling (see table 1.1) and in the share of the population that had secondary and higher education. In the widely cited framework proposed by Tinbergen (1975), to which we referred in chapter 1, it is exactly this increase in the supply of skilled workers that should offset, wholly or in part, the inequality-increasing changes in labor demand reflected in the education price effects. Yet our decompositions seem to suggest that, even when all other effects are held constant and only the (estimated) conditional distribution of the years of schooling is imported from the later to the earlier year, this effect tends more often to reinforce the rise in inequality than to dampen it. Because we found this result interesting, we named it the *MIDD effect,* after the Microeconomics of Income Distribution Dynamics project, and dedicate the next section entirely to its discussion.

Education and Inequality: The Paradox of Progress

Mean years of schooling rose in all seven economies analyzed in this volume. Apart from Argentina and Malaysia, which departed from comparatively high levels and experienced increases of 13 percent and 5 percent, respectively, all of the educational expansions were rather impressive. Table 1.1 reveals that mean years of schooling in the adult population grew by 23 percent in Mexico, 50 percent in Colombia, 58 percent in both Indonesia and Taiwan (China), and 66 percent in Brazil. Those performances refer to different periods, and it is not surprising that Brazil recorded the highest proportional increase, if one considers that it both started from the lowest base and had the longest time in which to achieve it. The evidence described in the case studies confirms that the impact of these additional years of schooling on mean household incomes was generally positive. As a result, the effect of simulating these educational expansions on the base year is generally poverty reducing. In fact, as shown in the Brazilian case study, this positive effect of higher educational endowments on household income per capita is composed of a direct effect (an increase in the number of years of schooling sold by active household members on the labor market, at unchanged returns) and of an indirect effect. The latter arises from two additional potential effects of more education. One is to reduce fertility rates and, thus, the number of children in households. The other is to increase labor-force participation. This last effect, by itself and combined with fewer children, is particularly pronounced for women.[9]

More surprising was the finding that the effect of these educational expansions on inequality measures was positive (that is, inequality increasing) more often than not. In fact, the only exceptions were Brazil and Taiwan, China, where the educational expansions were particularly large. Elsewhere, the effect of simulating the observed changes in the conditional distribution of years of schooling on the initial distribution was always to increase the Gini coefficient. At first sight, this effect might be unintuitive. When Langoni (1973) argued—using an early precursor to this microsimulation methodology—that some 35 percent of the total increase in Brazilian inequality between 1960 and 1970 was due to the increase in the country's levels of education, he was not widely believed. According to Almeida dos Reis and Paes de Barros (1991), Bacha and Taylor (1980) and Fishlow (1973) claimed that Langoni's result could not be correct. Yet Almeida dos Reis and Paes de Barros go on to conclude, in their own study, that "our results and the earlier findings for Brazil, Colombia, and East Africa indicate that the direct impact of an educational expansion is, in general, in the direction of increasing the degree of inequality, rather than in the direction of decreasing inequality" (Almeida dos Reis and Paes de Barros 1991, p. 140). How is this possible?

In this book, changes in the distribution of schooling are simulated very much like changes in fertility. Within groups of individuals defined by age, gender, and region, a rank-preserving transformation in the distribution of schooling is implemented. In the present case, individuals with the highest schooling in year t are given the highest schooling observed in year t', and so on.[10] Once the number of years of schooling has been modified in this way, then other variables that depend on schooling may also have to be modified. The same is true of occupational choices as well as of earnings and self-employment income. It may also be true of the number of children in case studies where fertility behavior was explicitly modeled.

This procedure for simulating changes in the distribution of schooling is completely flexible. It has absolutely no a priori implications for the resulting simulated changes in the distribution of household incomes. The income changes can come only from the nature of the changes in the distribution of schooling itself (for instance, if it became more unequal) or from the way in which this change translates into changes in earnings and household incomes. As regards the first possibility, one often encounters references to the existence of Kuznets curve in the distribution of schooling. According to that view, inequality in the distribution of the number of years of schooling would first increase with the average schooling level and would then decrease according to the following process: schooling first develops in some segment of the population, reaches some maximum for that segment, and then starts spreading to the rest of the population.[11]

In view of such a theory, it would be tempting to associate the observed inequality-increasing effect of schooling expansions in Indonesia and Mexico, for instance, with the upward-sloping part of the schooling Kuznets curve, whereas Brazil and Taiwan, China, would be on the downward-sloping side. This is simply not the case. In actual fact, the distribution of schooling levels in the population at working age became more equal in all seven economies. The difference across countries in the effect of more education on inequality must, therefore, lie in the mechanism of transmission from education to household incomes, rather than in the dynamics of the distribution of years of schooling itself.

Two interesting phenomena are at work. The first one has to do with the convexity of the returns to schooling. In all seven economies, wage earnings and self-employment incomes are convex functions of the number of years of schooling. In fact, even the logarithm of wages is often found to be convex: in some case studies, a quadratic specification is used for schooling, and the coefficient of the squared term generally is positive and significant. In other cases, dummies for individual years of schooling or educational splines are employed. All of these specifications are designed to allow the marginal returns to schooling to vary. And the empirical result is that these returns do vary and, in general, rise with education, so that even the log of wages is a convex function of years of schooling.

But this result is not necessary to explain the basic reason why more years of education may imply more inequality in incomes. What is required is that wages and other incomes themselves be convex functions of years of schooling.[12] If so, we can write the earnings function $y = f(e)$, where y is earnings (or self-employment income) and e denotes years of schooling. Let $f_e, f_{ee} > 0$. Now define an inequality measure $I(x): R^n \to R$, such that $I(x) = I(\lambda x)$, λ in R^+ and $I(x_1, \ldots, x_i, \ldots, x_j, \ldots, x_n) < I(x_1, \ldots, x_i - t, \ldots, x_j + t, \ldots, x_n)$, $t > 0$ as long as $x_1 < \ldots < x_i < \ldots < x_j < \ldots < x_n$.[13]

Finally, consider two ordered sets, Ω^L and Ω^H, of ordered pairs $(e_i, y_i)^j$, $j = L, H$, where the elements of Ω are ordered in increasing order of the first element, e. Let $e_i^H = \alpha e_i^L$, $\alpha > 1$. It is then easy to show that $I(e^H) = I(e^L)$ and $I(y^H) > I(y^L)$. In other words, if incomes are given by a strictly convex function of education, and if we scale up the distribution of education equiproportionately so as not to change its inequality, then the inequality in the distribution of income must rise. The key to the argument is that if $f_{ee} = 0$, $I(y)$ would not change either, by scale invariance and the definition of linearity. As soon as $f_{ee} > 0$, the same proportional increases in education translate into higher proportional increases in income for the more educated.

It is thus possible that substantial increases in the mean of the distribution of education lead to increases in income inequality.[14] In fact, if incomes are given by a strictly convex function of education (and nothing else), merely scaling up the educational distribution by a constant greater than 1 will necessarily raise income inequality. An example of this property was given by Lam (1999), who noted that if $\log y_i = \alpha + \beta S_i + u_i$, then $\mathrm{Var}(\log y_i) = \beta^2 \mathrm{Var}(S_i) + \mathrm{Var}(u_i)$. An increase in the mean of schooling S would increase its variance. For $\beta > 0$, this increase raises the variance of logarithms of income, which is a common income inequality measure.[15]

How can one then explain cases such as those of Brazil and Taiwan, China, where expansions in the endowment of education lowered income inequality? Note the number of strong assumptions made in the preceding paragraphs. First, we used as an example two distributions ranked by first-order stochastic dominance: Ω^L and Ω^H. In other words, every individual with a given rank in Ω^H has higher education than the individual with the same rank in Ω^L. This is a very strong assumption about the nature of the educational expansion. One can obviously raise the mean of the distribution of education by raising e for some individuals and not for others. If this process is such that it generates a sufficiently large decline in the inequality of the distribution of education, this effect might offset the inequality-increasing effect of climbing along a convex function and result in a decline in income inequality as well. Second, incomes are a function not only of education but also of other variables. If $y = f(e, z)$, the correlation between education and income will in general no longer be perfect. Nevertheless, while it remains positive, the gist of the argument will still apply.

The bottom line is that we should not be surprised that increases in the mean level of education (with returns kept constant) are associated with higher income inequality, even if the inequality in the distribution of education falls. This association is simply a result of the convexity of the earnings functions with respect to education. In fact, though it is possible for income inequality to fall as a result of educational expansions—as it did in Brazil and Taiwan, China— this effect will generally reflect a very substantial equalization in the distribution of years of schooling. Otherwise, the expected partial effect of educational expansions on income inequality is indeed positive, as was found for Argentina, Colombia, Indonesia, Malaysia, and Mexico.

This result is not new. Langoni (1973) and Almeida dos Reis and Paes de Barros (1991) found it for Brazil. Knight and Sabot (1983) report similar findings for East Africa, and Reyes (1988) does so for Colombia. Most recently, Lam (1999) notes this point when considering the evolution of income inequality in Brazil and South Africa, during periods of substantial rises in educational attainment. Finally, one should also note that this result does not, in and of itself, contradict Tinbergen's (1975) view that educational expansions should contribute to a reduction in inequality, because Tinbergen suggested that the inequality reduction would happen through the effect of increases in schooling levels on the equilibrium rates of return to education (which would fall as a response to higher supply). Here, in contrast, we are considering the partial effect of educational expansions, while keeping prices constant.

In terms of Tinbergen's race between demand and supply for skilled labor, however, it is interesting to note that in four of the seven economies—namely, Argentina, Indonesia, Malaysia, and Mexico—the effect of the price of education and the effect of quantities of education were both inequality increasing. That finding reflects a combination of two phenomena: the MIDD effect of climbing along a convex schedule of returns and the fact that demand for more educated workers has risen faster than supply over the period of study. This finding is, once again, very much in line with those reported for the United States and other industrial countries over the past decade (see, for example, Katz and Murphy 1992).

The second phenomenon that introduces some ambiguity in the evaluation of the distributional effect of the general progress in schooling comes from the (short-term) negative impact of schooling on labor supply. Consider a household in which a child was employed as a wage worker or in an informal family business in the initial year t. Imagine then that the simulation applying to year t the schooling distribution of year t' implies that this child is now going to school because her simulated schooling level is larger than her age minus the normal age for entering primary school. In the simulation methodology reported above, it was assumed in all case studies that a child in that situation had to be withdrawn from the labor market. But doing so does, of course, have some cost for the corresponding household. At the initial earnings level, it entails a loss of income. Households in this situation may thus find themselves relegated to the lowest centiles of the distribution of income, thereby contributing to a loss of mean income in those centiles and to the deterioration of the distribution of income. A process of this kind is indeed at work in Taiwan, China, and it considerably reduces the simulated equalizing effect of schooling progress there. The same process is also important for Indonesia.

It is very likely, then, that the observed schooling expansion in Indonesia and Taiwan, China, would not have been possible to the same extent without the dramatic increase in incomes brought about by economic growth. It is probably mostly because household incomes had risen substantially that longer schooling became possible for some children in poor households. This positive income elasticity of the demand for schooling suggests that economic growth and educational expansion were simultaneous and mutually reinforcing during the last decades of the 20th century, at least in Asia. The Latin American evidence, on the other hand, shows that, although growth certainly would seem to help the demand for schooling, it is not necessary for an educational expansion. It was in Brazil, where growth was negligible between 1976 and 1996, that we saw the largest proportional increase in mean years of schooling in our sample—66 percent—admittedly, from a very low initial level.

Conclusions

The first conclusion that arises from this comparative assessment of the findings reported in this volume is that the counterfactual microsimulation methodology described in chapter 2 appears to be a useful analytical tool. It has two main advantages over existing alternatives. First, it is informationally efficient, in the sense that it does not waste relevant information about changes in the distribution. Indeed, it allows for a very disaggregated analysis of changes in the distribution. Second, its counterfactual nature allows for the distinction between the effects due to changes in prices and those due to changes in quantities. In addition, among changes in quantities, it allows one to further distinguish those arising from changes in the structure of the population—be it demographically, educationally, or otherwise—and changes in occupational behavior.

The power to isolate price effects from sociodemographic effects and from occupational choice effects enabled the authors of the case studies to shed light on some aspects of the changes in the distributions of income that had gone largely unnoticed in previous analyses of the same economies. One example is the solution proposed by Bourguignon, Fournier, and Gurgand (in chapter 9) to the puzzle in Taiwan, China, of the falling earnings inequality and rising inequality in household income per capita. These changes turn out to have been largely driven by the entry into the labor market of a group of relatively highly educated women, who joined the middle ranks of the earnings distribution but contributed to increases in the incomes of the reasonably wealthy households from which they came. Another example is the finding by Ferreira and Paes de Barros (in chapter 4) that the apparent stability in the Brazilian income distribution between 1976 and 1996 hid a sharp deterioration in the incomes of the bottom 15 percent of the urban distribution. This deterioration was caused largely by a movement of poor household heads away from wage employment and into informal employment and unemployment. Yet another example is the extent to which increases in educational attainment in Mexico and Indonesia led to increases in inequality because of the MIDD effect.

Our second main conclusion concerns the nature of the specificity of individual country experiences with the dynamics of their income distributions. It is true that each seems to follow its own peculiar path in terms of inequality and poverty. Grand theories about universal laws of how inequality behaves over the process of development are probably less useful than the profession once thought. This is likely a result of the fact that the process of development itself differs a great deal across countries. Yet social scientists are always on the lookout for useful patterns, and we have found evidence that some of the bewildering variety of experiences of these economies actually arise from many diverse combinations of a few simple building blocks. Price effects, occupational-choice effects, and population effects are examples of such blocks.

More concretely, we found evidence that, in the last quarter of the 20th century, inequality was generally on the rise in the economies we considered in East Asia and Latin America. Steeper returns to human capital variables, principally education, generally contributed to this trend. In South America, so did a deterioration of labor markets. Unemployment rose, hours worked fell (particularly in Argentina), and informal employment grew. Kuznets-like effects were at work in Asia (particularly in Indonesia and Malaysia), where a population movement away from agriculture and toward industrial and service jobs in the cities contributed to higher inequality. Regional disparities grew in some countries in both regions (such as Malaysia and Mexico) but fell in others (such as Brazil and Indonesia). Educational expansions, which generally contributed to poverty reduction, were also found to be contributing to increases—rather than to declines—in inequality.

The good news in terms of inequality often came from women. Gender gaps in pay, when other characteristics were controlled for, declined almost everywhere. Fertility rates also fell, and wherever they were studied, these declines led to unambiguous declines in inequality. Combined with higher educational endowments for women, the falling numbers of dependent children led to frequent examples of higher female labor-force participation. Although this effect often had contradictory impacts in terms of inequality (it led to higher earnings inequality and lower household income inequality in Mexico but to the exact opposites in Taiwan, China), it was much less ambiguous in terms of poverty reduction. In Brazil, for instance, poor women joining the labor force were responsible for preventing substantial declines in the incomes of their households.

What are the policy implications of the main findings of this study? Given the relative importance of the increase in returns to education in accounting for rising inequalities during the period under consideration, it seems that reducing the disparities in the years of schooling between the least and the most educated should be a priority. Governments should continue to invest in the human capital asset base (particularly of the poor and the least educated) to minimize the undesirable repercussions of skill-biased technical innovations on poverty and the distribution of income. Because of the MIDD effect—convex returns implying that more education often means more income inequality, all else being held constant—this process will take time. It is interesting to note that the only economies with negative educational endowment effects were Brazil and Taiwan, China, which recorded some of the largest proportional increases in years of schooling. The facts that educational expansions may at first actually raise income inequality and that declines may take a long time to materialize should not discourage policymakers. The simple truth is that there is no alternative. Leaving the poor behind in education, as Brazil did for a long time (before the 1990s), only makes matters worse in the short term and delays the process of recovery. High-quality basic education for all is a necessity in every country that seeks equitable development.

The fact that educational expansions take a long time to reduce inequality does, however, imply that complementary policies need to be in place to protect the poor in the medium term. Safety nets aimed at credit-constrained families that cannot provide minimal levels of schooling, health, and nutrition to their children are particularly important. One set of programs that appears to perform this role quite effectively is the conditional cash-transfer programs, such as Bolsa Escola in Brazil and Progresa (now called Oportunidades) in Mexico. There is now an extensive (and recent) literature on the design and evaluation of these programs, and we will not go into it here. Morley and Coady (2003) review the current state of knowledge about the costs and benefits of these programs in a number of countries in Latin America.

A second set of policy implications arises from the divergence of conditions in rural areas relative to urban areas and from the absolute fall in rural real incomes, as found in Mexico. The danger that some of the poorest rural areas may be stuck in low-development, high-poverty traps suggests that policy actions may be needed to correct coordination failures and to get investment and growth moving again. In Mexico, agricultural workers suffered severe real income falls, as large as 45 percent, as a result of terms-of-trade reversals in their principal crops, including coffee and cocoa, and the elimination of agricultural price support schemes. Public policies may be able to play innovative roles in supporting the expansion of productive non-farm opportunities in rural areas and in addressing the seriously lagging asset base of rural households, particularly their human capital.

Finally, a general implication for policymakers is that a careful study of the dynamics of the income distribution in their own countries is likely to be a much better guide to action (or inaction) than exclusive reliance on the general results of cross-country regressions of poverty or inequality measures on GDP growth and other variables. The cross-country literature will often stake strong claims on the lack of statistical significance of a particular coefficient. Dollar and Kraay (2002), for instance, argue that growth is "good for the poor," because the coefficient on GDP per capita is not significantly different from 1 in a regression explaining the growth in the mean income of the poorest 20 percent of the population.

There are two main reasons policymakers should want to complement this kind of result with a more detailed investigation of the specific distributional mechanisms at work in their own countries. The first one is that the validity of such a general average result depends on the specification of the estimated regression. We have seen, for instance, that the *manner* in which the distribution of the years of schooling in the population evolves over time affects the distribution of income, both directly and through the response of skill prices in the labor market. Including mean years of schooling as an explanatory variable in the regression, as Dollar and Kraay (2002) do, clearly helps. But it does not capture the full distributional shift in education. In particular, a given change in mean years of schooling may be consistent both with increases and with reductions in the distance between the educational attainment of the poorest quintile and the average. If a component of this shift that is uncorrelated with mean years of schooling happens to be correlated with another explanatory variable (such as the growth rate in GDP per capita, which may affect returns to education differently along the distribution), then omitted variable biases would contaminate the estimated coefficients. Even if the omitted variable were uncorrelated with the included variables, its omission would increase the variance of the residuals (as compared with the fully specified regression), thereby upwardly biasing estimates of the standard errors and compromising inference. That some of these caveats apply to any known econometric estimation procedure does not invalidate them. Our first point is exactly that—although they are extremely useful, econometric results must always be interpreted with caution.

The second reason country studies are needed to supplement cross-country regressions is even stronger. Even if regressions are perfectly specified, endogeneity concerns are fully resolved, and omitted variables are unimportant; even then regression results only tell us something about conditional averages. In the particular example at hand, such results tell us that the number of poor people tends to grow at the same rate as the mean in their societies, on average. This average is taken over many countries. In some, the incomes of the poor grow faster, and in some, they grow more slowly. The incomes of the poor may have grown more slowly because labor-market opportunities have become scarcer, thereby leading to undesired declines in their hours of work (as in Argentina), or because the world market prices of their crops have fallen, hence depressing their local economies (as in southern Mexico). Or the incomes of the poor may have grown faster because they have stayed longer in school (as in Malaysia) or have migrated to booming urban labor markets (as in Indonesia).

We believe that, on average, growth is indeed good for the poor (and for everyone else). We also believe that the policies associated with higher growth rates that were highlighted in Dollar and Kraay (2002) and various other studies—such as good rule of law, openness to international trade, and developed financial markets—are extremely important. We believe that Dollar and Kraay were as careful as it was possible to be with their econometrics and, despite the possible caveats of the sort we raised above, that the evidence that has been amassed over the past 20 years on each of these variables is persuasive.

For any given country at any given time, however, other factors— such as institutional changes in the labor market, the specific nature of an expansion in education, or changes in fertility behavior and in female participation in the labor force—are also likely to matter a great deal. In designing policy for poverty reduction, governments should carefully study these dynamics inside their own countries, in addition to taking sound advice on policies for higher growth rates. Policies that encourage job creation in the least skilled segment of the labor markets, or the marginal reallocation of educational expenditure from tertiary institutions to primary schools, or legislation and investments that make it easier for poor women to work— if they so desire—may not shift coefficients in growth regressions any time soon. But such policies may be tremendously important for the reduction of poverty (and possibly inequality) in the specific countries for which they are designed. If they are well thought out and implemented, with the specific needs of the country in mind, they should be pursued as vigorously as openness to trade and deeper financial markets. There is no contradiction between them.

Notes

1. That is, the inverse cumulative distribution function, $F^{-1}(y)$, or Pen Parade.

2. One way to overcome this problem and, at the same time, estimate the impact of individual sociodemographic variables is to simulate their contribution *directly* (instead of as the result of a subtraction). Isolating the effect of individual attributes such as education or access to land without accounting for the correlation of that individual attribute with other characteristics of the person or for the correlation across other members of the household is an imperfect approach. Nonetheless, one can assess the potential importance of those factors by simulating changes in the marginal distribution of some of the characteristics while taking the other characteristics as given. The authors look at the impact of two population effects: the large rural-urban migration and the change in the structure of schooling (which became more equal in the period under study).

3. As usual, this estimate is partial because it assumes no effect on the returns to schooling from the rise in the supply of workers with more education.

4. This finding is a particularly stark example of the path dependence inherent in generalized Oaxaca-Blinder decompositions (see chapter 2).

5. Although these results are consistent with those found in other studies, they are more pronounced in this study. One possible explanation is that the Household Surveys (in contrast to the Labor-Force Surveys) do not have information on hours of work, tenure in the job, job mobility, and second jobs. It could be that the observed significant upward trend in returns to schooling is partly due to a systematic change in these variables that is correlated with years of schooling.

6. As we have argued earlier, it is an advantage of this approach that the decomposition results can be framed in terms of the entire distribution or of any functional thereof. Accordingly, the country chapters usually present these results in much more general terms than just for the Gini coefficient. We restrict our attention to it here in order to keep the amount of information manageable and because it does allow us to focus on the main messages.

7. As the chapter on Indonesia indicates, however, regional disparities between Java and the other islands actually reversed. It is, therefore, possible that, had the authors estimated a new decomposition using an initial year from much later in the period, the sign of the region coefficient might be changing again.

8. In the case of individual earnings in the United States, Juhn, Murphy, and Pierce (1993) interpret the observed increase in the variance of the residuals as a sign that unobserved "talents" were being paid a higher price. One supposes that the implicit justification is that unobserved talents may be associated with natural or biological characteristics—such as height or IQ—the distributions of which one might presume to be more stable.

9. See Ferreira and Leite (2004) for a simulation of these indirect effects on income of expanding female education in the Brazilian state of Ceará.

10. Given that many people have exactly the same level of schooling, this procedure may require selecting the people who must jump at a higher level. This selection is made randomly.

11. See Kanbur (2000) for a survey and discussion of this literature.

12. This situation is, of course, compatible with their logarithms being linear functions of years of schooling.

13. These two restrictions simply require that the inequality measure be scale invariant and satisfy the strict version of the Pigou-Dalton transfer axiom. Both are minimum standard requirements for reasonable inequality measures. See Cowell (1995).

14. This is what we call the *MIDD effect*, given its prevalence in our sample of countries and its importance in the dynamics of the income distributions that we observed.

15. Although, as it happens, this particular inequality measure does not actually satisfy the transfer principle.

References

Almeida dos Reis, José, and Ricardo Paes de Barros. 1991. "Wage Inequality and the Distribution of Education: A Study of the Evolution of Regional Differences in Inequality in Metropolitan Brazil." *Journal of Development Economics* 36: 117–43.

Bacha, Edmar, and Lance Taylor. 1980. "Brazilian Income Distribution in the 1960s: 'Facts,' Model Results, and the Controversy." In Lance Taylor, Edmar Bacha, Eliana Cardoso, and Frank Lysy, eds., *Models of Growth and Distribution for Brazil*. Oxford, U.K.: Oxford University Press.

Bound, John, and George Johnson. 1992. "Changes in the Structure of Wages in the 1980s: An Evaluation of Alternative Explanations." *American Economic Review* 82: 371–92.

Cowell, Frank A. 1995. *Measuring Inequality*, 2nd ed. Hemel Hempstead, U.K.: Harvester Wheatsheaf.

Dollar, David, and Aart Kraay. 2002. "Growth Is Good for the Poor." *Journal of Economic Growth* 7: 195–225.

Ferreira, Francisco H. G., and Phillippe G. Leite. 2004. "Educational Expansion and Income Distribution: A Micro-simulation for Ceará." In Rolph van der Hoeven and Anthony Shorrocks, eds. *Growth, Inequality, and Poverty*. New York: Oxford University Press.

Ferreira, Francisco H. G., Peter Lanjouw, and Marcelo Neri. 2003. "A Robust Poverty Profile for Brazil Using Multiple Data Sources." *Revista Brasileira de Economia* 57(1): 59–92.

Fishlow, Albert. 1973. "Distribuição de Renda no Brasil: Um Novo Exame." *Revista Dados*. 11: 10–80.

González-Rozada, Martín, and Alicia Menendez. 2002. "Why Have Poverty and Income Inequality Increased So Much? Argentina: 1991–2002." Princeton University, Princeton, N.J. Processed.

Juhn, Chinhui, Kevin Murphy, and Brooks Pierce. 1993. "Wage Inequality and the Rise in Returns to Skill." *Journal of Political Economy*. 101(3): 410–42.

Kanbur, Ravi. 2000. "Income Distribution and Development." In Anthony Atkinson and François Bourguignon, eds. *Handbook of Income Distribution*, Vol. 1. Amsterdam: North-Holland.

Katz, Lawrence, and Kevin Murphy. 1992. "Changes in Relative Wages, 1963–1987: Supply and Demand Factors." *Quarterly Journal of Economics* 107: 35–78.

Knight, John B., and Richard H. Sabot. 1983. "Educational Expansion and the Kuznets Effect." *American Economic Review* 73(5): 1132–36.

Lam, David. 1999. "Generating Extreme Inequality: Schooling, Earnings, and Intergenerational Transmission of Human Capital in South Africa and Brazil." Research Report 99-439. Population Studies Center, University of Michigan, Ann Arbor.

Langoni, Carlos G. 1973. *Distribuição de Renda e Desenvolvimento Econômico do Brasil.* Rio de Janeiro, Brazil: Expressão e Cultura.

Morley, Samuel, and David Coady. 2003. *From Social Assistance to Social Development: A Review of Targeted Education Subsidies in Developing Countries.* Washington, D.C.: International Food Policy Research Institute.

Reyes, A. 1988. "Evolución de la Distribución del Ingreso en Colombia." *Desarrollo y Sociedad* 21: 39–51.

Sánchez-Páramo, Carolina, and Norbert Schady. 2003. "Off and Running? Technology, Trade, and the Rising Demand for Skilled Workers in Latin America." Policy Research Working Paper 3015. World Bank, Washington, D.C.

Tan, Hong, and Geeta Batra. 1997. "Technology and Firm Size: Wage Differentials in Colombia, Mexico, and Taiwan (China)." *World Bank Economic Review* 11(1): 59–83.

Tinbergen, Jan. 1975. *Income Differences: Recent Research.* Oxford, U.K.: North-Holland.

Wood, Adrian. 1997. "Openness and Wage Inequality in Developing Countries: The Latin American Challenge to East Asian Conventional Wisdom." *World Bank Economic Review* 11(1): 33–57.

Index

Figures and tables are indicated by f and t, respectively.